THE INSIGHT GUIDES SERIES RECEIVED SPECIAL AWARDS FOR EXCELLENCE FROM THE PACIFIC AREA TRAVEL ASSOCIATION.

THAILAND

Ninth Edition

© 1989 APA PUBLICATIONS (HK) LTD
Printed in Singapore by APA Press Pte Ltd
Colour Separation in Singapore by Colourscan Pte Ltd

APA PUBLICATIONS

Publisher: Hans Johannes Hoefer
Managing Director: Julian Sale
General Manager: Henry Lee
Marketing Director: Aileen Lau
Editorial Director: Geoffrey Eu
Editorial Manager: Vivien Kim
Editorial Consultants: Brian Bell (Europe)
                            Heinz Vestner (German Editions)
Updating Coordinator: Hilary Cunningham (N. America)

Project Editors

Helen Abbott, Diana Ackland, Mohamed Amin, Ravindralal Anthonis, Roy Bailet, Louisa Cambell, Jon Carroll, Hilary Cunningham, John Eames, Janie Freeburg, Bikram Grewal, Virginia Hopkins, Samuel Israel, Jay Itzkowitz, Phil Jaratt, Tracy Johnson, Ben Kalb, Wilhelm Klein, Saul Lockhart, Sylvia Mayuga, Gordon McLauchlan, Kal Müller, Eric Oey, Daniel P. Reid, Kim Robinson, Ronn Ronck, Robert Seidenberg, Rolf Steinberg, Sriyani Tidball, Lisa Van Gruisen, Merin Wexler.

Contributing Writers

A.D. Aird, Ruth Armstrong, T. Terence Barrow, F. Lisa Beebe, Bruce Berger, Dor Bahadur Bista, Clinton V. Black, Star Black, Frena Bloomfield, John Borthwick, Roger Boschman, Tom Brosnahan, Jerry Carroll, Tom Chaffin, Nedra Chung, Tom Cole, Orman Day, Kunda Dixit, Richard Erdoes, Guillermo Gar-Oropeza, Ted Giannoulas, Barbara Gloudon, Harka Gurung, Sharifah Hamzah, Willard A. Hanna, Elizabeth Hawley, Sir Edmund Hillary, Tony Hillerman, Jerry Hopkins, Peter Hutton, Neil Jameson, Michael King, Michele Kort, Thomas Lucey, Leonard Lueras, Michael E. Macmillan, Derek Maitland, Buddy Mays, Craig McGregor, Reinhold Messner, Julie Michaels, M.R. Priya Rangsit, Al Read, Elizabeth V. Reyes, Victor Stafford Reid, Harry Rolnick, E.R. Sarachandra, Uli Schmetzer, Ilsa Sharp, Norman Sibley, Peter Spiro, Harold Stephens, Keith Stevens, Michael Stone, Desmond Tate, Colin Taylor, Deanna L. Thompson, Randy Udall, James Wade, Mallika Wanigasundara, William Warren, Cynthia Wee, Tony Wheeler, Linda White, H. Taft Wireback, Alfred A. Yuson, Paul Zach.

Contributing Photographers

Carole Allen, Ping Amranand, Tony Arruza, Marcello Bertinetti, Alberto Cassio, Pat Canova, Alain Compost, Ray Cranbourne, Alain Evrard, Ricardo Ferro, Lee Foster, Manfred Gottschalk, Werner Hahn, Dallas and John Heaton, Brent Hesselyn, Hans Hoefer, Luca Invernizzi, Ingo Jezierski, Wilhelm Klein, Dennis Lane, Max Lawrence, Lyle Lawson, Philip Little, Guy Marche, Antonio Martinelli, David Messent, Ben Nakayama, Vautier de Nanxe, Kal Müller, Günter Pfannmuller, Van Philips, Ronni Pinsler, Fitz Prenzel, G.P. Reichelt, Dan Rocovits, David Ryan, Frank Salmoiraghi, Thomas Schollhammer, Blair Seitz, David Stahl, Bill Wassman, Rendo Yap, Hisham Youssef.

Distributors

Australia and New Zealand: Prentice Hall of Australia, 7 Grosvenor Place, Brookvale, NSW 2100, Australia. **Benelux:** Utigeverij Cambium, Naarderstraat 11, 1251 AW Laren, The Netherlands. **Brazil and Portugal:** Cedibra Editora Brasileira Ltda, Rua Leonidia, 2-Rio de Janeiro, Brazil. **Denmark:** Copenhagen Book Centre Aps, Roskildevej 338, DK-2630 Tastrup, Denmark. **Germany:** RV Reise-und Verkehrsuerlag Gmbh, Neumarkter Strasse 18, 8000 Munchen 80, West Germany. **Hawaii:** Pacific Trade Group Inc., P.O. Box 1227, Kailua, Oahu, Hawaii 96734, U.S.A. **Hong Kong:** Far East Media Ltd., Vita Tower, 7th Floor, Block B, 29 Wong Chuk Hang Road, Hong Kong. **India and Nepal:** India Book Distributors, 107/108 Arcadia Building, 195 Narima Point, Rombay-400-021, India. **Indonesia:** Java Books, Box 55 J.K.C.P., Jakarta, Indonesia. **Israel:**

Steimatzky Ltd., P.O. Box 628, Tel Aviv 61006, Israel (Israel title only). **Italy:** Zanfi Editori SRL. Via Ganaceto 121, 41100 Modena, Italy. **Jamaica:** Novelty Trading Co., P.O. Box 80, 53 Hanover Street, Kingston, Jamaica. **Japan:** Charles E. Tuttle Co. Inc., 2-6 Suido 1-Chome, Bunkyo-ku, Tokyo 112, Japan. **Kenya:** Camerapix Publishers International Ltd., P.O. Box 45048, Nairobi, Kenya. **Korea:** Kyobo Book Centre Co., Ltd., P.O. Box Kwang Hwa Moon 1 658, Seoul, Korea. **Philippines:** National Book Store, 701 Rizal Avenue, Manila, Philippines. **Singapore:** MPH Distributors (S) Pte. Ltd., 601 Sims Drive #03-21 Pan-I Warehouse and Office Complex, S'pore 1438, Singapore. **Switzerland:** M.P.A. Agencies-Import SA, CH. du Croset 9, CH-1024, Ecublens, Switzerland. **Taiwan:** Caves Books Ltd., 103 Chungshan N. Road, Sec. 2, Taipei, Taiwan, Republic of China. **Thailand:** Far East Publications Ltd., 117/3 Soi Samahan, Sukhumvit 4 (South Nana), Bangkok, Thailand. **United Kingdom, Ireland and Europe (others):** Harrap Ltd., 19-23 Ludgate Hill, London EC4M 7PD, England, United Kingdom. **Mainland United States and Canada:** Graphic Arts Center Publishing, 3019 N.W. Yeon, P.O. Box 10306, Portland OR 97210, U.S.A. (The Pacific Northwest title only); Prentice Hall Press, Gulf & Western Building, One Gulf & Western Plaza, New York, NY 10023, U.S.A. (all other titles).

Chinese editions: Formosan Magazine Press Ltd., 6 Fl. No. 189, Yen Pin S. Road, Taipei, Taiwan, R.O.C. **French cditions:** Editions Gallimard, 5 rue Sébastien-Bottin, F-75007 Paris, France. **German editions:** Nelles Verlag GmbH, Schleissheirner Str. 371b, 8000 Munich 45, West Germany **Italian editions:** Zanfi Editori SLR. Via Ganaceto 121 41100 Modena, Italy. **Portuguese editions:** Cedibra Editora Brasileira Ltda, Rua Leonidia, 2-Rio de Janeiro, Brazil.

Advertising and Special Sales Representatives

Advertising carried in Insight Guides gives readers direct access to quality merchandise and travel-related services. These advertisements are inserted in the Guide in Brief section of each book. Advertisers are requested to contact their nearest representatives, listed below.
Special sales, for promotion purposes within the international travel industry and for educational purposes, are also available. The advertising representatives listed here also handle special sales. Alternatively, interested parties can contact Apa Publications, P.O. Box 219, Orchard Point Post Office, Singapore 9123.

Australia and New Zealand: Harve and Gullifer Pty. Ltd. 1 Fawkner St. Kilda 3181, Australia. Tel: (3) 525 3422; Tlx: 523259; Fax: (89) 4312837.
Canada: The Pacific Rim Agency, 6900 Cote Saint Luc Road, Suite 303, Montreal, Quebec, Canada H4V 2Y9. Tel: (514) 9311299; Tlx: 0525134 MTL; Fax: (514) 8615571.
Hawaii: HawaiianLMedia Sales; 1750 Kalakaua Ave., Suite 3-243, Honolulu, Hawaii 96826, U.S.A. Tel: (808) 9464483.
Hong Kong: C Cheney & Associates, 17th Floor, D'Aguilar Place, 1-30 D'Aguilar Street, Central, Hong Kong. Tel: 5-63079 CCAL HX.
India and Nepal, Pakistan and Bangladesh: Universal Media, CHA 2/718, 719 Kantipath, Lazimpat, Kathmandu-2, Nepal. Tel: 412911/414502; Tlx: 2229 KAJI NP ATTN MEDIA.
Indonesia: Media Investment Services, Setiabudi Bldg. 2, 4th Floor, Suite 407, Jl. Hr. Rasuna Said, Kuningan, Jakarta Selatan 12920, Indonesia. Tel: 5782723/5782752; Tlx: 62418 MEDIANETIA; Mata Graphic Design, Batujimbar, Sanur, Bali, Indonesia. Tel: (0361) 8073. (for Bali only)
Korea: Kaya Ad Inc., Rm. 402 Kunshin Annex B/D, 251-1 Dohwa Dong, Mapo-Ku, Seoul, Korea (121). Tel: (2) 7196906; Tlx: K 32144 KAYAAD; Fax: (2) 7199816.
Philippines: Torres Media Sales Inc., 21 Warbler St., Greenmeadows 1, Murphy, Quezon City, Metro Manila, Philippines. Tel: 722-02-43; Tlx: 23312 RHP PH.
Taiwan: Cheney Tan & Van Associates, 7th Floor, 10 Alley 4, Lane 545 Tun Hua South Road, Taipei, Taiwan. Tel: (2) 7002963; Tlx: 11491 FOROSAN; Fax: (2) 3821270.
Thailand: Cheney, Tan & Van Outrive, 17th Fl. Rajapark Bldg., 163 Asoke Rd., Bangkok 10110, Thailand. Tel: 2583244/2583259; Tlx: 20666 RAJAPAK TH.
Singapore and Malaysia: Cheney Tan Associates, 1 Goldhill Plaza, #02-01, Newton Rd., Singapore 1130, Singapore. Tel: 2549522; Tlx: RS 35983 CTAL.
Sri Lanka: Spectrum Lanka Advertising Ltd., 56 1/2 Ward Place, Colombo 7, Sr Lanka. Tel: 5984648/596227; Tlx: 21439 SPECTRM CE.
U.K., Ireland and Europe: Brian Taplin Associates, 32 Fishery Road, Boxmoor, Hemel Hempstead, Herts HP 1ND, U.K. Tel: (2)215635; Tlx:825454 CHARMAN.

APA PHOTO AGENCY PTE. LTD.

The Apa Photo Agency is S.E. Asia's leading stock photo archive, representing the work of professional photographers from all over the world. More than 150,000 original color transparencies are available for advertising, editorial and educational uses. We are linked with Tony Stone Worldwide, one of Europe's leading stock agencies, and their associate offices around the world:
Singapore: Apa Photo Agency Pte. Ltd., P.O. Box 219, Orchard Point Post Office, Singapore 9123, Singapore. **London:** Tony Stone Worldwide, 28 Finchley Rd.. St. John's Wood, London NW8 6ES, England. **North America & Canada:** Masterfile Inc., 415 Yonge St., Suite 200, Toronto M5B 2E7, Canada. **Paris:** Fotogram-Stone Agence Photographique, 45 rue de Richelieu, 75001 Paris, France. **Barcelona:** Fototec Torre Dels Pardais, 7 Barcelona 08026, Spain. **Johannesburg:** Color Library (Pty.) Ltd., P.O. Box 1659, Johannesburg, South Africa 2000. **Sydney:** The Photographic Library of Australia Pty. Ltd., 7 Ridge Street, North Sydney, New South Wales 2050, Australia. Tokyo: Orion Press, 55-1 Kanda Jimbocho, Chiyoda-ku, Tokyo 101, Japan.

E | F | G

Thailand

Created and photographed by Hans Hoefer
Compiled by
William Warren
Star Black
and M.R. Priya Rangsit

APA PUBLICATIONS

"I travel not to go anywhere, but to go," said Robert Louis Stevenson. "I travel for travel's sake. The great affair is to move." Well, yes, RLS has a point, nowhere more keenly established than in his *Travels with a Donkey*. But even Stevenson succumbed to the lure of a place — in his case, Samoa — and stayed; the great affair was also to sit, as though in a warm bath, and soak up deeply felt, pleasurable experiences.

Thailand put the same temptations, the same conundrum, in the path of the Apa Productions team in 1973: travel a lot, stay a lot, or both? The answer was "both," for to do justice to a country of such physical and cultural variety there could be no either/or.

Not that total immersion was any stranger to the originators of the Insight Guides series. *Bali* (1970), *Singapore* (1971) and *Malaysia* (1972) had all involved intensive travel, and intensive "soaking." The difference, this time, was the enormity of the challenge: a country the size of France (but nowhere near so compact, with a long tadpole's tail running south past Burma to Peninsular Malaysia) to be explored in every direction; a financial undertaking with only faith in the book's potential as collateral (earlier Insight Guides had been co-published or sponsored); and an awareness that much of Thailand was then completely off the beaten track in terms of tourist facilities and infrastructure.

The original team consisted of Apa founder and publisher **Hans Hoefer, Star Black** and **William Warren**, a long-time American resident in Bangkok. While Warren honed his acute observations on the "City of Angels" and the complexities of Thai culture and lifestyle, Hoefer and Black made four long sorties into the country's hinterland, south, northwest, east and northeast, covering more than 30,000 kilometers on highways, roads and back-of-beyond tracks.

The intrepid trio gathered masses of facts, impressions and experiences. Notes piled on notes. But even this was not enough. More writers with first-hand knowledge of Thailand were brought in — **Marcus Brooke, Robert Burrows, Jerry Dillon, Nancy Grace, Frank Green, John Stirling** and **Tony Wheeler.**

But time alters all places, and by the time of Thailand's Rattanakosin Bicentennial in 1982, *Thailand* the book was ready for major changes. So **Priya Rangsit,** great-granddaughter of the Thai King Chulalongkorn, was commissioned to write a thorough history of the land, while **David DeVoss, Aporanee Buatong** and **Kultida Wongsawat-**

| Hoefer | Black | Rangsit |

dichart of *Time Magazine's* Southeast Asia bureau updated and revised the text and the *Guide in Brief.*

A certain audacity is needed in any attempt to summarize the allure and impact of a country in little more than 300 pages. Hans Hoefer came adequately prepared for such a task. Born in southern Germany, Hoefer traveled extensively in Spain, Turkey, Jordan and Iran while gathering a handful of diplomas in printing, book production, design and photography at Krefeld, where he was subjected to the stern disciplines of the Bauhaus tradition. Arriving in Bali in 1967, he painted for a year before embarking on a project that was to change his life — the seminal *Guide to Bali,* first published in 1970 and the forerunner of the now internationally acclaimed Insight Guides, a series that has expanded since to include *Java, Singapore, Malaysia, Thailand, Philippines, Korea, Hawaii, Hong Kong, Nepal, Burma, Florida, Mexico, Jamaica, Sri Lanka* and *Taiwan.* Most books in the series have been translated into French and German, and some have also been published in Dutch, Japanese and Chinese.

Levine

California-born Star Black received degrees in art and English literature from Wellesley before going to live in Bangkok, traveling extensively in Southeast Asia, and writing the first three Insight Guides. She has since returned to the United States, where she now works as a freelance photographer in New York. She took the photographs for a book, *Texas Boots,* published by Penguin-Viking.

William Warren, one of the most knowledgeable *farang* (foreigners) resident in Bangkok, is a freelance writer and journalist. A regular contributor to Asia-oriented publications, Warren's books include *The*

DeVoss

Buatong

Van Outrive

Anderson

Legendary American and *The House on the Klong,* dealing with the life and art collections of Jim Thompson, the man who took Thai silk from village looms to the international marketplace.

M.R. Priyanandana Rangsit attended the School of Oriental and African Studies, London University, where she read Sanskrit and History of India and Southeast Asia, with emphasis on the ancient period. Priya is a free-lance writer whose works have appeared in *The Bangkok Post, The Nation, Vogue Magazine* (London), the *Monarchist,* and the *Taj Magazine* (Bombay). She belongs to one of Thailand's oldest literary families: her grandfather, Krom Muen Prince Bidyalongkorn, was regarded as the kingdom's "poet laureate," and her mother, V. na Pramuenmarg, was a renowned Thai novelist.

David DeVoss, *Time's* Bangkok bureau chief, first came to Asia in 1972 when he joined *Time's* Saigon bureau. He later covered Southeast Asia from Hong Kong. In early 1981 DeVoss moved to Bangkok, a city that he had visited nearly 50 times over the previous three years.

Expansion and updating of the book's *Guide in Brief* section were undertaken by Aporanee (Oi) Buatong, a graduate of the Chulalongkorn University and a Fulbright scholar in the United States (1983—1985) majoring in English literature, and Wongsawatdichart, a reporter and editorial assistant for *Time Magazine's* Southeast Asia bureau (Bangkok).

Editor **Charles Levine,** who coordinated

the efforts of *Thailand's* original contributors, worked with the Peace Corps in India for two years before settling in Bali (where he married a Balinese dancer) and subsequently working in Singapore as a senior editor with McGraw-Hill and, later, Apa Productions. His expertise with the blue pencil helped mould the textual character of many Insight Guides.

John Gottberg Anderson, Apa's managing editor for Asia, carried the book through its latter-day improvements. A former newspaper reporter and editor in Honolulu and Seattle, Anderson had visited Thailand frequently since first coming to Asia in 1976. He previously edited Insight Guides to *Burma, Nepal and Sri Lanka.*

Apa Productions marketing director **Yvan Van Outrive,** a resident of Bangkok, has been an invaluable source of advice and information in preparing the book's recent editions. His suggestions have helped Apa keep pace with the rapid and sweeping changes that take place almost everyday in Thailand.

All photos are taken by Hans Hoefer with the exception of the following: cover, pages 41 and 89 by **Bill Wassman,** pages 43 and 44-45 by **R. Ian Lloyd,** page 23 by **R.C.G. Varley** and page 25 by **John Heaton.** The historical photos appearing on pages 16—17, 32—33, 35 and 37 to 40 come from the **Collection of M.C. Piya Rangsit.** Additional acknowledgement is given to the following books as sources of historical material: *A History of Siam* by W.A.R. Wood (Bangkok: Siam Barnakich Press, 1933) for prints appearing on pages 24, 26 and 27; *1688: Revolution in Siam* by E.W. Hutchinson (Hong Kong: University Press, 1968) for photographs on pages 28 and 29; *Lords of Life* by Prince Chula Chakrabongse (London: Alvin Redman) for graphics on pages 30 and 34; *Louis and the King of Siam* by W.S. Bristave (London: Chatto and Windus, 1976) for photographs on page 36.

Sincere thanks are also due to Tourism Authority of Thailand, the Montien Hotel, the Thai Consulate in Singapore, General E. Black, Per Bang-Jensen, James Stanton, Henry Aronson, Vivien Loo, Leonard Lueras, Patrick (Shrimp) Gauvain, Sam Chan and the many unsung people who made this book possible.

— Apa Productions

TABLE OF CONTENTS

TABLE OF CONTENTS

11

CROSSROADS OF SOUTHEAST ASIA

Thailand's perhaps most celebrated landmark, pictured on hundreds of travel posters, rises high above the bank of the Chao Phya River across from Bangkok. From a distance, the towering central spire of Wat Arun, the Temple of Dawn, seems solidly coated with some strange glittering substance flashing like a gigantic jewel in the tropical sunlight. When examined closely, the imposing structure turns out to consist of countless bits of colored porcelain cunningly set in a vast mosaic.

A similar discovery lies in store for anyone who wants to get more than a distant, superficial glimpse of Thailand itself. Though unified culturally and politically, to a degree rare among the countries of Southeast Asia, Thailand nevertheless proves on closer acquaintance to be a kingdom of surprising diversity; and you are constantly being surprised by it the longer you stay.

For too long, perhaps, writers have emphasized the prettier, more picturesque Thailand, to the exclusion of almost everything else, and have been unable to resist such tempting labels as "The Land of Smiles." The description may be justified to the extent that Thais are remarkably friendly and more apt to smile than scowl on most occasions, sometimes even on solemn ones; but it is also misleading because it suggests that Thailand is an other-worldly Shangri-la where beaming faces flit charmingly in and out of the original stage set for *The King and I*. Such a preconception proves inadequate during one's initial encounter with Bangkok, where the fantastic temples and palaces of legend coexist with supermarkets, flyovers, luxury hotels, and air-conditioned shopping centers filled with every conceivable modern want.

Lying inland from the apex of the Gulf of Thailand, Bangkok — the country's international gateway, seat of government and monarchy, and booming metropolis — can also seduce the unwary into thinking that its highly westernized surface is an accurate reflection of the entire nation; yet Thailand is still basically a country of villages and towns following traditional ways; a full 80 percent of the population is engaged in agriculture. Tradition still exerts a powerful influence, even in the clamorous streets of the capital.

Diversity and a wide range of contrasts also characterize Thailand's geography. Within an area of 514,000 square kilometers — which makes the country roughly the size of France, or the states of California and New York combined — the landscape includes tropical rain forests, agriculturally rich plains, and forest-clad Himalayan hills. All these types of topography lie just 5° to 21° north of the equator, in the center of the geographical jigsaw puzzle of Southeast Asia.

THAILAND'S NEIGHBORS

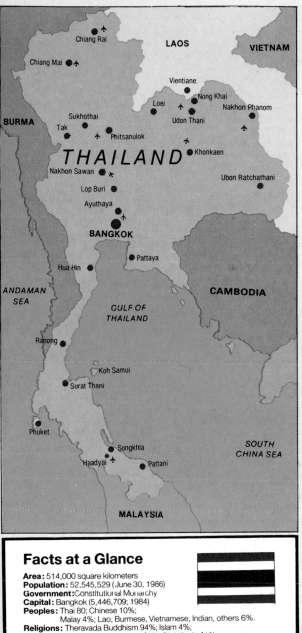

A closer look at Thailand's geography reveals a country that is richly endowed with natural resources. Under the canopies of its southern rain forests, a wide variety of flora and fauna abound: iridescent kingfisher, parakeet, pheasant, blue-tailed broadbill, flying squirrel and lizard, gibbon, dozens of species of snake, hundreds of species of butterfly, and nearly a thousand varieties of orchid. A cornucopia of fruits grows as well, wild in the jungles, or tended carefully on small family holdings and in larger plantations: nearly thirty varieties of banana and plantain, coconut, durian, orange, lime, custard apple, mango, papaya, breadfruit, jackfruit, mangosteen, rambutan, litchi, and *lamyai*.

In the North, Himalayan fold mountains crown the country at an average of 1,700 meters. In the teak forests covering their lower slopes, elephants move felled logs down the steep terrain to mountain streams, where they are lashed together into rafts and floated downriver to mills.

In the Central Plains from May to September, monsoon rains transform the landscape into a vast hydroponic basin, which nourishes an endless sea of rice, the country's staple and number one export. Through this region flows the Chao Phya River, carrying produce and people south to Bangkok, washing rich sediment down from the northern hills, and during the monsoon season pouring more water onto the rain-flooded rice fields. Though only about 300 kilometers long, the Chao Phya is Thailand's Mississippi, her Nile.

Across this landscape live Thailand's population of about 50 million people. Along with the ethnic Thais, who make up around 80 percent of the population, there are significant groups of Chinese (about 10 percent), Malays (about 4 percent), Lao, Mons, Khmers, Indians, and Burmese — reflecting this country's long and turbulent history at the crossroads of Southeast Asia.

Facts at a Glance

Area: 514,000 square kilometers
Population: 52,545,529 (June 30, 1986)
Government: Constitutional Monarchy
Capital: Bangkok (5,446,709; 1984)
Peoples: Thai 80; Chinese 10%;
    Malay 4%; Lao, Burmese, Vietnamese, Indian, others 6%.
Religions: Theravada Buddhism 94%; Islam 4%;
    Mahayana Buddhism 1½%; Christianity ½%.
Highest Point: Doi Inthanon (2,596 meters)
Currency: Baht (25.75 baht = 1 US$)
Electricity: 220 volts AC

FROM BAN CHIENG TO SUKHOTHAI

The Thai people have fiercely defended their country's independence for more than 800 years. They can boast the distinction of being the only country in Southeast Asia never to have been a European colony. Nor have they yet been divided by civil war, as tumultuous as Thai politics can be. Their shrewdness at international diplomacy has won them the admiration of far more powerful nations, and they have proved themselves adept at absorbing outside influences without losing their essential national identity.

Indeed, the name *Thai* means "free." Although the country was called "Siam" by foreigners from the 12th Century to the 20th, to its citizens it always carried the name of its capital—Sukhothai, Ayuthaya, etc. In the 19th Century, Siam was designated the official name of the Kingdom. This was changed to Thailand with the advent of democratic government in 1939.

The original homeland of the Thais is a topic of much dispute and few facts. Linguistic studies have indicated that southeastern China was their ancestral home; from there, they wandered to form communities in Yunnan, China's southernmost province. Historians once believed that the powerful Yunnanese kingdom of Nan-ch'ao (7th to 13th centuries) was a Thai principality, but this theory is no longer popular.

Long before the Thai people migrated into what is today called Thailand, however, the Menam Chao Phya valley was inhabited by a high civilization.

The Ban Chieng Culture

The first prehistoric discovery was accidentally made during World War II by a Dutch prisoner of war employed by the Japanese on the Siam-Burma "Death Railway." He uncovered Stone Age implements at Ban Kao in the western province of Kanchanaburi, which led to the finding of paleolithic and neolithic caves and cemeteries containing a wealth of pottery and tools.

By far the most important site, however, is the tiny village of Ban Chieng near Udon Thani in the northeast. Systematic excavation of Ban Chieng began only two decades ago, revealing painted pottery, jewelry, bronze and iron tools. If Carbon-14 dating is correct, the Bronze Age in Thailand corresponds to that of the Tigris-Euphrates valley civilization, which preceded the Bronze Age in Europe.

The identity of the Ban Chieng people is a mystery. Settlement began about 3600 B.C. and lasted until about 250 B.C. They farmed rice, domesticated their animals, and were skillful potters. Their red-painted pottery, decorated with fingerprint whorl patterns, was buried in funerary mounds as offerings to the dead. Beads of glass and semi-precious stones were also included. Similar sites were excavated in surrounding areas.

The Ban Chieng culture illustrates the high level of technology achieved by prehistoric man in Southeast Asia. It proves that China is not the sole birthplace of Far Eastern civilization, as previously surmised.

Indian Influence

Archaeological evidence is missing, but ancient chronicles discuss the presence of people of Indian origin around the 3rd Century B.C.

The Sinhalese Buddhist chronicle, the *Mahavamsa*, relates that India's great Emperor Ashoka (ruled 268 to 232 B.C.), the first royal patron of Buddhism, sent two missionaries to Suvannabhumi, the "land of gold" identified with Southeast Asia. By the beginning of the Christian era, maritime trading between India and the eastern shores had begun.

Buddhism and Hinduism, along with Indian ceremonial rites, iconography, law codes, cosmological and architectural treatises, were adopted *en bloc* by the Southeast Asian ruling elite and modified to suit local requirements and tastes. Sanskrit became the court language, while Pali was the language of the Buddhist canons. Native chiefs who wanted to consolidate their power and increase their prestige may have been responsible for this diffusion of culture by calling in brahmins (Indians of the priestly caste) to consecrate their rule.

This transmission at court level had a vital and permanent impact, especially in Cambodia. The Mons and Khmers were the first Indianized peoples to form settlements in

Preceding pages, procession of royal barges at King Prajadhipok's 1925 coronation. Left, a Stone Age skeleton unearthed at Ban Chieng.

present-day Thailand. The Mon influence is evident in the Buddhist art of the Dvaravati period (6th to 11th centuries); and the Khmers, famed as the builders of Cambodia's Angkor Wat, left many temples in Thailand's northeastern provinces.

Arrival of the Thais

Over the centuries, the Thais had migrated from Yunnan down rivers and streams into Southeast Asia. There, they branched off. The Shans, also known as "Great Thais," went to Upper Burma; the Ahom Thais established themselves in Assam; another group settled in Laos.

The greater number of "Little Thais" first settled in the north of modern Thailand,

around Chiang Mai and Chiang Saen, forming themselves into principalities. Some of these later became independent kingdoms embracing most of the area. The city of Chiang Mai was the capital of one of these kingdoms; and long after the main group of Thais moved farther down the peninsula to establish more powerful states, Chiang Mai continued to be ruled more or less autonomously, keeping a distinctive culture of its own.

By the 13th Century, the Thais had begun to emerge in dominance in the ruling class of the region, slowly absorbing the weakened empires of the Mons and Khmers. Their rise to power culminated circa 1238, when (according to inscriptions) the Khmers were expelled from Sukhothai.

The history of Peninsular Thailand is lesser known than that of the culturally richer north. The Isthmian region was once under the control of the mighty commercial and military empire of Sri Vijaya (7th to 13th centuries), whose capital was at Palembang in Sumatra. The fact that this island empire incorporated the Thai side of the Malaccan straits is proved by the discovery of a 775 A.D. inscription of a Sri Vijayan king at Chaiya, near the Kra Isthmus. The art of Sri Vijaya is heterogenous in character showing influences from India, Champa and Java. The empire disintegrated during the 13th Century and her dependencies were absorbed by Sukhothai.

Phra Ruang And
The 'Dawn' of Sukhothai

Sukhothai—"the dawn of happiness" and the first independent Thai kingdom—is considered the golden era of Thai history, and is often looked back upon with nostalgia as the ideal Thai state. It was the land of plenty, governed by just and paternal kings who ruled over peaceful, contented citizens. Sukhothai represented early Thai tribal society in its purest form.

Siamese tradition attributes the founding of the kingdom to Phra Ruang, a mythological hero comparable to King Arthur. Prior to his time, according to historical legend, the Thai people were forced to pay tribute to the Khmer rulers of Angkor. This tribute was exacted in the form of sacred water from a lake outside Lop Buri: the Khmer god-king needed holy water from all corners of the empire for his ceremonial rites.

Every three years, the water tribute was sent by bullock carts in large earthenware jars. The jars inevitably cracked en route, compelling the tribute payers to make second and third journeys to fill the required quota. When Phra Ruang came of age, he devised a new system of transporting water in sealed woven bamboo containers which arrived in Angkor intact.

This success aroused the curiosity of the Khmers, including the king himself. His chief astrologer said the ingenious Thai inventor was a person with supernatural powers, who constituted a threat to the empire. The king at once dispatched his gifted general, who had the magic ability of being

Left, an ancient rock inscription reminds of Cambodian influence 1,000 years ago. Right, elephant decorative figures at Wat Chang Rob, Kamphang Phet Province.

able to travel swiftly underground, to eliminate the Thai menace. Phra Ruang intuited danger and went to Sukhothai, where he concealed himself at Wat Mahathat as a Buddhist monk. The Khmer general coincidentally surfaced in the middle of the wat. There he encountered the monk, Phra Ruang, who used his inner spiritual power to transform the unsuspecting Khmer into stone!

From then on, Phra Ruang's fame spread far and wide. He left the monkhood, married the ruler of Sukhothai's daughter, and upon that monarch's death was invited to the throne by popular mandate. He assumed the title Sri Indraditya, sovereign of the newly independent Kingdom of Sukhothai.

Fact and fiction are inseparable in this

As a result, he was granted the name Phra Ramkamhaeng (Rama the Brave) by his parent.

The Sukhothai Kingdom at the time of Ramkamhaeng's accession was quite small, consisting of only the city and surrounding areas. By the end of his reign, he had increased its size tenfold: from Luang Prabang in the east through the central plains to the southern peninsula. The Mon state in Lower Burma also accepted his overlordship.

Ramkamhaeng was noted as an administrator, legislator and statesman, and sometimes as an amorous king. He is credited with the invention of Thai script, which he achieved by systematizing the Khmer alphabet with Thai words. The new script was

popular account. But there is no doubt that, since Sukhothai, Buddhism has been deeply rooted in the Thai way of life. Together with the monarchy, it provides a continuity lasting to the present day.

The Rule of Ramkamhaeng

The most famous king of Sukhothai was the founder's second son, Ramkamhaeng. He was the first Thai ruler to leave detailed epigraphical accounts of the Thai state, beginning with his own early life. He earned his title at age 19 on a campaign with his father against a neighboring state, in which, he saved the day by defeating the enemy leader in a hand-to-hand elephant combat.

employed for the first time in an inscription of 1292, in which Ramkamhaeng depicted the idyllic conditions of his kingdom—fertile land and plentiful food, free trade, prohibition of slavery, and guaranteed inheritance.

The king was a devout and conscientious Buddhist of the Theravada school practiced in Sukhothai. There remained, however, a trace of animism. Ramkamhaeng wrote about a mountain-dwelling ghost named Phra Khapung Phi, a spirit "above all others in the land." If correctly propiriated, he would bring prosperity to the country. The idea of a superior spirit looking after the nation survives today in the image of Phra Siam Devadhiraj, Siam's guardian angel.

One of the keys to Ramkamhaeng's success lays in his diplomatic relations with China. The Mongol Court pursued a "divide-and-rule" policy and supported the Thais' rise at the expense of the Khmers. Ramkamhaeng was said to have gone to China himself, and the *History of the Yuan* records seven missions from "Sien" (Sukhothai) between 1282 and 1323. Chinese craftsmen came to teach the Thais their secrets of glazing pottery, resulting in the production of the famous ceramic ware of Sawankhalok, whose kilns still remain.

The year Pagan fell to the armies of Kublai Khan in 1287, Ramkamhaeng formed a pact with two northern Thai princes, Mangrai of Chieng Rai and Ngam Muang of Phayao. The three agreed not to transgress but to protect each others' borders against common enemies. The alliance was maintained throughout their lifetimes,

The Founding of Chieng Mai
And the Decline of Sukhothai

It was Mangrai who completed Thai political ascendancy in the north by annexing the last Mon kingdom of Haripunjaya in about 1292. He first sent an agent provocateur to sow discontent, and when the time was right, his army "plucked the town like a ripe fruit."

Wishing to found a new capital, Mangrai invited his two allies to help him in selecting a site. The location they agreed upon as truly auspicious was one where two white sambars, two white barking deer, and a family of five white mice were seen together. On that spot by the river Mae Ping, Mangrai laid the foundation of Chiang Mai—"New Town"—in 1296. It became the capital of the Kingdom of Lanna Thai, "Land of the Million Rice Fields."

Tradition says Ramkamhaeng disappeared into the rapids at Sawankhalok. His son Lo Thai (ruled 1318 to 1347), preferring religion to war, proceeded to lose the feudatory states as fast as his father had gained them. He was called Dharmaraja, "the Pious King," an epithet which his successors bore after him. The relationship between Sukhothai and Sri Lanka, the center of orthodox Buddhism, became intensified during his rule; Lo Thai recorded that he built many monuments to house sacred relics of the Buddha newly obtained from Ceylon.

Lo Thai's son, Li Thai, was as concerned with moral affairs as his father. As heir to the throne, he composed a famous treatise on Buddhist cosmology, the *Traibhumikatha* or "Tales of the Three Worlds." When he became king in 1347 with the title Maha

Dharmaraja I, he declared that he ruled according to the 10 Royal Precepts of the Buddha. He pardoned criminals because he desired to become a Buddha—"to lead all creatures beyond the oceans of sorrow and transmigration."

This placing of religion over military might permitted the meteoric rise of one of Sukhothai's former vassal states, Ayuthaya. Gradually, this territory in the south extended control over the Menam Chao Phya valley until King Li Thai was forced to acknowledge Ayuthaya's suzerainty. Deprived of his independence, the pious king turned more to religion and eventually assumed the yellow robe. His family continued to rule for three more generations, merely as hereditary governors. When the

center of administration was transferred to Phitsanulok in 1378, Sukhothai became a deserted city.

The Sukhothai period saw the Thais, for the first time, developing a distinctive civilization with their own administrative institutions, art and architecture. Sukhothai Buddha images, characterized by refined facial features, lineal fluidity, and harmony of form, are considered to be the most beautiful and the most original of Thai artistic expressions.

Left, a stucco figure of Buddha, U-thong style, located at the front Vihara of Wat Maha-Thad, Sukhothai. Above, Wat Mahathat, principal shrine of Phitsanulok.

23

THE RISE AND FALL OF AYUTHAYA

History is ignorant of the anciestry of Ayuthaya's founder. But Thai folklore fills the lacuna:

The King of Traitrung unhappily discovered that his unmarried daughter had given birth to a child after eating an aubergine, which a vegetable gardener had fertilized with his own urine. The culprit—Nai Saen Pom, "Man With a Hundred Thousand Warts"—was summoned and banished from the city, along with the princess and her son. The god Indra, with his divine eye, saw the misery of the trio and decided to grant the

tal was blessed with several advantages. Situated on an island at the confluence of the Chao Phya, Lop Buri and Pasak rivers, not far from the sea and surrounded by fertile rice plains, it was an ideal center of administration and communications. Phya U-Tong officially established the city in 1350 after three years of preparation, when he assumed the title Ramatibodi I, King of Dvaravati .Sri Ayodhya. Within a few years, the king united the whole of central Siam, including Sukhothai, under his rule, and extended control to the Malay Peninsula and Lower

gardener three magic wishes. Saen Pom first asked for his warts to disappear; next, he prayed for a kingdom to rule over; and lastly, he wanted a cradle of gold for his son. All his desires came true! The child was henceforth known as Chao U-Tong, "Prince of the Golden Crib."

Historically, U-Tong was a principality in today's Suphan Buri. Its rulers were members of the prestigious line of Chiang Saen kings. During the reign of Phya U-Tong, a cholera outbreak forced the ruler to evacuate his people to the site of Ayodhya (Ayuthaya), an ancient Indianized settlement named after Rama's legendary kingdom in India.

The location of Phya U-Tong's new capi-

Burma. He and his successors pursued expansionist campaigns against Chiang Mai and Cambodia.

Ironically, although the Thais were responsible for the decline and eventual collapse of Angkor, the Ayuthaya kings adopted Khmer cultural influences from the very beginning. No longer the paternal and accessible rulers that the kings of Sukhothai had been, Ayuthaya's sovereigns were absolute monarchs—"Lords of Life" whose position was enhanced by trappings

Above, "Laying the foundation of Ayuthaya" took place in 1350. Right, a mural in the Ancient City near Bangkok depicts an army of ancient Ayuthaya on the march.

of royalty reflective of a Khmer *devaraja* (god-king). The *devaraja* concept was tempered by the tenets of Theravada Buddhism, wherein the king was not actually divine, but was the protector and supreme head of the religion. Nevertheless, Khmer court rituals and language were emulated at the Ayuthaya court. Brahmins officiated side by side with Buddhist monks at state ceremonies—a legacy which remains in modern Bangkok.

Ramatibodi I divided his administration into four sections: ministries of Royal

forces entered Angkor after a seige of seven months. The Khmer king abandoned his ancient capital in favor of Lovek and, later, Phnom Penh. The Siamese army returned from the campaign with a vast amount of booty and prisoners, including artists and brahmins.

The Reign of King Trailok

Two centuries of wars between Chiang Mai and Ayuthaya reached a climax during the reign of King Boroma Trailokanath, or

Household, Finance, Interior and Agriculture. This and his legislation provided a strong foundation for the kingdom, which persisted with Ayuthaya as its capital for 417 years.

Ramatibodi died in 1369. His son, Ramesuen, captured Chiang Mai in 1390—supposedly with the use of cannon, the first recorded use of this weapon in Siam. Ramesuen's army sacked Angkor three years later, and according to the *Pongsawadan*, the "Annals of Ayuthaya," 90,000 prisoners of war were taken. Given the economics of the time, manpower was more precious than gold.

The death blow to the Khmer capital was delivered in 1431 by Boromaraja II, whose

Trailok (1448–1488). In his campaigns against Maharaja Sutam Tilok, guile and occult complemented military might. A Burmese monk sent to spy for Trailok, for example, tricked Tilok into felling a sacred tree of Mangrai. As a result, a series of misfortunes befell him. Envoys sent to Tilok from Ayuthaya were discovered to have buried seven jars containing ingredients which, it was feared, would magically bring doom upon Chiang Mai. The jars were cast into the river, followed by the ambassadors, whose feet were weighted down with rocks. The fighting between these rival kingdoms led to the transfer of the Ayuthaya capital to Phitsanulok during the last 25 years of Trailok's reign, but ended in a stalemate.

Trailok is important for having introduced reforms which shaped the administrative and social structures of Siam until the 19th Century. He brought Ayuthaya's loosely controlled provinces under centralized rule, and regulated the grade of *sakdi na*—an ancient system of land ownership which stratified society and determined salary levels of the official hierarchy. Trailok also defined a system of corvee labor under which all able-bodied men were required to contribute part of each working year to the state. This system indirectly heightened the status of women, who were responsible for the welfare of their families in the absence of the menfolk.

Trailok's Palace Law of 1450 spelled out the relative ranks of members of the royal

Trailok helped to maintain the fluidity of Thai society. This persists today. Ranks of nobility were—and are—meritorious rather than hereditary. Titles of royal descendants, what's more, are not retained in perpetuity; they degenerate, reaching a common status within five generations.

Enter Portuguese and Burmese

The 16th Century was marked by the first arrival of Europeans and by continual conflict with the Burmese.

Affonso de Albuquerque of Portugal conquered Malacca in 1511, and soon thereafter his ships sailed to Siam. King Ramatibodi II (ruled 1491–1529) granted the Portuguese a permit to reside and trade within the king-

family, prescribed functions of officials, and regulated ceremonies. It also fixed punishments, which included death for "introducing amatory poems" in the palace or for whispering during a royal audience, and amputation of the foot of anyone kicking a palace door. While these sentences may not often have been carried out to the letter, they certainly exalted the aura of the king and dissuaded malefactors. Even royalty was not spared punishment, although the Palace Law stipulated that no menial hands could touch royal flesh. It was therefore the executioner's task to beat the condemned royalty at the nape of the neck with a sandalwood club.

On the whole, the rules fixed by King

dom, in return for arms and ammunition. Portuguese mercenaries fought in campaigns against Chiang Mai and taught the Thais the arts of cannon foundry and musketry.

But this did nothing to stem the rising tide of Burmese aggression. King Tabinshweti of Pegu, upon unifying the Burmese Empire, had cast his eyes toward Ayuthaya, already weakened by wars with Chiang Mai.

In 1549, when Tabinshweti attacked, King Mahachakrapat had just acceded to the throne. As the Burmese laid siege to his

Above, "Death of Queen Suryothai," a national heroine of the mid-16th Century. Right, Prince Naresuen engages the Burmese in a sea battle.

capital, Mahachakrapat led a sortie against them. Not only his sons, but his wife and daughter, accompanied him to the field of battle, mounted on elephants. Thai history proudly recalls how Queen Suriyothai, disguised as a warrior, galloped her mount between the king and his Burmese foe when she saw her husband in trouble. The queen saved the king's life, but lost her own in the process. A *chedi* enshrining her ashes can still be seen at Ayuthaya.

The Burmese invasion of 1549 was doomed to failure. Tabinshweti's armies withdrew, and Mahachakrapat refortified the kingdom's defenses with the help of the Portuguese. Three hundred wild elephants were captured and trained for further wars against Burma.

naung to rule Siam as a vassal state. His eldest son, Naresuen, was taken to Burma by Bayinnaung as a guarantee for Maha Thammaraja's good conduct. The boy was repatriated to Siam at the age of 15—and together with his younger brother, Ekatotsarot, he began immediately to gather armed followers.

Naresuen had gained an insight into Burmese armed strength and strategies during his formative years. He trained his troops in the art of guerrilla warfare; there hit-and-run tactics earned them the nicknames "Wild Tigers" and "Peeping Cats."

Naresuen's opportunity to reassert Siamese independence came following the death of Bayinnaung in 1581. Revolts in the Shan states and at Ava kept young King

Seven of the new war elephants were white ones. The Buddhist kings of Southeast Asia have always treasured the possession of white elephants. They are considered to be auspicious, enhancing royal prestige and ensuring the country's prosperity. When Burma's King Bayinnaung, who had succeeded his father-in-law, heard this, he launched another invasion.

In 1569, Ayuthaya fell to Bayinnaung's forces. The Burmese thoroughly sacked and plundered the city, and forcibly removed much of Ayuthaya's population to Burma. King Mahachakrapat was among the captives; he died before arriving in Pegu.

Maha Thammaraja, the defeated king's leading deputy, was appointed by Bayin-

Nandabayin busy at home when Naresuen declared Ayuthaya's freedom in 1584. During the following nine years, the Burmese made several attempts to resubjugate Siam, but Naresuen had taken thorough defensive measures and repulsed all invasions. On one of these occasions, he killed the Burmese crown prince in single combat mounted on elephants.

Naresuen assumed full kingship upon his father's death in 1590. He reconsolidated the Siamese kingdom, then turned the tables on Burma with repeated attacks which contributed to the disintegration of the Burmese Empire. The Khmers, who had been whittling away at Siam's eastern boundary during Ayuthaya's period of weakness, were also subdued. Under "Naresuen the Great," Ayuthaya prospered and became the thriving metropolis described by 17th Century European visitors.

Europe's 'Door to the East'

The reign of Naresuen's brother, Ekatotsarot, between 1605 and 1610, coincided with the arrival of the Dutch in Siam. Ekatotsarot was not interested in pursuing Naresuen's militaristic policies; instead, he sought to develop Ayuthaya's economy. To these ends, he took several measures to increase state revenue, among them the introduction of taxes on commerce. This gave him a reputation as a "covetous man" among Europeans.

The Dutch opened their first trading station at Ayuthaya in 1608. Keen to promote commercial relations, King Ekatotsarot in the same year sent emissaries to The Hague—the first recorded appearance of Thais in Europe.

During the reign of King Songham (1610–1628), the English arrived bearing a letter from James I. Like the Dutch, they were welcomed and allotted a plot of land on which to build a factory.

Europeans were primarily attracted to Siam as a door to the China trade. The nature of seasonal monsoons made direct sailing to China impossible, so Ayuthaya and her ports became entrepôts for goods traveling between Europe, India and the East Indies, and China and Japan. The Siamese home market was also quite substantial. The peace initiated by Naresuen had given rise to a surplus of wealth, which created a demand in Thai society for luxury items like Oriental porcelain and silk. The Japanese, who already had established a sizeable community of traders at Ayuthaya, paid silver bullion for local Siamese products such as hides, teak, tin and sugar.

Under the adventurer Yamada Nagamasa, who earned himself an official court rank, many Japanese gained employment as king's guards. These mercenaries played a key role in Thai history in 1628, when they helped King-to-be Prasattong to establish himself as regent to a boy-king, and subsequently to depose the rightful ruler. But when the shogun in Edo (Tokyo) refused to recognize him as Thai monarch, Prasattong took his revenge on the Japanese settlement in Ayuthaya. Several Japanese were killed; the rest hastily fled to Cambodia.

Prasattong ruled until 1655. He imposed a system of royal monopolies whereby all foreign trade was directly controlled by the king—represented by the Minister of Finance. (The minister's title, Phra Klang, was corrupted to "Barcalon" by European traders.) The importance of Ayuthaya as a trade center increased markedly during this period; because rare commodities were under state control, they could be procured only from royal warehouses in the capital.

The Dutch established maritime dominance in the Far East when they drove the Portuguese out of Malacca in 1641. Seven years later, in 1648, they made a show of naval force in the Gulf of Siam, thereby persuading Prasattong to agree to certain trade concessions and giving them virtual economic control in Siam. Prasattong's son, King Narai (ruled 1656 to 1688), despised the Dutch and welcomed the English as a

European ally to counter Holland's influence. But another Dutch blockade in 1664, this time at the mouth of the Chao Phya river, won them a monopoly on the hide trade and—for the first time in Thai history—extraterritorial privileges.

The 'Greek Favorite'

It was the French who gained greatest favor in King Narai's court. Their story is interwoven with that of one of the most

Above, King Narai (1656–1688) and right, Constantine Phaulkon. The "Greek Favorite's" manipulation of Narai won privileges for the French.

fascinating characters in Thai history, a Greek adventurer named Constantine Phaulkon.

French Jesuit missionaries first arrived at the court of Ayuthaya in 1665, and were permitted to open a center of worship. The king's friendliness and religious tolerance were taken by the bishops as a sign of his imminent conversion. Their exaggerated accounts excited the imagination of Louis XIV, who hoped that the salvation of Siamese heathens could be combined with French territorial acquisition. King Narai was delighted to receive a personal letter from the Sun King in 1673.

Enter Phaulkon. The son of a Greek innkeeper, he began his career with the East India Company as a cabin boy. He worked

his way east with the British, and arrived in Siam in 1678. A talented linguist, he learned the Thai language in just two years, and with the help of his English benefactors, he was hired as interpreter by the Barcalon. Within five years, Phaulkon had rapidly risen through the strata of Thai society to the very high rank of Phya Vijayendra. In this position, he had continual access to the king, whose confidence he slowly and surely cultivated.

The previous year, Phaulkon had fallen out of favor with the East India Company. He had also converted to Roman Catholicism in order to marry a Japanese woman of that faith. As Phaulkon moved firmly into the French camp, so did King Narai. He sent

two embassies to Louis' court, and the French reciprocated with a visit to Ayuthaya in 1685. While they failed to convert King Narai to Christianity, they did succeed in gaining many trade privileges.

Phaulkon, of course, served as interpreter during the French embassy. He secretly outlined to visiting Jesuit priests his plans to convert the entire country of Siam to Catholicism. To effect this, he said, he would need civilians and troops from France. Following another exchange of embassies between the courts of Louis and Narai, a French squadron—under the command of Marshal Desfarges—accompanied French and Thai delegations aboard warships to Siam. The small but disciplined and well-equipped French force of 500 soldiers was given landing rights by King Narai, under Phaulkon's advice. For his pains, Phaulkon was created a Count of France and a Knight of the Order of St. Michael.

Then the tables began to turn against Phaulkon. A number of high-ranking Siamese officials had privately been increasingly alarmed by the influence of the "Greek Favorite" over the king. Phaulkon's extravagant lifestyle was considered proof of his blatant robbery of the country. Contemporary European writers testify that at Phaulkon's Lop Buri mansion, the dinner table was laid for 40 guests every night, and a huge quantity of wine was consumed. His unpopularity was fueled not only by the ominous French military presence, but also by a rumor that Phaulkon had converted King Narai's adopted son to Christianity, with the intention of security his succession to the throne.

When Narai fell gravely ill in 1688, a nationalistic, anti-French movement took immediate action. Led by Phra Phetracha, a commander of the Royal Regiment of Elephants, the rebels confined the ailing king to his palace. Phaulkon was arrested for treason, and in June was executed outside Lop Buri. Narai died in July, and Phra Phetracha mounted the throne, declaring as his top priority the immediate withdrawal of French troops. The French forces had been diffused to man different garrisons, but Desfarges eventually agreed to remove his soldiers.

'The Most Beautiful City'

The presence of Europeans throughout Narai's reign gave the West most of its early knowledge of Siam. Voluminous literature was generated by Western visitors to Narai's court. Their attempts at cartography left a record of Ayuthaya's appearance, though few remains exist today. Royal palaces and hundreds of temples were within the walls surrounding the island on which the capital stood. Some Western visitors compared Ayuthaya to Venice and called it "the most beautiful city in the east." The Abbé de Choisy, an envoy of Louis XIV, was more reserved in his praise. "I have never seen anything fairer, despite the fact that the temples mark the only departure from unsophisticated nature," he wrote.

The kings who succeeded Narai terminated the open-door policy. A modest amount of trade was maintained and missionaries were permitted to remain; but Ayuthaya embarked on a course of isolation that lasted for well over 100 years. This left

acceded to the throne in 1758 after a bitter succession struggle with his brother, and surrounded himself with female company to ensure his pleasure. Meanwhile, a village headman united the Third Burmese Empire and assumed the royal title Alaungpaya. His invading Burmese armies were repelled in 1760 after Alaungpaya was wounded by his own cannon. But in 1767, a second Burmese invasion, led by Alaungpaya's son Hsinbyushin, succeeded in capturing Ayuthaya after a siege of 14 months.

In their hurry to withdraw from the conquered capital, the Burmese killed, looted and set fire to the whole city, thereby expunging four centuries of Thai civilization. Showing complete disregard for their common religion, the Burmese Buddhists plun-

the rulers free to concentrate mainly on religious and cultural affairs. Internal communications were strengthened with the linking of numerous waterways.

The reign of King Boromakot (1733–1758) began with a particularly violent struggle for power, but Boromakot's 25-year term was an unusually peaceful one and became known as Ayuthaya's Golden Age. Poets and artists abounded at his court, enabling literature and the arts to flourish as never before. During this period, Ceylon invited a delegation of Siamese monks to purify the Sinhalese Sangha, reversing the past religious roles of the two countries.

The tranquil days proved to be the calm before the storm. Boromakot's son Ekatat

dered Ayuthaya's rich temples, melting down all the available gold from Buddha images. Members of the royal family, along with 90,000 captives and the accumulated booty, were removed to Burma.

Taksin's Revenge

Despite their overwhelming victory, the Burmese didn't retain control of Siam for long. Giving meaning to an ancient proverb that "Ayuthaya never lacks good men," a young general named Phya Tak Sin gathered a small band of followers during the final Burmese siege of the Thai capital. He recognized the hopelessness of the Siamese situation under the effete king and his decadent entourage. So instead of waiting for the holocaust to envelop the city, he and his comrades broke through the Burmese encirclement and escaped to Chantaburi on the southeast coast of the Gulf of Siam. There, Phya Tak Sin assembled an army and navy. Seven months after the fall of Ayuthaya, he and his forces sailed back to the capital and expelled the Burmese occupation garrison.

Taksin, as he is popularly known, had barely spent a night at Ayuthaya when he decided to transfer the capital. He revealed to his troops that the old kings had appeared to him in a dream and told him to move. In fact, strategic considerations were probably more important than supernatural ones in Taksin's decision. A site nearer to the sea would facilitate foreign trade, ensure the procurement of arms, and make defense and withdrawal easier in case of renewed Burmese attack.

During the 17th Century, a small fishing village downstream had become an important trade and defense outpost for Ayuthaya. Known as Bangkok, "village of wild olive groves," it contained fortifications built by the French. The settlement straddled both sides of the Chao Phya river, at a place where a short-cut canal had widened into the main stream. On the west bank, at Thonburi, Taksin officially established his new capital and was proclaimed king.

The rule of Taksin was not an easy one. The lack of central authority since the fall of Ayuthaya had led to the rapid disintegration of the kingdom, and it fell upon Taksin to reunite the provinces. At the same time as he consolidated his power base at Thonburi, he contended with a series of Burmese invasions. These he resolutely repulsed.

Taksin ruled until 1782. In the last seven years of his reign, he relied heavily on two trusted generals, the brothers Chao Phya Chakri and Chao Phya Sarasih, who were given absolute command in military campaigns. They were responsible for liberating Chiang Mai and the rest of northern Thailand from Burmese rule, and for bringing Cambodia and most of present-day Laos under Thai suzerainty.

It was from the victorious Laotian campaign that Thailand obtained the famed Emerald Buddha. Chao Phya Chakri carried the Buddha from Vientiane to Thonburi in 1779. Carved of solid jadeite, the image was allegedly discovered at Chiang Rai in 1436 inside a pagoda struck asunder by lightning. The Emerald Buddha is regarded by Thais as the most sacred of all Buddha images, and is believed to guarantee the independence

and prosperity of the nation.

But while the Emerald Buddha was in good health, Taksin was not. At Thonburi, his personality underwent a slow metamorphosis from strong and just leader to cruel and unpredictable eccentric, due perhaps, to overexhaustion and the continuous strain of war and decision-making. He came to consider himself a *bodhisattva* or future Buddha, and flogged monks who refused to pay obeisance to him. Totally paranoid, he tortured his officials, his children, and even his wife to make them confess to imaginary crimes.

When a revolt broke out in March 1782, Taksin was forced to abdicate and enter a monastery. A minor official named Phya San, who engineered the revolt, offered the

vacant throne to Chao Phya Chakri upon his return from a Cambodian campaign. General Chakri assumed the kingship on April 6—a date still commemorated annually as Chakri Day—and established the reigning Chakri dynasty. Taksin, still regarded by an advisory council of generals as a potential threat to internal stability, was executed in the traditional royal manner. It is said that Chao Phya Chakri's eyes were filled with tears when he said farewell to his former king and patron.

Left, General Taksin in battle against Burmese conquerors in 1767. Above, an 18th Century European map of the Kingdom of Siam.

General Chakri took the name Ramati-bodi as the ruler of Siam. Later to be known as Rama I, he ruled from 1782 to 1809. His first action as king was to transfer his administrative headquarters across the river from Thonburi to Bangkok. There he set about to build his new palace according to the pattern at Ayuthaya. He assembled all surviving master craftsmen from the old city. The Grand Palace they built contained not only the residences of the king and royal family, but also incorporated the government and judicial offices and, most importantly, the

Royal Chapel.

The chapel, in fact, was the first permanent structure built by Rama I and the most elaborate. Constructed to house the Emerald Buddha, it took nearly three years to complete. When ready, the Emerald Buddha was brought from Thonburi and installed on a canopied throne in the Royal Chapel. As this was done, a new word was added to the lengthy official epithet of the capital city: Krung Thep Phra Maha Nakorn Amorn Rattanakosin (etc.). This was the "City of Angels, Abode of the Gem." The Rattanakosin Era was born.

Since this time, Thais have called their capital Krung Thep. But it continues to be known internationally as Bangkok.

One of Rama I's chief concerns was securing the borders of his country. Early in his reign, King Bodawpaya of Burma launched a series of military expeditions involving the largest number of troops in the history of Thai-Burmese wars. Siamese troops boldly attacked the invaders at strategic border points, routing the Burmese before they could do serious harm. After Bodawpaya, Burma became embroiled in British colonial conflicts and Siam was left more or less in peace.

Modern Thailand is indebted to Rama I for his assiduous cultural revival program. He appointed commissions of experts to review and assemble fragments of historical and religious treatises surviving the destruction of Ayuthaya in 1767.

Rama I perpetuated another Ayuthaya tradition by appointing his brother as *maha uparaja*, or deputy king, with powers almost equal to his own. His home, the Wang Na or "palace at the back," now houses the National Museum.

Because the royal regalia had been destroyed with everything else during the siege of Ayuthaya, Rama I had a new crown and regalia commissioned for his coronation. Similarly, in his old age, he commissioned a golden urn to be prepared for his body, according to ancient court protocol prescribing that the bodies of high-ranking royalty be placed in urns between the times of death and cremation.

The king was so pleased with the golden urn created by his craftsmen that he placed it in his bedroom to be able to admire it fully. Upon seeing this, one of his wives burst into tears: it was a bad omen, she said. "Nonsense," replied the king, laughing. "If I don't see it from the outside while I'm alive, how the hell do you think I can ever see it?"

Rama II and Rama III

Rama I's successors, Rama II and Rama III, completed the consolidation of the Siamese kingdom and the revival of the arts and culture of Ayuthaya. Best remembered as an artist, Rama II (1809–1824) was responsible for building and repairing numer-

Previous pages, young classical dancers at the royal court. Left, King Rama I (1782–1809). Right, century-old view of a city klong.

ous Bangkok monasteries. His most famous construction was Wat Arun, the Temple of Dawn.

During his father's reign, Rama II had already earned himself a name as a great poet. His magnum opus was the *Inao*, an epic poem adopted from a Javanese legend. His classic version of the *Ramakien*, or Thai Ramayana, was completed during his reign—with large sections composed by the king himself as well as by other poets. At this court, Rama II employed theatrical and classical dance troupes of the *khone* and

Anna and the King of Siam

With the help of Hollywood, Rama IV (ruled 1851–1868) became the most famous King of Siam. Best known as King Mongkut, he was portrayed in *The King and I* as a frivolous, bald-headed despot. But nothing could have been further from the truth. In fact, he was the first Thai king to understand Western culture and technology, and his reign has been described as "the bridge spanning the new and the old."

The younger brother of Rama III, Mong-

lakorn traditions to enact his compositions.

Rama II re-established relations with the West, suspended since the time of Narai, allowing the Portuguese to construct the first Western embassy in Bangkok. Rama III (ruled 1824–1851) continued to reopen Siam's doors to foreigners, successfully promoting trade with China. The ready availability of Chinese porcelain led him to decorate many of his temples, including Wat Arun, with porcelain fragments.

An extremely pious Buddhist, Rama III was labeled "austere and reactionary" by some Europeans. But he encouraged American missionaries to introduce Western medicine to his country—including small-pox vaccinations.

kut spent 27 years as a Buddhist monk prior to his accession to the throne. This gave him a unique opportunity to roam as a commoner among the populace. He learned to read Buddhist scriptures in the Pali language. Missionaries taught him Latin and English; thus able to read European texts, the monk Mongkut delved into many subjects: history, geography and the sciences, especially astronomy.

Mongkut realized that traditional Thai values would not save his country from Western encroachment. To the contrary, he believed that modernization would bring Siam in line with the West and reduce hostilities with foreigners. England was the first European country to benefit from this policy when a 1855 treaty granted extraterritorial privileges, a duty of only 3 percent on imports, and permission to bring in Indian opium duty-free. Other Western nations, including France and the United States, followed suit with similar treaties. And when Mongkut lifted the state monopoly on rice, that crop rapidly became Siam's leading export.

Rama IV wanted his children to gain the same benefits from the English language as himself. For this purpose, he engaged Anna Leonowens as an English teacher. The self-elevated governess greatly exaggerated her role at court in her autobiographical writings, misrepresenting the king as a cruel autocrat permanently involved in harem intrigues. Her residence in Siam (1862–1867)

The Beloved King Chulalongkorn

Mongkut's son, Chulalongkorn, was only 15 when he ascended the throne. But he reigned over Siam as Rama V for 42 years— longer than any other Thai king—and transformed his country from a backward Asian land to a modern 20th Century kingdom.

Chulalongkorn immediately revolutionized his court by ending the ancient custom of prostration and by allowing officials to sit on chairs during royal audiences. He abolished serfdom (in stages, giving owners and serfs time for readjustment) and replaced the age-old system of corvée labor with direct taxation.

His reign was truly a "revolution from the throne." When Chulalongkorn assumed

is hardly mentioned in Thai sources.

Mongkut's beloved hobby, astronomy, was the indirect cause of his death. From observatories at his favorite palaces, the Summer Palace at Bang Pa-in and the Palace on the Hill at Petchburi, he successfully calculated and predicted a total eclipse of the sun on August 18, 1868. European and Asian skeptics joined him on the southeastern coast of the Gulf of Siam as the moon blocked off the sun's light from the earth. Mongkut's triumph raised his esteem among Western residents and Eastern astrologers alike. But his satisfaction was short-lived. The king contracted malaria during the trip down the coast, and he died two months later.

power, Siam had no schools, roads, railways, hospitals, or well-equipped military forces. To achieve the enormous task of modernization, he brought in foreign advisors and sent his sons and other young men abroad for education. He also founded a palace school for children of the aristocracy, and followed this with the establishment of other schools and vocational centers. The only previous seats of learning in Siam had been the monasteries.

A watershed year was 1892, when the four

Above left, King Mongkut (1851–1868) and his favorite wife. Right, English teacher Anna Leonowens, whose exaggerated autobiography became the movie, "The King and I."

government ministries were expanded to 12; a post and telegraph office was established; and construction of the first railway was begun. Chulalongkorn's brothers were leading figures in his government, especially Prince Devawongse, the foreign minister, and Prince Damrong, the first interior minister and a historian who has come to be known as "the father of Thai history." Chulalongkorn's elder children returned home from their European schools in the 1890s and contributed to modernizing the army and navy; one of them became Siam's first minister of justice.

The first hospital, Siriraj, was opened in 1886 after years of opposition. Most of the Thai common folk preferred herbal re-

reign, Siam had given up 120,000 square kilometers of fringe territory. But that seemed a small price to pay for maintaining the peace and independence of the Thai heartland in the Menam Chao Phya basin.

King Chulalongkorn made two European tours during his reign, in 1897 and 1907. These led him to seek more spacious surroundings than those of the Grand Palace, so he built the Dusit Palace on the site of a fruit orchard. It was directly connected to the Grand Palace by the wide Rajdamnoen Avenue. At Dusit, he held intimate parties and even fancy-dress balls, often cooking the food himself.

Chulalongkorn's many reforms bore fruit within his lifetime. The economy of the

medies to *farang* medicine. Besides, there was a distinct shortage of qualified doctors. Eventually, the obstacles were overcome.

In foreign relations, Rama V had to compromise and give up parts of his kingdom to maintain Siam's freedom from foreign colonization. When France conquered Annam in 1883 and Britain annexed Upper Burma in 1886, Siam found itself sandwiched uncomfortably between two rival expansionist powers. Border conflicts and gunboat diplomacy forced Siam to surrender to France its claims to Laos and western Cambodia. Similarly, certain Malay Peninsula territories were ceded to Britain in exchange for renunciation of British extraterritorial rights in Siam. By the end of Chulalongkorn's

country flourished, and Thai peasantry—in comparison with their counterparts in French Indochina and British Burma—were very well off. It is no wonder that Chulalongkorn was posthumously named Piya Maharaj, "the Beloved Great King."

As Rama V, Chulalongkorn was conscious of worldwide democratic trends, but judged his country as yet unprepared for such a change. It is said that he brought progress to Siam "only through the judicious exercise of his absolute power."

Above left, King Chulalongkorn (1868–1910) and entourage in Heidelberg, Germany, in 1907. Right, Prince Damrong, "the father of Thai history."

Controversial Brilliance

King Chulalongkorn's successor, Vajiravudh, began his reign (1910–1925) with a lavish coronation. Oxford-educated and thoroughly anglicized, his Western-inspired reforms to modernize Siam considerably affected the structure of modern Thai society.

One of the first changes was a 1913 edict commanding his subjects to adopt surnames. In the absence of a clan or caste system, genealogy was not a Thai strong point. In the past, Thais only used first names, which the king considered uncivilized. The law generated much initial bewilderment, especially in rural areas, and Vajiravudh personally coined patronymics for hundreds of

tribution was the promotion of the nationalist concept. An accomplished author, he used literature and drama to foster nationalism by glorifying Thai legends and historical heroes in plays. Under a pseudonym, he also wrote essays extolling the virtues of the Thai nation.

At the outbreak of World War I, Siam maintained neutrality. Vajiravudh joined the Allies by sending a small expeditionary force to fight in Europe in 1917, thereby securing Siam's admittance to the League of Nations. The Thai flag, a white elephant against a red background, was flown with others at Versailles but the pachyderm was unfortunately mistaken for a small domestic animal. The incident greatly discomfited the

families.

To simplify his forebears' lengthy titles for foreigners, he invented the Chakri dynastic name, Rama, to be followed by the proper reign number. To start with, he proclaimed himself as Rama VI. As Thai standards of beauty did not conform to Western ideals of femininity, women were encouraged to keep their hair long instead of having it close-cropped, and to replace their dhotis or plus-fours with the *panung*, a Thai-style sarong. Primary education was made compulsory throughout the kingdom; Chulalongkorn University, the first in Siam, was founded and schools for both sexes flourished during his reign.

Rama VI's most significant political con-

king who then changed the flag to red, white and blue stripes to represent the nation, the religion and the monarchy—elements now recognized as essential to the structure of modern Thailand.

King Vajiravudh preferred individual ministerial consultations to summoning his appointed Cabinet. His regime was therefore criticized as autocratic and lacking in coordination. Members of his family were dissatisfied because he rarely saw them, enjoying more the company of his courtiers. To this

Above, Chulalongkorn's widow and family; Vajiravudh and Prajadhipok are at center top and lower right, respectively. Right, turn-of-the-century state visitors at Ayuthaya.

clique, he was overly generous. His extravagance soon emptied the reserve funds built up by Chulalongkorn; towards the end of his reign, the Treasury had to meet deficits caused by the ruler's personal expenses.

Vajiravudh married late. His only daughter was born one day before he died in 1925. He was succeeded by his youngest brother, Prajadhipok, who reaped the consequences of his predecessor's brilliant but controversial reign.

Prajadhipok's Short Reign

The early death of his elder brother propelled Prajadhipok to royal succession although he, being an old Étonian, would have preferred a soldier's career to a ruler's.

proving the welfare of his subjects. He was aware of the rising demand for greater participation in government by a small foreign-educated faction, but felt that the Siamese were, on the whole, not ready for democracy. In 1927, he publicly commented that the people must first be taught political consciousness before democracy could effectively be introduced.

The worldwide economic crisis of 1931 affected Siam's rice export. By the time Prajadhipok dropped the gold standard linking the Thai baht to the pound sterling, it was too late to stem the financial crisis. The government was forced to implement further economies by cutting the salary of junior personnel and by resorting to a retrenchment of the armed services. Thus, discontent

Once king, however, he stressed economy and efficiency within the government. Unlike his brother, he tried to cut public expenditure by reducing the Civil List and Royal Household expenses drastically. Prajadhipok's economic policies, combined with increased revenue from foreign trade, amply paid off.

In the early years of his reign, communications were improved by a wireless service and the Don Muang Airport began to operate an international air center. It was also during his reign that Siam saw the establishment of the Fine Arts Department, the National Library and the National Museum.

Hard-working and conscientious, Prajadhipok was personally concerned with im-

brewed among army officials and bureaucrats, who felt that their promotion was hindered.

Rumors and speculation were rampant during the 150th anniversary celebrations of the Chakri dynasty in April 1932. Prajadhipok was the last regal representative of traditional Thai kingship to preside over grand pageantry which featured a royal barge procession. Two months later on June 24, a coup d'etat ended the paternal but absolute rule of the king.

The coup was staged by the People's Party, a military and civilian group masterminded by foreign-educated Thais. The chief ideologist was Pridi Panomyong, a young lawyer trained in France. On the military side, Captain Luang Pibulsongram was responsible for gaining the support of important army colonels. With a few tanks, the 70 conspirators sparked off their "revolution" by occupying strategic areas and holding the senior princes hostages. Other army officers stood by and the public took no part in it, save as spectators. The king was out of Bangkok; he quickly returned to the capital and to avoid bloodshed, accepted the provisional constitution by which he "ceased to rule but continued to reign."

From Monarchy to Democracy

Absolute monarchy was quickly replaced by a Party dictatorship. Once in power, the new regime declared that Thais were insuf-

porters were from the intelligentsia. The latter was allowed to return in 1934 when he was cleared of all charges.

Meanwhile, King Prajadhipok was finding his new role increasingly painful. Constitutional differences with the government culminated in his decision to abdicate in 1935. In his farewell speech to the nation, he said that he had given up his absolute power to the whole of the Thai people and not to any particular group. At the time of the abdication, Prajadhipok was in England; he remained there with the title "Prince Sukhothai" until his death in 1941. Ananda Mahidol, his 10-year-old nephew studying in Switzerland, was proclaimed King. A Regency Council of three members was appointed to act during his minority.

ficiently educated to rule themselves; the new government's first 10 years was to be a trial period for democracy. In December 1932, the king signed the Parliament Constitution which promised universal suffrage and general elections every four years.

In 1933, the government was divided by Pridi's economic policy advocating the nationalization of all agricultural land. The plan was considered communistic and Pridi was maneuvered into temporary exile. A counter-coup in the same year reshuffled members of the Executive Council, with Pibul (Pibulsongram) gaining ascendency. Thai politics for the next two decades was alternately dominated by Pibul, who had the military backing, and Pridi, whose sup-

Aimlessness and Instability

The abrupt transplanting of Western democracy to a traditionally deep-rooted society resulted in political aimlessness and instability. The "permanent" constitution was revised several times; experiments with both unicameral and bicameral legislative systems were attempted. Unsuccessful democratic interludes usually paved the way for military intervention and dominance.

A series of governmental crises occurred

Above, the 1947 coronation of King Bhumibol Adulyadej. Here, he receives the scepter of sovereignty. Right, portraits of Thailand's influential generals.

40

between 1935 and 1938, enabling Pibul to assume control. Nationalism was intensified, economically as well as culturally, by his authoritarian regime. To demonstrate the new chauvinism, the name of the country was officially changed from Siam to Thailand. Pibul began a "civilizing campaign" which forced Western dress styles and social mores upon the masses. The chewing of betelnut, favored by Thais from time immemorial, was outlawed and people were told to wear shoes and hats in public. Even expectant mothers and serious casualties, if shoeless or hatless, were refused admittance into hospitals.

A pro-Ally underground resistance movement, the Seri Thai or Free Thai Movement, emerged. It received the active support of

younger brother King Bhumibol Adulyadej, the present monarch. The new king resumed his studies in Switzerland in 1946 and Prince Rangsit of Jainat, who had been released after six years of imprisonment, was appointed Regent until his death in 1951.

The military consolidated its power by a bloodless coup in 1947. One of the main figures was Colonel Sarit Thanarat, army commander of the First Division controlling the Bangkok area. This coup saw the emergence of a younger generation of army officers, Thai-educated and less westernized than the coup leaders of 1932. Communist uprisings in neighboring countries were considered threatening by upper and middle-class Thais, and this helped to justify two decades of military junta rule.

Pridi, who was acting as Regent, and was led by Seni Pramoj in the United States. The Japanese became increasingly disliked and when the tide turned against them, Pibul's collaborative government collapsed. To bring about reconciliation with the West, Seni Pramoj was appointed Prime Minister in 1945.

Seni government was soon replaced by that of Pridi, whose image had been improved by his war stance. King Ananda Mahidol, now aged 20, returned home to a tumultuous welcome in 1945. Only one year later, the young king was found shot dead in his bedroom. His tragic and unsolved death caused Pridi's political exit.

Ananda Mahidol was succeeded by his

Field Marshall Pibul returned to politics in 1948. His premiership was to last 10 years. His anti-communist foreign policy led to closer cooperation with the United States against the People's Republic of China. Thailand joined SEATO (South East Asia Treaty Organization) to combat communist aggression. American economic aid began in 1950, most of which was for military purposes. The total sum was to reach stupendous proportion, especially during the Vietnam War.

Subsequent to his world tour in 1955, Pibul decided to experiment with democracy by lifting the ban on political parties and permitting "Hyde Park" style free speeches. The democratic period misfired and two years later, a state of emergency was declared. His newly elected government was overthrown by Sarit.

Strong-man Politics

The 1957 coup saw the alignment of Sarit, General Thanom Kitticachorn and General Prapas Charusathien, a trio which controlled Thai politics from the later' 50s to the early' 70s. Sarit epitomized the strong-man concept in the past represented by certain kings. Although all trappings of democracy were abolished, his decisiveness and stress on discipline won popular support.

The military leaders, however, became involved in business activities, gradually controlling major finanical, industrial, commercial and foreign enterprises. Sarit's government declared economic development its national priority and implemented a six-year plan. A Board of Investment was set up to attract foreign capital. Recognizing the foreign exchange earning power of tourism, the Tourist Organization of Thailand was established. Sarit set in motion the machinery necessary for national development.

Upon his death in 1965, Sarit's aide General Thanom became Prime Minister and head of junta, with Prapas as the army commander-in-chief. The communist threat accounted for Thailand's complexity in the Vietnam war. By allowing the United States to build six air bases in 1965, American monetary aid was obtained for the construction of highways. But certain administrators allegedly siphoned funds to their private accounts.

The King proclaimed a new constitution in 1968 and the next year's general election saw Thanom democratically reassuming his premiership. But the internal situation soon deteriorated due to terrorist insurgency, resulting in the abrogation of the constitution and the proclamation of martial law. Student leaders' demand for an end to military dictatorship and a return of parliamentary democracy culminated in the student uprising of October 1973. Most of the agitators were from the left-wing Thammasat University. A clash between students and the army produced 69 dead and 800 wounded. Thanom's clique was forced to resign and go into exile.

This heralded an era of open politics from 1973 to 1976. It was, according to the Institute of Southeast Asian Studies, "a nightmare for the bureaucratics and military elite." Hundreds of pressure groups were formed, strikes and demonstrations were common occurrences, and elections led to brief coalition governments. Foreign policywise, the most successful government was that of Kukrit Pramoj. Kukrit started diplomatic relations with the People's Republic of China and strengthened Thailand's role in ASEAN (the Association of South East Asian Nations). In October 1976 another violent confrontation between the police and students led the army to seize control from the elected government.

The fall of Vietnam, Laos and Cambodia in 1975 resulted in the withdrawal of U.S. troops as well as equipment from Thailand. The arrival in Bangkok of GIs on "rest and recuperation" leaves from Vietnam, and their demand for distractions, had spawned a variety of entertainment facilities, temporarily boosting the local economy but leaving behind destitute Amerasian children. World opinion considered Thailand the next "domino" to fall to the communists. But the unity maintained by the King and the Buddhist religion prevented that from happening.

Ruling with Dharma

"We will reign with *dharma* (righteousness), for the benefits and happiness of the Siamese people," was the coronation pledge of King Bhumibol Adulyadej. The King alone provides stability and continuity lacking in the turbulent cycle of Thai politics. Tirelessly touring the land with Queen Sirikit to inspect and improve the welfare of the people, the King inspires universal reverence. As a constitutional monarch, he maintains neutrality at times of crises, and coupmakers have declared their loyalty to the Crown.

The King's moral authority was demonstrated in April 1981 when a group of army officers calling themselves the Young Turks staged a coup to overthrow the government of General Prem Tinsulanond. Although commanding formidable forces, their attempt quickly ended in failure when it was apparent that the group did not possess the King's tacit consent.

Bangkok celebrated her 200th birthday with the Rattanakosin Bicentennial celebrations in April 1982. The last 50 years have been extremely eventful. Thailand is today a front-line nation for the West in Asia, but it remains the "Land of the Free." In the words of the King: "We still stand here. We stand here for good of the world."

The 1982 Rattanakosin Celebration commemorated 200 years of Thai greatness. Right, a procession of the Grand Palace; and following pages, the royal barge on the Chao Phya.

Portraits of Contemporaries

Even a cursory glance at Thai history, such as the one presented on the previous pages, belies any simplified view of the country and the people. In the following pages we try to capture the more ineffable quality of the character of the Thai nation through a series of portraits of Thai contemporaries.

Whether it is a young monk out and about modern Bangkok in the gentle light of dawn carrying an alms bowl; a chic Thai businesswoman closing a deal with her more traditional compatriot wearing a silk *pasin* (full-length wraparound); or King Bhumibol rushing back by helicopter to an upcountry summer palace after a royal visit to a nearby village school — Thailand sparkles with remarkable individuals.

The King: A symbol from the distant past; a man vital to the present

His Majesty the King is to preside over a royal ceremony at Wat Phra Keo, the Temple of the Emerald Buddha. The crowd has begun to gather hours before the scheduled royal appearance, representing every walk of Thai life — elderly country women with cropped hair and betel-stained lips; farmers in blue homespun cotton; students in neatly pressed uniforms; society ladies in Thai silk dresses; office workers from nearby government buildings; and children brought by their parents to see their ruler. A few moments before the appointed time, a perceptible thrill runs through the crowd.

It is not the first time most of them have seen the king, for within his kingdom he is perhaps one of the most visible rulers in the world — constantly opening fairs, presiding over ceremonies, handing out diplomas, dropping out of the sky in a

The monarchy plays a vital role in Thai life; here the King is shown at the investiture of the Crown Prince.

helicopter — yet the same sense of reverence and excitement grips his subjects every time he appears. Swords clank, the honor guard snaps to attention, the crowd draws its breath — and today through the ornately carved doors that separate Wat Phra Keo from the compound of the Grand Palace steps a slim man in an immaculate white uniform, followed by a woman of breath-taking beauty in a shimmering traditional Thai-style dress. Their majesties, King Bhumibol and Queen Sirikit, have arrived.

The king of Thailand is both a symbol and a man. Born in the distant past in fabled Sukhothai, the symbol has endured through wars and revolutions, the fall of dynasties and the smashing of traditions and governments, both dictatorial and democratic, and through times of tribulation and prosperity. While the idea of kingship has faded in most other countries to that of a figurehead, in Thailand it remains the most powerful unifying force in the country, respected by all groups. Pictures of the king and queen hang in almost every house in the nation; and at the conclusion of every movie, no Thai in the audience would think of leaving the theater before standing at attention for a portrait of the king that is flashed on the screen while the national anthem is being played. The one thing the tolerant Thais will not forgive is any remark disrespectful of the monarchy.

The man himself is as extraordinary as the symbol. He was born in Cambridge, Massachusetts in 1927, where his father Prince Mahidol of Songkhla was studying medicine at Harvard University. His father, a son of King Rama V, was later regarded as the father of modern medicine in Thailand. At Prince Bhumibol's birth there seemed little chance of his ever becoming king. Between him and the throne, according to the laws of succession laid down by Rama V, stood any children the ruling Rama VII

might have, Bhumibol's own father, and his elder brother Prince Ananda. But Rama VII had no children, and Prince Mahidol died in 1929. On King Rama VII's abdication, Ananda, still a young student in Switzerland, became king, though he did not return to his kingdom until after the war. In 1947, he was killed under mysterious circumstances in the Grand Palace and his younger brother, Prince Bhumibol, ascended the throne as the ninth ruler of the Chakri dynasty.

Over the thirty years since his coronation, King Bhumibol has proved himself a worthy successor to his celebrated ancestors. With his beautiful Queen Sirikit, he has traveled to every part of the country and played an active role in solving many of its problems. The spacious grounds of Chitralada Palace where he lives — the old Grand Palace is used now only for ceremonial occasions and state receptions — include experimental rice fields and a dairy farm where the king, at his own expense, tests methods to improve the country's agriculture. He also supports an extensive program of artificial rain making for the drought-plagued Northeast, as well as schemes for improving the lot of the northern hilltribes. In addition to all this, he and the queen take part in the innumerable royal ceremonies that punctuate the year — the seasonal robing of the Emerald Buddha, the various Buddhist holy days, the opening of Parliament, the Armed Forces Day parade, to name only a few — plus the handing out of diplomas at the universities and countless royally sponsored weddings and cremations. If the Thais revere their king traditionally as a symbol, they have also come to feel a similar respect for the present ruler as a man, a fact which makes

On October 23, the anniversary of King Chulalongkorn's death, Thais pay homage to the revered king's memory at his equestrian statue in Bangkok.

the Thai monarchy stronger now than at any period since King Bhumibol's grandfather, Chulalongkorn (Rama V).

Buddhism: A total way of being

A young Buddhist monk walks with grave dignity along a city street in the pale light of early morning, a saffron-colored cloth satchel over one arm, a brass alms bowl in the other. The total number of monks in Thailand varies from season to season, swelling during the rainy season, the traditional time for a young man to enter the priesthood for a period that may range from two weeks to six months. While in the temple, he listens to sermons based on the Buddha's teachings, studies the Tripitaka *or Three Baskets (the teaching of Buddha in Pali), practices meditation, and learns the virtues of an ascetic life free of material possessions. Like the regular priests, he goes out at dawn to receive his morning meal from the devout almsgivers who thereby earn merit.*

A Buddhist monk, according to one authority, "must not only abstain from stealing, lying and idle talk, taking life, indulgence in sex, intoxicants, luxuries and frivolous amusements; he must also obey no less than 227 rules that govern all the minutiae of daily conduct and manners. He can have no possessions except the yellow robe, the alms bowl, and a few personal necessaries." He eats only two meals a day, the first early in the morning and the second before noon.

For all its spartan life, however a Buddhist *wat* (or "temple") in Thailand is by no means isolated from the "real" world. Most *wats* have schools

The spirit of Buddhism is omnipresent, most obviously in the thousands of temples throughout Thailand. This serene image is one of the three Buddhas situated in the front of Wat Prasingh, Chiang Mai.

of some sort attached to them — sometimes the only school in the village — and except during the period of Buddhist Lent, monks are free to travel from one temple to another at will. Moreover, the *wats* are open to anyone who wishes to retire to them. Monks also play an important part in many of the rituals of daily life, such as the blessing of a new building, a birthday, or a funeral.

To people outside, the *wat* and its priests offer an important opportunity for merit making, which ensures them of greater rewards after death. This is of special importance to women, for though an order of nuns once existed in Thailand (and now and then you still see survivors of it wearing white robes), it was discontinued some time ago, and the only way a woman can attain spiritual advancement is through earning merit; for this reason, an unusual number of the people attending the sabbath-day sermons are females, usually older ones. Besides giving food to the monks, the most popular way of earning merit is to make some needed repairs on the temple or, even better, replacing an old and derelict building with a new one.

The great majority — about 94 percent — of the Thai people are devout Buddhists, but religious tolerance is (and always has been) extended to most of the world's other religions. In Bangkok alone there are over a hundred mosques, reflecting the powerful presence of Islam in the provinces of the South bordering on Malaysia.

"Thai religion is no fire and brimstone affair from the pulpit," writes Valentine Chu in *Thailand Today*. "It is rather a way of being and looking at the world — philosophical, mystical, sometimes baffling to the Westerner — that permeates every part of one's existence." And it is a way of being that is remarkably alive today.

The basic form of Buddhism practiced in Thailand is Hinayana,

also called the Buddhism of the Lesser Vehicle, which originally came from India. This is the same form practiced in neighboring Burma, but even a casual visitor to temples in both places will quickly perceive many differences between them; for as they have done with most outside influences — Khmer temple decorations and Chinese food, for instance — the Thais over the centuries have evolved a Buddhism of their own, suited to the Thai temperament. As a philosopy — as distinct from a religion — Buddhism has played a profound role in shaping the Thai character, particularly their reactions to events. The Buddhist concept of earthly impermanence, its idea of the absurdity of trying to establish certainties in an ever fluid existence, has done much to create that relaxed, carefree charm that is one of the most appealing characteristics of the country. Tension, ulcers, nervous breakdowns, and the like are not unknown in Thailand, at least not in places like Bangkok; but that they are remarkably uncommon is in no small way due to the influence of Buddhism.

Spirits: A commonplace belief

An old woman, kneeling reverently before a small spirit house, clasps her hands in the prayerlike gesture called the wai. *Before the house she has placed burning incense sticks and a wreath of sweetly scented jasmine: these, she hopes, will persuade the spirit to look fondly on her and grant her wish — to win a lottery, perhaps, or get a grandson, or maybe just have good luck in general. Though the Thais are mostly Buddhist, other, older beliefs — in*

Tattoos are regarded as an effective means of warding off evil spirits, especially in rural parts of Thailand. This friendly fisherman from Chon Buri, shows off the Ramakien hero, Hanuman.

spirits, in astrology, in good and bad omens — also figure importantly in their lives.

Nearly every Thai male, and a large number of women as well, carries some sort of amulet, usually on a chain around his neck. Some wear as many as half a dozen charms, to protect them from all sorts of hazards, such as automobile accidents, gunfire, snakebite, and almost any other disaster one can think of. In the provinces, tattoos are regarded as effective in warding off evil. According to official Thai chronicles, the first Thai embassy to France, to the court of Louis XIV, amazed the king by telling him they possessed a magic charm that rendered them immune to bullets. A demonstration was arranged, and when the French squad fired, the chronicles continue, their bullets fell harmlessly to the ground without reaching their target.

Astrologers today are consulted regularly in Thailand to learn the most auspicious time for weddings, important journeys, moving into a new house, and even the promulgation of a constitution. Auspicious wedding dates seem to come in groups, and sometimes for three or four nights running, every available hall and hotel reception room in Bangkok is booked for nuptial banquets.

Many of the Thai's non-Buddhist beliefs are Brahman in origin, and even today Brahman priests — coming from the approximately four thousand Brahman families in the country — have an important place in Thai religious life and officiate at a number of major ceremonies. One of the most popular and impressive of these, the Plowing Ceremony, takes place every May on the Pramane Ground across from Bangkok's Temple of the Emerald Buddha. To inaugurate the first rice planting of the year, a team of sacred oxen draws a gilded plow, seeds are symbolically sown (and afterwards eagerly collected by farmers to bring them luck), and the head priest, after complex calculations, makes predictions on the forthcoming rainfall and the bounty of the next harvest. The Thai wedding ceremony, too, is almost entirely Brahman; and so are many of the rites attending a funeral.

The Thai word for spirit is *phi* and the variety of *phis* is immense, particularly in the countryside, outnumbering, so it is believed, the human population manyfold. One, a seductive female *phi*, is believed to reside in a certain kind of banana and to torment young men who come near. Another bothersome one takes possession of her victims and forces them to remove their clothes in public. (For some reason, the most destructive spirits all seem to be female.)

Stroll through the residential areas of any town in Thailand, including sophisticated Bangkok, and you will notice that in nearly every compound there is a miniature house, generally set on a post in a site selected after complex astrological consideration. In ordinary residences the small doll-like house may be a simple wooden structure that resembles a Thai dwelling; in grander establishments, hotels, and office buildings, it may be an elaborate mini-temple, made of cement and painted and gilded. In either case, the abode of the resident spirits of the compound, who have it in their power to favor or plague the human inhabitants, is regularly adorned with placative offerings of food, fresh flowers, and incense sticks. If calamity or ill luck befalls the compound, it may be necessary to call in an expert (frequently a Buddhist priest) who will consult the spirit to determine what is wrong.

One of the most famous spirit houses in Bangkok is in the compound of the Erawan Hotel, at the corner of Rajadamri and Ploenchit Roads. This shrine, honoring the Hindu god Shiva, was erected by the owners during the construction of the hotel, after several workers had been injured in a mysterious accidents; but the shrine soon acquired a widespread reputation for bringing good fortune to outsiders as well. As a result, believers asking for special favors nowadays so crowd the shrine that the hotel has built a special courtyard around it, and policemen are on hand on especially busy days.

A less well-known shrine in the capital, but highly regarded by its followers, is accessible only through a narrow, unmarked gate in a fashionable residential neighborhood. Its offerings consist entirely of phalluses, ranging from small to gargantuan, sculpted from wood, wax, stone, or cement with scrupulous fidelity to life.

To the average Thai, there is nothing inconsistent about the intermingling of such practices and beliefs with Buddhism. Their broad, easygoing tolerance makes it possible for them to accept, or at least to absorb, all such beliefs.

The Thai Woman: Gracefully balancing tradition and modernity

A Thai businesswomen, small, soft-spoken, gentle-mannered is the antithesis of the Western "career woman." According to an old Thai proverb, "A woman is the hind legs of the elephant," and Thai tradition requires that she honor and obey her husband, deferring to him in all matters, large and small. As if to ensure that she does so, Thai law forbids her to get a divorce, or dispose of property, without his consent.

During the drafting of the 1974 constitution a proposal that for the first time equality between men and women be clearly spelled out (made

Traditionally, the Thai woman has been regarded as "the hind legs of the elephant." Today, though, many of them are as up-to-date as their Western sisters and the old submissive stereotype is fast becoming the exception.

by the sole woman member of the drafting committee) was soundly defeated. From all this it would appear that the women of Thailand are sorely oppressed, and that a fertile field exists for proponents of Women's Lib. In truth, however, this is yet another example of how Thai appearances can be misleading; with a few activist exceptions, Thai women would be amazed at the suggestion that they are downtrodden, for they know just how much real power they have.

Without losing a bit of their feminity, almost without having to raise their voices, they have managed to prove that whatever their role in helping the elephant to move, it is at least as significant as that of the male's, and possibly more so; if they wanted to, they could cite another proverb: "All men are children, who must be cared for by their mothers."

The idea that the Asian woman is thoroughly subjugated and downtrodden probably had its origin in the old days of polygamy, when Western visitors were shocked by the seeming complacency with which the various wives accepted their relegated position within the family. But even then — in Thailand, at any rate — things were not quite what they seemed. The first wife often played an important part in the selection of the younger ones, and she usually got a number of more tangible rewards for being deprived of her husband's full attentions. In Thai family life today, it is the woman rather than the man who is more apt to be the dominant one, who handles the family finances and makes important decisions, although many Thai men scarcely know it.

If you rent a house in Thailand, you will probably pay your monthly check to a woman, no matter whose name might be on the title deed to the property; and if you move in business circles, especially in Bangkok, you will sooner or later have dealings with one of the famous "lady tycoons" who have been written about with wonder by several American magazines. The oldest and largest bus company in Bangkok is operated by a woman, and so is the largest fleet of ferry boats that ply the Chao Phya River; so, also, are at least three of the largest hotels in the capital. Whether she sits behind a desk actively directing a business operation, or she sits at home and "helps" her husband, the Thai woman exercises a power that is no less real for being unwritten into the law of the land. Indeed, some of them would prefer that it remains that way. "I don't understand what all the fuss is about," one lady owner of a big Bangkok jewelry shop said during the drafting of the constitution. "It's better to keep things the way they've always been. If it's all put down in black and white men might start thinking about it and then they would lose face. Let them keep their little proverbs; it doesn't do any harm."

The Civil Service: Once the main vocation for the well-educated

A civil servant. You will see him (or her) whenever you go into any government office, or into any public school or university, for teachers in Thailand are civil servants, too, and come under the same regulations as employees of the Internal Revenue Department. The civil service also includes the employees of the various government monopolies and business enterprises like the state railways, the lottery, the tobacco monopoly, and the telephone organization. Altogether they number in the hundreds of thousands, after farmers perhaps the largest single work force in the country — a massive, often cumbersome bureaucracy that administers the kingdom out of Bangkok.

Restful spots like this square near Wat Suthat still exist in Bangkok, only a a short walk from the government buildings of the Thai bureaucracy.

56

Civil service pay-scales are much lower than those of business and industry (a university lecturer with a Ph.D from abroad, for example, gets less than US$300 a month), but there is never a shortage of applications for even the lowest positions. One reason for this is that government service offers great security; civil servants are almost never fired, except in cases of blatant dishonesty or corruption. Another, more important, reason is that government service carries a high degree of social prestige. The Thais do not use "civil servant" when translating the Thai term into English; it comes out "government official," a lofty designation that covers everyone from the prime minister down to the lowly clerk earning a few hundred baht a month for doing anonymous paper work in some vast Kafkaesque office. Dating from the days of King Chulalongkorn's broad reform of the government administration in the latter part of the 19th century, acceptance into the civil service has been looked upon as an honor, a dependable way of earning respect from those outside in society at large. For young women in particular it was one of the few socially acceptable ways of earning a living, for business was regarded as unsuitable for any young woman from a good family.

There is not much doubt that this is another aspect of Thai life that is in the process of changing. The traditional Thai attitude that business was an activity best left to outsiders, such as the Chinese and Indian newcomers, is fast dying out, if it is not dead already; and the cost of living along with expanded job opportunities are sending many who in the past would have become civil servants into advertising and airline offices, trading companies, or in the case of teachers, into one of the private schools that offer better salaries than the government. It would certainly be inaccurate to say that being a "government official" has lost its appeal for the mass of Thais, but it is no longer the main avenue open to the well-educated and the ambitious.

The Military: A sprawling organization, active in all sectors of the country

The Thai soldier, like the civil servant, belongs to a rather sprawling, complex organization, which is often misunderstood by visitors who compare it to armies back home. In many ways, of course, it is the same, in that it has the job of defending the country: and Thai conscriptees serving their obligatory two-year terms before returning to civilian life fill most of the lower ranks. At the same time, however, the Thai army — more so than either the navy or the air force (though the same applies to them to a lesser degree) — is far more intimately involved in the business and government of the country than would be the case in most places in Western Europe or the United States.

High-ranking military officers sit on the boards of banks, own hotels, take part in business — at the same time as they actively pursue a military career. This has mainly resulted from army rule of the country almost continuously since the 1932 coup ending the absolute monarchy. However, one must not get the wrong impression that civilian influence and position were achieved purely by the use of force by military men otherwise unqualified. In certain cases, no doubt, this has happened; but not nearly as often as outsiders might think. Actually, the military in Thailand, as in several other developing nations, has evolved — whether by accident or design — into a career not unlike that of the civil service, and is one of the few careers in which a bright but poor

The military, exemplified by this bemedaled guard of honor, offers a popular career to bright but poor young men who want to get ahead; the army is an integral part of Thai society.

young man can achieve advancement on merit. The military establishment is now such an integral part of Thai society that is difficult to imagine life without it.

Rural life: The backbone of the country

A phu yai ban, *or Thai village headman, middle-aged usually, or older (experience and stability are counted as important qualities in a leader), must have a sharp perception of all the nuances of village life. Far more important to the villagers than the more modern government-appointed district officers, the head-man is the backbone of Thai rural society. Selected by his fellow villag-ers in an open election, the* phu yai ban *has a large role in village affairs: to speak for the village when negotia-tions are necessary with the outside world; to settle disputes of various kinds; to organize cooperative village undertakings; to listen; to under-stand.*

Most Thai villages, even those ly-ing a relatively short distance from large towns and cities, are remarkably insular; some have no electricity, and for many in the dry Northeast, the nearest fresh water may be an hour's walk away. Their concerns, like those of most insular people, are mainly inward and personal. When university students from Bangkok embarked on an ambitious "political education" plan in the countryside before the 1975 elections, some of them were surprised to discover that many villagers were totally uninterested in what was going on in Bangkok, and a number had no news of events in the capital or the country at large. An elderly couple from a village in the South, brought on

Farmers, like these taking a lunchbreak at harvest time near Phrae in North-Central Thailand, are still the backbone of the national life.

their first visit to the capital by their son who had made good in the big city, found only one thing that really im-pressed them in the noisy, confusing place: the electrically operated auto-matic doors of a department store. But even this turned out to be a some-what droll discovery, for when they returned to their village and told people about the doors, no one be-lieved them; one old villager had a good laugh at their story.

The land and the crops it pro-duces; the vagaries of weather; the local temple and the opportunities it offers for earning merit as well as the special pleasures of its fairs and cer-emonies; the strange spirits that lie everywhere in wait for the unwary; the love affairs and small scandals that provide occasional diversion from everyday cares; illness and death — these are the immediate concerns of rural life, as they have been from time immemorial. When one of the vil-lagers, generally one of the young men, leaves the village to try his luck in the city, his family views his depar-ture with a mixture of hope and sad-ness: hope because he may find a good job, in which case he will cer-tainly send money home each month; sadness because they know that a young man who leaves his village rarely ever comes back except to visit, and when he does he has changed beyond all recognition.

But the village and the *phu yai ban* will go on, as they always have; and as long as they last, so will the country.

Hilltribes: Seminomadic peoples living in the misty hills of the North

Wearing an enormous turban, a costume of heavy, shiny black mate-rial, and a large quantity of silver jewelry that flashes in the sun, a tribeswoman of the H'mong (popu-larly called the Meo), down from the hills for a look at the market of Chiang Mai, the nearest city to her

tiny hamlet, is an exotic, even a bizarre, sight in this otherwise wholly Thai marketplace. But no one pays her much attention; in the last decade the hilltribes have become a common sight in the cities of the North.

Approximately twenty distinct tribes of seminomadic peoples live in the mountains along the Burmese and Laotian borders of the North, and the tribes range from large, relatively sophisticated groups like the H'mong to tiny groups like the elusive Phi Thong Luang ("Spirits of the Yellow Leaves"), whose very existence was in doubt until an expedition tracked them down some years ago. Culturally, the tribes are of interest because their relative isolation has enabled them to retain almost unchanged customs and traditions that go back centuries. To the Thai government, they are a matter of concern because of their agricultural methods, which tend to deplete the land; their reliance on illegal opium as their chief cash crop; and their uncertain political loyalties.

For a long time, the main contact between the hilltribes and the outside world was the missionaries, mostly American, who elected to go and work among them, learning their languages and often living as far as five days' walk from the nearest civilization. As the government became more aware of the problems, actual and potential, presented by the tribes, it began to take more definite official steps; and now a sizeable tribal development program is underway. The king takes a personal interest in developing new crops for the tribespeople to grow — among them coffee, tea, and fruit trees — and the Border Patrol Police are establishing schools, while keeping the opium-rich

A girl of the Akha tribe, one of the several exotic hilltribes who inhabit Thailand's wild northern mountains. Basically nomadic, they are now being assimilated into the national life through novel programs.

area under surveillance. Moreover, the distinctive handicrafts of the tribes — encouraged first by the missionaries and now by Queen Sirikit's SUPPORT Foundation — are beginning to find popularity not only in Bangkok but also abroad, providing the hilltribes with another source of income.

The Chinese: Thailand's largest minority group excelling in trade and commerce

---

A Chinese storekeeper, sitting behind the counter of his miscellaneous-goods shop in one of the long, narrow, two- or three-story rows of shop houses that can be found in every town in Thailand. He lives with his family — a large family, usually — upstairs over the shop. Every day of the year he opens for business except for a short break at Chinese New Year, when the iron bars are drawn across the doors for two or three days and the family enjoys feasting, visiting ancestral graves, and the rare luxury of doing nothing.

Like every country in Southeast Asia, Thailand has had Chinese merchants since the earliest days of commerce. When King Rama I decided on Bangkok as his new capital, the site on which he wanted to build the Grand Palace was occupied by Chinese shops; he moved them a kilometer or so down the riverbank, where they settled and formed the nucleus of what is today Yaowaraj, the Chinese center of the capital. Throughout the 19th century and through the first half of the 20th, immigrants from China continued to pour into the country; only with the coming of the communist regime to mainland China did the flow turn into a trickle and finally stop altogether. As in other Asian countries these immigrants gravitated naturally toward trade — agriculture and government administration being already in the hands of the Thais. They opened banks, pawnshops, export-import

firms, and the innumerable little variety shops and restaurants that you find in even the smallest hamlet.

One thing, however, has long distinguished the Thai Chinese from their counterparts in most of the other countries in the region: they have been assimilated to a remarkable degree into the life of their adopted land. In part this has been due to deliberate government policy: all children, Chinese or otherwise, are required to learn the Thai language in primary school (Chinese language was not even taught at the university level until a few years ago), and the Chinese were encouraged, sometimes pressured, into taking Thai names if they wanted a passport, a government scholarship, or some other official document. Mostly, though, the lack of religious barriers, as exist in places like Malaysia and Indonesia, has encouraged Chinese and Thais to intermarry freely, so that today especially in the cities, it would be difficult to point with assurance to anyone and say that he or she were "pure" Thai. King Taksin who avenged Ayuthaya and established his capital at Thonburi had a Chinese mother; and most of the prominent Thai families have a Chinese branch somewhere on their genealogical tree.

The most outstanding result of this has been that the Thai Chinese have never really lived in an exclusive, separate world as they do elsewhere; even places like Yaowaraj, where the atmosphere is as Chinese as Hong Kong, have never been ghettoes, and the various Chinese associations are charitable rather than cultural in purpose. There is no deep-rooted anti-Chinese bias in Thailand, nor have there been any of the serious racial conflicts that have marred the

As this typical newsstand suggests, Thailand has a thriving communications industry, with dozens of daily newspapers and hundreds of magazines. There is also a large audience for popular novels on various subjects.

recent histories of neighboring countries. Only among the older generation will you find many people who think and speak of themselves specifically as "Chinese." The younger generation thinks of itself as Thai, if it considers such racial matters at all.

Literature: A testing ground for change

A popular novelist, a thin, rather intense woman in her early forties, the author of a half dozen successful romances, most of which have been adapted to the movies or television. All of her novels first appeared serially in a woman's magazine, and all appealed primarily to a female audience. A typical plot concerns a wellborn young girl who falls in love with a poor boy and is forbidden to marry him by her family; true love finally triumphs (after many chapters and many obstacles) as the boy at last convinces her parents of his sterling character.

Classical Thai literature, which mainly consists of the *Ramakien* (the Thai version of the Sanskrit epic *Ramayana*), folk tales in verse, and court poetry, is studied by university students, who also read some Thai translations of Western classics *(The Merchant of Venice* was translated by King Rama VI); but the general reading public prefers escapist, sentimental stories generally written by and for women. There are, however, a few exceptions to this rule, as well as some indications that an audience may exist for novels on more serious contemporary subjects. One of the exceptions is provided by M.R. Kukrit Pramoj, a versatile figure who has been a classical dancer, a movie star (he was in *The Ugly American)*, a newspaper editor, and a politician, and has written popular novels dealing with court life *(Four Reigns)* and with the struggle between Buddhism and communism *(Red Bamboo)*. Also several of the newer novelists have found a wide readership, especially

among students, for books about current social problems. In *Letters from Thailand,* a writer who uses the pseudonym of Botan, discusses the relationship between the Thai and the Chinese in Thailand and makes some sharp criticisms of both races. In *A Man Called Karn,* which won a SEATO prize and became a successful Thai movie, Suwanee Sukonta tells the story of an idealistic doctor who goes to work in the provinces and is defeated in the end by corrupt officials. Khamsing Srinawk, author of *The Politican and Other Stories,* is undoubtedly one of the best, if not the best, contemporary short-story writers in Thailand. The popularity of these and other similar works of literature in recent years has pointed out new directions to Thai writers and may lead to a literature that reflects the reality as opposed to the daydreams of the country.

The Movies: A kaleidoscope of Thai myth and legend

A Thai movie star, like movie stars everywhere, represents an ideal, a dream, of beauty rather than the reality commonly seen. She has pale, flawless skin and an artfully made-up face; she speaks in a soft, almost childlike voice, often hardly more than a whisper; her clothes are the latest fashion, and her jewels look expensive; she manages, somehow, to suggest purity and the promise of sex at the same time. She can be seen usually smiling demurely throughout the kingdom on calendars and on gigantic advertising billboards. At any given time she is making an average of ten movies simultaneously, playing more or less the same role in all of them.

Few foreign visitors go to see a Thai movie during their stay. This is

Mammoth movie billboards like this one are a common sight in Thailand, achieving what some foreign experts consider a unique form of pop art.

understandable in view of the language barrier, but it is also unfortunate, for popular arts like the movies reveal much about the contemporary culture and tastes of their country. There are five major movie studios in Thailand, all of them in Bangkok, and they produce several hundred films a year; though they have a larger audience in the capital than one might think considering the number of Western films being shown there, their greatest popularity is in the provinces, where the average price of a ticket is only five to ten baht and movies are the major entertainment.

Until fairly recently, most Thai movies were silent 16 mm films and the sound was provided by narrators — often a *single* narrator — who stood near the screen and spoke all the parts, or else recorded them on tape for distribution with the movie; as the narrators frequently had strong personalities of their own, people paid as much to hear them as to see the stars. In the last seven or eight years, however, more and more Thai movies have been made in 35 mm with sound track: producers have adopted the more sophisticated moviemaking techniques of the West; and a few directors have even experimented with departures from the tried-and-true story formulas of the past. But only a few, for the Thai-film audience knows what it wants.

To begin with, it wants familiar faces, the same stars over and over again, playing predictable roles. The two leading superstars of the present, Naowarat and Sorapong (their last names are rarely used, the first being sufficient to identify them) have been superstars for many years; they make twenty to thirty movies a year, usually together. Audiences also want the same stories, with only slight variations. The Cinderella theme is highly popular; poor girl (or boy) meets bright boy (or girl), encounters many difficulties along the way, finally gets him (or her) at the end when all the misunderstandings are cleared away.

Another popular story is the poor boy from the country who comes to the wicked city, is subjected to all sorts of temptations (usually sexual), finally settles for the virtuous girl who has loved him all along. Ghost stories, the gorier the better, are also favorites with Thai movie-goers. No matter how sad the theme, Thai audiences also insist on comic relief, and there are several slapstick comedians who are as much in demand as the superstars; and a good deal of singing and folk dancing is also considered a powerful asset. Finally, they want their money's worth in length — two and a half hours is common for a Thai film, and many go for three or more.

Whether they go to Thai or Western films, Thais have similar tastes; a foreign movie that is too "talky" or slow moving will have a short run, while comedies, musicals, and cowboy films attract large crowds. The two most popular western movies ever shown in Thailand have been *The Sound of Music* and *The Deer Hunter*.

Traditional Dance: The classical epitome

A group of students of Thai classical dance solemnly practice the complicated movements essential to this ancient form of theater. Most of them are girls, for traditionally the masked khon *dances were performed only by women in the inner court of the Royal Palace where no men were allowed, although nowadays young men also take part, especially in such athletic roles as Hanuman, the white monkey god. The students training in the school are also mostly young, for after a certain age it is difficult to train the body to do some of the contortions by which a dancer is judged; the fingers, for example, must be able to bend gracefully backward almost to the wrist.*

In a *khon* performance, masks, heavy makeup, and elaborate jeweled costumes and headdress subordinate and hide the individual personality of the dancer; to purists, it is a cardinal sin to smile or otherwise indicate the human being behind the role. Every gesture is highly stylized, immediately recognizable to a connoisseur though often not to an outsider; and a full-length performance can last for as long as eight hours.

The *khon* has never been an art form for the masses. Born in the royal palaces, and for many centuries only performed there, the *khon* was created for the pleasure of the king. It lives today in Thailand largely through the efforts of the Fine Arts Department, which has a school for training dancers and sponsors occasional performances at the National Theater in Bangkok. The excerpts presented at certain tourist restaurants are, like the Thai food served, but pale imitations of the originals, but worth seeing if only for the costumes.

Two more popular dance forms with the general Thai public are *lakhon*, which uses no masks and in which the movements are somewhat less stylized; and the *likay*, which might be described as a burlesque form of the classical dance, relying heavily on pitfalls and bawdy lyrics. A prominent feature of almost every provincial Thai fair, *likay* occupies a place roughly analogous to popular folk singing in the West. In the early part of the evening, low comedy fills the stage, but once the children have been put safely to bed, sex comes to the fore in a flurry of puns and double entendres which can keep the show going and the audiences wide awake until the wee hours of the morning.

The spectacular costumes and angular yet sinuous movements of the Thai classical dance are still a prominent part of the national culture; once only for royalty, the dances are now performed at the National Theater.

68

A City of Many Faces

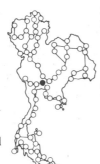

Some cities are easy: after only a few days you have a clear sense of their design, their personality, and you do not hesitate to set out boldly on explorations. Others are less accesible: they sprawl they are confusing, and they seem to have not one but a dozen personalities, often contrary. Almost every visitor without hesitation would put Bangkok in the second category. For this metropolis of over five million appears at first glance to be a bewildering conglomeration of new and old, East and West, serenity and chaos, the exotic and the commonplace — all thrown together haphazardly into a gigantic urban stew following no apparent recipe. Lying roughly midway between Taipei and New Delhi, Bangkok for several decades has also been at the hub of airline routes through South Asia, adding to its vitality.

You can stand at one moment in a hushed temple courtyard, lulled by the rhythmic chanting of priests and the silvery tinkle of bells, and at the next, risk life and limb crossing a street down which hurtles some of the most lethal traffic in Asia. You can start out with the most up-to-date city map and find yourself on streets that do not exist (at least on the map) — not little, unimportant streets either, but major thoroughfares, lined with shops that look as if they have been there for years.

Bangkok is not an orderly city. It never really has been during the present century, not even in what old

The spires of the Grand Palace glow in the evening light (previous pages), giving Bangkok an air of tranquillity that is belied by its sometimes chaotic traffic, which the policeman on the right tries to direct.

timers nostalgically look back on as "the good old days," by which they mean 20-odd years ago when there were as many pedicabs as automobiles, when many of today's avenues were narrow lanes bordered by *klongs* however smelly, and when going across town did not assume the proportions of a major expedition. Life may have been more leisurely in those days, but even so Bangkok was a city that had developed more by whim and historical vicissitude than by design, here spilling over into rice fields, there leaving almost untouched a scene from the 19th Century. And even then the "center" of Bangkok depended on who you were — government official or Chinese businessman, military or civilian, tourist or resident, rich or poor.

The biggest, most disorderly building boom in Bangkok's history started in the late 1950s, and a large part of what strikes the eye most forcibly today has appeared since then: the lofty office buildings, the air-conditioned supermarkets and shopping centers, nearly all the broad streets, movie theaters, and international hotels, the endless blocks of row shops following what one critic called the "egg-crate principle of design." Before the boom the now fashionable residential streets on either side of Sukhumvit Road were mostly agricultural; you could go by boat along Rama IV Road from where the Dusit Thani Hotel now stands to the river, and the newly built Erawan Hotel was regarded as rather inconveniently located on the city's outskirts.

After the boom, it seemed to some, a whole new Bangkok had emerged; and yet there were large areas around the old Grand Palace, in the Chinese district, and across the

A typical scene along crowded Yaowaraj Road, the heart of Bangkok's teeming Chinese district; except for the traffic, it still looks today very much as it did fifty years ago.

river in Thonburi (now included in the Greater Bangkok Metropolitan Area) that were hardly touched by the building fever, and still looked almost exactly as they did 50 years ago.

Today about one out of every ten Thais lives in Bangkok. About 90 percent of all the automobiles in the country are registered there. The metropolitan area is more than 40 times larger than Chiang Mai, Thailand's second city. At least 65 percent of Bangkok's population is of Chinese descent. The population has grown five-fold since World War II. About 80 percent of the country's university students study there, and the monarchy has reigned there for 200 years.

To many lovers of Bangkok, it is precisely its vital, changing, clashing, unpredictable nature that gives the city its special flavor. Quite apart from its celebrated tourist attractions, you are constantly being confronted, and sometimes amused, by unexpected sights: a narrow *klong* of soothing tranquillity, meandering in the shadow of a 400-room, supermodern hotel; a leafy tropical garden with full-sized trees and an elegant little Chinese pagoda on the roof of an otherwise commonplace row shop; a slightly derelict but still noble Victorian palace, with turrets and gingerbread, behind a cinema; a barbershop whimsically called the Darling and a restaurant the Puberty; an old woman calmly stringing ropes of jasmine blossoms on a busy sidewalk; a mammoth standing Buddha, three stories high, inadvertently glimpsed between two glass-and-cement office blocks; an apartment house built entirely in circles; a little Greek temple in the grounds of a hospital once the palace of a crown prince; a short-time hotel called the Bungalow Home Fun; a group of street urchins moving like ballet

Draped in a monk's robes and honored with offerings of flowers, this figure adorns the famous Wat Phra Keo.

dancers as they kick a rattan ball from one to another with the side of their feet; a vast movie poster in which a smiling woman's entrails spill down the side of a building; thousands of migratory swallows roosting unperturbed over one of the noisiest streets in the city; Thai classical dancers in the sunlight, on a velvet green lawn at a tea party. All in Bangkok.

* * *

As a possibly helpful clue to getting your bearings in the sprawl of present-day Bangkok, think of it as being roughly (very roughly) divided up as given below.

1. *Early Royal Bangkok*: The area around the Grand Palace, including Wat Phra Keo, Wat Po, Sanam Luang, Wat Suthat, Wat Rajabopitr, the Giant Swing.

2. *Later Royal Bangkok:* Chitralada Palace (the residence of the present king), the Marble Temple, Parliament, Dusit Zoo.

3. *Military Bangkok*: Actually a part of No. 2, the military having taken over many of the palaces and government offices built during the latter part of Rama V's reign in the Dusit area.

4. *Chinese Bangkok:* Yaowaraj Road and surrounding districts.

5. *Old Tourist Bangkok*: New Road, the Oriental Hotel, lower Suriwong and Silom Roads.

6. *New Tourist Bangkok*: Upper Silom and Suriwong Roads, around the Dusit Thani Hotel; Rajprasong, around the Erawan and President Hotels.

7. *New Residential Bangkok*: The streets leading off both sides of Sukhumvit Road, all the way to Prakanong and beyond.

8. *Even Newer Residential Bangkok*: Vast middle- and upper-income housing estates on the New Petchburi Road and on the superhighway leading north from the city.

9. *Principal Thai Markets*: Pratunam, Bangrak, Thevet, Klong Toey, to mention some of the largest.

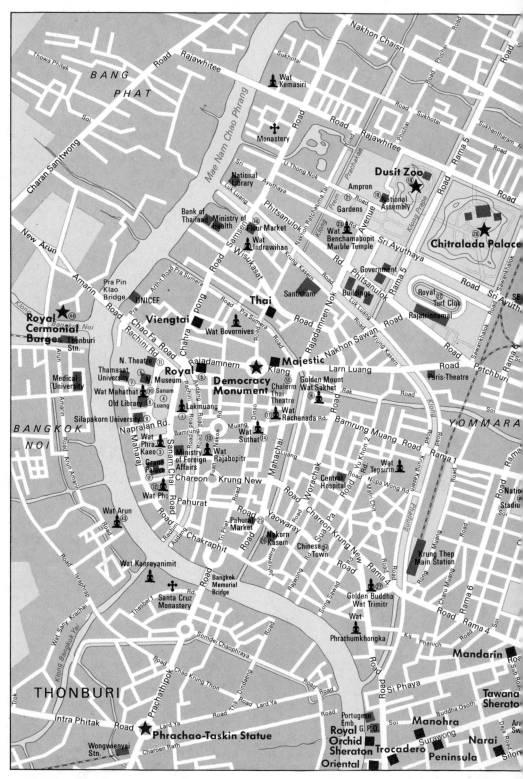

BANG PHAT

Thowa Phitek

Charan Sanitwong

New Arun

Amarin

Royal
Cermonial
Barges

BANGKOK
NOI

Medical
University

THONBURI

Rajawhitee Road

Wat Kemasiri

Monastery

National Library

Bank of Thailand
Ministry of Health

Flour Market

Wat Indrawihan

Pra Pin
Klao
Bridge

UNICEF

Viengtai

Wat Bovornives

Royal

Thai

Santitham

Thamasat University

N. Theatre

N. Museum

Wat Mahathat
Old Library

Sanam Luang

Silapakorn University

Napralan Rd.

Lakmuang

Wat Phra Kaeo

Grand Palace

Wat Pho

Wat Arun

Wat Kanrayanimit

Santa Cruz Monastery

Bangkok Memorial Bridge

Ministry of Foreign Affairs

Chareon

Democracy Monument

Wat Suthat

Wat Rajabopitr

Krung New

Pahurat

Pahurat Market

Nakorn Kasem

Chinese Town

Yaowaray

Majestic

Klang

Larn Luang

Chalerm Thai Theatre

Wat Rachanada

Golden Mount
Wat Sakhet

Paris-Theatre

Bamrung Muang Road

Central Hospital

Wat Tepsirin

Krung Thep Main Station

Golden Buddha
Wat Trimitr

Wat Phrathumkhongka

Intra Phitak Road

Phrachao-Taskin Statue

Wongwienyai Stn.

Nakhon Chaisri

Sukhotai

Rajawhitee Road

Dusit Zoo

Ampron

Gardens

National Assembly

Wat Benchamabopit
Marble Temple

Government Buildings

Royal Turf Club

Rajatronamai

Chitralada Palace

YOMMARA

Mandarin

Tawana Sheraton

Manohra

Narai

Peninsula

Royal Orchid Sheraton

Trocadero

Oriental

Portugese Emb.

G.P.O.

Surawong

National Library

Wisukasat

Phitsanulok

Sri Ayuthaya

Samsen Road

Phitsanulok

Rama 5

Sri Ayuth

Petchburi

Rama 1

Rama 6

Rama 4

Silom

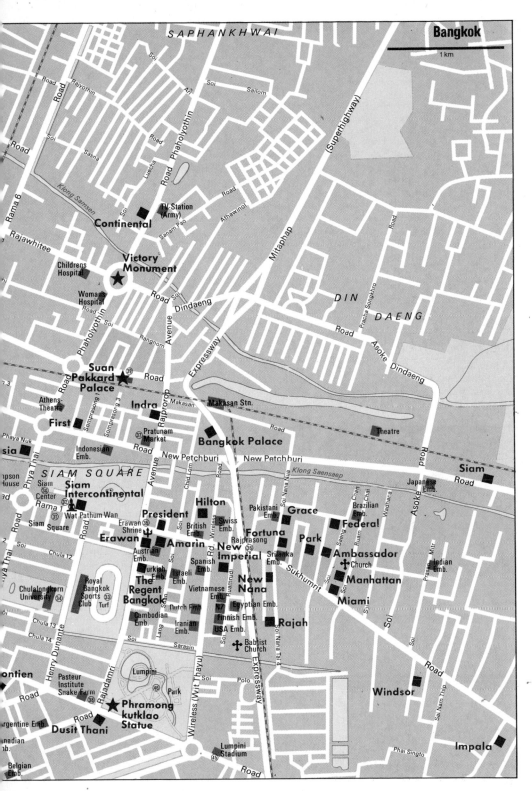

SAPHANKHWAI

Bangkok

1 km

TV Station
(Army)

Continental

**Victory
Monument**

Childrens
Hospital

Womans
Hospital

D I N

D A E N G

Athens
Theatre

**Suan
Pakkard
Palace**

Indra

First

Makasan Stn.

Bangkok Palace

Pratunam
Market

Indonesian
Emb.

Theatre

Siam

New Petchburi

New Petchburi

Klong Saensep

SIAM SQUARE

Siam
Center

**Siam
Intercontinental**

Wat Pathum Wan

Siam
Square

Erawan

Erawan
Shrine

President

Amarin

Hilton

British
Emb.

Swiss
Emb.

Pakistani
Emb.

Grace

Brazilian
Emb.

Federal

Japanese
Emb.

Fortuna

Park

Ambassador

Church

Austrian
Emb.

**New
Imperial**

Spanish
Emb.

Srilanka
Emb.

Indian
Emb.

Chulalongkorn
University

Royal
Bangkok
Sports
Club

Turkish
Emb.

Israeli
Emb.

**The
Regent
Bangkok**

Vietnamese
Emb.

**New
Nana**

Manhattan

Miami

Cambodian
Emb.

Dutch Emb.

N7

Egyptian Emb.

Finnish Emb.

Iranian
Emb.

USA Emb.

Rajah

Baptist
Church

Lumpini

Windsor

Pasteur
Institute
Snake Farm

Lumpini
Park

**Phramong
kutklao
Statue**

ontien

Dusit Thani

rgentine Emb.

nadian
b.

Lumpini
Stadium

Phai Singto

Impala

Belgian
Emb.

The Inner City

Look at any map of Bangkok. Locate the Grand Palace, Wat Phra Keo (Temple of the Emerald Buddha), and the broad expanse called Sanam Luang (Pramane Ground). In this vicinity, where the Chao Phya River arches dramatically, a narrow *klong* (canal) connects the sides of the oxbow, setting off an area roughly the shape of a mango. Surrounded by the waters of the river and the canal, this man-made island was the original Bangkok, its "inner city," as it were; and it is here that any exploration of Bangkok should start.

In this relatively small area in the heart of Bangkok you will find most of the sights that every visitor must include in his or her itinerary —those sights that really look like the pictures you remember from your schoolbooks and the scenes that linger from the film *The King and I.* If you approach this area from Democracy Monument on Rajadamnern

Avenue (King Rama V's version of the Champs Élysées), the tree-rimmed expanse of Sanam Luang will appear ahead, and there flashing in the sunlight rises Wat Phra Keo, a sight guaranteed to stir even the most jaded traveler.

A good place to start your tour of the inner city is at the official heart of Bangkok — for contrary to what many people think of the sprawling metropolis, it does have one: a small shrine not far from the Ministry of Defense across the entrance to Wat Phra Keo. In this shrine stands **Lakmuang**, a stone pillar placed there by Rama I at the beginning of his reign as the foundation stone of his new capital. Distances within the city are measured from this stone. Sheltered by a graceful, little temple-like building, Lakmuang is believed to have the power to grant many wishes, especially a winning ticket in the National Lottery or fertility to a childless

The numbers in the margin in this section refer to the map on pages 60-61

1..Lakmuang
ศาลเจ้าหลักเมือง

The Lakmuang Shrine, containing an ancient stone pillar placed there by King Rama I, is the official heart of Bangkok. Offerings of fragrant flowers and incense adorn the shrine (left), while in an adjoining room (right) a dancer awaits her performance, commissioned by a supplicant whose wishes have been granted. Not far away from the shrine, the fabled spires of the Grand Palace and Wat Phra Keo (facing page) gracefully pierce the sky.

couple. Floral offerings are always piled high around the pillar, and the air of the shrine is potent with the smell of incense. In an adjoining room a performance of Thai classical dance and music, by either amateurs or professionals, is usually under way, hired by supplicants whose wishes have been granted by the spirit of Lakmuang. The best times to visit the shrine are in the late afternoon, on holidays, and especially on the day before the drawing of the lottery.

The grounds of the **Grand Palace**, open to visitors daily from 8:30 am — 11:30 am and 1 pm — 3:30 pm (a certain decorum in dress is demanded), occupy part of a larger compound which also includes the Temple of the Emerald Buddha, used as the royal chapel. Here too is the Royal Collection of Weapons and the Coin Pavilion.

The palace compound right away introduces the visitor to Thailand's characteristic blend of temporal and spiritual elements.

Surrounded by high, crenellated walls and entered by the huge Piman Jayasri double gate, the Grand Palace was originally built by the first king of Bangkok in 1782; almost every subsequent king of the present Chakri dynasty has added to it, so that today the buildings of the Grand Palace present a melange of architectural styles ranging from Thai to Victorian. After the palace murder of King Ananda in 1946, his brother, the present King Bhumibol, moved to the more modern and comfortable Chitralada Palace; and the Grand Palace nowadays is used only for state banquets, presentation of ambassadorial credentials, and other royal ceremonies.

The royal residence of the Grand Palace, called the **Chakri Maha Prasad** — of which visitors are allowed to see only the reception rooms — was constructed during King Rama V's

2 The Grand Palace
พระบรมมหาราชวัง

Chakri Maha Prasad
พระที่นั่งจักรีมหาปราสาท

reign (1868-1910) to commemorate the hundredth anniversary of the Chakri dynasty. It is an impressive mixture of Thai and Western architecture — the roof being pure Thai, and the lower part of the building, designed by a British architect, being what might be called "Imperial Victorian." The top floor, under the tall central spire, contains a golden urn with ashes of the Chakri kings. The large reception rooms are decorated with pictures of past kings, busts of foreign royalty (most of whom Rama V met on his trips abroad), and a quantity of mostly European objets d'art. In the center of the building is the magnificent Chakri Throne Room, where the king receives foreign ambassadors on a niello throne under a nine-tiered white umbrella made originally for King Chulalongkorn.

The hall to the right (west) of the Chakri Maha Prasad is the **Dusit Maha Prasad,** built by Rama I in 1789. This is a splendid example of classic Thai architecture, with a four-tiered roof from which rises an elegant nine-tiered spire. The balcony on the north wing contains a throne once used by the king for outdoor receptions; the last occasion was when Rama VI received the oath of loyalty from his court after his coronation in 1911. Just outside the Dusit Maha Prasad is a beautiful little pavilion called the **Arporn Phimok Prasad,** "Disrobing Pavilion," built to the height of the king's palanquin, from which he alighted to take off his ceremonial hat and gown before proceeding to the audience hall. This graceful structure — the most exquisite pavilion in Thailand — was reproduced by Rama V at Bang Pa-In, his summer palace just south of Ayuthaya; and a replica of it was exhibited at the 1958 World Fair in Brussels.

To the left of the Chakri Maha

Dusit Maha Prasad
พระที่นั่งดุสิตมหาปราสาท

Arporn Phimok Prasad
พระที่นั่งอาภรณ์พิโมกข์ปราสาท

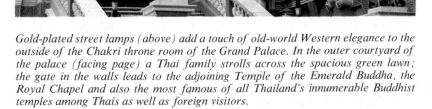

Gold-plated street lamps (above) add a touch of old-world Western elegance to the outside of the Chakri throne room of the Grand Palace. In the outer courtyard of the palace (facing page) a Thai family strolls across the spacious green lawn; the gate in the walls leads to the adjoining Temple of the Emerald Buddha, the Royal Chapel and also the most famous of all Thailand's innumerable Buddhist temples among Thais as well as foreign visitors.

Prasad is a door leading to the **Forbidden Quarters,** an area where the king's many wives used to live. The king himself was the only man ever allowed to enter the door which led to the harem's lovely garden of cool fountains, pavilions, and carefully pruned trees. Even today this inner section is closed to all visitors, except for once a year when the king throws a garden party on his birthday for diplomats and government officials. North of the women's quarters lies **Borompiman Hall,** built in a Western style of King Chulalongkorn as a residence for the then crown prince who later became Rama VI; it was in this building that the young King Ananda was killed.

The **Amarin Vinichai Hall,** just beyond the doorway leading to the former harem, is another of the palace's few remaining original buildings, having been built by Rama I. The splendidly painted audience hall

is used for coronations, and the king also uses it for some special ceremonies such as presenting medals to government officials. During these ceremonies, the throne is at first concealed by two curtains, called *Phra Visud* in Thai; the king takes his seat unseen by those in the hall; then a fanfare sounds, the curtains part dramatically, and the king appears adorned in fabulous regalia.

Wat Phra Keo, Temple of the Emerald Buddha, adjoins the Grand Palace and serves as the Royal Temple where the king performs his various religious duties. Beyond any doubt, it ranks among the world's great spectacles: a dazzling, dizzying collection of gilded spires and pavilions and mythological gods both awesome and delightful. It is what most foreigners expect to see when they come to Thailand, and it is the single most powerful image visitors take away when they leave. The temple

compound is open to the public free on Sundays and Buddhist holidays; on other days there is an admission charge: 50 baht for *farangs* (foreigners) and 10 baht for Thais.

For a full appreciation, Wat Phra Keo really deserves at least two visits. The first should be on one of the nonpublic days, when admission is charged; the compound is relatively uncrowded, and you can wander about at leisure inspecting its serene treasures. The second visit, however, should be on a public day, for only then can you witness the vital role the temple and its celebrated image play in the life of the Thai people. Then ardent worshipers who fill the sanctuary prostrate themselves on the marble floor before the golden altar; the air is alive with the noise of the supplicants, yet heavy with the smell of floral offerings and burning joss sticks. Bathed in a strange light, high on its pedestal, the small image looks serenely down from the focal point of all eyes as well as prayers. Only on days like this can you sense the power and the role the Emerald Buddha has had through the long years of Thai history.

Wat Phra Keo was originally built by King Rama I in 1782, in imitation of the Royal Temple of the Grand Palace in Ayuthaya, to house the celebrated Phra Keo, or Emerald Buddha. No one knows the precise origin of this 75-centimeter-high image, the most sacred in all Thailand, but some experts believe it to be of northern workmanship.

Today, in its blue-tiled sanctuary, the Emerald Buddha sits atop a gilded altar 11 meters high, almost lost in the swirls of smoke from joss sticks burned on days the temple is open to the public. Poised above the image is a nine-tiered umbrella, and on either side are crystal balls representing the sun and the moon. Three

The Emerald Buddha glows mysteriously (above), while a Chinese stone guardian keeps watch outside. The Royal Pantheon (opposite), open once a year, honors the Chakri dynasty, which still sits on Thailand's throne.

84

times a year, at the beginning of each new season, the king changes the Emerald Buddha's robes, donning it with a golden diamond-studded tunic for the hot season; a gilded robe flecked with blue for the rainy season; and a robe of enamel-coated solid gold from head to toe for the cool season.

A spectacular collection of structures crowds the compound of Wat Phra Keo: buildings, pavilions, *chedis* (pointed spires), *prangs* (rounded spires), and mythological gods and goddesses, most of which are gilded or encrusted with bits of porcelain or glass. A full listing of all the things to be seen would require another book, so we shall mention just a few of the highlights.

The walls of the cloister that surround the entire temple are painted with murals telling the story of the *Ramakien,* the Thai version of the *Ramayana* epic of Indian origin. The murals were originally painted during the reign of Rama III (1824-1850), but had to be restored by his two successors. In 1932, there was a more drastic restoration, during which many Western influences crept into the classic Thai style. The Fine Arts Department recently finished work on yet another restoration of the paintings, this time trying to achieve the original style. As you walk around the cloister the story starts on the left.

You will see that the *Ramakien* regales in epic battles, intrigues, and occasional scenes of low comedy, the most colorful character being the white monkey-god Hanuman, who is also a favourite in Thai classical dance performances. Marble slabs set in pillars in front of the paintings are inscribed with Thai poems describing each episode of the story.

On a broad, raised marble terrace — higher than the rest of the

compound because it was built on the ruins of some earlier buildings that were destroyed by fire during the reign of Rama I — are the Royal Pantheon, the library (Mondop), and a golden stupa erected by Rama IV. The **Royal Pantheon** contains life-size statues of the kings of the present dynasty and is open to the public only once a year, on Chakri Day, April 6. In front of it stand many marvelous gilded statues of mythological creatures, including the charming half-bird, half-woman *kinaree*. Behind the Pantheon is the library, surrounded by monuments commemorating the sacred white elephants, symbol of royal power, that were found in the kingdom during the reigns of the first five Chakri kings. Nearby is a large, detailed model of the famous Khmer temple of Angkor Wat, built by Rama IV to show his people what the temple looked like, during a period when it was located on Thai territory.

Wat Po is the popular name for Wat Phra Jetupon, the oldest and largest temple in Bangkok, covering nearly eight hectares. Located just south of the Grand Palace, it is divided into two sections, one containing the living quarters of the monks and the other the various religious buildings. The two parts are separated by the narrow Jetupon Road, down which, according to Thai legend, King Rama I marched on his way back from Cambodia to Thonburi on April 6, 1782, the day he officially founded the Chakri dynasty.

There are 16 gates in the huge, massive walls of Wat Po, but only two of them, both on Jetupon Road, are open to the public. The temple compound is so large, yet so crammed with buildings, pavilions, statues, and enclosed gardens, that it tends to overpower many visitors who fail to give it the attention it deserves.

The first temple building on this

Visitors entering the courtyard of Wat Po (above), Bangkok's oldest and largest temple, are guided through a maze of fascinating buildings and objects. Known as "Thailand's first university," the temple was filled by early kings with varied items aimed at the general edification of the people. It also contains some superlative examples of Thai art adorning the temple buildings, like the delicate ceramic mosaic pictured on the facing page.

site was built as long ago as the 16th century, but the place did not begin to achieve real importance until the establishment of Bangkok as the capital. Wat Po was a particular favorite of the first four Bangkok kings, all of whom added to its treasures; the four large *chedis* to the west of the main chapel are memorials to them, the earliest being the green-mosaic *chedi* built by Rama I, and the latest being the blue one built by Rama IV in the mid-19th century. All round the cloisters leading to the chapel are 91 other *chedis* — 71 small ones and 20 larger ones. The small ones contain the ashes of various royal descendants, while the larger ones hold relics of the Buddha. The admission fee is about 10 baht.

The vast quantity and variety of things to be seen at Wat Po are more meaningful if you bear in mind that the early kings regarded the temple as a primary source of public educa-tion—it is sometimes called "Thailand's first university." Objects were placed in the compound as a way of letting people acquire knowledge, not necessarily connected with Buddhism. The contorted figures on a little artificial mound just inside the main entrance, for example, illustrate methods of massage and meditation practiced by hermits. There are 20 small hills around the compound displaying stone specimens from different parts of Thailand for anyone's geological education. In most of the buildings are inscriptions or murals giving information on such diverse subjects as military defense, astrology, morality, literature, and archaeology. On the walls of a small open pavilion, which you pass on your way to the Reclining Buddha, are plaques that prescribe treatments for different ailments. The modern building to the left houses the head-quarters of the traditional-medicine

practitioners of Bangkok, and in the late afternoon (around 4:00 to 6:00 p.m.) each day people still flock for treatment by the old methods.

For most tourists the big attraction of the temple is the gigantic **Reclining Buddha,** the largest in Thailand, 46 meters long and 15 meters high and entirely covered with gold leaf. The soles of the feet, 15½ meters high, are marvelously inlaid with mother-of-pearl designs depicting the 108 auspicious signs of the Buddha. The inlaid feet are all the more fascinating, because to Buddhists and Hindus alike the lowest part of the anatomy would ordinarily represent what is spiritually least exalted. Make a point of looking closely at what remains of the mural paintings in the rather cramped and dimly lighted building that houses this great image; though in a bad state of repair, the murals rank among the finest traditional Thai paintings to be seen in Bangkok and show many fascinating vignettes of daily Thai life. In the courtyard outside the Reclining Buddha are stalls selling souvenirs, including stone-rubbings made from the reliefs depicting scenes from the *Ramakien* epic on the balustrades of the main chapel.

The huge, top-hatted stone figures (which supposedly represent Europeans) that guard the gates of Wat Po and the delightful little stone animals and pagodas all over the compound came to Thailand as ballast on the royal rice boats returning from trade with China.

One of the most beautiful, smaller buildings in the temple, near the four big *chedis,* is the library, entirely covered with pale bits of broken porcelain. Near it lies a walled Chinese garden that once contained crocodiles.

Past and present attractions of the Pramane Ground are (left) the Weekend Market, which once attracted throngs of bargain hunters, and (opposite) the National Museum, seen through a kaleidoscope of evening lights.

Between Wat Phra Keo and the beginning of Rajadamnern Avenue is a large oval expanse known alternatively as the **Sanam Luang** (Royal Field) and the **Pramane Ground** (Royal Cremation Ground). Traditionally, this space was used for royal cremations and such ceremonies as the annual plowing Ceremony in May which marks the start of the riceplanting season. The last king to be cremated there was Rama VIII, brother of the present ruler. In a significant departure from tradition, the bodies of those killed in the 1973 revolution were given a royally sponsored cremation in the field.

Mostly, however, it is used for less solemn purposes and, for the Thais, it is a favorite place to go *paitio* (take a leisurely stroll) in the late afternoon. During the week there are bicycles for rent, and sports teams play soccer in the central field. From around mid-February through April,

4. Sanam Luang
สนามหลวง

Reclining Buddha
พระไสยาสน์

when a dependable breeze springs up every afternoon to break the day's heat, the big attraction is kite-fighting, which starts about 4:30 p.m. when the many government offices in the vicinity close for the day. Watching a Thai kite-fight is one of the most pleasant ways of ending a day. A row of temporary restaurants springs up along the Thammasat University side of the field (so that the afternoon sun declines behind you), and spectators can lounge comfortably in reclining chairs with a beer and a wide choice of Thai snacks. Many of the restaurants have musical shows that go on into the evening. Although there are always a lot of children flying fanciful little kites in the shape of snakes and bats and dragons, the fights themselves are very much an adult affair: various business companies and governmental departments sponsor teams; there is an elaborate system of scoring; and

at the end of the season prizes are awarded.

Two kinds of kites oppose each other in a match — the *chula,* or "male" kite, sometimes as long as 2 meters and requiring a team of ten or more to fly it; and the *pukpao,* the "female," smaller and faster, flown by a single player. In a match, the field is divided in half, with *chula*'s territory located at the Wat Phra Keo end and the *pukpao*'s at the other. The object of the fight is for the big kites to cross the boundary, snare one of the small ones, and bring it successfully to earth in *chula* territory. Since the greatest amount of skill is required to maneuver the *chulas,* most of the action is at that end of the field.

The Sanam Luang was most noted for its **Weekend Market,** held every Saturday and Sunday except when the field was reserved for a special activity like the New Year's cele-

Weekend Market
ตลาดนัดสุดสัปดาห์

bration. Nothing in Bangkok quite compared with the Weekend Market. But the government felt that Pramane Ground, as a place of royal ceremony, should more fittingly be a large park than a marketplace. In preparation for the 1982 Ratanakosin Bicentennial, the market was disbanded and more trees planted.

Adjacent to the park, however, you will still find a surprising variety of strange goods for sale.

If you stand facing the market at the bridge that crosses Klong Lawd to Rajadamnern Avenue, on your left is the plant section. Here on both sides of the *klong* you can see a dazzling variety of the wild and hybrid orchids grown in Thailand, along with all sorts of other garden plants and supplies; the stalls nearest the bridge specialize in jungle plants brought from as far away as Chiang Mai. Across the street is the secondhand book section, offering a wide selection in European and Thai languages. The near side of the big field (toward Rajadamnern Avenue and the Royal Hotel) is devoted to foods, the far side (toward Napralan and Naprathat Roads) to cloth, clothing, and household goods. The central part of the field, perhaps the most fascinating of all, contains pets (look for the baby pythons); Thai handicrafts (musical instruments are a good buy); antiques (mostly fake but a few genuine discoveries lie in store); semiprecious gems; herbal medicines; and such miscellaneous treats as cobra-mongoose fights staged to boost the sales of patent medicines. Bargaining is definitely the rule at the Sanam Luang as nothing has a fixed price, but Thais claim that the prices on the whole are cheaper than in other markets. If you get tired, have an iced coffee (*o-liang*) or some chilled coconut juice (*nam maprao*).

Goods of all kinds were available at the Weekend Market, including the rich silk sarongs being sold by the Sikh merchant (above) from a portable shop. Along a gallery in Wat Mahathat, just across from the market, a row of gilded and berobed Buddha images (opposite) gaze serenely down in timeless contemplation: this temple is an important center of Buddhist instruction, specializing in meditation, and dates from the reign of the first Bangkok king.

Across from Sanam Luang, on the way from Wat Phra Keo to the National Museum, you first pass buildings belonging to **Silapakorn University**, the University of Fine Arts, located on Naprathat Road diagonally opposite the Grand Palace, where students are trained in painting, sculpture, archaeology, and architecture. The older part of this university was a former palace, and despite many modern additions there are still attractive shady courtyards where students can relax between classes. Frequent art exhibitions are held here, and there is a small but interesting archaeological museum. Next door is the pink-colored **National Library** and, in the same compound, **Wat Mahathat, Temple of the Great Relic**. Built during the reign of Rama I, it is an important Buddhist teaching institution, specializing in meditation. During his long period in the priesthood before

becoming king, Rama IV was abbot of this temple.

In the large area between the *wat* and the National Museum stands **Thammasat University**, founded just before World War II and now one of Thailand's leading educational institutions, especially in law and economics. The students of Thammasat tend to be less conservative than those of the older Chulalongkorn University; many leaders of the 1973 revolution came from Thammasat. In late 1976, there were further student demonstrations at Thammasat, which were violently suppressed, followed by a military takeover of the faltering government. Except for one quaint, rather Victorian administration building, there is little of architectural interest to be seen in Thammasat, but those who would like to sample Thai student attitudes will usually find a student willing to chat over a cup of coffee or a soft drink.

The **National Museum**, possibly the largest in Southeast Asia, located next to Thammasat University on Naprathat Road, consists of a group of older buildings, on either side of which two new wings were added in 1966. It is open everyday, except Monday and Friday, from 9:00 a.m. until noon, and from 1:00 until 4:00 p.m.; admission is free on Saturday and Sunday, and 5 baht on other days. On Tuesday, Wednesday, and Thursday mornings at 9:30 a.m., there is a special English-language tour of the museum, starting from the entry pavilion at the main gate and lasting about two hours.

Besides housing a vast treasure of antiquities, the museum has an interesting history of its own. The oldest buildings in the compound date from 1782 and were built as the palace of the second king, a sort of deputy ruler — a feature of the Thai monarchy in the early Bangkok period. Originally, the palace included a large park that went all the way to Wat Mahathat and covered the northern half of the present Pramane Grounds as well; however, the office of the second king was abolished during the reign of Rama V, who handed the buildings over to be used as a museum.

The first building to the left of the entrance is the **Sivamokkha Biman Hall**, which was originally an opensided audience hall. It now houses the prehistoric art collection, in particular the bronzes and handsome painted earthenware jars found in Ban Chiang in Northeast Thailand which are arousing much interest in the international world of archaeology. Also near the entrance is the **Buddhaisawan Chapel**, built by the second king as his private place of worship. It contains some well-preserved murals, depicting the life of the Buddha, and the famous *Phra*

Sivamokkha Biman Hall
พระที่นั่งศิวโมกข์พิมาน

Buddhaisawan Chapel
ตำหนักพุทธไธศวรรย์

National Museum in Brief

For the museum visitor in a hurry, the following are the main periods of Thai art, with a brief description of the principal characteristics of their statues or images, and the rooms where they are displayed.

Dvaravati (6th-11th centuries): Mon in appearance, with broad, usually smiling faces and tight curls, often showing Indian influence especially in the robes and the slightly curved bodies of standing figures. In rooms 32 and 33 you will find Dvaravati figures in terra-cotta, Buddha images, and lively groups of dancers and musicians.

Srivichaya (8th-13th centuries): Contemporaneous with Dvaravati but from areas farther south and strongly influenced by Javanese art. Bronzes are in room 35.

Lop Buri or *Khmer* (11th-14th centuries): Similar, sometimes identical, in style to the art of Cambodia, with many stone and bronze figures of Hindu deities as well as Buddha images. Figures look strong and masculine. Rooms 29 and 31.

Chiang Saen (12th-20th centuries): From North Thailand; rather plump, somewhat Chinese-looking faces and curled hair. Room 41.

Sukhothai (13th-15th centuries): The first purely Thai style and still regarded as the most original; images displaying long, flowing, idealized bodies and faces with enigmatic smiling expressions. Many of the features are based on descriptions in Sanskrit poetry of gods and heroes. Be sure to see the famous black bronze of the walking Buddha. Rooms 42 and 43.

Ayuthaya (15th-18th centuries): A mixture of styles with graceful but stylized figures, the lavish decoration reflecting the wealth and power of the kingdom. Rooms 44 and 45.

Bangkok or *Ratanakosin* (late 18th century to present): Round, rather sweet faces and elaborate Thai costumes; more decorative than figures of earlier periods; unfortunately not well represented.

The National Museum is housed partly in an old royal palace (below) and contains a comprehensive collection of Thai art.

Buddha Sihing, a bronze Sukhothai-style image greatly revered by the Thais. Another interesting building in the museum compound, behind the prehistoric-art pavilion, the **Tamnak Daeng**, or Red House, was the residence of an elder sister of King Rama I and was formerly located in the grounds of the Grand Palace; it has a fascinating collection of furniture used by early royalty.

The finely proportioned old palace of the second king, which formerly housed the museum's entire collection, now is limited to ethnological exhibits of elephant howdahs, ceramics, palanquins, royal furnishings, weapons, and similar objects. The Buddhist art collection, in the new wings on either side, includes exhibits from most Asian countries, but the greatest attraction, naturally, is the Thai collection, ranging from Dvaravati, the earliest period, up through Ratanakosin (Bangkok) art.

Brochures and pamphlets available at the entrance will help you understand the evolution of the various artistic styles.

If you turn left when you come out of the museum gate, you will see the **National Theater**, a huge building in a not entirely happy mixture of Thai and Western architecture. This is where performances of Thai classical dance are presented on certain occasions; check inside (or in the newspapers) to find out if one is scheduled during your stay, for they are full-length performances worth seeing. If not, you can visit the dancing school run by the Department of Fine Arts, called **Nattasin**, behind the National Theater in one of the old buildings of the second king's palace. Here students, mostly children, are trained in the complex gestures and steps of the *khon,* the masked dance dramas once performed only for the king and his court.

Other Bangkok
Temples and Sights

One of the most attractive small temples in Bangkok, an architectural curiosity visited by relatively few tourists, is **Wat Rajabopitr**, located near the Ministry of the Interior off Klong Lawd. You can easily recognize it by its distinctive doors, carved in relief with jaunty-looking soldiers wearing European-type uniforms. Built by King Chulalongkorn in 1863, the temple reflects the king's interest in Western art and in blending it with traditional Thai forms. The most prominent feature of Wat Rajabopitr is the tall, gilded *chedi*, covering a round vaulted room that contains a stone Buddha image seated on a *naga*, or sacred serpent, from Lop Buri. The lower part of the *chedi*, the circular cloister around it, and the outside of the *bot* (chapel) are completely covered with decorative pieces of colored Chinese porcelain, a delicate mixture of blue, yellow, red, and green, which con-

tributes greatly to the unique charm of this little temple. The doors and windows of the *bot* are inlaid with mother-of-pearl in designs depicting various honors bestowed by the king. In a recess beside one of the doors is a bas-relief of a god named Khio Kang, "the one with long teeth," who is supposed to guard this sanctuary. Four chapels, connected to the central gallery by small porticos, further enlarge the size of this colorful temple.

Wat Rajabopitr was built before King Chulalongkorn made his first trip to Europe, but even so, his strong interest in the West is apparent inside the vaulted *bot*, which appears Italian Gothic in inspiration and, to one observer, suggestive of "a rather ornate drawing room." The king was to carry this interest in mixing the native and the foreign even further when 40 years later he built Wat Benchamabopit.

13. Wat Rajabopitr
วัดราชบพิตร (สถิตมหาสีมาราม)

14. Giant Swing
เสาชิงช้า

14. Wat Suthat
วัดสุทัศน์ (เทพวราราม)

Bamrung Muang Road, beside the Ministry of the Interior (just north beyond Wat Rajabopitr and east of Wat Phra Keo) leads into the Square of the **Giant Swing**, *Sao Ching Cha* in Thai. Take a stroll down Bamrung Muang Road, for both sides are lined with old shops selling nothing but a variety of religious objects for temples or home shrines. The Swing itself consists of two gigantic red poles in the center of the square, joined at the top by a carved beam. The Swinging Ceremony, now no longer held, was a popular Brahminist ritual held in honor of the god, Phra Isuan, who was believed to visit the earth for ten days every January.

Wat Suthat, facing the Giant Swing, was started under the first Bangkok king and finished during the reign of its third (1824-1851). It is noted for its outstanding and enormous *bot* (chapel), said to be the tallest in Bangkok, and for its equally large *viharn* (hall for keeping sacred objects), surrounded by a gallery of gilded Buddha images. The principal Buddha image, called the *Phra Buddha Chakyamuni*, was cast in the 14th century and was originally in a temple at Sukhothai; impressed by its size and beauty, Rama I brought it down to Bangkok by river. The interior building that houses this image contains some monumental, finely carved doors, partly commissioned by Rama II, who, it is said, ordered the instruments used to be thrown into the river so that no one would be able to duplicate the fine carving. There are also excellent murals in the *bot* dating from the reign of Rama III which are in a better state of preservation than those in most Thai temples. Bronze horses and stone pagodas grace the lower courtyard. The *wat* is normally entered by Ti Thong (Dinso) Road.

Pigeons soar into the sky from the courtyard of Wat Rajabopitr (opposite); feeding them is regarded as a way of earning merit by those who go to the temple. The Giant Swing (above, left) is a relic of old Bangkok that survives in the modern city, where a unique Brahminist ceremony used to be held with teams swinging a full 180-degree arc. A dramatic bronze horse (above, right) raises its head silently against the brooding evening sky in the lower courtyard of Wat Suthat.

At the point where Rajadamnern Avenue crosses Klong Banglampoe, just outside the remains of what was once Bangkok's city wall, stand **Wat Sakhet** and the **Golden Mount**, one of the city's most imposing sights and for many years its highest point. Ayuthaya had had a great artificial hill, and King Rama III decided to reproduce it in Bangkok. Because of Bangkok's soft earth, however, he was never able to raise it to the desired height, and it was not until the reign of Chulalongkorn (Rama V) that the mount was completed — 78 meters high, the top level reached by a circular stairway of 318 steps. A gilded *chedi* at the top contains relics of the Buddha given to Rama V by Lord Curzon, the then Viceroy of India. The climb is fairly exhausting, especially on a hot day, but the view from the top spans all of Bangkok which lies supinely at its feet.

Wat Sakhet, at the bottom of the Mount, was originally built during the Ayuthaya period, when it was called Wat Sakae; according to legend, Rama I stopped here and ceremonially washed himself on the way back to Thonburi to be crowned, and the name of the temple was later changed to Sakhet, which means "the washing of hair." It also became noted, rather grimly, for cremations. By custom, the Pramane Ground could be used only for cremations of kings and other royalty; commoners had to be taken outside the city walls for the ceremony, and since Wat Sakhet stood just outside one of the main gates, it was a handy place.

Every November, Wat Sakhet and the Golden Mount are the scene of one of Bangkok's prettiest fairs. Food stalls and stage shows by the dozens are set up in the grounds; the mount is bathed in colored lights; and the devout make their way in candlelight processions to the top.

16. Wat Sakhet
วัดสระเกษ (มหาวรวิหาร)

16. Golden Mount
ภูเขาทอง

The man-made Golden Mount (above) was for years the highest point in Bangkok, and it still offers a panoramic view of the city. The Amulet Market (opposite) is where Thais go to buy the small votive plaques, often made of pressed terra cotta, that a large part of the population wear as a means of protection from a wide range of ills. Usually Buddha images, the amulets vary in price from a few baht to thousands, depending on their protective powers.

Even if the fair is not going on, the restaurants along the *klong* are pleasant places to relax in the late afternoon.

Across the street from the Golden Mount, behind the Chalerm Thai movie theater which is on Rajadamnern Avenue, and just a short way down Mahachai Road, hides **Wat Rachanada**, worth a visit because of its **Amulet Market.** This market used to be located in Wat Mahathat, near the National Museum, but was moved about a year ago. Thais are staunch believers in the protective powers of amulets, which they usually wear around the neck on a gold or silver chain, and great care is taken in the selection of precisely the right amulet. The majority of charms are Buddha images, often in pressed terra-cotta plaques covered in plastic, but there are likenesses of many other gods and goddesses who are supposed to have protective powers.

A ten-eyed deity, for example, protects not only from the front, but from the back and both sides as well. There are amulets that attract women to men, while others that act vice versa, and amulets that ward off bullets, or protect you from harm in car and airplane accidents. Some, believed to be especially powerful, sell for thousands of baht, and according to those who buy them, are worth the investment. The Thai methods of selecting an amulet are somewhat mysterious to an outsider, having, it would seem, little to do with either the charm's age or its visual beauty. Also, a visitor should keep in mind that the primary purpose of wearing an amulet, however far removed from Buddhism, is religious rather than decorative. Around the amulet stalls, gold- and silver-smiths sell chains for the amulets and a variety of other charms and Buddha images for home shrines.

After crossing the *klong* near the Golden Mount, Rajadamnern Avenue turns into a pleasant, tree-lined boulevard, that leads straight into the square in front of the old **National Assembly**. The square is dominated by an equestrian statue of King Chulalongkorn who had so much to do with the construction of this part of Bangkok. On the anniversary of his death, October 23, the square is crowded with students and government officials who lay wreaths at the statue in his honor. The area is also used for the trooping of the colors on the king's birthday and on armed forces day. To the left lies **Amporn Gardens**, a spacious park with fountains and trees, the setting for many royal social functions and fairs, among them the annual Red Cross Fair in January. Straight ahead across the square stands the imposing National Assembly, of white marble with a huge cupola in neoclassical style, built in 1907 by King Chulalongkorn as his Throne Hall. Special permission is required to go inside the building, which is decorated with huge murals depicting famous events in Thai history. In 1974, Parliament moved to new premises a short distance north.

Behind the old National Assembly is **Vimarn Mek**, billed as the world's largest golden teak building. As much a work of art as the treasures it holds, Vimarn Mek (Cloud Mansion), was built by King Chulalongkorn as a rural residence for his family in what was in 1900, the suburbs of Bangkok. The airy, 100-room home is filled with crystal, Faberge jewelry and other objects brought from Europe. Open daily; 50 baht admission.

King Chulalongkorn started a mass migration by royalty who also built their mansions in the neighborhood. Today, it has an air of gentility

18. National Assembly รัฐสภา

21. Amporn Gardens สวนอัมพร

The investiture of Crown Prince Vajiralongkorn several years ago took place at the former National Assembly (above) amid splendor and traditions that go far back to the earliest days of the Thai monarchy. Massive lions made of Italian marble (opposite) overlook the broad courtyard of Wat Benchamabopit, popularly known as the Marble Temple, which was built during the reign of King Chulalongkorn and which contains many unique architectural features.

98

with stately homes and buildings set along avenues shaded by tall trees.

Leaving the Royal Plaza, turn east on Sri Ayuthaya to arrive after a short distance at one of the city's most beautiful temples.

The newest of the royal temples in Bangkok, **Wat Benchamabopit**, the **Marble Temple**, was started by King Chulalongkorn in 1901 and finished ten years later, just after his death; the name means "Temple of the Fifth King." It is also one of the most unusual, for the architect, a half-brother of the king, made a number of departures from traditional style. The most obvious of these are the Carrara marble used on the main buildings; the enclosed courtyard; and the curved, yellow Chinese tiles of the roof. Two gigantic marble lions, or *singha*, guard the entrance to the *bot*. The marble courtyard has a Renaissance quality about it, with clouds of pigeons that

descend to eat bread thrown by visitors. Try to be there in the early morning or in the evening when the monks come to chant in the *bot*. In a gallery surrounding the courtyard are 51 Buddha images, slightly larger than life-size, in a variety of different styles and attitudes. All the periods of Thai Buddhist art are represented, as well as art from China, India, Japan, and Tibet. Some of the images are originals of the period; others were recast and enlarged from smaller images to achieve a uniform size. The principal Buddha image is a replica of a famous one in Phitsanulok called *Phra Buddha Chinaraj*.

Through the rear entrance of the courtyard is a huge Bodhi tree, 70-odd years old; it was brought as a seedling from a tree in South Thailand that came from Buddha Gaya in India, the Buddha's birthplace. A canal filled with large turtles (released there by people wishing to

23. Wat Benchamabopit
วัดเบญจมบพิตร (ราชวรวิหาร)

earn merit) separates the religious buildings from the monks' quarters where the present king spent his monkhood shortly after his coronation. Towards the front of the monks' section is a group of buildings called the **Royal Ordination Pavilions**, well worth seeing if you can find the man who has the key (not always an easy task). These buildings were originally located inside the compound of the Grand Palace.

* * *

Farther down Sri Ayuthaya Road stands **Chitralada Palace,** the residence of the king. Not much can be seen from the road except for a group of traditional Thai-style buildings used for entertaining, and the king's experimental dairy farm. The area between the Palace and the National Assembly is occupied by **Khao Din Zoo,** also popularly known as **Dusit Zoo.** The main entrance is on Rajawiti Road. *Khao Din* means "Mountain of Earth," and the place is so called because its central topographical feature is a man-made hill affording a view of the whole park. This is one of the most popular places in Bangkok for family outings, especially on weekends. Gibbons swing from the trees, there is a monkey show, and you can ride on an elephant. To meet the Thai demand for frequent snacks, there are many restaurants and food stalls. There is even a lake where young lovers can rent a rowboat. This is also the place where the royal white elephants are kept in a fancy enclosure all their own. By tradition, every white elephant found in Thailand belongs to the king, and after complicated and detailed examination to attest its whiteness, it is brought to Khao Din, where it receives lavish attention and special food; in the old days, the power of a

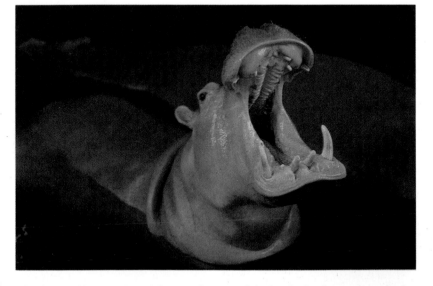

This hungry hippopotamus (above) is but one of the hundreds of animals on display at Dusit Zoo, a spacious park that is a popular place for city dwellers on weekends; the royal white elephants are also at the zoo in a special enclosure all their own. The narrow, twisting lanes of Bangkok's Chinatown offer an endless variety of surprising sights to a stroller, like the advertisements for a happy dentist and an expert palmist on the opposite page.

100

king was measured in part by the number of white elephants he possessed. Actually, as you will see, the elephants are not white at all, but albinos of pinkish hue, though in an odd way they do seem rather more regal than ordinary run-of-the-mill elephants!

The zoo also houses a fine collection of birds in a huge aviary on the "Mountain of Earth," and a large variety of other animals such as giraffes, kangaroos, crocodiles, quaint little mouse-deer (native to Thailand), and even bears, for whom blocks of ice are thoughtfully provided. The zoo is open from 7:00 a.m. until 6.00 p.m. everyday. Admission is only several baht.

* * *

24. Yaowaraj
ย่านเยาวราช (ไชน่าทาวน์)

The **Chinatown** of Bangkok is a large and rather ill-defined area, on either side of two large streets, Charoen Krung (New Road) and Yaowaraj, with Suapa (Rajawong) Road

found somewhat in the middle of the area. By day, these crowded, boisterous streets reach a noise level impressive even by Bangkok standards, though a certain degree of relief can be attained by turning off into one of the narrow, twisting lanes that teem with shops doing a brisk business selling everything imaginable, from motorcycles to birds' nests, Chinese paper lanterns, and ancient remedies of the Celestial Kingdom. Some of Bangkok's leading banks and commercial firms still have their headquarters in this district, reminders of the days when nearly all trade was in the hands of Chinese, Thailand's largest minority and a third of Bangkok's population; but most have now opened branch offices elsewhere.

Yaowaraj is famous for its gold shops — hundreds of them, one after another, looking exactly alike and for the most part selling articles at

almost the same prices since the price of gold is fixed by the government. People from all over Bangkok come here to invest their money in gold chains which are, rather confusingly for a tourist, sold by the baht — referring in this case to a weight and not the coin. If they prosper, the customers come back and exchange the first chain for a heavier one; if they encounter difficulties, Yaowaraj also has a large number of convenient pawn shops. At night, Yaowaraj quiets down a bit, but another phenomenon replaces the action on the street — thousands of small, migratory birds come to roost on the telephone wires and power lines above the street.

Another part of Chinatown that attracts people from all over is **Pahurat,** the cloth section. (It can be reached by walking west on narrow Soi Wanit, located just below and parallel to Yaowaraj Road, and going past Chakrawat and Chakraphet Roads, beyond the King's Theater.) Despite the location, a large proportion of the shop owners here are turbaned Sikhs from India. Fabric prices, especially of imported goods from Japan and Europe, are generally much cheaper than in other parts of the city.

In the heart of Yaowaraj, as Chinatown is called for short — also not far from the King's and Queen's Theaters — is an area of narrow, claustrophobic old streets known as **Nakorn Kasem,** the **Thieves Market** in many guidebooks. This is something of a misnomer, since it happens to be an eminently respectable district on the whole, with no more than its fair share of thieves in the legal sense of the word. The majority of its small shops sell such emphatically unromantic articles as toilets, water pumps, and lighting fixtures; but its lure for tourists is its close to two

26. Nakorn Kasem
เวิ้งนครเกษม

25. Pahurat Market
ตลาดผ้าพาหุรัด

Chinatown's Thieves' Market (above) contains a fascinating collection of goods for sale, including antique porcelains and Laotian war drums as well as ordinary water pumps. Wat Trimitr's immense Golden Buddha (opposite) is made of $5\frac{1}{2}$ tonnes of solid gold; disguised for centuries by a drab stucco covering, the priceless statue was only discovered by accident when the outer covering cracked as the image was being moved to a new location.

dozen antique shops that spill out treasures along the sidewalks. There was a time, not too many years ago, when every antique lover in search of a bargain was obliged to go to Nakorn Kasem, and many a treasure was uncovered in its dusty, dimly lighted shops. To a large extent, that has now changed; many old Nakorn Kasem dealers have struck it rich and opened flashy, new air-conditioned shops over on the other side of Bangkok in the tourist centers; but there are still things to be discovered by the buyer with a sharp eye and a gift for tough bargaining (as a general rule, every price can be talked down at least 20 percent). The best bargains are in Chinese items — porcelains, furniture inlaid with mother-of-pearl, rosewood screens, snuff bottles. Besides antiques, shops sell new but charming (and cheap) brass and copper oil lanterns and bell-shaped temple lighting fixtures.

Just east of the point where Yaowaraj Road meets Charoen Krung Road (not far from Hua Lampong Railway Station) is **Wat Trimitr,** worth visiting to see its famous **Golden Buddha,** found by accident when a construction company was extending the port of Bangkok. Entirely covered in stucco when it was discovered, the figure was moved to a temporary shelter at Wat Trimitr while a building was constructed to house it. On the night before it was scheduled to be moved by crane to the new building, torrential rain soaked the stucco covering, and during the move the image was accidentally dropped into soft mud — the stucco cracked, revealing the pure gold beneath. When the covering was removed, the whole Sukhothai image, three meters high and weighing about 5½ tonnes, was discovered to be made of gold. Experts believe it was probably originally in an Ayuthaya temple and cov-

Experts believe the Golden Buddha was camouflaged to keep the invading Burmese from finding it in early Ayuthaya.

ered with the stucco to conceal its value from the invading Burmese in the 18th century; the ruse worked so well that it remained hidden from the Thais as well for nearly 200 years.

* * *

New Road (Charoen Krung) one of the oldest roads in Bangkok in fact, used to be the center of the tourist and *farang* ("foreigner") shops, but a decade or so ago, this aspect of the city began to shift over to the Rajprasong-Ploenchit area. Now the most significant landmarks left are the G.P.O., the Portuguese, Finnish, and French embassies, the Oriental Hotel (down Oriental Lane which passes the Monaco Consulate and leads to the river), and the **Bangrak Market,** one of the city's busiest. To reach the latter walk south down New Road past Oriental Lane and you will see on your right between the road and the river, dozens of stalls selling mountains of fresh fruits and vege-

tables, along with other food. People come here from all over Bangkok in the belief that the produce is fresher and cheaper, because it comes by boat straight from the farms and orchards upriver. The variety of fruit is bound to stagger anyone from a temperate country. Bananas come in more than ten kinds (the small firm ones are best for cooking), and huge, sweet pineapples and papayas are only a few bant each. A tropical grape, developed at the agriculture university, is now available all year round in both red and green varieties. However, the two fruits most prized by the Thais are mangoes and durians, both of which appear on the market only in the hot season. If the only mangoes you have ever eaten are the Caribbean or Mexican varieties, you are in for a treat, for the pale Thai mangoes have an infinitely more delicate flavor. The Thais eat them green in a salad or dipped in sugar; or

Charoen Krung
ถนนเจริญกรุง

29. Bangkrak Market
ตลาดบางรัก

104

Modern Bangkok

ripe as a sweet along with glutinous (sticky) rice and coconut milk. Durian is a large, spiky, pungent prehistoric-looking fruit that you either like or loathe; nobody seems neutral about it. If you have a taste for it, be prepared to pay anywhere from 20 baht for one of the ordinary to several hundred for a superior *kanyao* ("long stem"), the most prized of all. If you are having your first durian, it might be helpful to remember that a very ripe fruit at room temperature tastes much stronger than a chilled one just ripening.

Located a few blocks farther south on New Road, **Wat Yannawa** has the unusual shape of an ark.

Besides the many temples and traditional sights, new tourist Bangkok invites exploration and shopping.

To the left (west) of the picturesque Siam Intercontinental Hotel on Rama I Road stands **Siam Center,** an airconditioned shopping center with four levels of shops catering to tourists. Behind it is the residence of the king's mother and an office building housing the Princess Mother's Charities. On the second floor of the small building (enter from Phya Thai Road) is a store selling northern hill-tribe handicrafts — fine pieces of embroidery, homespun cloth, basket-work, sling bags; prices here are cheaper than in most of the tourist-oriented shops selling the same things, and the money goes to the welfare of the tribes.

To the right (east) of the Siam Intercontinental Hotel, just beyond a primary school, stands **Wat Pathum Wan,** also called "The Lotus Temple," because of the great number of lotuses and water lilies blooming in the large pond behind it. The *bot* contains some attractive murals done

Only a short stroll from the Oriental Hotel, Bangrak Market (left) is noted for its fresh fruits, flowers and vegetables that are brought along the nearby Chao Phya River from neighboring farms and orchards.

during the period of Rama V (1868-1910). However, the temple itself was built by Rama IV and was part of a large park which also included a palace where the king came in the summer to escape the heat of the Grand Palace — this part of Bangkok then being "in the country." The palace is gone now, but despite ominous rumors of "development" — in Bangkok always meaning a new shopping center or hotel — much of the park still remains, its ponds and islands and large trees something of an anachronism in this busy commercial area. A peculiar distinction of Wat Pathum Wan is that it is the most popular temple in Bangkok among taxi drivers for having their vehicles blessed against accidents.

The large shopping area across from the Siam Intercontinental, extending from Phya Thai Road to Henri Dunant Road, is called **Siam Square**. This is a highly popular place with Thais, since it has three large movie theaters — the Siam, Lido, Scala — plus dozens of relatively inexpensive Thai and Chinese restaurants and coffee shops. There are also some good bookshops (the D.K. Bookshop has a wide range of paperbacks), antique shops, men's and women's tailors specializing in mod fashions, and the British Council, a striking example of modern architecture in red, white, and blue.

Along Henri Dunant Road (still called by Thais by its old name of Sanam Ma, "Race Course Road") are found two important old Bangkok institutions. On the left, walking south away from Siam Square, you come upon the **Royal Bangkok Sports Club**, a multinational private club with sports facilities — golf course, swimming pool, tennis courts — and racing on Saturdays during all but the rainiest months. The club is closed to non-members, but the racing is open to the public through separate entrances. You get your money's worth: the program commences at noon and consists of 15 races.

Across the road from the Sports Club stand the spectacular temple-like buildings of the Faculty of Arts of **Chulalongkorn University**, the country's oldest and most prestigious institution of higher learning. The campus extends from Henri Dunant to Phya Thai Road and has 14 faculties. Built in a mixture of Thai and Western styles, with spacious yellow-roofed pavilions, an open gallery, and an assembly hall, the university was founded by King Rama VI (1911-1925) and named for his father, King Chulalongkorn.

* * *

This area of Bangkok is for serious shoppers. North of Chulalongkorn University is **Siam Square**, a warren of shops selling everything from books to seashells. West, across Phya Thai Road is the enormous Mahboonkrong Center containing a department store, two cinemas and myriad shops.

Travel east on Rama I to **Rajprasong** intersection. The magnet here is the **Erawan Shrine**. To improve their fortunes or pass their exams, Thais make offerings at a statue of the Hindu god, Brahma. Originally erected by the Erawan Hotel to counter a spate of bad luck, the shrine is redolent with incense smoke and jasmine. To repay the god for wishes granted, they leave wooden elephants at the god's feet or hire a resident troupe to dance. Day or night, it provides a fascinating spectacle, an enclave of peace amid the din of one of the city's busiest streets.

Nearby is another cluster of shopping malls. The showcase is the **Peninsula Plaza** on Rajdamri Road near the Regent Hotel. **Galleries Lafayette** and other prestige shops sell luxury items from around the world.

A short distance east of the Shrine on Ploenchit Road is Amarin

Plaza with McDonalds for those who miss American cuisine. Up the road, where Ploenchit and Chidlom meet is the largest of the Central Department stores. **Central** has a large section selling Thai products for those who forgot to buy souvenirs elsewhere.

North of the Shrine, on Rajdamri Road is **Rajdamri Arcade** and **Bangkok Bazaar**. Both have the air of a market with numerous small shops crammed into a small space and vendors of various goods spilling off the sidewalks.

The pair serve as a link between the chic shops of **Rajprasong** and the bazaar atmosphere of a vast, sprawling **Pratunam**, one block north, a favourite shopping place for many Thais. *Pratunam* means "Water Door," referring to the lock at the bridge to prevent **Klong Saen Sap** on the right (east) from being flooded by the one on the left (west) which leads to the Chao Phya River. Under the

bridge there are shops selling straw goods, and you can hire a boat here to make the trip up Klong Saen Sap, one of the few really busy *klongs* left in Bangkok. The noodle shops of Pratunam Market are popular late at night after the bars and movie theaters close.

* * *

South of the shopping areas along Rama I Road, at the corner of Henri Dunant and Rama VI Roads, stands the **Pasteur Institute**, part of the Thai Red Cross and open everyday except Sunday. Locals (as may the visitor) come here to have cholera, smallpox and typhoid inoculations, as well as rabies treatment, for moderate fees; but it has become a tourist attraction because of the **Snake Farm** behind the main administration building. Here, under huge, shady rain trees (also called monkeypods), three large, deep pits contain hun-

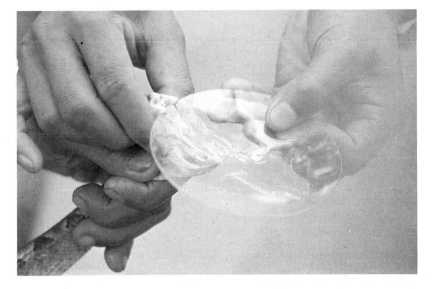

The Erawan Shrine (opposite) honors a Hindu deity and is one of the most popular of Bangkok's innumerable shrines; piles of sweet-smelling jasmine wreaths are offered by those in search of favors. Lethal snakes (above) are milked every Thursday at the Pasteur Institute; the pale yellow venom is injected into horses to produce serum which is subsequently sent all over the country to treat those bitten by cobras, vipers, and banded kraits.

dreds of poisonous snakes used in the production of anti-snakebite serum, mostly sent to the provinces where cases of snakebite are common in the rice fields. The principal species kept at the farm are king cobras (some of them four meters long), ordinary cobras, banded kraits, and Russell vipers. A different kind of serum is produced from each, and it is essential to know what kind of snake has bitten you, since krait serum, for example, is not effective against cobra bite, and vice versa. Every Thursday morning, around 10 o'clock, the snakes are "milked" by a pair of workers, who go into the pits, as if they were going into a coffee shop, and nonchalantly pick up suitable snakes. Though it may give you a case of the gooseflesh, viewing the handling of such legendary serpents can be a rewarding, eye-opening experience. One worker inserts a glass plate under the fangs of the selected snake while the other holds its neck and presses the venom sacs just behind the eyes, whereupon a pale, yellowish liquid is deposited on the glass. "By nature snakes are not aggressive and will attack human beings only under provocation," reads a bulletin produced by the Snake Farm. And although nature intended the venom for animals the snake can eat, and the men are skilled at their job, accidents have been known to happen. A few years ago an ill-tempered king cobra — not as potent as a banded krait, but more dangerous because of the amount of venom it can produce — bit a worker who was cleaning the pit. The man *was* saved by prompt treatment. After the men have extracted the venom, it is injected into horses kept for the purpose in a stable near the pits. The horses are periodically bled and tested for potency, and when the desired antibodies have been developed in the horse-blood, the serum is separated and freeze-dried for shipment to the provinces and to a number of surrounding countries with similar venomous snakes.

For plant lovers, especially from temperate lands, visiting a tropical country can be a dream come true. **Tropical gardens** virtually know no seasons, and countries like Thailand are perennially abloom.

Unfortunately for those who like to look at other people's gardens, however, Bangkok tends to be a city of high walls, many of them studded with intimidating bits of broken glass, so a drive through a residential area is not very rewarding. Bangkok has no botanical garden per se (the closest thing being the agricultural college, Kasetsart University, on the city's edge off Route 1 near Don Muang Airport), but a number of flower markets and private estates open to the public amply present the country's floral riches. One famous private garden that is open to the public is at **Suan Pakkard Palace** on Sri Ayuthaya Road (just east of the intersection with Phaya Thai Road), the splendid residence of Princess Chumbhot of Nagara Svarg, one of Thailand's leading gardeners and art collectors. Actually, the beautifully landscaped grounds (*suan* means "garden") containing numerous plants the princess brought from all over the world as well as from the Thai jungle, are only part of the reason for visiting Suan Pakkard, for it has a great diversity of other treasures. Five old, traditional Thai houses overlooking the garden contain a large collection, made all the more charming by its presentation without the stuffiness of a museum, of Buddha images, Khmer statues, old paintings, porcelain, musical instruments, and the regalia of the late Prince Chumbhot. At the back of the garden stands an exquisite little lacquer pavilion, which Prince Chumbhot discovered in a temple

39. Suan Pakkard Palace
วังสวนผักกาด

In the manicured gardens of Suan Pakkard Palace, maintained by Princess Chumbot, sits an exquisitely decorated lacquer pavilion, originally found in a temple near Ayuthaya.

near Ayuthaya, brought in pieces to Bangkok, and had carefully restored. The pavilion's black, gold panels are considered masterpieces of Thai decorative art. In various other buildings at Suan Pakkard are found collections of seashells, mineral crystals, and painted pottery and bronze objects from the prehistoric burial ground at Ban Chiang in Northeast Thailand. The palace is open every day except Sundays and admission is 30 baht.

Plant lovers who fail to be in Bangkok on one of the days of the Weekend Market at the Sanam Luang can visit the permanent **Flower Market in Thevet** (or Theves) district where many of the plant dealers have stalls during the week. (Tell the taxi driver you want to go to *talat dokmai Thevet.*) On a pretty street that runs down to the river and is shaded by flamboyant trees (a showy relative of the poinciana), about 50 plant shops spill out onto the road selling all the ornamentals used in Bangkok gardens. Across Klong Krung Kasem that runs behind the shops is the principal coconut market of Bangkok, where the barges from plantations come to unload their produce; note the large, handsome, cone-shaped baskets which are used only for loading and measuring coconuts. The arched bridge across the *klong* in the middle of the flower market is a good place for picture taking.

The flower that comes closest to being Thailand's national flower, expressing through its multicolored petal, leaf, and stem much of the character of the land, is the **Orchid.** Nearly a thousand species grow native to the country, and the home cultivation of hybrid varieties has long been a popular hobby. Just about every Thai house you see, even in a slum, has at least one pot of orchids, hanging somewhere. In the past decade,

40. Thevet Market
ตลาดดอกไม้เทเวศน์

Tame pelicans and sea gulls have the run of Suan Pakkard's carefully trimmed green lawns.

orchid growing has turned into a booming commercial enterprise. Today hardly a plane leaves Bangkok for Europe that does not carry a cargo of cut flowers or whole plants destined for German or French florists or cultivators.

Orchid lovers can visit one of the numerous nurseries where orchids are grown commercially for export. The majority of these are over in Thonburi or along the superhighway leading to the airport, where the air and water are fresher and cleaner, but nurseries can be found scattered throughout the city. Most have no objection to visitors coming to look about, though it is usually a good idea to have a Thai along to help interpret questions. Some of the larger nurseries are Phairot's Orchids (376 Satupradit Road, Yanawa); T. Orchids (30/71 Suthisanvinichai Road); Napa Orchid (9 Soi Santisuk); and CY Orchid (458/1 Sukhumvit).

The **Siam Society** on Soi 21 (Soi Asoke), off Sukhumvit Road, is a royally sponsored group founded in 1904 to promote studies in the history, botany, zoology, anthropology, and linguistics of Thailand. The society publishes a scholarly journal containing articles by experts on those subjects, and also special books on specific subjects like the orchids of Thailand, Thai customs, and gardening; copies of these are on sale at the society's headquarters, and there is an excellent reference library for anyone doing research on Thailand.

Any visitor interested in the culture of North Thailand should go to see the Kamthieng House in the Siam Society compound. This lovely old house, which is approximately 120 years old, was the ancestral home of a prominent family in Chiang Mai, one of whom donated it to the society. With the help of a grant from the Asia Foundation, it was dismantled,

The Siam Society
สยามสมาคม

brought to Bangkok, and carefully reassembled in a garden composed mostly of traditional Thai plants. It was decided to use it as an ethnological museum devoted to the folk art and other aspects of northern culture, a needed addition to Bangkok since the National Museum has no such collection. Among the things on display are various everyday objects of farmers and fishermen, fine wood carvings from temples and houses in the North, lacquerware, and hill tribe costumes. Notice in particular the beautifully carved teak lintels from traditional domestic houses, which are fast vanishing in the North. These were placed over the doorway leading to the inner main room of the house and are called in northern dialect *ham yon*, meaning "sacred testicles" — so named because the inner room was believed to contain not only the ancestral spirits of the family but also the virility of the present inhabitants.

When an old northern house is dismantled, or when a new owner moves in, the *ham yon* are often symbolically castrated by beating them severely to destroy the powerful magic accumulated in them under the old owner. A guide to the Kamthieng House and the collection in it is available in the library of the society. The society also intermittently organizes excellent tours around the country, which the visitor on a longer stay may be able to join.

* * *

On Klong Maha Nag at the end of Soi Kasemsong II, across from the National Stadium on Rama I Road, stands **Jim Thompson's House,** open daily except weekends from 9 a.m. to 5 p.m. This is the Thai-style house — or, to be more precise, a collection of seven Thai-style houses joined together — built by the remarkable American who came to Thailand at the end of World War II

Plant lovers are in store for a treat in Thailand, where lush tropical gardens are perennially in bloom. One of the dealers at the Thevet flower market (opposite) shows off a friendly smile as well as a specimen. Jim Thompson's House (above) was the home of the American who revived the Thai silk industry after World War II ; assembled from seven teak Thai-style houses, it contains an extensive collection of beautifully displayed Asian antiquities.

1. Jim Thompson's
บ้านทรงไทยของ จิม ทอมป์สัน

and started the Thai silk industry. In 1967, while on a visit to the Cameron Highlands in Peninsular Malaysia, Thompson mysteriously disappeared; despite an extensive search, no trace at all has ever been found of him.

Besides his contribution to the silk business, Thompson will also be remembered for his fabulous collection of Asian Art and the house in which he displayed it and which his heirs have decided to keep as he left it. "Not only have you beautiful things," Somerset Maugham once wrote Thompson after dining with him, "but what is more rare, you have displayed them beautifully." Scattered about the lovely teak-paneled rooms of the house are hundreds of pieces of Chinese blue-and-white Ming export ware; splendid Cambodian stone figures; the largest public collection of Bencharong ("five colors"), a multi-colored porcelain made in China for export only to Thailand; wooden Burmese statues; rare 17th-century Thai stone Buddha images; a dining table once used for card games by King Rama V; and such oddities as a charming little "mouse palace," an ornately carved cage for keeping white mice as pets. The garden around the house is a luxuriant tropical mini-jungle, and looking across the *klong* from the terrace, you can see the houses of some of Thompson's first silk weavers, with brilliant ropes of silk thread hanging out to dry in the sun. There are volunteer guides to explain the collection to visitors, and admission is 20 baht, which goes to a favorite charity of Thompson, the local School for the Blind. (The Thai-style houses you pass on your way to the house, incidentally, are not part of the Thompson estate; they were built by the daughter of one of his weavers as rental houses.) The Thompson Silk Company is on Suriwongse Road.

Seventy-nine meters tall, the spire of Wat Arun (above), encrusted with a glittering mosaic of broken bits of glass and ceramic, looms loftily above the Chao Phya River. The tower was raised on the site of an older one during the reign of King Rama II. The temple compound also contains many other outstanding artistic treasures, like the delicate gold-and-black lacquered doors (opposite) depicting armed but smiling soldiers.

Across the River

Wat Arun, Temple of Dawn, is located across from Bangkok in the sister city of Thonburi, and is most interesting and easily reached by water-taxi from any of the landing stages along the river. (The closest ferrying point is at Tha Tien, just on the opposite bank, where boats leave very frequently in the morning.) An older temple, called Wat Chaeng, was on this site when King Taksin established his capital at Thonburi, and he used it as the royal *wat,* the palace being located nearby. King Rama II of Bangkok, in the early years of the 19th century, decided to enlarge the temple and raise the height of the central tower from 15 to its present 79 meters, making it one of the tallest religious structures in the country. Because of the soft earth, this engineering feat took years to carry out and was finally completed during the reign of his successor. The great *prang* (rounded spire) is completely

covered with pieces of multicolored Chinese porcelain embedded in cement. The builders ran out of porcelain for this large edifice, compelling Rama III to call upon his subjects to contribute any broken crockery they could find to complete the decoration; he was rewarded with thousands of pieces. You can climb about halfway up the tower by one of four steep staircases and get a fine view of the temple compound and the river — though anyone suffering from vertigo should think twice before doing so.

Some good murals cover the inside of the *bot,* guarded by two giant masked gods. There is a large amount of the charming statuary similar to that found in Wat Po, and many lovely pavilions.

A visit to Wat Arun can be combined with one to the **Royal Barges**, also on the Thonburi side on Klong Bangkok Noi, farther north up the river. (Look on the map for the Thonburi Railway Station which sits near the mouth of the *klong.*) These splendidly carved boats were used by the king when he made his royal *kathin* at the end of the rainy season, bringing robes and gifts from the Grand Palace to the monks of Wat Arun. The king sat high on a throne in the largest barge in a procession of dozens, while brilliantly costumed oarsmen chanted as they moved upriver. Discontinued in 1967, this spectacle was revived for the Chakri dynasty's Bicentennial celebration in 1982. The Royal Thai Navy lavished more than US$440,000 for restoration of the barges, with special attention going to *Sri Supannahong,* the oldest and most richly carved. Nearly 43 meters long, it requires a crew of 54 oarsmen, two steermen, two officers, one flagman, one rhythm keeper, and one singer who chants to the cadence of the oars. Two seven-tiered umbrellas are placed, one in front of and the other behind, the golden pavilion that shelters the king. The gilded bird's head that forms the prow of the barge represents a *hansa,* or sacred swan.

Waterways

While on the Thonburi side, a trip to the **Floating Market** on Klong Dao Kanong will provide a glimpse of the still-active waterborne life of Thailand. Bangkok was once dubbed the Venice of the East, so numerous and important were its canals and rivers, which crisscrossed the entire area to form an extensive transportation network. In fact, up until the last century there were probably fewer roads than waterways in the area. Lying at sea level and flood-prone a good part of the year, Bangkok and the surrounding plain lent themselves naturally to water travel.

Though many *klong*s, especially in Bangkok, have been filled in to make way for the motorcar, thus diminishing considerably in recent years of progress the area's waterborne life, a lot of it still goes on, both on the main artery of the Chao Phya and on the extant canals.

Long-time foreign residents of Bangkok may advise you against going to the Floating Market in Thonburi, the early-morning attraction that, after the numerous temples, probably remains Thailand's most celebrated spectacle. Old hands will tell you that it is not what it used to be, that it has become something of a tourist trap. And in a way they are right: in the 20-odd years since the market was discovered by the tour agencies, it has certainly lost a good deal of its original innocence; and the Thais who bring things to sell there have not remained immune to the lure of the yen, the mark, and the dollar. (It would be a miracle indeed were the reverse true.) All the same, remember that the old-timers are speaking from the experience of having watched the change; visitors seeing it for the first time are nearly always delighted and count it among the highlights of their stay, the commercialism notwithstanding.

Floating Market
ตลาดน้ำ

Endlessly interesting traffic moves along the Chao Phya River flowing through the heart of Bangkok.

The easiest way to see the market is to take one of the tours which leave daily from the landing near the Oriental Hotel down Oriental Avenue, off Charoen Krung (New Road); these usually go to the Floating Market first and, on the way back, stop for a look at the Royal Barges and Wat Arun. The tour starts early in the morning, around 7:00 a.m., and usually finishes around 11:00 a.m. If you want to go on your own, you can arrange to hire a private boat at the same place, or at one of the other landing stages along the river, but this is likely to turn out to be more expensive unless you have a Thai friend along to haggle over the price of the outing.

To reach the Floating Market from the Oriental landing, the boat goes south down the Chao Phya River to the Krungthep Bridge, then turns right (west) into Klong Dao Kanong, which leads through smaller *klong*s and eventually to the center of the

market on Klong Dan, near Wat Sai. An early start is essential because the market reaches its peak of activity about 7:30 a.m. An hour later, it is merely another Thonburi *klong*, though with rather more souvenir shops than others. If you get there in time, however, you see hundreds of boats, loaded with fruits, vegetables, dried fish, rice, and other produce, paddled by pretty girls wearing broadbrimmed lampshade hats and looking as if they had been carefully selected for eager tourists to photograph. Other boats sell ready-to-eat foods: the inevitable noodles, of course; fried bananas; fresh coconut milk; and little custardlike sweets wrapped in banana leaf. The market presents a colorful and exotic scene; and even if there are almost as many tourist boats as vendors' on some mornings, it is still not the sort of sight you will see anywhere else in the world.

Concerned over criticism about the growing commercialization of the Thonburi Floating Market, the Tourist Authority of Thailand (T.A.T.) encourages visitors to go to another water market outside of Bangkok on a *klong* called **Damnern Saduak**, in Ratchaburi Province, about an hour's drive to the southwest of the city. This is now being scheduled by many tours as part of the trip to the great *chedi* in Nakhon Pathom and the Bridge on the River Kwai in Kanchanaburi. Aside from being far less crowded with tourists than the Thonburi Floating Market, the one at Damnern Saduak has the added advantage of lasting until around 10:00 a.m.; it is especially famous for its fruits which come from surrounding orchards, particularly large, succulent grapefruitlike pomelos, called *sam-o* in Thai. (The route to this market leaves Bangkok across the Memorial Bridge, follows Route 4 to Nakhon Pathom, and 25 km farther turns left on Route 325 for Damnern Saduak, which is on the road to Samut Songkram.)

Damnern Saduak
ดำเนินสะดวก (ตลาดน้ำ)

Klong Dao Kanong
คลองดาวกะนอง

There are other more customary **water tours** which set out on the Chao Phya and on *klong*s in Thonburi, like Bangkok Yai and Bangkok Noi, which remain much as they were fifty years ago. Without traffic lights and smoggy jams to hang you up, the boats breeze past Thai-style houses, orchards, and temples along the river banks. Seen from the river, which has played such an important part in its history, the Bangkok area takes on a completely different aspect. From a new and dramatic angle, you see such fine old European buildings as the French and Portuguese Embassies just up from the Oriental Hotel, faded old shop buildings, gaudily decorated Chinese temples, the Royal Landing Stage with its Thai-style pavilion, and the spires of the Grand Palace and Wat Phra Keo. The river life itself presents an endlessly interesting spectacle: huge rice and sand barges, so heavily loaded that the prow is almost level with the water, with families cheerfully cooking meals on deck; ferry boats packed with commuters, going back and forth between Bangkok and Thonburi; ships belonging to the Royal Thai Navy; and innumerable other craft of all shapes and sizes.

The same rules apply to taking a motorboat on the main river as on a *klong*. The small sleek boats are called *hang yao*, and they usually rent by the hour, unless you take the regular water-taxis that go up and down the *klong*s on fairly regular routes and are not for charter. The price for chartering your own "long-tail" should be 200 to 300 baht an hour, but this can depend on a number of factors; in any case, be sure to settle on a price before you set off. If you are intrepid and want to try the regular commuters' boats on the main river, ask for the *rua rew*, or fast boats, as the public launches are re-

ferred to. All the regular taxis and public launches are extremely inexpensive.

On the Chao Phya, you can also take larger, more comfortable (and more expensive) boats which are especially hired to tourists; these are fine for traveling on the river itself, but a *hang yao* is better for exploring the narrower, shallower *klong*s. The Oriental landing is the most common place to hire a large boat — most of the boatmen here speak some English and are accustomed to taking tourists — but you could also get on at the landing near Silapakorn University if you happen to be in the Grand Palace end of town.

The Supatra Company Ltd (254 Arun Amarin Road Thonburi), have daily river cruises on single-deck boats for parties of 15 to 25 people, or on double-deck boats for groups of 30 to 40. You can choose your own destination or choose from set cruises to standard attractions like Wat Arun or into the countryside.

The Oriental Hotel owns a luxury ship — the Oriental Queen — which sails up the river daily, except Mondays, to Ayuthaya, passengers returning by air-conditioned bus; or you can travel up by bus and return by river, in either case ending the trip at 5:00 p.m. The price per person is set at 650 baht, including lunch. (The adventuresome traveler can try the inexpensive commuter's water route to Ayuthaya: from Tha Tien ferry point near Wat Po, take a *rua kao*, or white boat, to Baan Phan, and then transfer to a *hang yao* for the trip downriver.) On Wednesday evenings the Oriental Queen becomes the Jazz Riverboat and cruises on the river from 8:00 until 11:00 p.m.; the fare includes dinner and dancing. And a young American has done up a rice

Bangkok's surviving waterways still offer one of the best ways to see the traditional life of the city. A long-tail motorboat (opposite) races through one of the narrow canals that lead out into the countryside.

barge that he calls the Tassaneeya Nava for sunset cruises and a Thai dinner. Reservations must be made at least one day in advance. Call direct (tel. 234.8620 ext. Oriental Queen), or book through travel agencies and leading hotels.

One of the most scenic *klongs* for exploring residential Bangkok is **klong Saen Sap,** a lotus-choked waterway than runs from Bangkapi east to the rice fields beyond. One of the early Bangkok kings supposedly had this canal dug in order to sail war boats all the way to the gulf and thence to Cambodia. Other excellent places in Bangkok to pick up motorboats are at the Ekamai Bridge on Soi 63 off Sukhumvit and at Prakanong Klong Tan Bridge on Soi 71 off Sukhumvit. If you go from Pratunam to Bangkapi, you will see more Western-style houses than Thai ones, but it does pass a number of picturesque Muslim settlements. If you take a boat out of the center of town at Soi 63 or Soi 71 and head southerly toward Prakanong and beyond, you soon enter real countryside where good-sized villages live entirely on waterborne commerce. Boats make available a vast range of goods: hot dishes served up from a floating restaurant; the daily newspaper; a piece of cloth for a new dress. Once along certain *klong*s in Bangkok — and perhaps still today in other places — floating prostitutes, known as "water babies," housed in little curtained boats paddled by discreet boatmen, plied their age-old trade. The people who live on the *klong*s not only use them for shopping and traveling, but also for bathing and washing — but not, as many visitors seem to think, for drinking; for that, there are boats which supply fresh water in large earthenware jars.

Other interesting boat trips may be made north to Rangsit, famous for its noodles; south to the Port of Bangkok; and to the *wat*s both north and south along the Chao Phya. For more details consult the T.A.T.

Klong Saen Sap
คลองแสนแสบ

Thai Boxing

A Thai boxing ring *look*s like one anywhere else in the world, but what goes on inside is uniquely Thai: a mixture of ballet, gymnastics, and mayhem in which just about anything goes short of biting. The difference is apparent as soon as the fighters enter the arena; they wear the familiar gloves and boxing trunks, but also a colored cord around their head and biceps (usually containing a lucky amulet), often a jasmine wreath around their neck, and they are barefoot. Before the fight starts they go through an odd, slow-motion little dance, designed to show off their talents in a stylized form. To an outsider, the dances may look pretty much the same, but in fact each boxing camp has its own distinctive version and connoisseurs can tell immediately which camp a fighter comes from. A four-piece orchestra composed of a Java pipe, cymbals, and a pair of long drums accompanies the dance and also the fight itself, following the action and stepping up the tempo as the blows fly and the excitement rises.

Thai boxing originated in the Ayuthaya period when it was transformed from a self-defensive art into a spectator sport. A curious combination of balletic grace and murderous ferocity, accompanied and whipped up by the music, makes it a thrilling sport to watch. "Wrestling, judo, throwing, butting, biting, spitting, and kicking your opponent while he is down" are forbidden by the rules; but a fighter can use his feet, elbows, legs, knees, and shoulders — almost every part of his body. The bare feet are the favored means of attack, and the art aptly has been dubbed eight-arm pugilism. You do not have to watch a fight long before you realize that diminutive size is no measure of a Thai boxer's capacity to inflict injury. A well-delivered kick (often to

Thai-style boxing combines ballet, gymnastics, and more than a little mayhem; anything goes, short of biting.

the groin) can floor an opponent; it is an open secret in martial arts' circles that a good Thai boxer is virtually unstoppable.

Until about 40 years ago, Thai boxers did not wear gloves but bound their hands with hemp, in which ground glass was sometimes put for added effect. It was also the custom for the fight to go on for as long as both fighters could stand up. Now there are five rounds of fixed three-minute duration, no ground glass, and if one fighter appears to be injured the referee stops the bout. Thai boxing can be seen in Bangkok at **Rajadamnern Stadium** (Rajadamnern Avenue), starting around 5:00 p.m. on Monday, Wednesday, Thursday, and Sunday and at **Lumpini Stadium** (Rama IV Road) on Tuesday, Wednesday, Friday, and Saturday. Two Thai fighters have held the World Flyweight Championship, and as a result Western-style boxing now rivals the older Thai-style; programs in Bangkok's boxing stadiums now usually include both styles. Fans also avidly follow championship matches abroad, and if you happen to be in the capital when an international bout appears over TV, you will find almost all the streets deserted and crowds huddled around every set.

Although programs at the Bangkok stadiums start around 5:00 p.m., the main fight of Thai boxing takes place around 7:00 p.m. Ringside seats cost about 100 baht, but you can sit in the bleachers for less than half that. If you sit in the cheaper seats — in Bangkok often separated by wire mesh from the expensive ringside seats, to protect the better-paying (and presumably more sedate) customers from the masses who hurtle bottles when angered by a referee's decision — you will also get an introduction to another aspect of Thailand: a strong love of gambling.

Rajadamnern Stadium
สนามมวยราชดำเนิน

45. Lumpini Stadium
สนามมวยลุมพินี

Bangkok at Night

When night falls, a different Bangkok emerges. **Bangkok at night** has many faces, offering just about any form of amusement you could want somewhere in the city. Some areas are transformed into an unbroken neon forest of bars and nightclubs, with touts hawking their attractions at each doorway; restaurants, movie theaters, and massage parlors are jammed, especially on weekends; and almost any taxi driver you encounter in the vicinity of a big hotel is prepared to offer, sometimes on a card printed in several languages, a mind-boggling menu of vices catering to every imaginable taste, and not couched in innuendoes either.

While no part of the city's night life could be described as strictly *farang*, meaning that Thai patrons rarely go there, certain areas do have a predominantly European clientele. Foremost among these is **Patpong**, a short, privately owned street that runs between Silom and Suriwong Roads a short walk from the Dusit Thani Hotel. Twenty years ago Patpong boasted only one or two rather sedate nightclubs and a couple of good restaurants; now it is nearly all night spots from one end to the other, spilling over to Patpong II, which runs parallel, and to the gay bars of Patpong III. Patpong clubs change name, ownership, and decor with bewildering frequency, so that printed guides become obsolete almost before the ink dries, but at any given time they run the gamut from raunchy to reasonably refined. Most of them have some gimmick to attract customers: topless go-go dancing, old movies, dart-throwing contests, and "special shows" that are occasionally raided by police (who do not, however, arrest the customers). Several better massage parlors are located on Patpong II. If you happen to see delectable-looking young ladies loitering around the sidewalks, incidentally, especially between Patpong and the Dusit Thani on Silom, the chances are good that they are not ladies at all but what the Thais called *kra-toeys*, or transvestites, some of whom could fool even a sober expert.

In the years when Bangkok was the leading rest and recreation center for the American military in Vietnam, a similar stretch of night life sprang up along the New Petchburi Road, starting roughly around the intersection of Soi Asoke (Soi 21) and generally referred to as **The Strip**. There were clubs with names like The San Francisco and Jack's American Star Bar, featuring soul food and country music, and massage palaces that looked like a cross between a bowling alley and a mansion. There were also innumerable "short time" hotels, almost as much a feature of Bangkok's evening world (and afternoon, too) as the massage parlors; they were discreet, motel-like establishments where you could drive your car straight into a garage adjoining the room, and a curtain came down immediately to conceal it. Thousands of such places are all over Bangkok, catering to every pocketbook, and many are full from mid-morning until late in the evening. The ones in the Sukhumvit-New Petchburi Road areas are among the fanciest; one has mirrors on the ceilings as well as on the walls, and a control board over the bed with push buttons for lights, music, air conditioning, and *sanuk* (if you press *sanuk* the bed begins to undulate slowly). With the passing of the American soldiers, a good deal of the ethnic life has gone out of The Strip, but most of the bars and massage parlors are still there, the customers now being mostly Thai. Latterly, the New Petchburi Road has become better known for its large outdoor restaurants specializing in sea-

Patpong Road, a center of nightlife, offers topless go-go clubs, restaurants, massage parlors, and just about every other kind of evening entertainment, ranging from the raunchy to the reasonably refined.

Patpong
ย่านพัฒนพงศ์
The Strip
โชว์ (ตามบาร์หรือไนท์คลับ)

Klong Toey
คลองเตย

Massage parlor
สถาน อาบ อบ นวด

food and for a couple of huge establishments where you dine in private rooms and are hand-fed by scantily clad waitresses.

For those whose night tastes run to the really basic, there is another strip of bars at **Klong Toey**, Bangkok's port area, just before the customs gate that leads to the docks. Patronized mostly by the crews of ships, these have an atmosphere reminiscent of the Shanghai dives of bad old movies. They are not recommended for the squeamish, for couples, or for anyone too arthritic to dodge a beer bottle during one of the melèes that occasionally break out.

When Thais go out in the evening they tend to do so in large, masculine groups, leaving wives and girl friends at home. (The wives are not left entirely uneducated, however; on Rajadamnern Avenue, there are a number of "day clubs" — indistinguishable from nightclubs except that they are open at lunchtime — and you often see parties of respectable-looking matrons having lunch in them.) Generally, eight or ten male friends from work or school will go to a Thai or Chinese restaurant after which, fortified by several bottles of *mekong*, they will pass a few hours in a night club or a massage parlor; the evening will end, almost always, with a late-night snack at a noodle shop or in one of the large markets — Pratunam is a favorite gathering spot. Or they might spend the evening bowling, a sport that has achieved great popularity in the last decade all over the country. The younger, better-heeled, more westernized set enjoy going to the clubs in the large hotels — usually *with* their girl friends — and dancing until closing time.

When night falls, Bangkok shows a different face. The go-go girl on the left is one of the thousands to be found in bars scattered all over the city, catering to every taste and to every pocketbook.

Whether the **massage parlor** originated in Bangkok, as some local enthusiasts claim, or whether they have merely reached their apotheosis here is a question best left for scholarly debate. Certainly they have been a feature of the city for as long as 20 years, and they now number in the hundreds, from rather suspicious-looking establishments in dark, narrow streets to glass-and-marble palaces that the sybaritic Romans might have envied. And they *do* really offer massages, either pure and simple or with such local embellishments as the method called, for reasons totally mysterious, B-course, in which the massuese does the job with her entire body as well as her hands. In the larger massage parlors, the girls are on display behind a one-way glass show window and customers select the one they want by her number, rather as you would select a fish from the tank in a seafood restaurant. You then proceed to a comfortable private room that contains a massage table and a bath tub with hot water; refreshments such as beer and soft drinks can be ordered. The usual length of a massage is an hour and prices vary from around 100 baht to several hundred, depending on the grandeur of the establishment; the girl gets part of the fee, but a tip is expected — small in the case of a simple massage, more if it has been accompanied by what are euphemistically referred to as "special services." To clear up one persistent misunderstanding: massage parlors are not brothels, and massage girls are not per se prostitutes. The price you pay for a massage in most places entitles you to precisely that and no more. Whatever arrangements you may make with your masseuse are strictly between you and her. On the other hand, the popularity of massage parlors with Thais as well as *farang*s, can scarcely be credited solely to a passion for bodily health or greater cleanliness.

Southeast of Bangkok

Bangkok is the hub of Thailand, not merely for commerce and government but also for tourism. Though today more and more visitors venture upcountry into the far provinces, the great majority still do their sightseeing in the city itself or within a radius of about 100 kilometers. For this reason many of the major newer attractions, like the Ancient City, the Rose Garden, and the Crocodile Farm, have been located within easy driving distance of the capital, adding to the Bangkok area's standard and traditional sights such as Bang Pa-in and the ruins of Ayuthaya which lie on the southern rim of Thailand's Central Plains. The most popular resorts on the East Coast of the Gulf of Thailand are also conveniently reached from Bangkok for a weekend outing. Excellent highways now lead out of Bangkok in all directions, and a trip that used to take three or four hours — to Ayuthaya, for example —

can now be made in just over an hour, thus enabling a visitor with a limited amount of time to cover a lot of ground in a few days. In the following pages we cover the main attractions near Bangkok — each of which can be visited in a day's round trip from the capital. The places of interest are covered in a counterclockwise spiral, starting southeast of the city.

**

The **CROCODILE FARM** is located in Samut Prakarn Province, near the river-mouth town of Pak Nam, half an hour's drive (30 km) southeast of Bangkok on the old Sukhumvit Highway (Route 3). A brochure describes it as "a happy marriage between wildlife conservation and commercial enterprise," and while the crocodiles that get turned into ladies' handbags might argue about the first part, no one can deny the second. Starting three decades ago with about 10,000 baht (less than

1. Crocodile Farm
ฟาร์มจระเข้

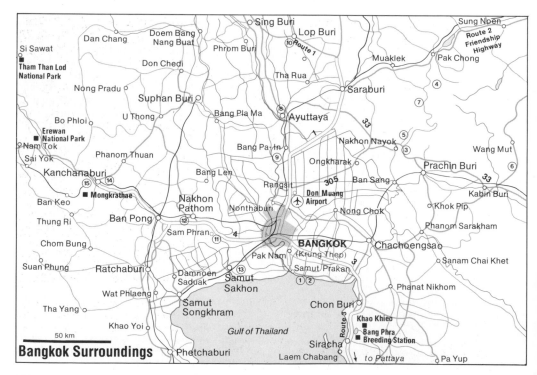

Bangkok Surroundings

The numbers in the margin in this section refer to the map on page 96.

US$5,000), the owner now has three farms (two in the Northeast) worth 100 million baht (US$4.4 million). At present the Samut Prakarn farm has about 20,000 crocodiles including both fresh- and saltwater Thai varieties, as well as some South American caimans and Nile River crocodiles. The highlight of a visit to the farm is a show in which handlers go into a pond teeming with crocodiles and toss them about rather roughly; a few overly sensitive visitors may feel that this is adding insult to injury, considering what lies in store for the beasts at the end of their show business career, but most find it exciting. After the crocodiles are skinned, incidentally, their meat is sold to various restaurants in Samut Prakarn and Bangkok, where diners claim it tastes like frog. Besides crocodiles, the farm also has other zoological amusements. There are two elephants for those who want to ride them; some charming gibbons (now on Thailand's protected species list); a collection of poisonous snakes; and a small zoo that contains lions, tigers, a tame python, a huge black bear, and an elephant that has been taught to do a somewhat ungainly dance to a Thai folk song. Children love it.

Also in Samut Prakarn, a few kilometers from the Crocodile Farm, is an attraction called the **ANCIENT CITY** which bills itself, maybe correctly, as "the world's largest outdoor museum." The brainchild of a Bangkok millionaire with a passion for Thai art and history, it took around three years to construct in what used to be open rice fields, the whole thing being roughly the shape of a map of Thailand and covering some 80 hectares. There are scale replicas (some full size, others one-third the size of the original) of famous monuments and temples from all parts of the kingdom, some of them recon-

Man and beast put on a hair-raising show at the Crocodile Farm (left). The Ancient City contains a monumental re-creation of Thai ruins and temples, and a collection of art, including this standing Buddha image (above).

structions of buildings that no longer exist, like the Grand Palace and Royal Chapel of Ayuthaya, and some copies of real places like the huge temple of Khao Phra Viharn on the Thai-Cambodian border, which was awarded to Cambodia by the World Court some years ago after a long dispute over its ownership. Experts from the National Museum worked as consultants on the reproductions to ensure accuracy of historical detail. At present there are more than 60 constructions, covering 15 centuries of Thai history, and more are planned. In addition to the monuments, the Ancient City also has a model Thai village, in which you can see artisans at work on various native handicrafts, such as lacquerware, ceramics, and paper umbrellas; its own version of the Floating Market, picturesquely staged for photographers; assorted shops for buying souvenirs; and a Thai restaurant. The king of Thailand has visited the place several times to bring royal visitors, among the first of whom, in 1972, were Queen Elizabeth and Prince Philip on their state visit to the country. On Rajadamnern Avenue, facing the Democracy Monument, is a booking office for bus trips to Ancient City; air-conditioned buses make the 33-km trip twice daily.

* * *

Located near enough to Bangkok for a comfortably paced day's trip, the eastern province of **NA-KHON NAYOK** features waterfalls, a pretty park, and picturesque temples. The most scenic route to this province lies along Road 305, which branches off Route 1 north of Bangkok, runs northeast along the canal to Ongkharak, and then goes on above rice fields and small rivers to Nakhon Nayok town, a total of about 140 km

from the capital. From the town Road 33 goes northwest and then, within a few kilometers, another road leads off to the right towards two waterfalls and Wang Takrai Park. After 11 km you reach an intersection: straight ahead takes you to **SALIKA WATERFALL.** Near the parking lot are pleasant outdoor restaurants and stalls selling fruits and drinks. The waterfall itself is impressive around the end of the rainy season (September to November).

Turning left at the intersection takes you to **WANG TAKRAI PARK.** On the way stop at the **Temple of Chao Pau Khun Dan,** named after one of King Naresuan's advisers whose spirit is believed to protect the area. Prince Chumbhot (of Suan Pakkard Palace in Bangkok) established the 80-hectare **Wang Takrai Park** in the 1950s; a statue of him now stands on the opposite bank of the small river flowing through the park. Prin-

3. Nakhon Nayok
นครนายก (จังหวัด, ตัวเมือง)

4. Salika Waterfall
น้ำตกสาลิกา

5. Wang Takrai Park
วังตะไกร้

Gold leaf adorns the sacred rock of the Temple of Chao Pau Khun Dan (right). In the countryside near Bangkok (opposite) a boy enjoys a ride on a companionable albino buffalo.

cess Chumbhot, wife of the founder, has carefully managed the planting of many varieties of flowers and trees, including some imported species. Cultivated gardens among tall trees line both banks of the main stream that flows through the 2-km-long park. Bungalows are also for rent in this picturesque botanical garden.

Before driving back to Bangkok, visitors can have a meal at the park restaurant. On the way out at the park entrance, the road on the left crosses a river and continues 5 km to **NANG RONG WATERFALL**, an inviting three-part cascade situated in a steep valley, where open-air restaurants and fruit stalls await visitors.

* * *

KHAO YAI NATIONAL PARK, the nearest hill resort to Bangkok, lying 205 km north of the capital, covers 2,000 sq km in four provinces. The government has provided this

cool retreat with bungalows, motels, restaurants, an 18-hole golf course, and many nature trails and roads. You can drive to Khao Yai ("Big Mountain") in about three to four hours directly from Bangkok by taking Route 1 north towards Saraburi. Near Saraburi, about 107 km from the capital, the Friendship Highway (Route 2) heads northeast and about 58 km from Saraburi, Dhanarajata Road goes another 24 km to the foot of the park. At that point the road begins to climb and twist among the hills for 16 km until it reaches **Nong Khing Village** atop one of Khao Yai's peaks. At Nong Khing dine at the Khao Yai Restaurant and check out the accommodations for overnight stays: 16 two-bedroom and four three-bedroom luxury bungalows with bathrooms, sitting rooms, and servants' quarters; another 14 one-bedroom and four two-bedroom motel units; and cheapest of all for

large groups, the tourist houses that sleep up to ten people each. (You can book rooms through the T.O.T.)

Khao Yai's highest peaks lie east in the Korat sector: Khao Lam is 1,328 meters high and Khao Kheo 1,270 meters. Evergreen and deciduous trees, the latter dropping many of their leaves during the arid hot season, palms, and bamboo provide ample greenery throughout the park. At night temperatures may drop to below 15°C, depending on the season. Monkeys, gibbons, and langurs are commonly seen in the trees. Wild, but not considered dangerous, elephants, bears, gaurs, tigers, boars, and deer also roam the huge, protected reserve. After dark you can "hunt" for deer with flashlights.

From Nong Khing hike over the many trails to Orchid and Hew Suwat Waterfalls. If you camp in the park, notify officials as to where you want to camp and take mosquito nets.

A city greater than the London or Paris of its time, early European residents were forced to admit — but in 1767 the Burmese besieged and so utterly destroyed **AYUTHAYA** that it was never rebuilt. Today, located 85 km north of Bangkok, its ruins stand as a fascinating link with Thailand's past.

Ayuthaya's site had been carefully chosen to make it defensible. Built at the junction of three rivers, it was necessary only to cut a canal across the loop of the Chao Phya to convert Ayuthaya into an island. In the four centuries following its foundation in 1350, a great mass of temples and palaces, linked by canals, was erected on and around the man-made island. Its glittering opulence which astonished foreign visitors enticed the Burmese to savagely tear it apart in search of booty.

Today Ayuthaya is a bustling country town sprawled along the

8. Ayuthaya
อยุธยา (ตัวเมือง)

Lakeside bungalows (above), maintained by the Tourist Authority of Thailand, rim the edge of a peaceful lake in Khao Yai National Park, which covers 2,000 square kilometers in four provinces. The park contains kilometers of scenic walking trails where nature lovers can see a variety of native animals and plant life; an 18-hole golf course and a motel are also available. For most of the year the weather is cool, making it a popular retreat.

main street from the **Pridi Damrong Bridge** to a little beyond the **Chandrakasem Palace.** The majority of Ayuthaya's visitors cover the town in a day trip from Bangkok. Should you feel Ayuthaya's long history requires more time to absorb, there is a single motel and a pair of Chinese hotels across from the Chandrakasem Palace. The hotels are clean but spartan, and inexpensive. Open-air food stalls in the market area can look after the inner self in delicious fashion; or for a more romantic meal Ayuthaya can boast not one, but two, floating restaurants. Berthed slightly up- or downstream from the Pridi Damrong Bridge, the restaurants serve excellent sour hot beef, and you can eat while watching the waters rustle by.

The obvious way to arrive at a waterborne city is by boat and there are frequent river connections with Ayuthaya from Bang Pa-in. The fare is only 8 baht for the 40-minute trip,

and a pleasant way to travel is by road to Bang Pa-in and thence by water. Alternatively, convenient bus and train services run from Bangkok, both taking one and a half hours. The excellent road from Bangkok will whisk you to Ayuthaya in about 90 minutes once you have extricated yourself from Bangkok's eternal traffic jams. It is also possible to travel all the way to Ayuthaya by riverboat, and tours can be arranged in Bangkok (see "Bangkok Water Tours").

Once in Ayuthaya a circular river tour in a long-tailed boat can be easily arranged on the landing stage close to Chandrakasem Palace. This is the best introduction to the ruined city and the only way to reach some of the more isolated sites on the mainland side of the river. A boat hired for about an hour should not cost more than 40 to 50 baht.

As you start out on your boat tour, close to the junction of the Nam

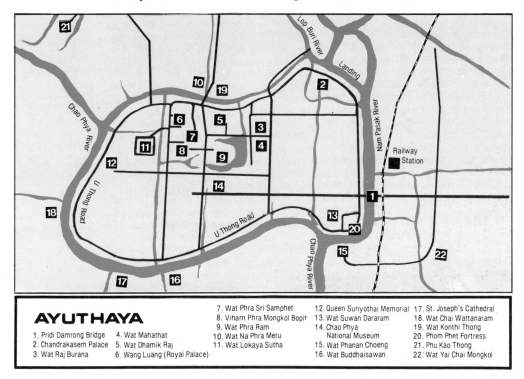

AYUTHAYA

1. Pridi Damrong Bridge
2. Chandrakasem Palace
3. Wat Raj Burana
4. Wat Mahathat
5. Wat Dhamik Raj
6. Wang Luang (Royal Palace)
7. Wat Phra Sri Samphet
8. Viharn Phra Mongkol Bopit
9. Wat Phra Ram
10. Wat Na Phra Meru
11. Wat Lokaya Sutha
12. Queen Suriyothai Memorial
13. Wat Suwan Dararam
14. Chao Phya National Museum
15. Wat Phanan Choeng
16. Wat Buddhaisawan
17. St. Joseph's Cathedral
18. Wat Chai Wattanaram
19. Wat Konthi Thong
20. Phom Phet Fortress
21. Phu Kao Thong
22. Wat Yai Chai Mongkol

Pasak and Chao Phya Rivers you pass the imposing **Wat Phanan Choeng.** Established 26 years prior to Ayuthaya, it houses a huge seated Buddha, so tightly crowded against the roof that he appears to be holding it up. Wat Phanan Choeng was a favorite of the Chinese traders of Ayuthaya who would pray there before setting out on long voyages — it still has an unmistakably Chinese atmosphere.

Ayuthaya was at one time surrounded by walls with stout fortifications. Only portions remain, one of the best examples of which is at **Phom Phet,** across the river from Wat Phanan Choeng.

Upstream from Wat Phanan Choeng, the recently restored **Wat Buddhaisawan** stands serenely on the riverbank. Farther upstream, the restored Catholic **Cathedral of St. Joseph** is a reminder of the large European population of the city when it was in its prime. At the bend of the river stands one of Ayuthaya's most eloquently romantic ruins, **Wat Chai Wattanaram.** A Buddha keeps solitary watch, perched on a high pedestal in front of the ruins. The stately *prang* with its surrounding *chedis* and rows of headless Buddhas have an almost lost-city feeling in their jungly, overgrown isolation. They make a fine contrast to the restored **Memorial to Queen Suriyothai** on the city-side of the river. The valiant Ayuthaya queen, dressed as a man, astride an elephant accompanied her king to battle and gave her own life to save his.

The junction of the Chao Phya and Lop Buri Rivers marks the section of the Chao Phya that was bypassed. Over the centuries the river has become narrower and shallower, so much so that it looks more like an artificial canal. Children splash in the water or paddle by adeptly in small boats; gaggles of geese drift imperiously across the murky water. Lines of saffron robes hanging out to dry mark the site of a riverside monastery; even the ubiquitous spirit houses stand semisubmerged. The riverside seems to virtually throb with activity as the boat passes under the last few bridges and arrives back at the landing stage near Chandrakasem Palace.

Chandrakasem Palace was known as the Palace of the Front, and was originally constructed outside the city walls. Built close to the junction of the old rivers and the new bypass, it had an important, defensive function — it was built by King Naresuan, the first ruler of Ayuthaya, to gain control over their northern rival, Chiang Mai. The Burmese burnt and destroyed the palace but King Mongkut later rebuilt it. It now houses a small museum. The palace looks out onto the noisiest part of town, where a continuous stream of vehicles passes by, including what must be the least silenced motor *samlors* in all of Thailand.

The old royal palace, **Wang Luang,** was completely leveled by the Burmese. The bricks were later removed to Bangkok to rebuild the capital, so now only scattered foundations among the trees mark the palace site. Close by stands the royal temple of **Wat Phra Sri Sanphet,** enclosed within the area of Wang Luang rather like the Temple of the Emerald Buddha stands within the Grand Palace compound in Bangkok. The gold-leafed Buddha, *Phra Sri Sanphet*, that gave the *wat* its name, was irreparably damaged by the Burmese. Today the three central *chedis* of the *wat* have been restored and stand in regal contrast to the surrounding ruins.

For centuries after Ayuthaya's fall, a huge bronze Buddha sat unsheltered near Wat Phra Sri Sanphet. His flame of knowledge and one of his arms had been broken by the collapsing roof of his temple. Twenty

Waterborne commerce and travel once dominated the rich, flat plains around Ayuthaya. Typical Thai river barges, filled to the brim, are towed upriver in long processions.

Wat Phanan Choeng
วัดพนัญเชิง

Wat Buddhaisawan
วัดพุทธไธศวรรย์

St. Joseph's Cathedral
วัดคริสต์ของ เซนต์ โยเซฟ

Wang Luang
วังหลวง

Wat Chai Wattanaram
วัดชัย วัฒนาราม

Wat Phra Sri Sanphet
วัดพระศรีสรรเพชญ

Queen Suriyothai Memorial
อนุสาวรีย์สมเด็จพระศรีสุริโยทัย

years ago **Viharn Phra Mongkol Bo-pitr** was built around the restored statue. With a large car park, and rows of souvenir stalls facing it, this is an often-used starting point for Ayuthaya tours. Apart from the cluster of souvenir shops and postcard emporiums, a line of antique specialists can also be found close by. They sell all sorts and sizes of "genuine" antique Buddhas.

In the same area is **Wat Phra Ram,** one of the older temples, begun in 1369 by the son of Ayuthaya's founder; in later years it was completely restored twice. Elephant gates still stand at intervals around the old walls, and the central terrace is dominated by a crumbling *prang* to which cling a gallery of stucco *nagas, garudas* (mythical sun-birds), and statues of the Buddha. Wat Phra Ram's *prang* shimmers, reflected in the pool, Beung Phra Ram, that almost surrounds the temple. Once a marshy

swamp the pool was dug out to provide fill for the temple sites.

Two of Ayuthaya's finest temples stand side by side across the lake from Wat Phra Ram. Built by the seventh king of Ayuthaya as a memorial to his brothers, **Wat Raj Burana** contained many fine images and items of royal jewelry which were discovered during a 1958 restoration. The two *chedis* at the crossroads contain the ashes of the royal brothers, Princes Ai and Yo. Across the road, **Wat Mahathat** has little remaining apart from the base of its huge *prang.* Originally built to a height of 46 meters, it later collapsed; undeterred the people of Ayuthaya rebuilt it four meters higher.

Why is it that ruins are always so much more appealing than restorations? **Wat Dhamik Raj** is an excellent example of this. Around a precariously leaning *chedi,* rows of lions growl defiance at the encroaching

vegetation; but it is too late — already some of the statues lie shattered and greenery sprouts from the heads of others. Beside the *chedi*, the high walls and columns of the *wat* reverently enclose a solid mass of plant life.

Wat Suwan Dararam was built towards the close of the Ayuthaya period and has been beautifully restored and preserved. The walls of the *bot* have foundations that dip in the center, typical of the architecture of that time. Delicately carved columns support the roof, and the inside walls are decorated with brilliantly hued frescoes. Still used as a temple today, the *wat* has a seemingly magical effect in the early evening as the monks chant their devotions.

Across the river from the old palace stands another restored building, **Wat Na Phra Meru.** Here a small

Buddha, seated in the "European

manner" in contrast to the yoga position of Ayuthaya Buddhas. Found in the ruins of Wat Mahathat, the statue is believed to have originally come from Nakhon Pathom. The *bot* contains an Ayuthaya-style seated Buddha on the altar.

A winding road from Queen Suriyothai's *chedi* leads to **Wat Lokaya Sutha.** Little remains here, apart from a massive reclining Buddha, calmly contemplating the view, freed from the claustrophobic walls which once encompassed him. A scattering of food stalls stand close by, their owners gazing back with equal equanimity.

A path runs down to the river close to the bridge leading to Wat Na Phra Meru. The precarious pathway of planks and boards snakes its way along and across the river, rising in the middle just enough for a boat to sneak underneath. On the other bank the bouncing planks lead right into a

Wat Suwan Dararam
วัดสุวรรณดาราราม

Wat Lokaya Sutha
วัดโลกยะสุธา

Wat Na Phra Meru
วัด ณ พระเมรุ

The ruins of Ayuthaya have an evocative, haunting quality, recalling the splendors of the old capital, destroyed by Burmese invaders in the 18th century. At Wat Raj Burana (above and opposite), once one of the city's largest and grandest temples, one sees shattered Buddha images and the lonely remains of a once-noble doorway framing a memory of past glory. The ancient city contains kilometers of such relics, which are carefully preserved today.

monastery, its temple gong hung in a riverside tower. A robed monk will show you through to the back door from where you can walk across to the secluded ruins of **Wat Konthi Thong.** Many more relics can be seen in ᶠine **Chao Phya Museum** ᵈe the city. At the road is a ᶦouses ᶦng — ᵃnsion. **ʸai Chai** ᶜhedi. In elephant- the crown The *chedi* e Phu Kao of Ayuthaya ᵗory. Contem- line the court- ᵃnt contrast to ᵃya the **Phu Kao** ᵗer known as the

Golden Mount Chedi, towers incongruously over the flat countryside — its upper terraces commanding a pastoral view of the rice paddies. Built by the Burmese after their earlier and less destructive conquest in 1549, it was later remodeled by the Siamese in their own style. To mark 2,500 years of Buddhism, a 2,500 gram gold ball was mounted on top of the *chedi* spire in 1956.

Going in the opposite direction to the Golden Mount, the road runs to the only **Elephant Kraal** left in Thailand. This kraal is a reminder of the days when elephants were not only caught and trained to work in the jungles, but were also an essential requisite for a strong army. Standing at the edge of the huge pit, one can still imagine the thunder of the mighty beasts that helped raise Ayuthaya to its peak, but could not stay its downfall from a great kingdom to a mere country town.

BANG PA-IN, a charming collection of palaces and pavilions once used by the kings of Thailand as a summer retreat, lies a short distance downriver from the ruins of Ayuthaya; it can be reached by water on a tour boat like the Oriental Queen or by road in about an hour from Bangkok. The rulers of Ayuthaya used Bang Pa-in in the hot season as long ago as the 17th century, but the buildings one sees today date from the late 19th- and early 20th-century reigns of Rama V and Rama VI, who used to come up from Bangkok. A pretty palace on a lake in a mixture of Italian and Victorian styles, built by Rama V, is closed to the public; but visitors can see an ornate Chinese-style palace in which the king stayed during visits. A Thai-style pavilion called the **Aisawan Tippaya Asna** in the middle of the lake as one enters the grounds, is regarded as one of the finest examples of Thai architecture.

The former summer capital of Siam, **LOP BURI** lies 155 km north of Bangkok. You can drive to Lop Buri from Bangkok in less than four hours. The journey through the fertile rice bowl of Thailand is a pleasant one. Just 10 km north of Ayuthaya, the hills of the Korat plateau appear on the horizon — the first break in the flatness of the Central Plains.

Artifacts of the Neolithic and Bronze Ages have been found in quantity in Lop Buri, testifying to the great antiquity of the city. In the Dvaravati period (6th to 11th centuries) it was a major town. At the height of the power of the kings of Angkor (11th and 12th centuries), it was a provincial capital of the Khmer empire. Then came the Thais, who put their imprint on most of the old buildings which now survive.

Tentative contacts with Dutch and Portuguese explorers came in the 16th century, but it was not until the mid

9. Bang Pa-in
วังบางปะอิน

10. Lop Buri
ลพบุรี (ตัวเมือง, จังหวัด)

Aisawan Tippaya
พระที่นั่งไอศวรรย์ทิพยอาสน์

The summer palace of Bang Pa-in (above) is a charming collection of palaces and pavilions in a variety of architectural styles. Among them is an elegant little pavilion, the most photographed structure in all the country, which seems to float on shimmering surface of the lake. Boldly sculptured faces (opposite) stare from a corner of Prang Sam Yod, part of a Khmer-style temple in Lop Buri, once a provincial capital of the Khmer empire.

Lop Buri Palace
วังละบุรี (นารายณ์ราชนิเวศน์)

Suttha Sawa Pavilion
ตำหนักสุทธาสวรรค์

Dusit Maha Prasat Hall
พระที่นั่งดุสิตมหาปราสาท

1700s that Ayuthaya became a bustling international city with missionaries from Italy and Spain and traders from Britain, Indonesia and China. Some French architects even ventured as far as Lop Buri, where King Narai retreated each summer to escape Ayuthaya's humidity.

However, Narai was one of the most luckless kings of the Ayuthaya dynasty. The last scenes of his life were played out in Lop Buri in the **Suttha Sawan Pavilion.** In May 1688, as he lay mortally ill in this pavilion, a regimental commander, Phra Phetracha, seized the throne. According to one tradition, the dying king was attended by only ten royal pages who remained loyal to him. Realizing that the rebels might never allow them to leave the palace alive, the king called in a Buddhist abbot to ordain the pages as monks, so that the saffron robe of Buddhism would guarantee their safety. In return, he offered the Suttha Sawan Pavilion to the monkhood as a temple. The truth of this tradition is attested by the actions of a later king, Mongkut, when he came to reoccupy the Lop Buri palace in the 19th century — he had to offer other lands to the Buddhist authorities in exchange for the palace and its grounds.

The grounds of the **Lop Buri Palace** (Narai Raja Niwes Palace) are enclosed by massive walls which still dominate the center of the modern town. The inner side of the walls flanking the gates are honeycombed with hundreds of leaf-shaped niches meant to contain small lamps fed by coconut oil. In the heyday of the palace, they were lighted on state and religious occasions.

Of King Narai's buildings, the only one which has substantially survived is the **Dusit Maha Prasat Hall**. This was built for the audience granted by the king in 1685 to Che-

valier de Chaumont, ambassador of Louis XIV. It is recorded that the walls of the front structure were panelled with mirrors given by the French king. Holes for the mirrors can still be seen.

Another surviving building of the Narai period is the **Chantra Paisan Pavilion** also in the palace grounds. Now part of the Fine Arts Museum, it was the first structure built by King Narai, and was later restored by King Mongkut. The wooden decorations of the roof are not in good proportions, somewhat spoiling the overall effect, but the classic Ayuthaya-period curve of the base is good. The sagging line of the multiple roofs is also classical and designed for elegance.

Adjoining the Chantra Paisan Pavilion is the **Phiman Mongkut Pavilion** — a three-storied mansion in the colonial style built in the mid-19th century by King Mongkut. The immensely thick walls and high ceilings show how the summer heat was averted most effectively before air conditioning arrived. The mansion, small but full of character, and also part of the Fine Arts Museum, displays a mixed bag of bronzes, Chinese and Sukhothai porcelain, coins, Buddhist fans, and shadow-play puppets. Yet some of the pieces, particularly the Ayuthaya bronze heads and Benchurong porcelain, are extremely fine. On the top floor are displayed some of King Mongkut's personal effects. They reveal the character of this remarkable man who, though Siam's "Lord of Life," led a Spartan existence.

Other buildings in the palace complex which should be visited are the eight bijou houses behind the museum. In King Mongkut's time they accommodated the court ladies, their children, and servants. One of the buildings has now been converted into a **Farmer's Museum**, which displays the traditional implements of Thai agriculture.

King Narai had a Greek adviser,

Constantine Phaulkon, whom the king ennobled with the title of *Chao Phya Vijayendra* ("The Noble Victorious Lord"). Though not officially the foreign minister, it was Phaulkon who managed Siam's relations with the European powers. However, his ambition also led him to meddle in domestic matters, making him most unpopular with the Buddhist clergy and also with officials of King Narai's government. When the king lay dying in his pavilion, Phra Phetracha seized power and had Phaulkon beheaded.

The remains of a grand palace in Lop Buri, said to have belonged to Phaulkon, rival those of the royal palace. Located just north of Narai's palace, and now overgrown with weeds, the buildings show traces of European influence — straight-sided walls and pedimental decorations over Western-style windows. The estate is now kept locked to prevent vandalism, and also possibly to hide from visitors the shocking neglect of the ruins. Hopefully, restoration work will be undertaken before it is too late.

Of particular interest in Lop Buri are two important relics of the Khmer (Cambodian) and pre-Khmer periods. One, located just west of the railroad and north of the town's main road, is a 13th-century laterite-block shrine with three spires which give it its Thai name of **Phra Prang Sam Yod** ("Sacred Three Spires"). Restored in 1926 by the Fine Arts Department, the stone carvings on the towers and the door columns are particularly fine. The second is the Hindu Spire (**Prang Khaek** in Thai) in the center of the town — also of great antiquity. A group of three laterite spires, it was probably built during the 11th century and restored by King Narai in the 17th century.

A slow-motion ride on an elephant is one of the offerings at the Rose Garden, a newer tourist attraction for people who want a quick survey of Thai life all in one place.

Chantra Paisan Pavilion
หลับพลา จันทรไพศาล

Phiman Mongkut Pavilion
หลับพลาพิมานมงกุฎ

Phra Prang Sam Yod
พระปรางค์สามยอด

Prang Khaek
ปรางค์แขก

Farmers Museum
พิพิธภัณฑ์เกษตรกร

West of Bangkok

11. Rose Garden
สวนสามพราน

Located on the bucolic Tachin River, less than an hour's drive west from Bangkok, the **ROSE GARDEN** is the brainchild of a former lord mayor of the capital. The garden, known as *Suan Sam Phran* in Thai, lies 32 km west of the capital on Route 4, the road to famous Nakhon Pathom. It covers a large area of well landscaped gardens — yes, there are roses, and healthy ones, too — and includes a modern hotel with convention rooms, traditional Thai-style houses for rent by the night, several first-rate restaurants, a swimming pool, a golf course, a bowling alley, facilities for boating and waterskiing on the river, and a model Thai village where each afternoon a cultural show is performed for tourists. To a discerning traveler, it might sound a bit calculated and "cute," but somehow it is not; the whole thing is done with such good taste, the gardens are so beautiful,

and the quality of the food served so high, that many jaded tourists who come with reluctance leave with praise.

A display that might catch your interest at the cultural show because of its novelty to Westerners is the sport of *takraw*. In fact, you may come across it in Bangkok: a group of boys or men, standing in a circle casually keeping a rattan ball aloft by knocking it from one to another using any part of the body except the hands. *Takraw* might be called the national sport; certainly it is the national pastime, for men of all ages spend their leisure playing *takraw*. There are semiprofessional *takraw* teams, too, who put on performances at various fairs and parties. If you are in Bangkok during the kite-fighting season, you can see the teams in action at the Rajadamnern Avenue end of Sanam Luang every weekday afternoon. Using the sides

of the feet is the preferred method of keeping the ball aloft, but a real star also uses his elbows, head, and shoulders, making the whole thing look as effortless as a great dancer going through his paces.

A visit to the Rose Garden can be arranged in Bangkok through the Rose Garden booking office, 264/4 Siam Square.

Just 54 km west of Bangkok beyond the Rose Garden on Route 4 is the town of **NAKHON PATHOM**. As you drive toward Nakhon Pathom, a colossal landmark seems to rise above the town and tower over the surrounding countryside. Standing 127 meters high, **Phra Pathom Chedi** is the tallest Buddhist monument in the world.

The original Phra Pathom Chedi was small and was built more than a thousand years ago during the Mon empire when culture flourished in the Nakhon Pathom area. In 1057, King Anawrahta of Burma besieged the town, leaving it in ruins for the next hundred years. It was not until King Mongkut had visited the old *chedi* and was impressed by its significance as the oldest Buddhist monument in Thailand, that restoration of the temple began in 1853. However, the original structure was found to be in such a state of collapse that repair proved impossible, and a new *chedi* was built to cover the old one. This too collapsed in a rainstorm, and eventually the present building was completed by King Chulalongkorn.

Set in a huge square park, the massive *chedi* rests upon a circular terrace dotted with examples of trees connected with the Buddha's life. In November each year, a gay fair in the temple grounds attracts crowds from far and near.

In the days of canal travel, a royal visit to Nakhon Pathom was more than a day's journey, and so it is

12. Nakhon Pathom
นครปฐม (ตัวเมือง, จังหวัด)

Phra Pathom Chedi
พระปฐมเจดีย์

The tallest Buddhist monument in the world (above) towers like a cathedral over Nakhon Pathom. Each November a country fair (right) lights up the spire. Samut Sakhon (far right) is a typical Thai seaport.

138

not surprising that various palaces and residences were built there. **Sanam Chand Palace** has a fine *sala* (formerly a meeting pavilion) — now used for government offices — and a building in a most unusual Thai interpretation of English Tudor architecture, used appropriately as a setting for Shakespearean drama. In front of this building stands a statue of Yaleh, the pet dog of King Rama VI. The fierce dog, unpopular with the court, was poisoned by the king's attendants. Even as a statue, Yaleh looks insufferable.

13. Samut Sakhon
สมุทรสาคร (ตัวเมือง, จังหวัด)

A good way to approach the port of **SAMUT SAKHON**, for a view of Thailand's coastal life, is by the branch railway connecting it with Thonburi, Bangkok's sister city. The line, called the Mae Klong Railway, runs at a loss, but has been reprieved from extinction because of its usefulness to the population of the three provinces west of Bangkok. For a few baht, you can take the "express" which leaves approximately every hour, from Wong Wien Yai station in Thonburi. The express train moves at a leisurely pace. The 40-minute journey passes first through the suburbs, then through thriving vegetable gardens, groves of coconut and areca palms, and rice fields.

A busy fishing port, Samut Sakhon (also called Mahachai) lies at the meeting of the Tachin River, the Mahachai Canal, and the Gulf of Thailand. The main landing stage on the riverbank has a clock tower and a restaurant which, as might be expected, serves excellent seafood, including grilled crab with vegetables. Nearby at the main **Fish Market** fishermen unload hauls of fish, crabs, squids, and prawns from their boats.

At the fish market pier, you can hire a boat with an outboard engine for a 40-baht round trip to Samut Sakhon's principal temple, **Wat**

Chom Long, at the mouth of the Tachin River. Most of the buildings are modern except for an old *viharn* immediately to the right of the temple's river landing. The *viharn* dates back about a century. The extensive grounds overlooking the water are charmingly laid out with shrubs and flowering trees. There is also a bronze statue of King Chulalongkorn commemorating his visit to the temple. His homburg hat does not in the least detract from his immense dignity.

* * *

An odd-looking railway bridge crosses the Meklang River a few kilometers from **KANCHANABURI**. The bridge leaves the bank over a series of elliptical spans; in the center of the river the spans become awkwardly rectangular, without apparent reason, and then revert to their elliptical way before disappearing into the forest on the other side. Crossing over the bridge flows a constant stream of

pedestrians taking vegetables home from the market or just out for a walk. Occasionally a motorcycle buzzes across the bridge skirting between the railway tracks. When the river's other name is mentioned, the mystery behind the strange pattern of spans becomes clear. The Meklang River, also known as the Kwai Yai, is spanned by the infamous **Bridge on the River Kwai**. And we soon learn that towards the end of World War II the central spans were knocked out by Allied bombers and later rebuilt with those incongruous angular replacements.

Kanchanaburi town, in the province of the same name, is about 122 km northwest of Bangkok, past Nakhon Pathom, and not far from the Thai border with Burma. It was from here that the Japanese put to work Allied prisoners of war to construct 415 km of rail leading to the Three Pagodas Pass at the Burmese

Wat Chom Long
วัดชมล่อง

15. River Kwai Bridge
สะพานข้ามแม่น้ำแคว

14. Kanachanaburi
กาญจนบุรี (ตัวเมือง, จังหวัด)

Lashed together into rafts (above), newly cut bamboo poles float downstream to market. Though peaceful-looking today, the waterway is spanned by the infamous Bridge on the River Kwai, built by Allied prisoners during World War II. Mute testimony to their suffering is offered by the Kanchanaburi Allied Cemetery (opposite) where 6,982 of those who labored on the notorious "Death Railway" lie buried in neatly labeled graves near the river.

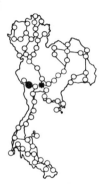

border. It is estimated that 100,000 oppressed laborers as well as 16,000 Allied prisoners of war lost their lives due to beatings, starvation, disease, and exhaustion when constructing the railroad. In Kanchanaburi, endless rows of war graves mark the resting places of 6,982 of those Allied soldiers.

Although the Bridge on the River Kwai probably owes much of its fame to the novel by Pierre Boulle and later to the film, it is worth a visit from an historical point of view. It can be reached by boat or *samlor* from Kanchanaburi. The Kanchanaburi Tourist Bureau, located on the main street of Kanchanaburi opposite the Allied War Cemetery, can arrange tours to the bridge and surroundings. A combined boat landing and restaurant is moored near the bridge and provides an excellent vantage point to watch for the occasional train to cross. The pedestrian path over the bridge is not as unsafe as it looks — niches between the spans provide an escape in case of an unexpected train. A steam locomotive used shortly after the war is displayed beside the tiny Kwai Bridge station platform, along with an ingenious Japanese supply truck that could run on road or rails.

The entire railway was bought by the Thai government from the Allies for 50 million baht. It was a "pig in a poke" purchase, as the British had already dismantled several kilometers of track at the Burmese border, and the whole line was in need of considerable repair. The prisoners had done their utmost to make the worst possible job of constructing the railway. Quite apart from frequent bombings, the wooden supports were often rotting even before they were put in place.

Shortly before the end of the war, British bombers from Ceylon suc-

ceeded in destroying the fourth, fifth, and sixth spans of the bridge. As war reparations, the Japanese replaced these three spans by two larger ones — the "Made in Japan" signs on the newer girders strike an ironic note. Today, the quiet little railway runs peacefully from nowhere to nowhere.

There was one fortunate outcome during construction of the railway: a Dutch prisoner of war discovered what he thought to be evidence of Neolithic remains nearby. However, not until 1961 did a Thai-Danish archaeological search party confirm the find and open a whole new page of Thai prehistory. A small museum close to the original excavations has many of the finds on exhibition, including a skeleton from one of the burial sites. The bulk of the finds from this first Neolithic site to be found in this part of Southeast Asia is on display in the National Museum in Bangkok. Sugar cane has long over-grown the archaeological site, but university students still manage to conduct diggings from time to time. The dusty little town of Ban Keo near the site, and a couple of kilometers walk from the small museum, lies 30 km north of Kanchanaburi and can be reached by bus or train from the provincial town.

Long before it assumed its strategic role in the last war. Kanchanaburi had been a continual battlefield between the warring Siamese and Burmese, and evidence of old battlements can still be seen. North of Ban Keo, before the station of Wang Po, are the ruins of the Khmer town of **MUANG SING**, City of the Lion.

The Kanchanaburi area is bountifully blessed with caves and waterfalls, and if you have the time, you will find the **ERAWAN FALLS,** or "Elephant Falls," about 67 km north of Kanchanaburi and a magnificent sight. The tranquil setting of these

Muang Sing
เมืองสิงห์

Erawan Falls
น้ำตกเอราวัณ

An old locomotive chugs across the River Kwai Bridge, which inspired the famous novel.

falls creates one of the most beautiful spots in Thailand.

Alternatively, you could catch the train from Kanchanaburi west to Nam Tok, the railway terminal, where you can stay overnight. Near Nam Tok, are the **KAO PANG FALLS** where the water trips down over a series of limestone steps. From here you can take a three-hour boat ride to the **SAI YOK FALLS** where the water plunges directly into the river. On the way to Sai Yok, the river passes the **CAVE OF THAM KUNG** with its impressive stalactites and stalagmites. It would take several days further travel by river and a long trek on foot to reach the aged pagodas that mark the Three Pagodas Pass and the border with Burma.

To experience fully the beauty of the River Kwai, spend several days on its banks. Thirty-two km from Kanchanaburi is the River Kwai

Farm; 80 km away is the River Kwai Village Hotel. Upriver lies a newer concept in river living: flotels, thatched houses built on bamboo rafts. There are 10 of these rafthouse complexes on the Kwai Noi branch of the river. They can be reached by a three-hour boat journey or by road. Stays must be booked at Bangkok reservation offices.

Many hotels and rafthouses offer treks into the jungle to visit caves, waterfalls, Karen and Mon villages. Traces of the Death Railway still run through beautiful bamboo forests.

The State Railways of Thailand offers an all-day trip from Bangkok's Hualampong Station to the Nakorn Pathom chedi, the Bridge, the POW cemetery, Khao Phang waterfalls, and travels a short stretch of the Death Railway to its terminus at Nam Tok. Saturdays, Sundays, holidays; 60 baht.

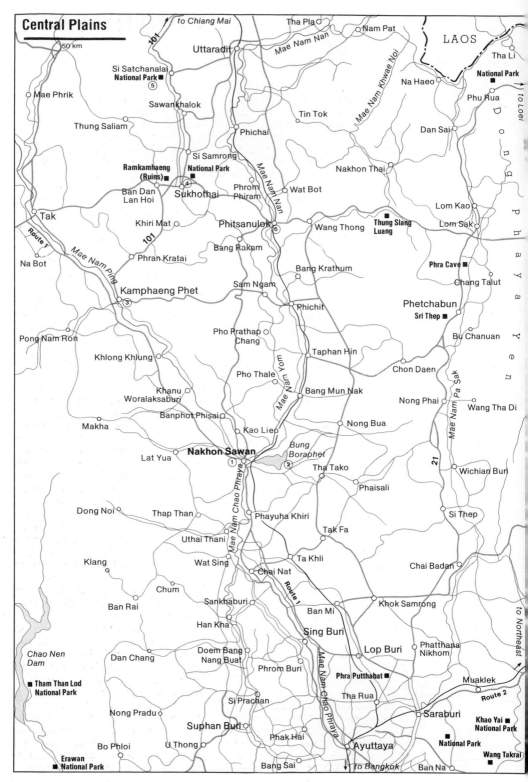

Central Plains

50 km

to Chiang Mai

LAOS

Tha Pla
Nam Pat
Tha Li

Uttaradit

National Park ■

Mae Nam Nan

Si Satchanalai
National Park ■
⑤

Phu Rua

to Loei

Sawankhalok

Tin Tok

Mae Phrik

Na Haeo

Mae Nam Khwae Noi

Dan Sai

Thung Saliam

Phichai

Si Samrong

Nakhon Thai

Wat Bot

Ramkamhaeng
(Ruins) ■
National Park ■
④

Phrom
Phiram

Lom Kao

Ban Dan
Lan Hoi

Sukhothai

Tak

Khiri Mat

Phitsanulok
⑥

Wang Thong

Thung Slang
Luang

Lom Sak

101

Route 1

Bang Rakam

Phra Cave ■

Chang Talut

Na Bot

Mae Nam Ping

Phran Kratai

Sam Ngam

Bang Krathum

Phetchabun
Sri Thep ■

Kamphaeng Phet
③

Phichit

Bu Chanuan

Pong Nam Ron

Pho Prathap
Chang

Taphan Hin

Chon Daen

Khlong Khlung

Pho Thale

Bang Mun Nak

Nong Phai

Wang Tha Di

Khanu
Woralaksaburi

Mae Nam Pa Sak

Makha

Banphot Phisai

Kao Liep

Nong Bua

Lat Yua

Nakhon Sawan
①

*Bung
Boraphet*
②

Tha Tako

Wichian Buri

21

Phaisali

Dong Noi

Thap Than

Phayuha Khiri

Si Thep

Uthai Thani

Tak Fa

Klang

Wat Sing

Ta Khli

Chai Badan

Chum

Chai Nat

Ban Rai

Sankhaburi

Ban Mi

Khok Samrong

Route 1

Han Kha

Sing Buri

*Chao Nen
Dam*

Dan Chang

Doem Bang
Nang Buat

Lop Buri

Phatthana
Nikhom

■ **Tham Than Lod**
National Park

Phrom Buri

Phra Putthabat ■

Muaklek

to Northeast

Nong Pradu

Si Prachan

Tha Rua

Saraburi

Route 2

Suphan Buri

Phak Hai

Khao Yai
National Park ■

Bo Phloi

U Thong

■ **National Park**

Erawan
■ **National Park**

Bang Sai

Ayuttaya

Wang Takrai ■

to Bangkok

Ban Na

146

A cluster of simple, thatched-roof farmhouses, almost hidden amid tall, graceful plumes of bamboo swaying lazily in the breeze: like a small island in the vast, acid-green sea that stretches for seemingly endless kilometers in all directions, broken only by similar islands of darker green or, occasionally, by the swooping orange roof and glittering gilt of a Buddhist temple that flashes out of the sea like an improbable jewel. This rippling expanse is the traditional source of Thailand's wealth, the intricately diked and dependably watered rice fields that have fed its people for more than 700 years, that still produce the kingdom's number one export to less fortunate neighboring countries. These are the Central Plains, the fertile heart of the country toward which the early Thais steadily, inevitably migrated from the mountains of the North and the jungles of the South, coming here to found their greatest cities.

If you drive across the Central Plains toward the end of the dry season in May, the fields are alive with blue-shirted, straw-hatted farmers and broad-backed water buffaloes, turning the cracked and arid earth. A month or so later, when the rains have come, water flickers in the shallow paddies, and the young rice plants are of a vivid green that almost hurts the eye with its intensity. In late October the rains cease with dramatic suddenness. The grain turns golden, and it is harvest time; the people reappear from the little hidden hamlets, from the temples where they have been passing the wet months as monks, from the city where they have been doing seasonal work; for it is upon the harvest that their lives depend, upon which to a very real extent the whole

The colossal seated Buddha at Wat Si Chum meditates stolidly on the ruins of Sukhothai (previous pages). Here was founded the first truly Thai nation, built on the prosperity and stability of the Central Plains.

country depends. And so to the fields come just about all the able-bodied members of every farming family. Later, when the crop is in, there is time for festivals, for relaxation; and the air over the Central Plains is hazy for hundreds of kilometers with smoke from burning fields, as the earth is prepared for another cycle of cultivation. So it has been for ages; so it will continue to be, despite governments and politics and the rise and fall of cities.

Several major rivers water this fertile heartland, most notably the broad Chao Phya which flows like an artery from the North all the way to the Gulf of Thailand, just below Bangkok, feeding the paddies through an incredibly complex network of streams and man-made canals. Thai history has moved down these rivers, through these rich fields, and its remains are scattered about like an archaeological scrapbook: the Angkor-style towers of Lop Buri, where the Khmers once ruled to reap the bounty of the Plains; the sprawling ruins farther south near Bangkok of once great Ayuthaya — precariously leaning pagodas and the shells of palaces, half-submerged beneath the rampant vegetation that always lies in wait to take over when man turns his back (see "Bangkok Surroundings"). The smog-enshrouded immensity of Bangkok, latest of the capitals to be built on the prosperity of the Central Plains, shimmers on the horizon, half-threat, half-dream, tantalizingly near, yet in many ways as remote from the life of the farmers' fields as the moon.

Broad superhighways such as National Route 1 now slice through the fields carrying flashy cars, roaring trucks, and air-conditioned tour buses to all parts of the country. Jumbo jets scream overhead, fluttering the rice stalks, on their way to and from Bangkok's Don Muang Airport. And even within the fields themselves the wail of the transistor radio, that harbinger of the modern world, sometimes breaks the traditional silence.

Yet for all these 20th-century intrusions, there is a strong sense of timelessness about this part of Thailand, for fundamentally it has changed remarkably little over the centuries. The cities like Bangkok, and the larger towns with their mass-produced row shops, have the look of temporary aberrations, huddling along the highways as if for reassurance of their reality. Outside them, though, the Central Plains is still basically a region of small, self-contained little hamlets, each with its carefully ordered way of life revolving around family, fields and temple, wary of city folks with their strange ways.

These hamlets may be simple, but they are not, in terms of Thai life, poor. In the mountainous North and the often-parched Northeast, farming can be a perilous, unpredictable occupation and land can often slip into the hands of the moneylenders. In the Central Plains, on the other hand, nature has always been generous; land tends to stay in the same family for generations; and such inequities of distribution as there may be have never loomed large among the country's problems. There is a feeling of solidity, of continuity, about the plain wooden houses, set high on sturdy poles above the family's domestic animals: the pigs, chickens, and water buffalo. Not as many of the young people of this region decide in despair to leave the land and seek their fortunes in the capital, and the elders are inclined to be conservative in both political and social matters. Though chemical fertilizers and mechanized equipment could double the crop yield, farmers prefer their traditional methods, reasoning that if one crop is sufficient to feed their family and yield a small profit why worry with double cropping. Though a noted inventor

In the country's rice bowl, transplanting the rice seedlings into the muddy fields is a communal affair, with time for levity and enjoyment.

149

in Bangkok is reportedly working to perfect something called a "mechanical buffalo" to do the work of ploughing the paddies, the news does not greatly excite the hamlet dwellers; they still place their trust in the slow, patient animal whose broad back can seat several small children and whose dependable strength has turned their fields for countless generations. Many more young Central Plains farmers returning from progressive agricultural schools today are questioning the old methods, and to ask whether this rich earth will be forever adequate to feed a population that has grown from 17.5 million just after World War II to about 46.5 million today, not to mention having enough left over for export.

The hamlets of the Central Plains reveal Thai life at its purest, least diluted by the outside cultures of neighboring countries and the Western world. To begin with, more than in any other part of the country you still see houses in the classic style of Thai architecture, the plain but elegant domestic equivalent of the magnificent temples that reached their full flowering at Ayuthaya: the paneled walls slanting slightly inward to achieve an oddly graceful effect and the steep roof seeming to strain toward the sky. The faces of the people, too, are less likely to show the imprint of the Chinese and the Lao, the Burmese and the Malay, all the races that have intermingled with the Thai in the cities and in the border regions. In the hamlets, with their extended families, their communal approach to farming, their reliance on the village temple as a source of social as well as spiritual sustenance, their deeply rooted sense of independence, the strongest, most enduring aspects of the Thai character can be seen more clearly than anywhere else.

Another cheerful farmer works in rice fields soon to sprout into a "vast, acid-green sea" of plants.

The numbers in the margin in this section refer to the map on page 128.

Wat Chomkiri Nagaproth
วัดจอมคีรีนาคพรต

2. Bung Borapet
บึงบรเพ็ด

1. Nakhon Sawan
นครสวรรค์ (ตัวเมือง, จังหวัด)

3. Kamphang Phet
กำแพงเพชร (ตัวเมือง, จังหวัด)

Phom Seti
ป้อมเศรษฐี

Centuries of weathering have removed the stucco covering of this laterite image of the Buddha in the old fortified town of Kamphang Phet. revealing the serene elegance underneath.

Reaching one's destination in the Central Plains, as in most other parts of Thailand, is generally quick and comfortable. The main cities in the center are linked with the capital by road, rail, and air. Of these three modes, the most recently developed is travel by coach. A number of "super-bus" companies now offer rapid trips by air-conditioned coaches to most major destinations in Thailand. The standard of service on these vehicles is generally excellent. Snacks of the airline type are served by stewardesses, and soothing music is played on a tape deck. A Coach Tour Association of Thailand has been formed with 18 member companies. Among them, Grand Tour, Pat Tour, and Siam Coach cater particularly for foreign passengers.

The State Railway takes the traveler at a more leisurely pace through the Central Plains on a line slightly to the east of Route 1. The railway passes through Ayuthaya, Nakhon Sawan, Phitsanulok, and Uttaradit on its way to Chiang Mai. On the Northern Express, air-conditioned first class sleepers are available, as well as couchettes in the first and second class. A restaurant car serves excellent Thai food and European breakfasts. Thai Airways Co. provides frequent service to the Central Plains and North, its main destinations in the Central Plains being Phitsanulok and Uttaradit.

* * *

NAKHON SAWAN has always been an important commercial entrepot because of its location at the meeting of roads and rivers connecting North and Central Thailand. The Ping, Yom, and Nan Rivers, which flow through the northern highlands, meet above Nakhon Sawan. Under its old name of Paknam Po, the town played a vital role in the teak trade, for it was here that the great teak rafts, which had sometimes been traveling for two or three years from the northern forests, were broken up into smaller rafts for floating down to Bangkok on the Chao Phya River. Teak rafts may still be seen on the river above Nakhon Sawan, but they are not as numerous as they were in the heyday of Thailand's teak trade.

There are few traces of Nakhon Sawan's past in the modern commercial town. The most notable shrine is outside the town, across the bridge over the Chao Phya River. Here on a small hill stands **Wat Chomkiri Nagaproth**. The main structure dates from the Sukhothai period, but the Buddha image, seated on a throne supported by demons, is of the Ayuthaya period. Behind the main shrine is a massive, finely adorned bronze bell, about 100 years old, supported on modern brick pillars.

A favorite outing for those living in and around Nakhon Sawan is a trip to **BUNG BORAPET**, the seasonal lake located 2 km to the east. This low-lying area acts as a catchment during the rainy season. At the height of the monsoon in September and October, the lake covers an area of some 120 sq km. The best time to visit the lake is on a moonlit night in the cool season when you can picnic on the island in the middle of the waters.

* * *

The "new" city of **KAMPHANG PHET** lies 3 km off Route 1, on the east bank of the Ping River about 120 km northwest of Nakhon Sawan. This city was built by King Li Thai (1347-1368) of the Sukhothai dynasty to replace the older town of Chakangrao on the opposite bank. Both served as garrison towns for Sukhothai. On the right-hand side of the approach road to Kamphang Phet are the remains of a laterite fort, **Phom Seti**, built to defend the first and older city. Farther along the road is the well-restored *chedi* of **Wat Ched Klang Tung**, also a relic of the fomer city of Chakangrao.

Crossing a bridge over the Ping, you come to the modern town. A short distance from the center, with its numerous rice and noodle eating-houses, is the well-designed **Provincial Museum** containing one of the finest bronzes of Siva in Thailand. This life-sized image was cast on the orders of the governor of Kamphang Phet in the first quarter of the 16th century. Early in the reign of King Chulalongkorn (1868-1910), a German visitor to the town saw the image and decided to remove its head and two hands. The governor at the time, too afraid to arrest a *farang* (foreigner), quickly sent word to Bangkok that the priceless fragments were on their way there by boat. Officials in Bangkok detained the German, who declared that he was going to give the fragments to the Berlin Museum.

King Chulalongkorn (whose skillful diplomacy saved Thailand from much more serious threats from the West) found a way to placate the German as well as keep the cultural treasures for his country. He promised to send an exact copy of the whole Siva image to Germany, so the fragments could remain in Thailand. And so it was done. The copy of the bronze is still in Berlin, while the head and hands of the image in the Kamphang Phet museum have been skilfully restored. Other exhibits in the museum include pre-Sukhothai bronzes, stucco Buddha heads from monuments in the neighborhood, and some fine ceramics.

For a tour of the fortifications and temples, a car or coach is necessary since they are a considerable distance from the modern town. A visit to **King Li Thai's fortifications** reveals why the town was called Kamphang Phet or "Diamond Wall"

Old Kamphang Phet dates from the 14th-century Sukhothai dynasty, the first true Thai kingdom. This fragment of a massive Buddha image (above) sits in evocative solitude among the tumbled stones of its vanished temple. Numerous other remains of buildings and statues, like the fallen Buddha head on the right, lie scattered about the luxuriant undergrowth covering much of the old site, mute relics of the rise and fall of past kingdoms.

Wat Chang Rob
วัดช้างรอบ

Wat Phra Si Iriyaboth
วัดพระศรีอิริยาบถ

— the massive ramparts of earth topped by laterite rise six meters above the outer moat, now overgrown with water hyacinths.

The chief monuments of Kamphang Phet lie northwest of the walled city. The monks who built them were a forest-dwelling sect, strongly influenced by teachers from Sri Lanka. Their temples, constructed solidly of laterite, show Ceylonese influence. However, most of them underwent changes during heavy restoration in the Ayuthaya period. The familiar themes of Buddhist architecture are repeated in the ordination halls, *viharn*s, and *chedi*s of these temples. Two temples are of special interest and should be visited even on a rapid tour.

Wat Phra Si Iriyaboth derives its name from Buddha images which are depicted in four postures (*si* meaning "four," and *iriyaboth*, "postures") on the central square *mondop* (sanc-

tuary). The standing image is largely intact, with the original stucco coating on its head and lower part of the body. This is an impressive and unaltered example of Sukhothai sculpture. Unfortunately the other images (in the sitting, walking, and sleeping postures) are in very poor condition. The whole temple stands on a platform encircled by the original laterite railing and walls.

The other temple, **Wat Chang Rob**, or Shrine of the Elephants, consists of the base of a great laterite stupa surrounded by elephant caryatids — a theme borrowed from Sri Lanka. The row of elephants on the south side is almost complete, but several are missing on the other flanks of the stupa. Unfortunately, the spire of the great monument has vanished, but the ruins of a crypt on the upper level of the stupa can still be inspected. The pillars of the former *viharn* also remain.

Magical Center of Old Siam

4. Sukhothai
สุโขทัย (ตัวเมือง, จังหวัด)

Non Prasat
·นอนปราสาท

Ramkamhaeng
พิพิธภัณฑ์สถานแห่งชาติรามคำแหง

Wat Mahathat
วัดมหาธาตุ

As you head towards the ancient city of **SUKHOTHAI** northeast of Kamphang Phet, you pass through "new" Sukhothai, a dreary and dusty collection of shop houses. About 12 km farther on, the road enters the city limits of old Sukhothai through the **Kamphang-hak ("Broken Wall") Gate.** The remains of the massive walls reveal that the Maginot Line concept was not new: the capital was protected by no less than three rows of earthen ramparts and two moats which enclosed the inner city.

A short distance from Kamphang-hak Gate is the **Ramkamhaeng National Museum**, a good starting point for a tour of the enclave. The museum contains a fine collection of Sukhothai sculpture, ceramics, and other artifacts, and also has exhibits from other periods. The entrance hall is dominated by an impressive bronze image of the walking Buddha. This style of image is regarded as the finest sculptural innovation of the Sukhothai period (1230-1440?) — there had been earlier essays in high and low relief, but the Sukhothai sculptors were the first to create walking Buddha images in the round.

In this period, the Thais adopted Theravada Buddhism and invited monastic help from Sri Lanka. But Hindu influence remained strong as is revealed by the two bronze images of Hindu gods which flank the walking Buddha in the museum. The one on the right, with the combined attributes of Vishnu and Siva, is specially fine. Also worth noting is a stone torso of an *Apsara*, or divinity, in the Khmer style. (Look behind the statue; in spite of ugly iron struts, you can still see the superb detail of its costume.)

Farmers take a lunch break, just as their ancestors did more than 600 years ago, near the statue of the walking Buddha at Wat Chetuphon in Sukhothai. This image is regarded as one of the finest of its type.

An important object proudly displayed on the mezzanine floor is a copy of the famous stone inscription of King Ramkamhaeng — the original and most prized exhibit of the National Museum in Bangkok. It was at the **Non Prasat (Palace Mound)** — now merely a slightly raised terrace of earth and brick — that the famous stone inscription was found. In 1833, then Crown Prince Mongkut discovered the stone which had been inscribed in the year 1292. On it, King Ramkamhaeng had recorded his conquests in surrounding kingdoms, and also the fact that in 1283 he devised the Siamese alphabet, an achievement which has outlasted most of his conquests. Once situated on the Non Prasat was the stone throne of King Ramkamhaeng, and although there is little to be seen now apart from the walled terrace, this was the numinous center of old Siam. Alexander Griswold notes: "The political significance of the throne can scarcely be exaggerated, for the king sat on it when he discussed affairs of state . . . and when he received his vassals who came to do homage." The stone throne, called the *Manangasila*, is now in the Temple of the Emerald Buddha in Bangkok.

Within the walls of Sukhothai are the ruins of some twenty *wats* and monasteries, the greatest of them being **Wat Mahathat.** It is not definitely known who founded this shrine, which Griswold called "the magical and spiritual center of the kingdom," but it is presumed to have been King Sri Indraditya (1220?-1250), the first king of the Sukhothai dynasty. Wat Mahathat owes its present form to a remodeling completed by King Lo Thai around 1345. The original design — as the Fine Arts Department discovered a few years ago when making some repairs — was a quincunx of laterite towers standing on a laterite platform. The four axial towers, which can still be seen, are of the Khmer style but with stucco decorations added by King Lo Thai. The central tower is now hidden in the basement of Lo Thai's "lotus bud" tower. The axial towers were linked to the central tower by laterite buttresses which are still visible. The principal Buddha image, cast in bronze by King Li Thai (1347-1368) is now in Bangkok at Wat Suthat. The stucco frieze of walking monks around the base of the main tower is unusual.

Of the 20 other shrines within the walls, and some 70 more in the neighborhood, many repeat familiar architectural themes. The following short list, drawn up with the help of Professor Prince Subhadradis Diskul, an authority on the history and art of Sukhothai, indicates the monuments of special interest (for more detailed information, a guide to Sukhothai, published in English by the Fine Arts Department, is available at the museum.)

Wat Sri Sawai, southwest of Wat Mahathat, was originally a Hindu shrine which contained an image of Siva. Triple towers remain, built in a modified Khmer style; and the stucco decoration, added to the towers in the 15th century, showing mythical birds and divinities, is particularly fine.

Wat Sra Sri, on the way to the southern gate of the city has a spire (*chedi*) of the Sri Lankan type. The ordination hall (*bot*) lies on an island to the east of the spire. The ruins of the main shrine consist of six rows of columns, which lead up to a well-restored seated Buddha image. Achille Clarac comments: "The detail, balance, and harmony of the proportions and decoration of Wat Sra Sri, and the beauty of the area where it stands, bear witness to the unusual and refined aesthetic sense of the architects of the Sukhothai period."

Located immediately north of Wat Mahathat, **Wat Chana Songgram** and **Wat Trakuan** have particularly fine Sri Lankan-style *chedis*,

Wat Sra Sri
วัดสระศรี

Wat Chana Songgram
วัดชนะสงคราม
Wat Trakuan
วัดตระควร
Wat Sri Sawai
วัดศรีไสว

Sukhothai, dating from the 14th century, was the capital of the first Thai nation. Wat Mahathat (above), "the magical and spiritual center of the kingdom," was built partly in the style of the Khmers, whose powerful kingdoms preceded those of the Thais. Around the base of the temple's main tower is a stucco frieze of walking monks (right) that indicates the high degree of artistry that characterized this short-lived but influential city.

Wat Phra Phai Luang
วัดพระพายหลวง

of which only the lower parts still stand. Wat Trakuan has revealed many bronze images of the Chiang Saen period, which pre-dates Sukhothai.

Leaving the walled city by the northern San Luang, or "Royal Shrine," gate and traveling about a kilometer, you arrive at the important shrine of **Wat Phra Phai Luang**. It originally consisted of three laterite towers covered with stucco, probably built in the late 12th century when Sukhothai was still part of the Khmer empire. This shrine might have been the original center of Sukhothai, since Wat Mahathat is of a later period. A fragmentary seated stone Buddha image, accurately dated to 1191 in the reign of the Khmer King Jayavarman VII, was found here and is now in the grounds of the town's Ramkamhaeng Museum. During restoration by the Fine Arts Department in the mid-1960s, a large stucco im-

age of the Buddha in the central tower collapsed, disclosing numerous smaller images inside. Some date these images to the second half of the 13th century.

To the east of the main shrine lies a pyramidal brick stupa. Originally it contained seated Buddha images in stucco on each story, dating from the late 13th century. Later the niches were covered over with bricks, which were removed during a restoration started in 1953. When heads of the stucco Buddha images appeared on the antique market in Bangkok, it was realized that the stupa was being pillaged. A team from the Fine Arts Department was dispatched to the site, but most of the damage had already been done. Those heads (facially of the Chiang Saen style) which have not left the country are in private collections in Thailand or in the reserves of the National Museum in Bangkok.

Beyond Wat Phra Phai Luang is **Wat Si Chum**, which has one of the largest seated Buddha images in the kingdom. The *mondop*, or enclosing shrine, was built in the second half of the 14th century, but the image itself, called *Phra Achana*, or "The Venerable," is believed to be the one mentioned in King Ramkamhaeng's inscription. There is a stairway within the walls of the *mondop* which leads to a space behind the head of the image. The ceiling of the stairway is made up of more than 50 carved slate slabs illustrating scenes from Buddhist folklore. Their function is to turn the ritual climbing of the stairs into a symbolic ascent to Buddhahood.

South of the walled city is another group of shrines and monasteries. One of the most interesting is **Wat Chetupon**, where the protecting wall of the *viharn* is made of slate slabs shaped in imitation of wood. The gates are also formed of huge slabs of slate which was mined in the nearby hills. On a small scale, they resemble the megaliths of England's Stonehenge. The bridges across the moat which surrounds the temple are also made of stone slabs. On the central tower of Wat Chetupon are Buddha images in the standing, reclining, walking, and sitting postures. The walking Buddha here is regarded as one of the finest of its type.

"To the west of the city of Sukhothai," says King Ramkamhaeng's inscription, "is a forested area where the king has made offerings . . . In the forest is a large, tall, and beautiful *viharn* which contains an 18 cubit image of the standing Buddha." This is now identified as **Wat Saphan Hin**, "Monastery of the Stone Bridge." It is so called because it is approached by a stairway of large stone slabs. The image is situated on the crest of a low hill and can be seen at a considerable

Wat Si Chum
วัดศรีชุม

Wat Saphan Hin
วัดสะพานหิน

Wat Chetupon
วัดเชตุพน

Vendors near Sukhothai's ruins sell amulets and semiprecious stones (above, left), tokens of the spiritual power radiating from the kingdom. Decorated sherds (above, right) lie at the site of an ancient kiln in which potters from China produced the distinctive Sawankhalok stoneware, exported all over Southeast Asia. In Sukhothai's twin city (right) of Si Satchanalai rise the impressive stucco-covered walls of Wat Chedi Chet Thaew.

Wat Pa Mamuang
วัดผะมาเมือง

Wat Chang Lom
วัดช้างล้อม

5. Si Satchanalai
ศรีสัชนาลัย (ตัวเมือง, อำเภอ)

distance. It is 12½ meters high, with its hand raised in the attitude of "giving protection." This is almost certainly the image described by King Ramkamhaeng.

Many other monuments are to be found in this western area. They were probably built by monks from Sri Lanka who preferred to locate their monasteries in the forest. Another monument worth visiting, near the road not far from the western gate of Sukhothai, is **Wat Pa Mamuang**, "Shrine of the Mango Grove," where King Li Thai installed a famous monk of the Theravada sect in 1361. Still standing are the foundations of the shrine and the ruins of the main *chedi*.

* * *

About 55 km north of the modern town of Sukhothai along a new concrete highway lies the old city of **SI**

SATCHANALAI. Founded at the same time as Sukhothai in the middle of the 13th century, it served as the seat of the viceroys of Sukhothai and was always mentioned as the twin city of the capital.

To reach the walled city, cross over the newly constructed bridge or hire a sampan, the only way until recently to get across the river.

The first and most important monument to visit in Si Satchanalai is **Wat Chang Lom**. There can be little doubt that this is the "Elephant-girdled Shrine" described in King Ramkamhaeng's stone inscription. The great king records that he started to build it in 1285 to house some exceptionally holy relics of the Lord Buddha, and that it was finished six years later. It is the only surviving stupa which can be attributed with virtual certainty to King Ramkamhaeng. Built of laterite and stucco, it is a large bell-shaped spire of the Sri

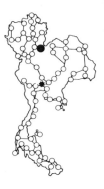

Lankan type standing on a two-story, square basement. The upper tier contains niches for Buddha images, now mostly empty, while the lower level contains 39 elephant caryatids, built of laterite blocks. Enough of them remain to give a good idea of the original design.

South of the Elephant Shrine are the ruins of **Wat Chedi Chet Thaew,** which include seven rows of stupas, believed to contain the ashes of the viceroys of Si Satchanalai. One of the stupas has a stucco image of the Buddha sheltered by the Naga (divine serpent), which is in unusually good repair.

Farther south still, and close to the massive walls of the city, are the remains of **Wat Nang Phy**, "Temple of the Queen." This is worth visiting, if only for the fine stucco decoration on one of the external walls. Dating probably from the 16th century, this stucco work has some affinities with European baroque.

Other temples worth visiting include **Wat Khao Phanom Pleung** and **Wat Khao Suwan Kiri,** set on two scenic hills linked by a walkway. **Wat Prasi Ratana Mahathat,** one of the most beautiful temples, lies 2 km southeast of the old city and must be reached by a ferry. In Si Satchanalai it is possible to buy genuine antique Sawankhalok ceramics.

* * *

PHITSANULOK, a city famous in Thailand for 500 years, now has only a few survivals from its past, because of a disastrous fire about 1960 which razed most of the old town. The new city is a rather dull collection of recently built shop houses. However, nothing can detract from its superb location, spanning the Nan River with its quays shaded by flowering trees, and its houseboats moored beside the steep banks of the river. Phitsanulok also boasts a first-class

Wat Chedi Chet Thaew
วัดเจดีย์เจ็ดแถว

6. Phitsanulok
พิษณุโลก

Wat Nang Phy
วัดนางพี

Intricate floral patterns (above, left) adorn the walls of Wat Chedi Chet Thaew at Si Satchanalai. The sanctity of a seated Buddha (above, right) is guarded by the seven heads of a divine serpent, or naga, at Wat Prasit Ratana Mahathat, also at Si Satchanalai. A young boy enjoys his ride on a merry-go-round (right) at a country fair near Phitsanulok, one of the contemporary scenes that bring to life the ancient ruins one sees in the Thai countryside.

hotel, the Amarin Nakorn, which is air conditioned and offers Western-style cuisine.

The great fire fortunately spared **Wat Mahathat**, the principal shrine in Phitsanulok. It is still a focus of piety, as it has been for several centuries. *Phra Buddha Chinaraj*, the image in the main *bot*, is venerated all over Thailand. Regrettably, this has given rise to a busy traffic in religious objects and souvenirs. The much-revered image is seated, has a round face in the Sukhothai style, a rather corpulent body, and fingers of equal length. There were two other bronze images of the same style in Wat Mahathat, but they were taken to Wat Bovornives in Bangkok.

The *bot* which enshrines the *Phra Buddha Chinaraj* gives the visitor an idea of the ancient style of Thai religious architecture. The three-tiered room of the *bot* sweeps down steeply to low side walls, focusing attention on the gleaming image at the end of the nave.

On either side of the image are two wooden pulpits of superb late-Ayuthaya workmanship. The large one on the left is meant for a chapter of monks chanting the Buddhist texts in ancient Pali, while the smaller pulpit on the other side accommodates one monk who translates the chanting into Thai (since few of the congregation would understand Pali). Before leaving the *bot*, note the main doors from the late 18th century inlaid with mother-of-pearl.

The *prang* (spire) in the center of the temple complex was rebuilt in the Khmer style by King Borom Trai Lokanat. The cloisters surrounding the *prang* are well worth visiting since they contain Buddha images of various periods, some of them of great artistic value. There is also a repository of objects including rare Thai and Chinese ceramics.

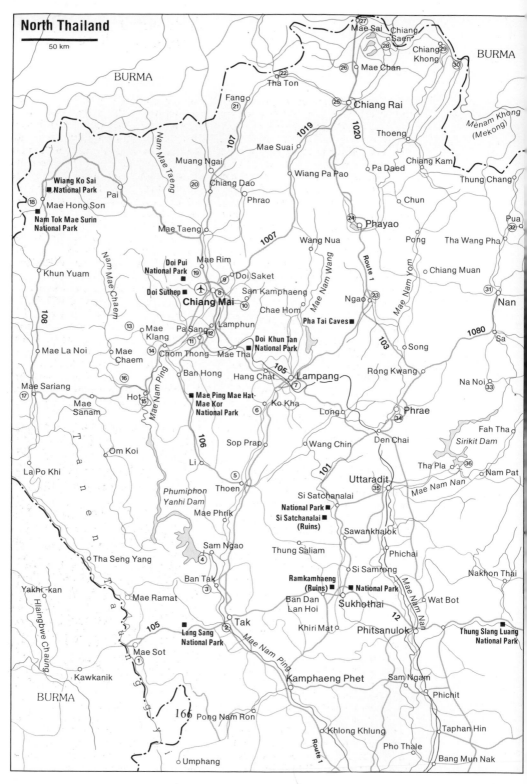

North Thailand

50 km

BURMA

BURMA

BURMA

Mae Sai ㉗
Chiang Saen
㉘
Chiang ㉙
Khong
㉚

Mae Chan ㉖

Tha Ton ㉒

Fango ㉑

Chiang Rai ㉕

Thoeng

Mènam Khong (Mekong)

Mae Suai

1019

1020

Chiang Kam

Pa Daed

Thung Chang

Muang Ngai

Wiang Pa Pao

Chun

Wiang Ko Sai ■ National Park

Pai

Chiang Dao ⑳

Phrao

1007

Pua ㉜

Mae Hong Son ⑱

Nam Tok Mae Surin National Park

Mae Taeng

Wang Nua

Phayao ㉔

Pong

Tha Wang Pha

Chiang Muan

Khun Yuam

Doi Pui National Park ⑲

Mae Rim

Doi Saket ⑧

Route 1

㉛ Nan

Doi Suthep ■

Chiang Mai

San Kamphaeng

⑩

Chae Hom

Ngao ㉓

103

Song

Sa

Pha Tai Caves ■

Mae Klang ⑬

Pa Sang ⑫

Lamphun

Doi Khun Tan National Park

1080

Mae Chaem ⑭

Chom Thong ⑪

Mae Tha

Rong Kwang

Na Noi ㉝

Mae La Noi

Ban Hong

Hang Chat

Lampang ⑦

108

Mae Sariang ⑰

Mae Sanam

Hot ⑮

Mae Ping Mae Hat- Mae Kor National Park ■

Ko Kha

Long

Phrae ㉞

Den Chai

Fah Tha Sirikit Dam

Om Koi

106

Sop Prap

Wang Chin

Tha Pla ㊱

Nam Pat

La Po Khi

Li

Thoen ⑤

101

Uttaradit ㉟

Mae Nam Nan

Phumiphon Yanhi Dam

Mae Phrik

Si Satchanalai

National Park ■

Sawankhalok

Nakhon Thai

Tha Seng Yang

Sam Ngao ④

Thung Saliam

Phichai

Yakhi -kan

Ban Tak ③

Si Samrong

12

Wat Bot

Mae Ramat

Ramkamhaeng (Ruins) ■

■ National Park

Sukhothai

Thung Slang Luang National Park ■

105

Lang Sang National Park ■

Tak ②

Ban Dan Lan Hoi

Khiri Mat

Phitsanulok

Mae Sot ①

Kawkanik

Kamphaeng Phet

Sam Ngam

Phichit

BURMA

166

Pong Nam Ron

Khlong Khlung

Taphan Hin

Umphang

Pho Thale

Bang Mun Nak

Another group of simple houses, but different in architecture, and in atmosphere, than those we saw on the Central Plains. Different in setting, too: this village is even more remote than the farming hamlets of the Central Plains; its surrounding ocean consists not of rice fields, but of rocky hills and mist-covered mountains, a wild and almost roadless terrain where distances are measured in walking hours rather than in kilometers. In these jungled mountains, secret, sketchily-mapped, and all but inaccessible to outsiders, live unusual people: Meo tribesmen who wear vast black turbans and clanking silver jewelry; Yao tribespeople who wear finely worked embroidery and speak a language that until recently only a handful of foreign missionaries could interpret; and several almost legendary small nomadic groups, like the Phi Thong Luang, "Spirits of the Yellow Leaves," whom some thought to exist only in myth until an expedition came across their jungle home and thrust them into the modern world.

Here, also, in lost valleys where fields of forbidden poppies grow, begins a complex trail of illicit activity that ends on the streets of many major Western cities. The poppies and the opium by-product were outlawed in Thailand more than 20 years ago, but the problem is not that simple: it is hard for the authorities to adequately patrol this wild terrain, but easy for offenders to slip back and forth across the borders with Burma and Laos, which form the notorious "Golden Triangle" mentioned in so many narcotics news stories. Recent efforts, however, are meeting with growing success. From his winter palace on Doi Suthep, overlooking the northern capital of Chiang Mai, the king personally directs an ambitious crop-substitution program aimed at the hillpeople who traditionally derived their main income from the poppy plant. Missionaries and organizations, such as the royally sponsored Hill Tribe Founda-

tion, are finding markets for the fine handicrafts of the tribespeople. And members of the elite Border Patrol Police are dropping by helicopter into the remote mountain villages not only to enforce the law but to set up schools and bring modern medicine for the first time. The hilltribes are still an exotic thread on the fringe of Thai life, but gradually they are being woven into the national fabric, venturing to the larger cities in the North, some even to distant Bangkok, breaking through their traditional shell of isolation.

But the North has more to offer than strange hilltribes and jungled wilderness. It is also a place rich in history, with great kingdoms, legendary rulers, and artistic achievement that go back beyond the founding of the first Thai capital at Sukhothai in the 13th century. The celebrated Emerald Buddha, the most venerated of all the images in Thailand, was

In Thailand's North, as in the rest of the kingdom, rice is the staple food. Here a farmer near Mae Sariang, close to the Burmese border, threshes the grain in a huge basket that measures more than two meters across.

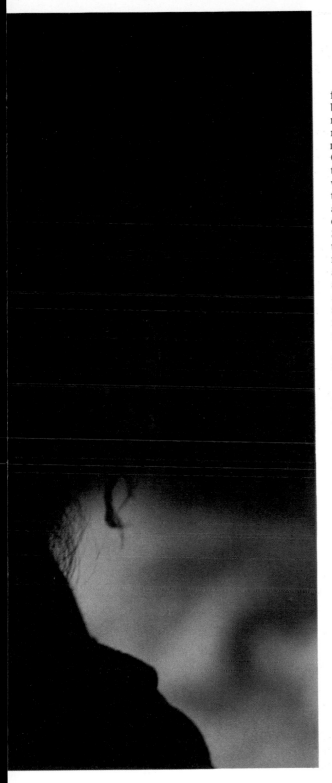

found in the North (most experts also believe it was made there) and spent much of its early existence in various northern temples. According to a northern legend, King Mangrai of Chiang Saen, who ruled the North in the 13th century, was so powerful that when he decided to found a new capital, the future Chiang Mai, he was able to call on royal friends from other parts of the country, including Sukhothai, to assist him in the selection of a suitable location. The eminent surveyors knew they had found an auspicious site when they heard of a place where an extraordinary assembly of rare animals had been seen: two white sambar deer (a variety now extinct), two white barking deer, and a white mouse with a family of five. King Mangrai, so the story goes, immediately ordered Chiang Mai to be built on the spot.

The North has been the scene of epic battles, of Burmese invasions, of the rise and fall of independent kingdoms, only distantly related to the ruling cities of the central part of the present-day country. Until the early part of this century, it was accessible from Bangkok only by a complicated river trip or by a journey of several weeks on elephant back. There are still old residents in the capital who remember the great day when the northern railway line was finally opened in the late 1920s, after more than ten years of tunneling and blasting through the mountains. It is not surprising, then, that the region has retained a distinct flavor all its own, one still so strong that tourists from other parts of Thailand come here almost as if to another country, marveling at the profusion and beauty of the temples with their splendid teak carvings and intricate Burmese-

Fabulous, almost medieval costumes are daily dress to the exotic hilltribes who inhabit the wild mountains of Thailand's North. The life-style of this Meo woman is changing, but she retains much of her distinctive culture.

inspired decorations (there are more than a hundred in moderate-sized Chiang Mai alone); the splendor of the wild orchids that grow so profusely in the hills; the gentle good manners of the people (among whose hospitable habits it is to place a basin of cool water outside their gates for the benefit of thirsty passing strangers); the fabled good looks of the girls; and the novelty of having to bundle up in a sweater in the cool season. Ancient handicrafts which have either succumbed to the machine or which never even existed in other regions still thrive here: delicate lacquerware, thin silver bowls pounded into complex designs over wooden molds, supple handwoven cottons and shimmering silk, expertly carved teak, paper umbrellas painted in bold designs, and fine celadon stoneware.

Nor is the culture of the North something that has been artificially preserved for the pleasure of the tourists, who have flocked to the North and turned it into Thailand's leading provincial attraction. In fact, for all their gracious manners, the northerners have a perceptible sense of superiority toward the aggressive newcomers of Bangkok and are quite firm in their ideas of what they will and will not accept in the interests of "development." At the height of the Vietnam War, for instance, when Thailand was a major rest and recreation spot for American servicemen, some profit-minded operators in the capital got the idea of turning Chiang Mai into a hillstation for pleasures. The Chiang Mai city fathers politely turned down the offer; if the soldiers wanted to enjoy northern culture as it was, they replied, they were welcome to come, but if they were after the kind of things Bangkok specialized in they would be far happier there. End of discussion.

Mae Hong Son market. An elderly woman of Burmese origin thoughtfully puffs on an old-style cheroot as she goes about her business.

Along with its manners, handicrafts, and relative serenity, the North has also kept its love of festivals, which are observed with greater frequency and enthusiasm than anywhere else in Thailand. A visitor who comes in the winter months — that is, between October and the end of January — is almost certain to come across some kind of celebration, ranging from the famous Loy Krathong water festival, when Chiang Mai hotels are booked for months in advance, to localized affairs, like the bringing in of the garlic crop in Lamphun, when one of the local beauties is chosen "Miss Garlic."

The North is also a region of great natural wealth and scenic beauty. Vast hardwood forests cover much of it, the working of which still requires the services of trained elephants, which drag the huge logs downhill to the banks of rivers, to be floated down to mills below. Mines for minerals such as wolfram have been sunk in the mountains, producing booming new industries. In the high-altitude fields grow tobacco, coffee, tea, strawberries, garlic, and a delectable fruit called *lamyai*, whose annual harvest is, inevitably, the occasion for a festival. Experimental crops being tested on Doi Inthanon, Thailand's highest mountain, include apples, peaches, plums, and other temperate fruits. The production of cut flowers is another new industry, and in the winter season the florist shops of Bangkok are filled with unfamiliar gladiolus, snapdragons, carnations and other blossoms which, like so many things in the North, seem strange and special.

Getting to the North is now much easier than in the days of travel by boat and elephant. Thai Airways'

Near Mae Sariang, a Karen tribeswoman trudges through the burnt stumps of a former forest cleared by the nomadic hilltribe. Efforts are being made to get the tribes to replace their traditional opium with other crops.

domestic service offers at least five flights daily from Bangkok to the North. These include at least two direct flights to Chiang Mai every day, and other flights with touchdowns in the provincial capitals of Lampang, Phrae, Phitsanulok, and Chiang Rai.

Several trains and many buses leave Bangkok daily for northern destinations. The best train, the Daily Express, departs Bangkok in the late afternoon, stops at Ayuthaya, Lop Buri, Nakhon Sawan, Phichit, Phitsanulok, Uttaradit, Den Chai, Lampang, and Lamphun, and arrives in Chiang Mai early the next morning. Reservations for seats and sleepers should be made well in advance during school holidays and especially around the mid-April Songkran or winter Loy Krathong festival when hotels in Chiang Mai are full.

If the express train is fully booked, one can still travel comfortably and inexpensively to the North by air-conditioned buses. Every day, three buses leave Bangkok's northern terminal on Phaholyothin Road for an express ride to Chiang Mai. The first bus pulls out at the invigorating hour of 5:25 a.m. Eight non-air-conditioned but quite modern and breezy buses also make the 700-km trip in about nine hours (compared with 15 hours by train). From the northern terminal one can also go by bus to Chiang Rai, Lampang, Bhumibol Dam (Tak), and Sukhothai.

For travelers with cars, Route 1 leaves the Central Plains around Kamphang Phet, passes the northern gateway province of Tak, and follows the Wang River north-northeast to Lampang. From Lampang you can branch off on the all-weather road to Chiang Mai or continue on Route 1 to Chiang Rai. You should try to make several sidetrips on the North's scenic secondary roads. Occasional reports of insurgent activities along roads in the North should not necessarily deter your explorations. Most of these incidents occur in very remote areas and involve soldiers, government officials, or road construction crews, but not travelers.

Try to visit the North during the cool season (late November to February) when the days are usually bright and sunny but not too hot, and the nights cool enough for sweaters and jackets. Blue skies and clear air allow for good photography, and the evening chill makes you appreciate the warming effect of Chiang Mai's *kow tom* (hot rice porridge with egg and meat).

Travel beyond the North into Burma is not yet legally possible as the Burmese government does not issue visas for overland entry from Thailand. For years travelers have been allowed to cross the Mekong River from Chiang Khong over to Ban Houei Sai in Laos. Now, with relations between the two countries soured, it is no longer possible to enter Laos from here.

A hunter armed with an old flintlock (left) goes in search of birds near the town of Hot. Leaves serve a variety of purposes in Thailand, from thatching a house to serving as an emergency hat (above) in a downpour.

Gateway to the North

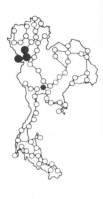

One of the first interesting places to explore in the North provides a touch of Burma: the town of **MAE SOT** near the Burmese border just west of Tak. Tak itself, the gateway to the North, has little of interest, but can be the point of departure for trips to Mae Sot and the Bhumibol Dam.

Although truck drivers make offerings at the spirit house below Phawoh Mountain for a safe passage, as you approach Mae Sot, Road 105 sweeps through forests into a peaceful valley dotted with miniature farmhouses, white *chedi*s, and ornate Burmese-style temples.

A confusion of short streets, sidewalk stalls, bicycles, and pedestrian shoppers: Mae Sot thrives as a backwoods trading post. The town even boasts a short airstrip. Shops advertize their wares in Thai, Chinese, Burmese, and English. At the Siam Hotel one finds dramatic (if tasteless) wood carvings for sale.

From Mae Sot a 5-km drive takes you to the Burmese border. On the way an ornate Burmese temple can be visited. This temple has a rectangular roof with red shingles and silverwork piled heavenward into a tower. Within the sanctuary are four Buddha images, one of which has gold jewelry spilling out from its earlobes. After seeing this temple you can drive to the Moei River which forms the border with Burma and the point at which the Pan Asian Highway may someday enter Thailand, linking Southeast Asia with Europe by road.

On the way to Tak from Mae Sot, if time allows, stop at the *nik-horn*, or "settlement," for Lisu, Lahu, and Meo hilltribes on Doi Mussu. About 12 km outside of Tak lies Luang Larn National Park where waterfalls hide behind bamboo groves. Road 105 soon rejoins Route 1 going north to Tak.

1. Mae Sot
แม่สอด (อำเภอ, ตัวเมือง)

This scenic winding road (above, left) leads to the bustling little town of Mae Sot, on the border of Burma; one day it may form part of Asia's great Route 1 which will take overland travelers all the way from Istanbul to Singapore. Shy Karen girls (above, right), members of one of the hilltribes who live in the surrounding hills, come down to hawk fruits and vegetables beside the road and get a look at the outside world passing by.

176

TAK was a prosperous riverine junction for goods coming from Chiang Mai to Bangkok before the era of the highway; but today travelers enter Tak not by ferrying sampans, but along a small road that weaves through tiny manicured gardens and around a pond near the provincial offices. A broad, drab esplanade separates the market and the old wooden houses from the Ping River, so as to prevent too much flooding from the notorious Ping floods in the rainy season.

Tak is a peaceful place, offering few sights other than the river at sunset and two temples in the northern part of town. These are **Wat Phrae** and **Wat Sibunruang**, the latter of which has a gold-topped *chedi* and contains *Phra Buddhamon,* an early Sukhothai image. For an overnight stay in Tak, choose from several inexpensive hotels: Tawee Sak, Tak, Charoen Suk, and the air-conditioned

Bhumibhol.

Off Route 1, about 20 km past Tak on the left, lies the village of **BAN TAK**. Tiny and undisturbed, Ban Tak stretches precariously over the Ping River. Houses on stilts and a rickety bamboo footbridge look down upon children swimming eagerly against the current of the Ping. At sunset the Ping turns silver, and boatmen drift like silhouettes in a shadow-play across the reflected light.

BHUMIBOL DAM (also called Yanhee Dam), lies north of Ban Tak about 29 km on a turnoff on the left off Route 1. With permission, you can drive across the 154-meter-high cement arch to view the reservoir which stretches more than 100 km northwest to Hot District, not far from Chiang Mai. This huge dam generates enough power to help light Bangkok and 37 of Thailand's widely scattered 72 provinces. The nearby

With the water level controlled by the huge Bhumibol Dam (above), the catchment area near Ban Tak is calm and shallow enough to allow a bamboo footbridge (left) to span the waters.

Bhumibol Guest House complex consists of nine facilities, two of them air-conditioned. House 100, with both air conditioning and reasonable charges, contains 26 rooms. Below the Bhumibol Dam lies a mini-city of workers' quarters, a school, the Energy Authority offices, a restaurant, and swimming pier. The area surrounding the dam has resort potential, but to date, the only tourist incursion is an 18-hole golf course.

About 63 km beyond the Bhumibol Dam turnoff, Road 106 crosses Route 1 at **THOEN**. Although Thoen can be passed rapidly, it does cherish a small claim to fame as the home of lucky stones. Each *pohng kham* contains a variety of colors and internal "scenes." Some pieces are clear and have strange, crystalline formations inside — resembling wisps of blue hair, jungle moss, or even a city skyline.

From Thoen to Lampang, Route 1 undulates over teak-covered hills and a mountain pass sprinkled with spirit houses before dipping into the broad, cattle-grazing Yom River Valley of Lampang. About 18 km south of Lampang, Route 1 crosses the road to **KO KHA**. By turning left, passing the town, crossing the Wang River, and bearing left for 1 km, you will reach the elegant old temple, **Wat Lampang Luang**. Cherished by scholars for its antiquity and delicate artwork, the temple compound is all that remains of a fortressed city that flourished more than a millennium ago; it is believed to have been founded by a Lop Buri princess, Chama Dewi, who bore two sons: one became king of Lampang, the other king of Lamphun. The *wat*, entirely rebuilt in the 16th century, wove a golden pattern through the history of the North's ruling families. About 200 years ago, Burmese invaders occupied the temple. According to legend, Thai at-

6. Ko Kha
เกาะคา (ตัวเมือง, อำเภอ)

Wat Lampang Luang
วัดลำปางหลวง

5. Thoen
เถิน (ตัวเมือง, อำเภอ)

Wat Pha Sang
วัดไฟเสาง

Wat Phra Keo DonTau
วัดพระแก้วดอนเตื้อ

7. Lampang
ลำปาง (ตัวเมือง, จังหวัด)

Wat Chedi Sao Phra
วัดเจดีย์เสาพระ

tackers sneaked through a drain to surprise and overwhelm their enemy. A hole in the balustrade is said to have been caused by the cannon-shot that killed a Burmese general.

The temple's museum features lacquered bookcases, wooden *tong* emblems that hang from poles like stiff flags, and many jeweled Buddhas. Most revered is a small "Emerald Buddha" believed to have been carved from the same jasper stone as its famous counterpart in Bangkok. Some eaves have been carted off to antique collections, but the wooden facade of the *viharn* remains a fine example of northern carving. A bronze Lop Buri Buddha sits in the dark interior.

About 18 km past Ko Kha, Route 1 enters the provincial capital of **LAMPANG**. Half the size of Chiang Mai and far less developed, Lampang epitomizes the bucolic peacefulness of North Thailand. In no other Thai city do horse-drawn carriages continue to resist the march of taxis. The graceful old railway station takes the viewer several decades back in time.

Two Burmese-style temples in the town are worth visiting. Seven chapels, one for each day of the week, stand at the base of the *chedi* in **Wat Pha Sang**, on the left bank of the Wang River. On the right bank, **Wat Phra Keo Don Tau** presents a lovely fusion of Burmese and local architecture. In the 18th-century chapel, columns soar to great heights; the ceilings are a kaleidoscope of inlaid enamel, mother-of-pearl, and cut glass. For an overnight stay, Lampang has several modern hotels: the Siam, Sri Sangar, Lampang, and Asia Lampang. North of town stand the twenty chalky spires of **Wat Chedi Sao Phra** set in the rice fields. Approximately 100 km farther north of Lampang lies Chiang Mai.

The countryside temple of Lampang Luang (far left), one of Thailand's oldest, is adorned with intricate decorations (above). Village musicians (left) perform at the ordination ceremony of a new monk.

Chiang Mai: Flower of the North

The cacophonous whine of thousands of motorcycles and *thuk-thuks* (three-wheeled, motorized pickups) hammers at the eardrums; countless souvenir shops, their wares spilling onto the streets, make a complementary visual assault. Only a few years ago a small, relaxed place, the town today has an overlay of tinsel modernity which, fortunately, fails to completely hide the real **CHIANG MAI**. Situated 710 km north of Bangkok in a valley 305 meters above sea level, Chiang Mai makes a pleasant dry-season escape from the sticky humidity of the capital. The second largest city of Thailand, with an amazing array of handicrafts, impressive mountain scenery, historical temples, and colorful hilltribes, still greets visitors with a graceful *wai*, making comfortable friends out of those who arrive as strangers.

On the green mass of nearby Doi Suthep, which rises like a backdrop

to the town, Wat Prathat appears with crystalline clarity through the chill morning air, which in December could almost be described as cold. At breakfast-time a minibus (perhaps by the moat) is already filling with a group of hardy travelers setting off for a three-day jungle walk from Fang, 150 km to the north. The murky moat beside the food stalls offers little hope of fish, but two young boys, undaunted, dangle lines in the water. An elderly monk, well aware that this is Chiang Mai's best breakfasting spot, returns the courtesy of his meal with a blessing for the kneeling waitresses. Another day begins in Chiang Mai.

Getting around Chiang Mai is a breeze; buses charge a standard one baht for any journey in town. Some follow such circuitous routes that your baht buys a complete town tour. *Thuk-thuk*s should not cost more than two or four baht for most rides;

8. Chiang Mai
เชียงใหม่ (ตัวเมือง, จังหวัด)

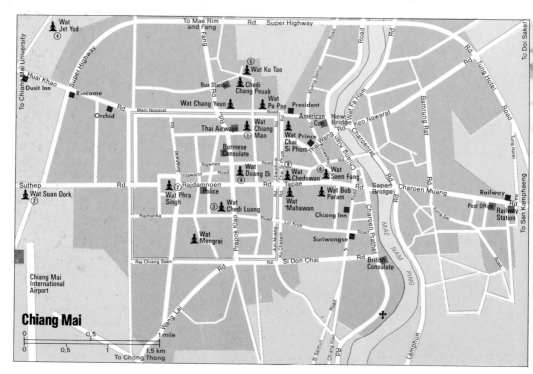

Chiang Mai

Cool, leisurely
Chiang Mai
combines small-city
charm with a
multitude of
fascinating things
to see and do.

Wat Chiang Man
วัดเชียงแมน

just hail one going your way. Pedal *samlors* provide a more leisurely way of seeing Chiang Mai; or hire a push bicycle and pedal yourself. The tour agents around the eastern moat gate do a thriving business renting push bicycles and motorcycles. The Tourist Organization of Thailand has a branch in Chiang Mai at 135 Praisanee Road for further tips on enjoying your stay.

Chiang Mai's history is as old as that of the Thais themselves. In the 13th century, when Thais were fleeing en masse from southern China, King Mangrai ruled a Thai Kingdom around Chiang Rai. When Kublai Khan sacked Pagan in 1287, Mangrai formed a life-long alliance with the kings of Sukhothai. With his southern boundaries secure, Mangrai captured the old Mon Kingdom at Haripunjaya in 1292, and thereafter founded his new capital at Chiang Mai in 1298.

Chiang Mai, with its moat and walls, was at first a great city, repelling invaders and overshadowing both the Mons and Khmers to the east. But less than a century after its founding, Chiang Mai's relations with Ayuthaya became strained. For the next 400 years its southern borders were unsafe and hostile. Ayuthaya crushed in the 16th century an invasion by Chiang Mai, and from 1550 to 1650 Chiang Mai's power began to wane. The Burmese invaded in the early 18th century. Fighting continued until 1775, and although the Burmese were finally defeated, the inhabitants of Chiang Mai were so dazed and exhausted from centuries of warfare that they drifted away, leaving Chiang Mai deserted until 1796, when it came under the sway of Siam. The present moat in Chiang Mai dates from soon after the re-establishment of the city, but only the patch of coal at the southeast corner is original; all the other fragments of the wall and gates are reconstructions.

The low rays of the morning sun

brilliantly illumine the *bot* of **Wat Chiang Man.** Behind it the *chedi* is supported by rows of fine elephant buttresses. In this the oldest temple in Chiang Mai, built by Mengrai who resided there during the construction of the city, two ancient and much venerated Buddha images are kept in the abbot's quarters. The images can be seen on request. One is a crystal Buddha (*Phra Sae Tang Tamani*), a small image brought by Mengrai to Chiang Mai from Lamphun where it was said to have been for 600 years. Apart from a short sojourn in Ayuthaya, the image has remained in Chiang Mai ever since, and each April 1 it is ceremoniously paraded through the town. The other sacred image is a stone Buddha (*Phra Sila*) in bas-relief, believed to have originated in India around the 8th century. These two statues apparently have the power to bring rain.

In Chiang Mai's most important

"The second largest city of Thailand still greets visitors with the graceful gesture of the wai, *making comfortable friends out of those who arrive as strangers." A statue at Wat Prasingh (above) extends a welcome.*

temple, **Wat Prasingh**, founded in 1345, the spacious grounds seem to shut out the bustle of traffic on the main road in town which runs right up to it. The *wat* contains a collection of buildings, including a fine library. The small chapel behind the ancient *chedi* shelters the main Buddha image which has a long and undoubtedly much embroidered history. Claimed to be more than 1,500 years old and to have originated in Sri Lanka, it is said to have arrived in Siam during the Sukhothai period and eventually to have found its way to Chiang Mai. As the statue is in the Sukhothai style, and as there are similar images in Bangkok and Nakhon Si Thammarat, it is hard to say how much truth there is in the story: any one of the "copies" could be the original. What is certain is that the head of the Chiang Mai image was stolen in 1922, and that the present head is a replica.

The crumbling base of a huge *chedi* is visible to the southeast of Wat Prasingh. In 1545 a violent earthquake shook Chiang Mai, toppling the 90-meter-high, 500-year-old pagoda of **Wat Chedi Luang**. This monstrous *chedi* was never repaired. For a reported 84 years the restless Emerald Buddha was housed in this *wat;* King Mangrai is romantically said to have been killed nearby by a bolt of lightning. Close to the entrance to the *wat* stands a tall gum tree: should it fall, legend insists, Chiang Mai will suffer a great misfortune. The "spirit of the city," a town boundary post, is sheltered in a small building near the fateful gum.

Located outside the city walls, **Wat Jet Yod** suffered damage from a more mortal cause. Begun in 1453 its square *chedi* has, as the name describes, seven spires. Having been built in imitation of a temple in the Burmese capital of Pagan did not stop the

Wat Prasingh
วัดพระสิงห์

Wat Chedi Luang
วัดเจดีย์หลวง

Wat Jet Yod
วัดเจ็ดยอด

Strikingly carved gilded doors (above, left) lead into a building at Chiang Mai's most important temple, Wat Prasingh. The city has many other attractive temples, such as Wat Duang Di (above, right), where the main spire is inlaid with colored mirrors, and framed by a parasol and stylized guardian lions. Slender chedis containing the ashes of Chiang Mai's royal family rise gracefully in the compound of Wat Suan Dok (right).

Burmese from severely damaging it during one of their periodic invasions in 1566.

Chiang Mai proper has still more temples worthy of a visit. **Wat Koo Tao**, hidden away behind the bus station, has a strange bulbous *chedi*, like a pile of diminishing spheres. **Wat Saen Fang**, with its unusual monastery, is reached by a narrow lane guarded by long *naga*s. The mass of small *chedi*s at **Wat Suan Dok** contain the ashes of Chiang Mai's royal family, and the huge central *chedi* is said to hold no less than eight relics of Lord Buddha. **Wat Chedovan**, close to the east gate, has three tiled *chedi*s and a menagerie of mythical animals which almost come alive in the slanting rays of the morning sun.

A hairpin switchback ride climbs 12 km uphill to Chiang Mai's best-known temple. Seven-headed *naga*s snarl menacingly at visitors, their ceramic tails undulating up the 290 steps leading to **Wat Prathat (Doi Suthep)**. From this hilltop lookout at 1,000 meters, Thailand's northern metropolis appears like a toy below.

The sidetrip to Doi Suthep and its gilded temple can make an interesting morning excursion from Chiang Mai. The road to the mountain sanctuary leaves the old city at its northwest corner and crosses the plain studded with rice fields. (Transportation can be arranged at the White Elephant Gate.) After passing a large hospital, the road comes to the fairly new **Chiang Mai University**, officially opened in 1965 on its 200-hectare campus. A little farther on, an arboretum cultivates many of North Thailand's species of trees. About 7 km from town, where the road turns to begin its climb of Doi Suthep, is the entrance to the **Chiang Mai Zoo**. Started as the private collection of Mr. Harold Young and his son, the popular zoo was donated to

the town; it houses most of the region's wild animals.

After beginning its ascent, the road passes the statue of the monk Krupan Srivichai, who in 1934 began construction on the first road to the temple to make it more accessible to pilgrims. The completed road reaches the foot of the temple, where cars must be left. The temple on the summit is reached by the staircase of 290 steps flanked by *naga* balustrades. The two sanctuaries, the temple, and the cloister were built in the 16th century. Since then, the buildings have been maintained through gifts from pilgrims.

The outside pediment between the two doors leading to the cloister has been heavily restored, but inside the two sanctuaries are sumptuously decorated facades with murals depicting Buddhist tales. There are also Buddha images in the Sukhothai and the Chiang Saen styles. The 24-meter-high *chedi* is surrounded by gilded bronze parasols and covered with engraved gold tiles.

From the parking area of Wat Prathat, a road continues to ascend for about 5 km to **Bhubing Palace**, the summer palace of King Bhumibol. Situated at an elevation of about 1,300 meters, the palace grounds are completely furnished with audience halls, guest houses, dining rooms, kitchens, and official suites to carry on the royal affairs at this remote hilltop retreat. On weekends and holidays, when the royal family is absent, the public may visit the grounds and its well-tended gardens aflame with roses, orchids, hibiscus, and double-headed bougainvilleas; but the buildings cannot be entered.

About 400 meters before the palace entrance, a track goes 2 km to a crossroads, and from there the left branch leads to a **Meo village**. The first 2 km can be covered by jeep, but

Bhubing Palace
ตำหนักภูพิงค์ราชนิเวศน์

Meo Village
หมู่บ้านแม้ว

the remainder must be done on foot; although the track descends steeply, it takes only about 10 minutes to cover. On the way one passes smiling tribesmen carrying fresh game they have shot, or perhaps a few tribeswomen heading home. The Meo village consists of several huts perched all along the hillside; the people are extremely friendly and eager to talk and ask questions. Grubby faced children in bright red and black costumes wave happily at you; each seems to carry around their neck half their weight in jewelry. These people are members of one of the hilltribes that adds so much color to North Thailand. A nomadic people, groups of whom are also found in neighboring Burma and Laos, the Meo once depended on opium cultivation for their livelihood. While the government began persuading them to turn to less harmful crops, it discovered in the process that the tribes are a major tourist attraction. The Meo women, small and active, wear heavy dark-blue skirts embroidered with bands of red and white. Because of its relative accessibility, this village receives far more visitors than most other tribal villages. For those who lack the time to go deeper into Thailand, this Meo village offers a typical example of hilltribe life; the disadvantage, however, results from their exposure to tourists, which has made them pecuniary-minded, and they now insist on payment for being photographed. This, however, is unusual in Thailand. Most tour operators, such as Diethelm, can arrange excursions to more untouched, less frequented hilltribe villages. Outings can include roughing it on three-day treks into the surrounding Himalayan foothills.

Another place to see the hilltribes is at the **Old Chiang Mai Cultural Center** south of town. Here,

Old Chiang Mai
Cultural Center
ศูนย์วัฒนธรรมดั้งเดิมเชียงใหม่

In evening light people pay homage at the famous sanctuary atop Doi Suthep (far left). The young girl (left) and the old man puffing a cigarette through a water pipe (above) live in the Meo village nearby.

Handicrafts

every night, while sitting cross-legged on the floor, you can indulge in a northern Thai style banquet *(kantoke)* and watch and listen to traditional Thai dances and songs. This is followed by an excellent genuine hill-tribes show during which you can chance to see the costumes and the dances of the seven tribes in the area (Meo, Red and White Karen, Lisu, Lahu, Yao, and Akha). The Center also contains representative houses which have been built and which are occupied by the several tribes. Although the setting is obviously artificial, it is nonetheless worthwhile.

Elephants are still used in the forests around Chiang Mai. Just off the main road, 58 km to the north, an enterprising lumber camp owner puts on a **daily elephant work show**. Arrive early to see the huge beasts having a morning scrub in the river before getting down to a few hours of hard log hauling.

What would anyone do with a half-life-size wooden elephant? There must be a good answer, for every other Chiang Mai handicrafts shop seems to have one. Chiang Mai's range of carvings is enormous; elephants from matchbox size up to those big ones are available. Visit Chiang Mai Carving on Rat Chiang Saen Road where 200 youngsters spend their mornings chiseling teak elephants, dolls, and furniture. All the carvers learn their skills at home, since the company cannot afford taking risks on a novice. Only one designer draws the patterns for the carvers. Buyers should patronize such established carving shops since much of the teak hawked on the street is green and cracks within a few months. Teak salad bowls or trays are equally plentiful, if you want something smallish and utilitarian.

Each of Chiang Mai's other prolific crafts seems to have its own

Elephant Show
การแสดงของช้าง

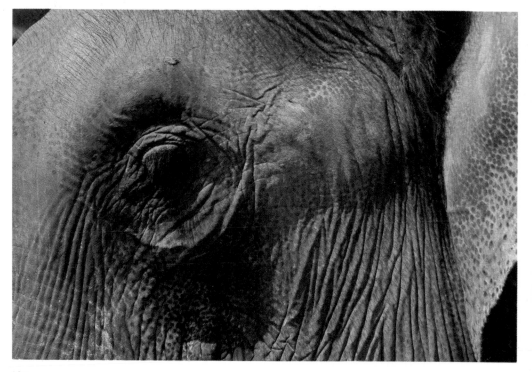

section of the city; but a good place to get a glimpse of the entire range of crafted goods that awaits the shopper is along **Tapae Road** near the eastern gate, where shops sell everything. In one stop you can buy lacquerware, silk, cotton, clothes, and jewelry. One of the more popular of these all-purpose centers is Hudson Enterprises, run by a very English gentleman, Roy Hudson, who was active in Southeast Asia during the war and eventually settled in Chiang Mai to become the resident expert on everything in North Thailand. In the evening, Tapae Road and nearby Chang Kian Road become shopping malls, rivaling London's Carnaby Street, as vendors lay out their wares in front of the tour coaches preparing to return to Bangkok.

After you have whetted your appetite for further exploring the treasures of Thailand's handicraft capital, you can investigate each craft more closely. Near the south gate is the **silversmiths' street, Wualai Road**, where all manner of jewelry and silver objects are crafted. The shops may look modern, but in the back rooms bare-chested, muscular smiths pound away at silver bowls propped on iron pegs. They hammer out intricate patterns of hilltribe-inspired designs, as well as scenes from the familiar *Ramakien* epic and stories of the Buddha's many incarnations. A number of Chiang Mai shops also sell, besides the work of city artisans, the less refined silverwork of the hilltribes. Most tribes prefer silver to paper for money; the women usually wear their wealth in heavy chunky necklaces and earrings.

Just beyond the silver shops, farther out on the road to Chom Thong,

You can look an elephant in the eye at the pachyderm's training school north of Chiang Mai. Elephants are still used in the teak forests of the North, where the terrain is rugged and the loads are mammoth.

the traditional **lacquerware industry** still flourishes. Village artisans first shape bamboo strips into a framework. Over this frame, layers of lacquer must be applied, dried, and then polished with a special ash and clay compound. The artisans laboriously build up layer upon layer of lacquer to make a beautiful black and gold tray, plate, or bowl, or a brightly colored orange, green, and yellow container. The similarity to the lacquerware of Burma results from the cultural intermingling that has taken place in this area for centuries. Much of the antique lacquerware found on the market, in fact, comes from Burma.

Chiang Mai's **umbrella-making and silk-weaving areas** are centered east of the city, over the river and past the ungainly Railway Hotel. Except for the rice fields, the drive presents an almost European vignette with an old, tree-lined road, orchards, and distant mountains. After 9 km a left turn enters the one-street village of **Bor Sang**, where freshly dyed paper umbrellas dry in front of every other house, providing a visual feast for passersby. The homes double as shops selling handbags and brocaded shirts in addition to the cheerful-looking umbrellas which they manufacture in a true cottage industry.

Umbrella production begins with a cane stem carefully cut and trimmed by young men deft with their cleavers. Young girls form bamboo strips into frames, over which translucent paper locally made from a special tree is meticulously pasted. Some of the painters seem less careful, chatting or glancing over at the TV next door, as they sketch zigzags and rose patterns with a two-toned brush onto the translucent umbrellas.

Three kilometers beyond the turnoff to Bor Sang, silk and cotton weaving on traditional Thai looms occupies many women in the district town of **San Kamphaeng.** Here North Thailand's best-known craft is on display in shops that are a panoply of

shiny colors, orchestrated by the steady rattle of the hand looms in adjoining rooms. Apart from small modern additions, such as a piece of wire, or a nail, the looms have changed little in the past 50 years or more. Young girls frequently do the weaving, as a friend or a suitor lingers nearby. With concentration, a weaver produces about six meters of finished cloth per day. Only young eyes can function for long in the scant light that pierces the latticework of the bamboo walls which enclose the dirt-floored weaving area. Like the cloth shops in Pa Sang (see below), San Kamphaeng's stores are also full of former or hopeful beauty contestants.

Just east of San Kamphaeng one can stroll through the ruins of a pottery-making center where, 300 years ago, Chinese craftsmen fired a distinctive regional pottery called Sawankhalok pottery, the modern recreation of which is called **Thai celadon.** Clay and feldspar found in this area are particularly good for pottery making and give it its distinctive characteristics. Nowadays, such stoneware is again made at the Thai Celadon Factory on the Fang Road (several kilometers north of Chiang Mai) and at the Chiang Mai Sankalok Factory (in Chiang Mai). Tours of the former are conducted every day except on Monday. Here one can watch workers in faded blue shirts turn bowls, inscribe intricate designs on them, and then fire them to give the characteristic cracked look to the deep green or brown glazing. A small showroom offers a selection of pieces for sale.

A short drive about 13 km beyond San Kamphaeng takes you to Doi Saket where the lotus pond named Nong Bua is a favorite weekend retreat from Chiang Mai for *pai-tio.* An excellent new highway now continues from Doi Saket to Chiang Rai. This more than halves the driving time between Chiang Mai and Chiang Rai.

For the impecunious, **Pa Sang** 36 km south of Chiang Mai, specializes in less fine but equally eye-appealing **Thai cotton.** In an area reputed to have the most beautiful girls in Thailand, this village claims to have the prettiest of the lot. Local tailors will turn your silk or cotton purchases into clothes; ready-made shirts, blouses, and dresses can be picked up at bargain-basement prices in Chiang Mai or in the surrounding villages.

Not everything is sparkling new; Chiang Mai is also a treasure trove for the **antique hunter.** Those little metal weights in the shape of elephants and birds on sale in many shops are opium measures. Unhappily the plethora of antiques available in Chiang Mai is indicative of the economic misfortunes of neighboring Burma. Many of the antiques on sale here are smuggled from Burma to be exchanged on the black market for consumer goods.

Chiang Mai is the center of handicrafts in Thailand. A silversmith (left) hammers out paper-thin bowls covered with delicate designs; in the village of Bor Sang (above), paper umbrellas dry in the sun.

Be careful on the streets of Chiang Mai on April 13 and for several days thereafter, for a sudden deluge of water can fall on you despite clear blue skies. The reason behind the unexpected local downpour is Songkran, the Thai new year. Coming at the hottest part of the dry season, Songkran is celebrated especially enthusiastically in Chiang Mai when the weather is hottest and driest. How better to celebrate a dry season festival than by throwing water on everybody and anybody?

Chiang Mai has a wide variety of hotels, ranging from the luxurious Rincome, Suriwongse, and the Chiang Inn where doubles cost several hundred baht, down to the old-fashioned Station Hotel and the friendly guest houses where a pleasant room with bathroom is only 40 to 60 baht. Popular guest houses are Poung Keo (called "PK") and Saitum near the east moat, or the favorite of the budget traveler, Je T'aime, in a quiet setting across the river from the town center. Several new hotels have recently been constructed or are in the works. Indeed, Chiang Mai has become a buyer's market for hotels.

At night a busy band of food stalls by the old east gate to the city provide a long menu of some of the cheapest and tastiest food in Thailand. Darets restaurant has a tempting array of fruits to be fed through their blender for delicious iced drinks, and their watermelon and orange combination has to be tasted to be believed. Here too is the Thai-German dairy stall where the results of a successful attempt to introduce dairy produce to Thailand are sold. They always have a crowd of people in the morning, breakfasting on the best bacon and eggs in Southeast Asia.

Confusingly two of Chiang Mai's most popular eating places have the same name. If you glance back at those frenetic food stalls the one with the biggest crowds is Pat's. Perhaps it is due to their energetic waitresses who, if they see you heading towards another stall, will blithely rush out to steer you in the right direction, even taking your order at another stall then asking you to transfer. On the other side of the moat and a hundred or so meters north stands the other Pat's. This one is Pat's Tavern Grill and is a popular restaurant for those in need of Western nourishment or a well-stocked bar.

If you want some authenticity in your northern eating, then opt for Aroon Rai and its flanking restaurants on the other side of the moat for real northern Thai cuisine at very reasonable prices. But make sure a glass of water is at hand: such food can be fiery.

At the Rincome Hotel or at Old Chiang Mai one can enjoy a traditional *kantoke* dinner. Sitting on the floor around a low table, (from which the name comes) guests are served a variety of curries with the northern staple, glutinous rice, and exotic dances are performed while you dine.

Mae Sa Valley, 16 km north of Chiang Mai on Highway 1096 offers the peace of the northern hills. A number of bungalow complexes line the banks of the Mae Sa River. Further up the valley are the beautiful Mae Sa Waterfalls, a series of cataracts. There is also an elephant training camp and ample opportunity for long hikes into the surrounding hills.

Beware lest you are overtaken by the fate that befell Thomas Samuel who, at the start of the 17th century, was one of the first Westerners to visit the City of Flowers. His employers, the East India Company, ordered him several times to leave the city but Samuel had fallen in love with Chiang Mai, was taken prisoner when the Burmese invaded in 1615, and died in Burma.

A sienna sunset softens the lines on one of the most venerable temples in North Thailand, Wat Haripoonchai, in Lamphun. The oldest building is the gold-topped chedi, the base of which dates from the ninth century.

Chiang Mai has hotels and restaurants to suit the needs and tastes of all kinds of travelers.

Sidetrip to Lamphun

Several interesting sidetrips may be made from Chiang Mai. These include excursions to Lamphun, Mae Hong Son and Doi Inthanon, Fang, and the Chiang Rai area.

* * *

The road to **LAMPHUN**, situated 26 km south of Chiang Mai, leaves Chiang Mai across the Nawarat Bridge and then turns to follow the Ping River. About 4 km from the bridge, a turn on the right at the Shell station leads to a dirt road and a small diversion. The dirt road passes the five-tiered *chedi* of the Burmese-style Wat Chedi Liem, then goes by Wat Pa Peu on the right and finally arrives after 4 km at the gates of the **McKean Leprosarium.** There, several hundred lepers and their dependents receive treatment and care in a park-like setting on a secluded peninsula framed by the Ping and one of its tributaries. Visitors need not fear contagion.

Lamphun itself is famed for two old *wats*, attractive women, and young and fecund *lamyai* fruit trees. Located on the right bank of the Kuang River, a tributary of the Ping, the provincial town was once situated on the main road to Chiang Mai; but now a new highway bypasses Lamphun, which is perhaps a blessing in disguise, because the town has managed to preserve a mellow upcountry atmosphere, appropriate to its historical significance. Lamphun was once the seat of the Haripunjaya kingdom. On the site of the original palace now stands Wat Prathat Haripoonchai, on the left side of Lamphun's main street.

You should enter **Wat Prathat Haripoonchai** through its riverside entrance, because the temple faces that way. Large statues of lions guard its main entrances, overlooking the waters of the Kuang. Inside the large compound, monks study in a large

Buddhist school, set among the monuments and buildings which date as far back as the late 9th century. This makes the *wat* one of the most venerable in North Thailand. The base of the 50-meter-high gold-topped *chedi* in the center of the courtyard is the oldest structure in the temple. Ten centuries younger, but still respectably old, the gilded-roofed library stands to the left of a *sala* that shelters one of the largest bronze gongs in the world. The *sala* was restored in 1915 after damage by fire. The somewhat disorganized temple museum contains a representative sampling of several styles of old Buddhist art, including a rare silver Buddha head. Another small building close by is garishly illustrated with frescoes showing the good getting their reward and the bad their just deserts.

A kilometer west of Lamphun's old moat, stands **Wat Kukut,** also known as **Wat Chama Devi**, which has uninteresting buildings, but a pair of unusual *chedi*s. The larger *chedi* consists of five tiers, each of which contains three niches, each holding a Buddha statue — making an impressive display of 15 Buddha images on each side, or 60 Buddhas in all gazing from their ancient domicile. This *chedi* is thought to have been built by Chama Devi, the fabled princess of Lop Buri and queen of Lamphun.

Before leaving Lamphun province, fruit lovers and horticulturists may visit **TONKHAM** village to see the "10,000-baht *lamyai* tree" which annually nets its owner that handsome sum through the sale of its fruit and seeds.

The trip to Lamphun can also be combined with a visit to **PA SANG,** about 12 km southwest of Lamphun on Road 106, which is the center for cotton weaving around Chiang Mai.

Wat Chama Devi
วัดจามเทวี

Wat Kukut
วัดกู่กุฏ

A young monk (above, center), taking a stroll with two companions. Many Thai men become novitiates at an early age, and almost all of them become monks for a short period of time sometime in their life to study Buddhist scriptures. Frothy Mae Klang Waterfall (right), in Doi Inthanon Park, is one of the numerous picturesque cascades in the North; paths in the park lead up to panoramic views.

Sidetrip to Hot and Mae Hong Son

Mae Klang Waterfall
น้ำตกแม่กลาง

Pakau Na Waterfall
น้ำตกพระโกนา

13. Doi Inthanon
National Park
อุทยานแห่งชาติดอยอินทนนท์

Doi Inthanon
ดอยอินทนนท์

From Chiang Mai, Thai Airways several times weekly offers a bumpy, 40-minute flight over cloud-covered hills to **MAE HONG SON.** By land, a bus leaves Chiang Mai Gate daily at around 7:00 a.m. for the 11-hour, 368-km horseshoe journey, which passes through Hot and Mae Sariang, then goes north through jungle, past the Shan settlement of Khun Yuam, to arrive at Mae Hong Son by dusk. However, you are more flexible in a car, and if time does not allow you to make the full trip to Mae Hong Son, you can drive down to Hot and back in a leisurely half-day.

By road, the excursion to Mae Hong Son heads south from Chiang Mai on Road 108, and just before the 57-km-stone turns right and goes 10 km to the entrance of **DOI IN-THANON NATIONAL PARK,** named after its prime attraction, Doi Inthanon, the highest mountain in the country at 2,596 meters. Girls rush out to sell bead necklaces, and cold beer is served in small shops on the river's edge below **MAE KLANG WATERFALL.** From the shops you walk up 20 meters to see this powerful cataract and its loud fusion of muddy brown water and white spray. Clearly marked footpaths branch up the rocky hills; one leads around a corner of boulders to a full view of the wider falls, **PAKAU NA,** which slides over its broad, craggy slopes for 120 meters like a liquid highway. Another path weaves up to nearby Doi Hua Chang which provides helicopter views of the broad farmlands south of Chiang Mai. On the leafy dome of Hua Chang plants quiver in the humid heat. The peak of Doi Inthanon hides behind a curtain of clouds 25 km away; you can glimpse sections of the new road which climbs to the signal station on its summit.

DOI INTHANON is a limestone knob in the long geological range that

stretches southeast from Yunnan in southern China and resurfaces as far south as Irian Jaya. But Doi Inthanon, Thailand's tallest peak, is a mere foothill in this southern extension of the Himalayan range. The trumpeting of work-elephants still echoes from the slopes of Inthanon, where Karen and Meo tribesmen dwell in isolated villages. They have been slowly moving out, as the mountain is now a national reserve.

By making prior arrangements with park authorities in Chiang Mai, you can take a three- to five-day hike on foot or by pony up the mountain. Simple campsites along the route are maintained by the Wildlife Association, affording simple accommodation for trekkers. During the climb you can observe rare birds and enjoy nature under a broad canopy of trees. Rather than a barren peak, the summit is lightly forested, complete with picnic tables.

At the 58-km-stone on Road 108, which is about 1 km south of the park turnoff, lies the town of **CHOM THONG.** The town's distinction rests with elegant **Wat Phra Thai Si Chom Thong,** where glints of subdued light accentuate an unusually beautiful collection of bronze Buddhas. The monastery creaks with old age, as the slumping boughs of its courtyard trees do. The Burmese-style *chedi* dates from 1451, and the sanctuary itself was built by only 50 years later. The broad stairway leading to a facade of wood carvings is actually the back entrance.

A large *prang,* carved deeply with a profusion of floral patterns entwined with birds and *naga* serpents, dominates this temple compound. Four standing Buddhas, clothed like celestial kings, flank the *prang.* Although much of the decoration in the temple reflects the Burmese penchant for elaboration, the

North Thailand is rich in teak, and the temples of the region are usually adorned with intricately carved and gilded pieces of wood. Wat Phra Thai Si Chom Thong (above) is noted for its elegance, as well as for its collection of bronze Buddha images. The temple's Burmese-style chedi *dates from the mid-15th century, and the sanctuary is only a little less ancient. Splendid woodcarvings and Burmese decorations abound in the compound.*

Ancient Hot
ฮอดเดิม

Wang Lung
วังหลัง

15. Hot
ฮอด (ตัวเมือง, อำเภอ)

central Buddha image with its protective *naga* seems extremely Thai, and resembles the famed image at Wat Prasingh in Chiang Mai. On either side of the *prang* stand enshrined collections of miniature gold and silver Buddha images, some bejeweled and metallic, others carved of crystal.

Continuing south on Road 108, you will see many northern touches: rambling, stylized elephants carved on the back of bullock carts; *lamyai* trees and green bean-patches; giant plaited baskets which farmers use to thresh harvested rice; and shady, thatched-roof *sala*s dotting the rice fields.

HOT, lying 88 km southwest of Chiang Mai on Road 108, seems like the preview of a new town yet to come. Hot once lay 15 km farther south at the mouth of the Ping River, until the rising reservoir behind the Bhumibol Dam submerged its site. Shop houses,

hotels, and restaurants were constructed hastily in this new town.

Farther south on Road 1012 lies the **site of ancient Hot.** Cracked, rain-washed *chedi*s dot the landscape like dignified relics from the time when Hot was part of the early kingdoms of the North. Excavations at these sites have unearthed gold jewelry, amulets, and lively stucco carvings, now on display in the Chiang Mai Museum.

Road 1012 goes on to **WANG LUNG** a tiny village that earns its keep by selling dried fish caught in the catchment area created by Bhumibol Dam. Karen people have settled much of this area. Their necks hidden by a profusion of black beads, and their bodices covered with thick, colored patchwork, Karen tribeswomen walk into the tiny town to buy provisions.

You can hire a boat at Wang Lung for an hour's ride among the bamboo- and reed-covered islands at

Karen girls at Hot decorate their daily dress with black-bead necklaces and novel bracelets made of white shirt buttons.

the estuary of the Mae Ping and out onto the vast expanse of water at the upper end of the reservoir. Reflections of ruined *chedi*s and strangely eroded cliffs enliven remote mountain scenes; but unless you speak Thai you will need a guide.

From Hot, Road 108 strikes out west across the Chaem River, following its right bank toward Mae Sariang. About 17 km from Hot, the road passes **OB LUANG GORGE,** called Thailand's version of the Grand Canyon, though it could be considered so only in miniature. Stop at the *sala* for a look into the deep, ragged incision in rock, cut over the ages by the river.

After the gorge, the road continues to wriggle like a belly dancer. Butterflies and plumed blossoms brighten the way. Lovers of hot springs should turn left 4 km after the gorge and drive another 5 km to reach a lonely sulfur spring with a

small campsite. Chances are nobody will be there.

The drive to the Mae Sariang district seat is more exciting than the town itself. The road goes like a roller coaster over the mountains. Not even motorbikes can reach the small leaf-and-bamboo huts tucked away in these hills. Most of the villages in the area belong to the Skaw Karen, one of the largest groups of hillpeople in Thailand, who have settled all the way down the Thai-Burmese frontier as far south as Chumphon. In the moist valleys they plant wet rice on steep terraces. The nomadic Karen burn away the forest to make clearings to plant new crops. This slash-and-burn technique has scarred the mountainsides and caused extensive erosion. On the slopes, black tree stumps stand out like whiskers on a green background of rice sprouts. In places the road skirts around high banks of red earth. Fresh mounds of

16. Ob Luang Gorge

Incised in rock over the ages, Ob Luang Gorge (above, left) has been perhaps optimistically dubbed Thailand's Grand Canyon. On past, the road to Mae Sariang traverses hilly terrain, hugging the slopes, and affords tranquil views of Karen villages (above, right). Giant stone lions (facing page) flank a forgotten stairway leading up to the hilltop temple of Doi Kong Mou, above the remote and serene little town of Mae Hong Son.

mud on the asphalt show that land-slides are not uncommon, because the banks cannot always hold back the runoff. The solution to this problem is the pine tree. Though it is not the tree one associates with tropical Thailand, the pine is well suited for re-building the soil. Its roots form an extensive earth-holding network un-derground, and its seeds do not burn. Before reaching the highest point on the road (at about 1,130 meters) on the way to Mae Sariang, you pass the Thai-Danish Reforestation Camp which resembles a tropical Christmas tree farm.

Hemmed in by mountains, **MAE SARIANG** lies 103 km west of Hot at the bend where Road 108 curves north. Only a Burmese-style temple and Karen handicraft shops distin-guish this small district seat and border trading post.

Road 108 continues north on a ough track from Mae Sariang

through mountain scenery that is among the most breathtaking in Thailand, reaching **MAE HONG SON** 171 km later. Mae Hong Son fits into Thailand like the overlooked last piece of a jigsaw puzzle. Secluded by jungle ridges and framed on the north and west by the Shan states of Burma, the province peacefully bene-fits from years of relative neglect by the outside world. This is the place for seekers of old-world serenity. The presence of Karen, Meo, Lawa, Shan, Lisu, Lahu, and Burmese, all of whom easily outnumber the ethnic Thais, adds intrigue to the ill-kept secret that Mae Hong Son lies on bor-der smuggling routes.

The town bustles only in the early morning. By 7:30 a.m., when half the market is deserted, sellers busily pack their bunches of long beans, dried fish, chips of fried pig skin, cabbages, carrot-size chilies, cheroot tobacco, and betel nut. By

Sidetrip to Fang

8:00 a.m. the market has emptied. Over the town's small buildings loom the deep-green mountains, which are separated by hidden valley hollows. Some of the peaks are usually obscured by heavy clouds or dark gray curtains of falling rain.

A commanding view of the town of Mae Hong Son and the surrounding countryside is afforded from Doi Kongmou which lies about 250 meters above the habitation. At night, the *chedis* of **Wat Phrathat Doi Kongmou** atop the hill light up like timid beacons of civilization in this remote corner of Thailand.

To return overland to Chiang Mai, you must retrace your steps on Road 108 via Mae Sariang and Hot. There will eventually be a shorter route on a surfaced road through Pai to Mae Taeng 40 km north of Chiang Mai. A Thai Airways flight can also return you to Chiang Mai, completing this northern excursion.

To reach the border outpost of **FANG** take Road 107 north from Chiang Mai (beginning at the Elephant Gate), past the Thai Celadon Factory and continuing on to Mae Rim, 13 km from Chiang Mai. Left from Mae Rim is the drive to **MAE SA WATERFALL.** At the nearby royal *sala* the Thai government occasionally stages performances of working elephants in preparation for visits by the royal family and their guests.

Road 107 continues north through rice fields and small villages. Up ahead on the right one can see the outline of Chiang Dao Mountain. Slowly, the road leaves flat farmland, enters the Mae Ping Gorge, then follows the river's right bank through scenic countryside. About 60 km from Chiang Mai on Road 107, a dirt road branches left and goes to **DOI CHIANG DAO,** which is at an elevation of 2,186 meters. You need a jeep or a scrambler motorcycle to negoti-

21. Fang
ฝาง

19. Mae Sa Waterfall
น้ำตกแม่สา

20. Doi Chiang Dao
ดอยเชียงดาว

Non-Thai peoples, such as this woman and child (above, left) from a rare hilltribe subgroup, outnumber the ethnic Thais in Mae Hong Son, adding to the distinctive charm of the place. Fractured light (above, right) filters through a hole in the grotto roof of Chiang Dao cave, north of Chiang Mai. Visitors can take local transportation (opposite) for a breathtaking boat trip through the rapids on the river between Chiang Rai and Tha Thon.

20. Chiang Dao Cave
ถ้ำเชียงดาว

ate this 9-km-long track which emerges at a lookout spot 1,000 meters up on the mountainside. From the government station there, officials trek out to assist hilltribes living on the slopes of Doi Chiang Dao and the neighboring mountains. At the near-by nursery, horticulturists experiment with new strains of tea that someday may be cultivated throughout the region. The government's agricultural aid on Doi Chiang Dao is aimed at eradicating opium cultivation.

Farther north on Road 107 is the town of Chiang Dao, located 72 km from Chiang Mai; at the end of town a dirt road leads off to the left going 6 km to **CHIANG DAO CAVE.** Buddha statues and a small white *chedi* with many spires grace the cave site.

After visiting the cave, the drive goes on to **FANG,** located 152 km from Chiang Mai. The district around Fang combines the elements of the Wild West with the mysteries of the East. During the 1950s the district witnessed a "black-gold rush," following a minor discovery of crude oil; but production never matched expectation. Now the only get-rich-quick gamble is illegal, dangerous, and reprehensible: smuggling opium. Located on the Burmese border adjacent to the infamous Golden Triangle, Fang is a natural conduit for opium. To help seal off an otherwise hopelessly porous border, the government allowed remnants of Chiang Kai-shek's Kuomintang Army to settle in Fang and act as an auxiliary border patrol. The Hunanese-speaking soldiers fled China in the late 1940s.

Dressed in distinctively embroidered clothing, Yao hilltribes also live in the mountains around Fang. The women wear black hats decorated with red or magenta woolen balls, while babies carried on their mothers' backs sport little embroidered

Sidetrip to Chiang Rai

caps. Young girls may spend an entire year embroidering large pantspanels for their weddings. To appreciate the meaning and cultural context of this handicraft, read Jacqueline Butler's *Yao Embroidery*.

The government has worked extensively with the Yao, promoting crops as substitutes for the more lucrative opium. One Yao headman, leader of a 15-house village, proudly listed his new produce: potatoes, corn, garlic, chickens, and pigs. His eyes widened as he happily described the size of the breeding pig presented to the village by the king. About 8 km northeast of Fang is an agricultural station near the hot springs of Baw Nam Rawn.

From Fang a rough road leads north 24 km to **THA THON** on the Burmese border, where you can rent a boat for a five- to six-hour exciting journey down the Mae Kok River to Chiang Rai.

After visiting Fang, you may want to continue exploring the far northern crown of Thailand, tucked between Burma and Laos — the area which is called the Golden Triangle. As the crow flies, **CHIANG RAI** lies only 65-odd km to the east of Fang; but at present Road 1001, which wriggles east from below Fang through Mae Suai toward Chiang Rai, is unsurfaced and in poor condition. This means that a sidetrip to Chiang Rai begins in Chiang Mai, the focal point for the North.

Chiang Rai is linked to Chiang Mai by air; each day Thai Airways flies from Bangkok to Chiang Rai, with a stopover at Chiang Mai. Otherwise, the standard way to Chiang Rai is via Route 1, which continues north from Lampang.

Route 1 twists around and over mountains on its way to **NGAO** 81 km northeast of Lampang. At the highest point in the road, below twin

22. Tha Thon
ท่าทอน

23. Ngao
งาว (ตัวเมือง, อำเภอ)

On the road from Lampang to Ngao: spirit houses cluster at the highest point in the road (right); a recess at the FIO elephant school (above); finally, limestone formations in Tham Pha Thai cave (facing page).

rocky peaks, drivers stop, or if in a hurry just blow their horns or *wai,* to pay respects to the *phi*s believed to inhabit the pass. Scores of spirit houses, some simple like farmers' houses, others as elaborate as the Marble Temple, cluster along the roadside.

Teak saplings line Route 1 between Lampang and Ngao, thanks to the Forest Industry Organization (FIO). The FIO also runs an elephant training school about 54 km from Lampang, 1½ km west of the highway behind Pang-la village. Visitors can watch the mahouts put their young pachyderms through mounting, marching, and log-dragging drills until noon. If made to train beyond noon, the elephants stamp their feet in protest until they are allowed to lumber off to their stalls for a snack of sugar cane.

About 19 km before the district town of Ngao, a left turn leads in less than 1 km to a small grove of teak trees and a refreshment stand that mark the entrance to **THAM PHA THAI** probably the most interesting cave in Thailand. The climb up to the cave covers 283 concrete steps, some broken by roots or rocks, past the monks' quarters, to the huge arched entrance to the grotto. In front of the entrance stands a white *chedi*; a gilded Buddha image inside sits near the sunlit edge. Most striking, though, is the colossal stalagmite rising like a white explosion from a sea of limestone. Often a young novice monk will lead visitors down into the cave and point out bizarre limestone formations which, with a little imagination, can resemble a throne, a rabbit, or a turtle. Slithering green snakes wrap themselves around electric wires or coil up in crevices. The novice guide explains that these snakes are protected and have never bitten anyone. The 400-

meter walk into the cave ends at a small mound of bat guano. Light streaks down from a jagged opening in the cave roof, projecting the silhouettes of flying bats onto the cavern walls.

About 12 km before Ngao, on the left of Route 1, Burmese-style **Wat Chong Kram** exudes charm in the face of alarming decrepitude. The ceiling is gradually becoming more crooked as its supporting pillars sink into the mud; as one guidebook has advised, "See it before it falls down!"

Route 1 continues through Ngao and then goes 49 km farther to **PHAYAO,** a district town lying on the eastern shore of a shallow lake at the foot of a 1,700-meter-high mountain. Although quite small and outwardly undistinguished, Phayao holds interest for archaeologists, as the town was rebuilt in the 11th century on a more ancient deserted site. Judging from the remains of a moat

and eight city gates which enclose an area measuring about 2 km square, scholars believe the older site may predate the Bronze Age. Between the lake and the road, as you leave Phayao, sits **Wat Si Khom Kham,** considered by scholars the most important temple in the area for its 400-year-old, 16-meter-high Buddha image inside a *viharn*. Local legend claims that a *naga* king in disguise gave a young couple gold for sculpting this large image.

From Phayao Route 1 continues north 94 km to the provincial capital of **CHIANG RAI,** located in Thailand's northernmost province, at an elevation of about 580 meters. Although linked to Bangkok 940 km away by daily Thai Airways flights, and strategically important because of its location near the borders with Burma and Laos, Chiang Rai has taken the slow path to commercial development. King Mangrai who

Wat Si Khom Kham
วัดศรีคมคำ

Wat Chong Kram
วัดช่องคราม

25. Chiang Rai
เชียงราย (ตัวเมือง, จังหวัด)
24. Phayao
พะเยาว์ (ตัวเมือง, อำเภอ)

Upcountry buses go almost everywhere (above), sometimes at hair-raising speeds, passing such rural sights as this pack of elephants slowly commuting to work. A closeup of Yao embroidery (right) shows the intricate and colorful patterns which the hilltribe women excel in making to decorate their clothes. Tribal embroidery is now being used by many high-fashion designers in Bangkok boutiques and makes an excellent souvenir of the North.

26. Mae Chan
แม่จัน (ตัวเมือง, อำเภอ)

Wat Prasingh
วัดพระสิงห์

Wat Phra Keo
วัดพระแก้ว

also established Chiang Mai as a walled city, founded Chiang Rai in 1262. Legend claims that the king decided to conquer regions south of his seat of empire located at Chiang Saen after his favorite elephant ran away in a southerly direction. The search for the elephant led to the banks of the Kok River, where the king decided to build Chiang Rai. A statue of King Mangrai now stands north of Chiang Rai along the road to Mae Chan.

Two temples in Chiang Rai are of interest: Wat Prasing and Wat Phra Keo. Both share the distinction of having once sheltered famous images. The *chedi* and *viharn* at **Wat Prasingh,** where legend holds that an important Theravada image was located, have been restored too many times to allow accurate dating, but documents suggest the 15th century or earlier. **Wat Phra Keo,** situated behind Wat Prasingh, is believed to

have been the original residence of the Emerald Buddha which is now in Bangkok at the royal temple of the same name. To the west of Wat Phra Keo rises Ngam Muang Hill. Inside the *wat* atop the hill, a reliquary is believed to contain the bones of King Mangrai, placed there by one' of his sons.

From Chiang Rai, Road 110 goes 29 km north to **MAE CHAN.** (Check on road conditions.) Formerly a center for silverwork, the tiny district town now serves as a trading post for Akha and Yao hillpeople who sell their goods and buy manufactured items. You can still view some silver and other tribal handicrafts at the shops of Lao Tzan, a Yao merchant, and Lao Taa, who is half Lisu and half Haw Chinese (like the Kuomintang soldiers).

More about Hilltribes

About 2km beyond Mae Chan, a dirt road on the left off Road 110 leads through a valley noted for its fragrant rice, and then ascends to Doi Thong (or "The Flag Mountain"). From the Mae Kam community development station on the mountain, government officials go out to assist local hillpeople in agricultural and village projects. The trail leading from the Mae Kam center continues on to Ko Saen Chai, an **Akha village.** Considered to be among the least sophisticated of the hilltribes, the Akha nevertheless seem to have beaten the West in one trend: Akha women were wearing miniskirts long before they became fashionable elsewhere. The Akha, who inhabit Thailand only in Chiang Rai province, build characteristic wooden swings and hold swinging ceremonies around their New Year to bring good luck and to enhance the fertility of the soil. Akha women embroider their black shirts and hats with bright cloth beads and silver ornaments.

Chiang Rai province hosts, besides the Akha, other hilltribe groups: the Yao, the Blue and White Meo, Lisu, Lahu, Lahu Shi, and Skaw and P'wo Karen. Each main group speaks its own language, and follows animist customs (based on a belief in spirits) as well as adhering to other more recently adopted religious beliefs. Most of the tribes came to Thailand from China via Burma and Laos within the last 100 years. The Meo are probably the best known of these hillpeoples, partly due to the proximity of several Meo villages to Chiang Mai, and also because of the tribal insurgency in the 1960s known as the Meo War.

Basically shy and clannish, the hillpeople tend to settle at specific altitudes, some building villages only above 1,000 meters. Although members of some tribes have embraced

Akha village
หมู่บ้านชาวเขาอาข่า

At Mae Kam community development center, the government assists the hilltribe people living nearby. Among them are an Akha boy (above), a Yao girl with her little brother (right), and Lisu girls (facing page).

Lahu
ลาฮู

Karen
กะเหรี่ยง

Yao
เย้า

Meo
แม้ว

Lisu
ลีซู (หรือ ลีซอ)

Islam, Buddhism, or Christianity in response to missionary work, most retain strong animist convictions. They protect their homes and villages with altars, fertility symbols, totems, and objects of sympathetic magic (including model airplanes), to ward off evil spirits.

About 70,000 **Karen** in Thailand live in Mae Hong Son, Chiang Mai, Chiang Rai, and Lamphun. They are of Tibeto-Burman stock. Many are Christians and have beliefs bearing some resemblance to early Christianity, leading to speculation about their origin and antiquity which remains a mystery. The Karen are endogamous and matrilineal.

Nearly 20,000 **Lisu,** also of Tibeto-Burman origin, live in North Thailand going as far south as Tak, where one group lives near a Black Lahu tribe. Different hilltribes often live peacefully in close proximity. The Lisu come originally from the upper

reaches of the Salween River. The Lisu are patrilineal and have strong animist beliefs; each village has a folk healer and exorcist *(tongpa)*. Along with the Meo, the Lisu have been major opium cultivators.

The **Lahu** are famed for their hunting skills. Some groups reportedly recognize a "man-god" who must qualify himself through physical and magical feats. **Yao** villages celebrate the Chinese lunar new year by slaughtering a pig, drinking great quantities of rice wine, and making merry for days. The **Meo** practice a courting ritual in which boys and girls standing in separate lines throw balls to each other to "break the ice."

Gradually all the tribes are assimilating Thai culture through trade contacts and education in *nikhorn* ("settlement") schools built by the government. The sale of their crafts has improved the economics of many

Apex of the
Golden Triangle

of the tribes. Organizations like the Thai Hill-Crafts Foundation (with offices in Bangkok and Chiang Rai) and the Border Patrol Police have found domestic and foreign markets for the colorful and distinctive tribal crafts. Many shops in Bangkok and other cities sell hilltribe jewelry, embroidery, shoulder bags, and weaving.

From Mae Chan Road 101 continues 34 km due north to **MAE SAI** at the northernmost point in Thailand. Mae Sai and Chiang Saen lie at the apex of the Golden Triangle. This district on the frontier does a thriving business selling a variety of goods, especially shoes, to Burmese who cross the border on shopping sprees. Many Thais from Chiang Rai *pai-tio* in Mae Sai and browse over smuggled items from Laos and Burma. Supplies of liquor and cigarettes from Laos have dwindled, although gems still arrive from Burma.

On returning south toward Mae Chan, a swing northeast on Road 1010 goes to the ancient capital of **CHIANG SAEN.** Scholars believe the town was founded around the end of the 13th century and strongly fortified about 100 years later. The Burmese captured it in the 16th century, but the first king of the Chakri dynasty later recaptured it. Fearing history would repeat itself with another Burmese invasion, however, Rama I ordered the town destroyed. Chiang Saen remained deserted until the reign of Rama V, and in 1957 the town became a district seat. Chiang Saen's lovely setting on the Mekong River strongly enhances the charm of its old temples. Just west of the town stands **Wat Pa Sak,** whose name derives from the use of 300 teak *(sak)* trunks for the original enclosure. The temple's foundation was laid in 1295 during the reign of King Ramkamhaeng. Earlier Srivichaya and Dva-

28. Chiang Saen
เชียงแสน (ตัวเมือง, อำเภอ)
27. Mae Sai
แม่สาย (ตัวเมือง, อำเภอ) •

Wat Pa Sak
วัดป่าสัก

This merchant in Mae Chan (above, left) still sells handsome silver bracelets by weight, in the traditional way; the far north offers a multitude of bargains in fine handicrafts and Thai and Burmese antiques. In a pond near the ancient city of Chiang Saen (above, right), local fishermen employ a small-scale version of the same poled nets used traditionally along the distant shores of the Gulf of Thailand to the south.

ravati influences, along with the predominant Sukhothai style, are evident in the *that* ("reliquary"), the clothing of the deities, and in the stucco walking Buddhas. Located about 1 km west of the town gate, **Wat Prathat Chom Kitti** occupies a hill commanding a good view of Chiang Saen. Local chronicles suggest that the old *that* with a leaning top was first built around the 10th century and subsequently restored at least twice. Below this temple lies a ruined *chedi* in **Wat Chom Chang.** From there a staircase leads farther downhill toward town. Close to the western gate of town stand **Wat Chedi Luang** and a branch of the National Museum. The 60-meter-tall 13th-century *chedi* stands out in style as well as size; its bricks rise from an octagonal base to a bell-shaped top. In the grounds of the museum one can see a good assortment of bronze Buddhas and other Chiang Saen art.

The most scenic return trip from Chiang Saen to Chiang Rai is via water in a long-tail boat down the Mekong River as far as **CHIANG KHONG,** a three-hour trip after the rainy season when the river is high. Be sure to check on security conditions before setting out. The river follows an approximately S-shaped path, first flowing southeast to the mouth of the Kok River, then curving north between beautiful mountains, then finally south again for 20 thrilling kilometers down deep narrow sections, through rapids and eddies beneath steep, jungled mountainsides. At Chiang Khong, the river widens slightly. Set on left-bank hills, the Laotian town of **BAN HOUEI SAI** lies opposite the Chiang Khong district seat. Laotian government officials still work in fortifications built by the French who named the town Fort Carnot. Until recently, relations between Thailand and Laos were

A Buddha image (left) in the small museum at Chiang Saen displays the style of that period: Chinese features and curled hair. The ghostly ramparts of a French citadel (above) guard Ban Houei Sai in Laos.

Excursion through the Nan Valley

cordial, and a ferry carried visitors across the river to Ban Houei San. The town proper has few sights to offer other than watching the hilltribe people coming back and forth to visit the market and hospital here. Nevertheless, this trip used to be popular due to the availability of daily flights from Ban Houei San to the beautiful royal capital at Luang Prabang, with connections onward to Vientiane, and then back into northeast Thailand. Unfortunately, this free movement ceased when tension arose between Bangkok and the new Pathet Lao government.

From Chiang Khong Road 1021 goes to Thoeng; Road 1020 then returns to the provincial capital of Chiang Rai.

From Chiang Rai, one can continue eastward across North Thailand toward **NAN.** One must follow Route 1 cross-country from the provincial capital south through Phayao and on to Ngao, where road 103 branches southwest to the Song and Rong Kwang districts of Phrae province. Phrae province, which was once notorious for its hired gunmen, is now better known for its tobacco plantations. At Rong Kwang, Road 101 heads northeast 96 km to Nan. Taxis travel this route taking passengers who disembarked from the train in Den Chai for Phrae and Nan. Nan is now linked by air with Chiang Mai about five times a week on a shuttle that touches down at Phitsanulok.

Road 101 winds through sparsely settled hills and teak reserves. You may see some elephants dragging logs alongside the road. The government, through reforestation, is trying to reduce dependence on teak imports, but the trees take long to grow. Beyond Sa District, 24 km before Nan, the road begins to parallel the Nan River flowing southward a few kilo-

31. Nan
น่าน (ตัวเมือง, จังหวัด)

meters to the east. The fertile Nan valley supports rice and corn. The provincial capital, seat of an independent kingdom until this century, lies on the right bank of the river.

Nan's town walls were rebuilt in 1857 to replace the original walls destroyed in a severe flood 40 years earlier. The walls are roughly circular, indicating Mon influence in the late 14th century, when the town was established. The first recorded settlement of Nan province dates back to 1282 when Khun Fong, brother of the founder of Vientiane, set up a court in Wora Nakhon, 70 km north of the present provincial capital. Nan's inaccessibility helped it remain relatively free, although it did fall occasionally under the sway of Chiang Mai, the Burmese (for 200 years), and other powers — until 1931 when the province came fully under the control of Bangkok. The presence of Thai Army soldiers in Nan indicates that there are security problems in the remote districts. Nan town, though, is safe. The Thevarat Hotel has air-conditioned rooms although Nan is usually cool. Around 5:00 a.m. the main market begins to bustle; look for rattan products, famous Nan tangerines, and crafts sold by Yao women. Just south of the *sala klang* government offices stands the town's most interesting temple, **Wat Phumin,** built in 1596 and extensively restored in the 19th century. The carved doors are nearly comparable to the famous doors of the *viharn* of Bangkok's Wat Suthat (now kept in the National Museum). Although the *wat's* murals were inexpertly restored, they tell an interesting story of the kingdom, with scenes depicting the arrival of foreigners, and even some bawdy comic portrayals. Inside the unusual cross-shaped hall are four gilded stucco images facing the cardinal directions.

The isolated but rice-rich Nan valley (left) was once the center of an early independent kingdom; not until 1931 did the Bangkok government gain full control of the province. Nan boasts many venerable temples, such as Wat Phumin (above), which is perhaps the most famous in the area. Inside the temple, murals tell stories of the ancient kingdom, including the arrival of foreigners and even a few bawdy portrayals thrown in for comic relief.

The "Elephant-Supported Temple" or **Wat Chang Kham** is located in what was the center of the old walled city, now opposite the provincial administrative offices. Actually, it is an old *chedi* supported by elephant buttresses, seven elephants per side under the second tier of the base. A Nan prince built the *viharn* in 1547. Two walking and one standing Buddha images in front of the main altar are good examples of the Sukhothai style. An inscription dated 1547 records the installation of the *viharn*'s principal image in that year. On the reverse side is a prophecy about the fifth (future) Buddha, Sri Ariyametteya Bodhisattva.

Two life-size Sukhothai Buddhas, dated 1427, reside in **Wat Phya Phu**. One bears an inscription telling that it was cast in the fourth lunar month of that year. The total of five similar images at both *wats* was chosen to ensure that the then prince would be reborn as a man in the lifetime of the future fifth Buddha, and also to attest that Buddhism would last 5,000 years.

Wat Suan Tan, the only temple in the North with a *prang* (rounded ornate spire), also features an interesting 500-year-old bronze seated Buddha in its *viharn*. In 1450, the conquering King Tiloka of Chiang Mai gave the people of Nan seven days to collect enough metal for a new image, then he set a 100-day deadline for refugee Sukhothai artists to fashion it. The image is called *Phra Khao Thong Thip*.

Across the river from Wat Suan Tan, 3 km southeast of town on a small hill, sits **Wat Chae Haeng**. There, during the fourth lunar month, Nan residents hold a boisterous fair, complete with fireworks. The temple's name, meaning "to soak the parched," refers to an incident in the life of Buddha which the pious believe

Wat Chang Kham
วัดช้างค้ำ

Wat Suan Tan
วัดสวนตาล

Wat Chae Haeng
วัดแช่แห้ง

Wat Phya Phu
วัดหญ้าภู่

predicted that this spot would shelter relics.

Southwest of town, down a dirt track off Road 101, **Wat Khao Noi** affords a good view of Nan from a small mountain. A golden parasol tops the old Chiang Saen *chedi* there. This temple hosts an annual fair in the sixth lunar month.

Those who are not deterred by the sight of passing military convoys filled with weapon-toting troops can venture 60 km north of Nan town to to the district of **PHUA.** There, missionaries and civil servants, including a district officer with a price on his head, attend to the needs of several thousand people from the hilltribes and other ethnic minorities living in resettlement camps. The government has relocated these people to isolate them from insurgents, but life in the Phua valley does not particularly suit hillpeople.

A more scenic and relaxed side-trip goes south from Nan on Road 101 to Sa, then on the dirt road due south to Na Noi. A few kilometers beyond Na Noi lies **SAO DIN CANYON,** a small but striking arrangement of wind-carved rock, used as a film setting in many Thai movies. From the canyon, return to Road 101, pass the junction with Road 103 at Rong Kwang and drive 31 km to **PHRAE.** There, located on Road 1022 about 8 km east of town is **Wat Prathat Cho Mae,** on a small hill surrounded by orchards. The high-ceilinged *viharn* and parts of the courtyard were recently renovated.

From Phrae Road 101 follows the Yom River. Around Sung Men you may see hundreds of people digging and panning for gems, when news or rumors of new finds send them scurrying in search of instant wealth. About 10 km beyond Sung Men lies Den Chai. From there the shortest way to Uttaradit, the next provincial town, is by train. By car you have to take Road 101 to Si Satchanalai, then turn east on Road 102 for a total of just over 130 km to reach Uttaradit.

Most of the buildings in **UTTA-RADIT** seem new, and they are. A fire in 1967 burned most of the city to the ground. From Uttaradit town, which lies between the rail line and the Nan River, you can travel east 55 km to **SIRIKIT DAM,** named after the queen. Completed in 1973, the dam generates power and provides great amounts of sorely needed water during the dry season to farms around Uttaradit. Below the dam, near Pak Pat village, stands the tallest teak tree in Thailand.

From Uttaradit one could begin a trip to the Northeast, by going to Sukhothai and taking Road 12 east through Phitsanulok to Lom Sak, then going north on Road 203 to Loei. Or from Sukhothai you can return to Bangkok by continuing down Road 101 to Kamphang Phet, then picking up Route 1 for the rest of the way south to the capital.

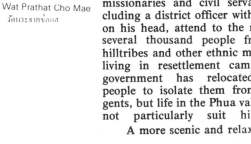

A monk poses pensively beside the beautifully carved doors of Wat Phumin in Nan (left). Hardly a stone has been left unturned or a hill unexplored in the gem country just southwest of Phrae (above).

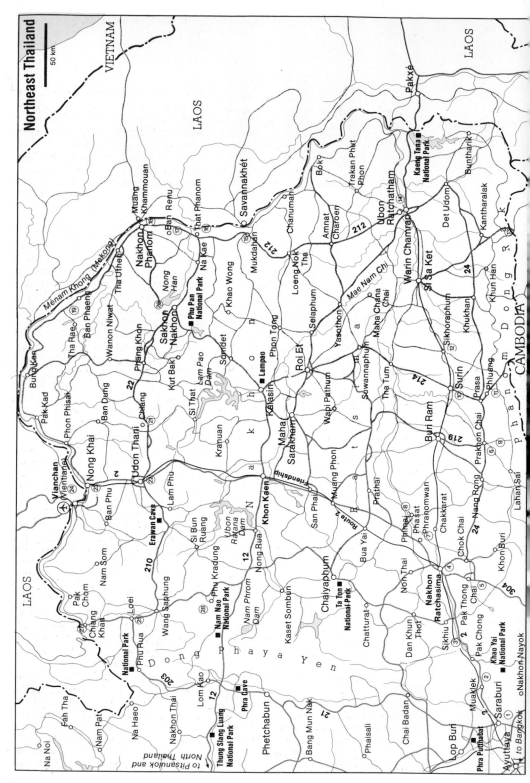

Northeast Thailand

50 km

214

Thailand's age-old problem area, the Northeast is now undergoing many changes and the future is brighter.

A Thai village of little romantic appeal: a tired-looking, dusty place where a few scrawny chickens peck in the shade of mean houses; not the sort of place likely to appear on any picture postcard. It is all too characteristic of hundreds of other villages in the Northeast, a region other Thais call *Issan*, and one that has been Thailand's chronic problem area, where nature and neglect have combined for too long to make life hard for the gentle-natured inhabitants. Many of them of Lao extraction, whose ancestors drifted across the great Mekong River which forms the natural border today, they retain the Lao quality of sweet passivity in the face of adversity. Historically, they have had ample opportunity to put the quality to use, for the Northeast has not been an easy place to live. The soil is thin and infertile, producing as much dissatisfaction as crops; there is either not enough rain or too much, and the Mekong can be a terror at flood-time; and because of inadequate transportation few industries chose to settle here. Traditionally, northeasterners have been drawn to the magnet of Bangkok, leaving their poor villages behind to fill the most menial of unskilled jobs in the capital — servants, day-laborers, pedicab drivers.

The basic agricultural products of the Northeast are poor-soil staples like cotton and jute; mulberry trees, too, are grown to feed the worms that spin the silk that travels far away, light years in terms of life in the Northeast, to adorn a beautiful woman in New York or Paris. Small wonder that the Northeast also has a tradition of dissident politicians whose demands for social reform have been louder than those from

With Cambodia's frontier closed, the Northeast of Thailand is the only place in Asia where one can see great Khmer-style ruins, such as the ancient stones of Muang Tham (previous pages), near the border.

most other parts of the country. It is the area that most idealistic younger Thais have in mind these days when they talk about the need for improvements in the national life.

Changes are being made, however, and the future of the Northeast is beginning to look brighter than ever before in recent history. In the late 1950s, the modern Friendship Highway, a joint Thai-American undertaking, for the first time made this region, a high plateau on which about one-third of the country's population live, easily accessible in the rainy season as well as the dry, providing farmers and manufacturers with a way of getting their goods to the all-important markets of Bangkok throughout the year. Former Prime Minister Sarit Thanarat, himself a northeasterner, initiated many projects to help the people; dams to control flooding and to expand irrigation; roads linking remote villages; rural electrification; better medical facilities; and experimental agricultural stations. The establishment of several large American military bases during the Vietnam War, whatever their moral and political shortcomings, at least pumped new and needed money into the region and made boom towns out of once sleepy places like Nakhon Ratchasima (Korat), Ubon, and Udon. A northeastern university has been opened at Khon Kaen to serve the students of the area and introduce new ideas at the local level. A northeastern doctor, Krasae Channawong, a member of the new generation, won the Magsaysay Award (the Asian equivalent of the Nobel Prize) for his pioneering work in rural medicine and birth control in the impoverished village of Muang Phon where he grew up. There is a growing sense of achievement and purpose in Issan, and the day may not be far off when the name is no longer synonymous with poverty and problems.

For reasons that should be plain, the Northeast does not usually

figure prominently on anybody's list of travel destinations in Thailand. But even this may be changing, too, thanks to some extraordinary discoveries being made at Ban Chiang concerning the region's distant past that someday could conceivably result in schoolchildren all over the world memorizing details about the place.

The more recent past of Northeast Thailand, covering a millennium, may also lure visitors interested in archaeology. Parts of the region were ruled by the Khmers during their great period at the time they built Angkor Wat, and a number of major Khmer temples still exist on the Thai side of the border. One, Pimai, not far from Nakhon Ratchasima (Korat), the largest city in the Northeast, has been carefully restored by the Department of Fine Arts; dubbed the "Angkor Wat of Thailand," it is already an important tourist attraction. If Angkor itself remains closed to outsiders, the Northeast may be the best available place in Asia to view the remains of this splendid culture.

Nor is the Northeast completely devoid of fine natural scenery that is the equal of anything the North has to offer. Among more adventurous Thai tourists, a popular hot-season undertaking is a trip to Loei Province to climb 1,500-meter Phu Kradung Mountain. The ascent is a mild endurance test, but the rewards are breathtaking views, a parklike plateau forested with pine trees, and a dramatic drop in the temperature. During Thailand's cool season, Loei in general, and Phu Kradung in particular, usually register the lowest temperatures in the kingdom.

The Northeast is a region in the

All over Thailand, and particularly in the transitory Northeast, the traditional and the modern coexist in harmony. The Buddhist religion exerts a powerful and stabilizing influence in everyday village life.

midst of transition. The conventional traveler in search of the picturesque and the romantic would probably be best advised to miss it and concentrate on the other areas of Thailand; for those who want to see something of contemporary problems, however, and thus get a more balanced view of the country as a whole, it is an essential part of the itinerary.

* * *

Travel in the Northeast today is generally fast and easy over a terrain that in most places slopes gently from an elevation of 250 meters above sea level in the northwest corner to less than 100 meters in the southeast.

Thai Airways flies from Bangkok to Nakhon Phanom, Udon, Ubon, Khon Kaen, and Loei in the Northeast.

Scores of buses depart Bangkok's Northern Terminal on Phaholyothin Road every day for direct trips to most northeastern provincial capitals with many stops along the way. Connections are available upcountry for buses to practically any town in the Northeast. It is surprising how many small towns are served by large, modern buses. The inside of a provincial bus may resemble a rolling market, but it gets you there. Even remote villages can be reached by small, converted pickup trucks, "baht buses." For luxury travel, there is air-conditioned bus service to Nakhon Phanom and Surin.

The state railway has two lines to the Northeast beginning in Bangkok and branching at Nakhon Ratchasima (Korat): one goes east to Ubon and the other almost due north

Rice is harvested by hand near Nakhon Phanom, as in most places throughout Thailand and Southeast Asia. The yield each year depends on the vagaries of the monsoon.

218

Superhighway to the Korat Plateau

Teppitakpunnaram
วัดเทพพิทักษ์ปุณนาราม

3. Lam Ta
Kong Dam
เขื่อนลำตะคอง

The numbers in the margin in this section refer to the map on page 186.

1. Saraburi
สระบุรี

Phra Ngam Cave
ถ้ำพระงาม

2. Muak Lek Valley
หุบเขามวกเหล็ก

to Nong Khai. Express trains with sleeper provision (book as far as ten days in advance of weekend or holiday travel) leave Bangkok every evening at 6:30 p.m. for Nong Khai and at 7:30 p.m. for Ubon. Each stops at provincial capitals and major district towns enroute. On the eastern line that lies below the Northeast and above the Eastern Gulf Coast, an ordinary train leaves Bangkok every morning at 8:00 a.m. for the Cambodian border town of Aranyaprathet.

* * *

The good roads of the Northeast invite travel by car, which undoubtedly is the best way to see the many out-of-the-way sights of this part of the country. Choose from two basic itineraries. Route 2 begins near Saraburi, north-northeast of Bangkok, and runs through the heart of the Northeast. Also called the *Mitraparb* or "Friendship" Highway, this road passes most of the big provincial capitals and ends at Nong Khai on the Mekong. For a more leisurely trip through rural Issan, take the "Elephant's Ear" route through Surin and Ubon for about four days along the scenic and ethnically interesting periphery of the Northeast.

The Friendship Highway or Route 2, the main road through the Northeast, begins about 105 km from Bangkok, just before the town of Saraburi. About 20 km after the Saraburi turnoff on Route 2, a dirt road on the right leads to an experimental farm run by the Kesetsart Agricultural University of Bangkok and beyond to **PHRA NGAM CAVE ("Beautiful Buddha Image" Cave)** where a Dvaravati-era image may be seen. There are many other caves nearby, most of them unexplored.

Another 15 km leads to **MUAK LEK VALLEY**. Once known for malaria, Muak Lek has been transformed from an unhealthy jungle into dairy land that features a small Arboretum Garden Department where roses bloom around a blue

stream and a roadside stand from which the Thai Danish Dairy sells fresh milk products, including yoghurt.

* * *

About 43 km east of Saraburi, a sign points to **Wat Teppitakpunnaram** where a monumental white Buddha sits on a green mountain like an alabaster relic. The countryside in this area belongs to Khao Yai ("Big Mountain") National Park, hidden 40 km to the south (see "Bangkok Surroundings"). Route 2 continues northeast up the Korat Plateau, passing the reservoir of **LAM TA KONG DAM**. Soon the blue lake disappears and scrub brush, typical vegetation of the dry Northeast, begins to dominate the scenery. Past the district town of Pak Chong 62 km from Saraburi, going another 86 km leads to the provincial capital of Korat, now officially called Nakhon Ratchasima.

A warrior (opposite) charges into mock battle on elephant back, at the elephant roundup in Surin. An alabaster Buddha (above), at Wat Teppitakpunnaram, dominates the last hill before the Korat Plateau.

Richest and largest city in the Northeast, **NAKHON RATCHA-SIMA (KORAT)** serves as a trade, communications, and military center for the region. It is also the capital of the most densely populated up-country province in Thailand with over 1½ million people living in the province of Nakhon Ratchasima. Korat grew rapidly in the 1960s with the buildup of its Royal Thai Air Force Base where American fighter-bombers operated during the Indo-china War.

Although a busy commercial center, Korat has not forgotten its past. A statue of national heroine Khunying Mo (Tao Suranari) presides over the town square and the whitewashed ramparts of the old city wall. Khunying Mo was the wife of an assistant provincial governor in the early 19th century, when Prince Anu of Vientiane led his army into Korat. After taking the city, the prince threatened to enslave its residents. Khunying Mo rallied the women of Korat who enticed many of the Laotian soldiers to a drunken revelry and then killed them. Shortly thereafter, Prince Anu, who meanwhile had gone to attack Saraburi, was thus forced to withdraw to Vientiane.

With comfortable hotels such as the Chomsurang, Korat, Sri Pattana, Chompon, and Thai Pokaphan, which have air-conditioned rooms; a big night market; and at least five cinemas with films fresh from Bangkok; Korat makes a comfortable and convenient base for sidetrips.

To visit an important nearby silk production center, take Road 304 south towards Kabin Buri. After 27 km lies the town of **PAK THONG-CHAI** which produces silk thread for the weaving industry of Bangkok. (Road 304 also provides an alternative return route to Bangkok.)

4. Nakhon Ratchasima
นครราชสีมา
(ตัวเมือง, จังหวัด)

5. Pak Thongchai
ปักธงชัย (ตัวเมือง, อำเภอ)

Major Khmer Ruins

Korat's main nearby attractions, though, are two sites created nine centuries ago by Khmer architects. Both Prasat Phranomwan and Pimai lie north of Korat off Route 2. A drive north about 14 km from the provincial capital to a dirt road that leads off to the right 4 km takes you to the isolated and peaceful monastery of **PRASAT PHRANOMWAN**. Heavy stone galleries reveal the Khmer penchant for false windows with stone mullions. Romantic zigzags, rather than straight lines, cover the carved stones. An uncommon stillness pervades the place, broken only by the footsteps of resident monks. Unlike the majority of Khmer ruins, this one contains an active temple. Behind its well-preserved vaulted entrance, the original dark sanctuary is filled with many more recent Buddha images of different styles, most of them covered with patches of gold leaf. Full-grown trees sprout from the oldest chambers. The presence of older monks reminds visitors that donations are needed to help with the upkeep of the site.

Farther north 34 km on Route 2, lies the turnoff on the right that goes about 10 km east to the ruins of **PIMAI**, which along with the elephant roundup at Surin and the cool plateau of Phu Kradung, are the main tourist attractions of the Northeast. A sense of contemporary organization emerges among the awesome *prang*s and galleries of Pimai. Red paint spells danger where an incredibly heavy stone lintel balances precariously. Another sign informs the visitor that an ancient library vanished here. These are the only ruins in Thailand with hours; they close at 4:30 p.m. to prevent plundering.

King Jayavarman VII, last of the great Angkor monarchs, who had his face chiseled in dozens of eerie

Glittering like a silver ribbon, the Friendship Highway (facing page) is playing an important role in opening up the Northeast for development. The region also boasts numerous Khmer ruins that date from the same period as Angkor Wat, such as the standing Buddha image (above, left) at Prasat Phranomwan and Pimai (above, right), both near the city of Korat. The remains of Pimai have become one of the major tourist attractions of the Northeast.

angles on the towers of Angkor Thom, could easily have traveled from his palace along a 240-km road to Pimai, at the western extent of his kingdom. During his reign (A.D. 1181-1201), Pimai prospered within a walled rectangular area 1,000 meters long by 560 meters wide, situated on an artificial island created by linking the Moun River and one of its tributaries by means of a canal. Like the shrines at Angkor, the monuments at Pimai which endure in stone were never inhabited. Shops, pilgrim shelters, libraries, and houses were built of wood and have long since disintegrated.

The old city gate, probably the main entrance to the sanctuary, still stands at the end of the main street in the village of Pimai. Along the street near the Moun River Bridge, the Fine Arts Department maintains an open-air museum displaying some of the more beautifully carved lintels and statues found in the area.

Before leaving the area, see *Sai Ngam*, "Beautiful Banyan Tree," 1 km east of the temple on an irrigation reservoir; it has an extraordinary umbrella of dense leaves and roots which local people revere as a shelter for special spirits.

* * *

From Pimai you can continue north on Route 2 to Khon Kaen and beyond directly to the Mekong at Nong Khai. But, for a better look at the rural Northeast, more Khmer temples, and folksy Issan atmosphere, try the "Elephant's Ear" journey roughly running parallel to the Cambodian and Laotian borders.

For the longer route through the region, you return to Korat and from there take Road 24 dipping south and then east at Chok Chai. Farther east about 80 km Road 218 branches north to the town of Buri Ram. Stay on Road 24 for another

6. Prasat Phnom Rung
ปราสาทหินพนมรุ้ง

18 km, then at Ban Ta Ko turn right at the sign for Prasat Phnom Rung. Follow the road to Ban Wan, bear left, and soon you reach Khmer hilltop temple ruins.

Three full ponds, essential elements of Khmer monumental architecture, and pretty farmland surround **PRASAT PHNOM RUNG**. Historians believe this temple was an important station between Angkor and Pimai during the 11th and 12th centuries. Several generations must have elapsed during its construction, since several of the stone lintels resemble the early Baphuon style while the *naga*s date from the later Angkor Wat period. A stone inscription in Sanskrit mentions King Suryavarman II who built Angkor Wat.

Although damaged by plunder, the main *prang* of Phnom Rung and its galleries and chapels still reflect the geometric precision of Angkor architecture; there are symmetrical doors and windows and antechapels that face the four cardinal points. The monumental staircase, interrupted by landings, exudes the sense of mass and power typical of Khmer design. Look for the sandstone bas-reliefs of elephants and enthroned Hindu deities.

Monks of the Dharmayuti sect maintain the temple. During the Songkran festival in April, country folk walk in processions up the main staircase.

* * *

Going farther east on Road 24 to Prakhon Chai takes you near another site worth visiting. These second ruins can be reached by going south on Road 2075 about 1 km to a smaller road which branches right (west) near a modern temple. Follow it for 12 km to Ban Chorake, "Village of Crocodiles," then another 1 km to the Khmer temple ruins of Muang Tham.

A reassembled lintel at Pimai (left) reveals skillful carving that shows scenes of the ancient Khmer kingdom and its godlike kings, whose rule once extended over this part of Thailand. Although the splendor has been gone from such ruins for centuries, daily life continues undisturbed in and around them. At Muang Tham (above), villagers and monks from a nearby temple enjoy an outing among the tumbled remains of the once-great civilization.

Other Khmer Temples

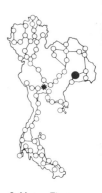

MUANG THAM or Lower Temple sits on a mossy lawn like an art historian's daydream. Older than Prasat Phnom Rung, its cornerstones were laid in the 10th century and the temple finished about a hundred years later. Thick jungle surrounded Muang Tham until recently, when a group of families migrated there from Ubon, cleared the area and founded a large village.

At dusk, women fetch water from the lotus-filled ponds and young novices of the monastery wander among the meter-thick walls, perhaps to meditate or to enjoy watching their teenage contemporaries practice Thai boxing in the courtyards.

Five *prang*s, surrounded by galleries, protected by walls, and now shaded by trees, constitute Muang Tham. A beautiful lintel on the ground shows Krishna standing on the head of Kirtimukha and holding up Mount Govardhana. The central shrines have crumbled, but the temple retains hints of vivid detail. The huge rectangular stone blocks that form the outer walls contain drilled circular holes probably used for stone figures shaped like lotus buds.

Road 24 continues 38 km to the town of Prasat. To see more Khmer art, turn right on Road 214 and go about 4 km south to the Mon-Khmer village of Ban Pluang. A track between the 30- and 31-km-stones (from Surin) branches east 500 meters to **PRASAT BAN PLUANG**, a small temple that features excellent carving. Drive back to Prasat and continue 29 km north on Road 214 to the town of Surin.

* * *

Located on an old Mon-Khmer site, **SURIN** was known primarily for silk raising until the T.A.T. organized an annual elephant roundup

9. Muang Tham
เมืองธรรม

11. Prasat Ban Pluang
ปราสาทบ้านปลวง

10. Surin
สุรินทร์ (ตัวเมือง, จังหวัด)

Armies of elephant-borne warriors charge each other thunderously at the annual Elephant Roundup in Surin province, one of Southeast Asia's leading tourist attractions. The lofty Khmer-style sanctuary of Khao Phra Viharn (right) sits impressively atop a mountain just a few hundred meters beyond the Thai border with Cambodia. Hopefully, some day the temple, of great historical and artistic interest, will be open again to visits from Thailand.

Wat Ra Ngeng
วัดระเจ็ง

Si Sa Ket
ศรีสะเกษ

13. Khao Phra Viharn
เขาพระวิหาร

12. Sikoraphum
ศรีขรภูมิ (ตัวเมือง, อำเภอ)

there in early November. The people of Surin are famed for their skill at training elephants. During the well-publicized roundup, local mahouts put their pachyderms through a variety of acts and demonstrations. Special buses and a train from Bangkok take tourists to the popular event.

A direct rail line connects Surin to the next province in the Northeast which borders on Cambodia, **SI SA KET**. Traveling by car is less direct. When Road 24 is improved as far as Khukhan, you will be able to drive easily from Khukhan on Road 220 all the way into Si Sa Ket town. Otherwise, you must drive north on Road 214 from Surin to Suwanphum, then southeast to Rasi Salai, crossing the Moun River twice in the process, and on to Si Sa Ket. At the start of either roundabout trip to Si Sa Ket, you can detour to **SIKORAPHUM** 31 km northeast of

Surin, via Roads 2077 and 2079, to see **Wat Ra Ngeng**, an 11th-century Khmer temple in a lovely natural setting. Four *prang*s are set at the corners of a square; a fifth graces the center and has beautifully carved pillars and a lintel which frame the door.

The province of Si Sa Ket's former main attraction no longer lies in Thailand. In 1963 the World Court awarded to Cambodia the splendid cliffside temple complex of **KHAO PHRA VIHARN**. If relations between Bangkok and Phnom Penh allow, you may be able to visit Khao Phra Viharn, which can be reached from Si Sa Ket along a 63-km drive southeast to Kantharalak, then straight into the jungle on another 37-km leg to the border.

Khao Phra Viharn stretches almost a kilometer in length. Its awesome stairs alternate between hewn bedrock and imported stones

placed there before the days of Angkor Wat. They rise in a succession of layers, each marked by an increasingly large *gopura*, or gate, and end at the topmost sanctuary that honors the god Siva.

To the east of the first *gopura*, a trail descends through the jungle to the Cambodian plains. Before the second *gopura*, a sacred pond cut in the rock was found to contain a 45-kilogram fish that now rests in Phnom Penh's National Museum.

The second *gopura*, shaped like a Greek cross, is superbly carved in the Khmer style of the 11th century. Its lintels show Vishnu in a scene from the Hindu myth of creation. The stairs continue up, in a symbolic ascent to heaven, past another purificatory basin, to the first courtyard with its two palaces and *gopura*, finally up to the second and third courtyards and the main sanctuary.

UBON (sometimes spelled Ubol) lies 680 km east of Bangkok and sports the full name of Ubon Ratchathani, meaning "Royal Town of the Lotus Flower." Its size and opulence contrast strongly with the surrounding countryside. Office buildings, multistory construction sites, and some of the most well-endowed *wats* in the Northeast rise abruptly behind the banks of the Moun. The river flows eastward, emptying into the Mekong about 100 km downstream from Ubon. Much of the town's growth coincided with the buildup of the Royal Thai Air Force Base during the 1960s when squadrons of American planes flew missions over Indochina from there. The Pathumratana, Bordin, SiamWatana, and Ubon hotels offer air-conditioned rooms that are welcome in the hot season when the Northeast generally is hotter than the Bangkok area.

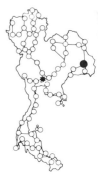

14. Ubon
อุบลราชธานี

Ubon province was the country's largest in area until its western half was split off and designated Thailand's 72nd province, Yasothorn. Ubon province still has a population well over one million, ranking third in that department after Bangkok and Korat.

* * *

Allow a full day for the trip north from Ubon to Nakhon Phanom. First, drive 76 km on Road 212 to Amnat Charoen. The dry land looks barely arable but somehow produces the rice that turns golden brown in late October and the kenaf that stands in bunches against the farmhouses.

Beyond Amnat Charoen about 2 km on the left side, shine the golden tiles of **Wat Phra Mongkol.** Behind an arbor, about 300 meters off the road the temple shelters a new 4½-meter-high Buddha image.

Continuing north on Road 212

about 88 km takes you to the district town of **MUKDAHAN** on the right bank of the wide and sluggish Mekong River, opposite the Laotian town of Savannakhet. Take the road to the river, turn right, and visit **Wat Sri Nongkran,** a buff-colored temple built by Vietnamese refugees in 1956. The gates present a curious mixture of Thai contours, Vietnamese script, and Chinese-inspired dragons. Farther down the river bank stands the colorful **Wat Jok Keo.** An unsophisticated but vibrant mural enlivens its small *prang.*

From Mukdahan, 55 km north lies **THAT PHANOM.** The road is in good condition, straight and flat. You feel far upcountry, and you are. Traffic consists of an occasional motorcycle. Uncultivated brush interspersed with rice fields rushes by. Black-shirted farmers balance produce-laden baskets from the ends of long poles. You drive close to the

Fanciful folk art decorates many of the temples of the Northeast, such as the relatively new Wat Sri Mongkran (opposite), which was built by Vietnamese refugees in a mixture of styles. The mighty Mekong River (above), one of Asia's great waterways, sweeps around the Northeast of Thailand for about 1,000 kilometers, forming most of its border with Laos. Viewed from Nakhon Phanom, the distant hills of Laos rise hazily above the Mekong River basin.

Mekong River all the way up to the village and temple of That Phanom.

Thousands of pilgrims from Northeast Thailand and Laos used to make an annual pilgrimage to **Wat That Phanom** to worship and make offerings at the base of the spire that was built around the 9th century and restored several times thereafter. But in mid 1975 disaster struck again when the spire collapsed after four days of torrential monsoon rains. But in 1979 the temple was restored again making it well worth a visit for those interested in history or simply seeking a beautiful riverside setting.

For a short and pleasant side-trip into the countryside, 7 km north of That Phanom and 8 km inland is **BAN RENU.** Like several small weaving villages in North Thailand, Ban Renu is famous for pretty girls and cloth. Embroidered shirts, northeastern *ikat* sarongs (in which the material is predyed in patterns), head

rests, and long dresses hang outside a dozen shops on the main street. The people are friendly bargainers. **Wat Prathat Renu,** the village's temple, features an extremely pretty spire covered with finely painted reliefs in bright blues, reds, and yellows as well as in pastels. Portraits of elephant riders, angels, guardians, and foot soldiers convey a vibrant realism that distinguishes such contemporary temple art in the Northeast.

* * *

Farther north about 45 km on Road 212 lies **NAKHON PHANOM.** On a fresh morning in Nakhon Phanom, a chain of powder-gray mountains can be seen behind the little Laotian town of Thakhek across the wide Mekong over 25,000 Vietnamese refugees crossed over the river during the 1950s and '60s to settle in this province. Although security precautions complicated their resettlement, many Vietnamese have pros-

Wat Prathat Renu
วัดพระธาตุเรณู

18. Nakhon Phanom
นครพนม (ตัวเมือง, จังหวัด)

17. Ban Renu
บ้านเรณู

230

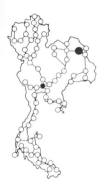

19. Tha Rae
ท่าแร่

20. Sakon Nakhon
สกลนคร (ตัวเมือง, จังหวัด)

pered financially in the town's own markets, and seem to have matched the overseas Chinese in business acumen.

During the Indochina war, American rescue and reconnaissance missions flew from the Royal Thai Air Force Base hidden behind grassy mounds 12 km west of town. NKP, as the Americans dubbed the base, was also a listening post for radio and electronic sensor devices. At that time you could buy at the market an appropriate symbol of such technologically sophisticated activity set in rural Thailand: fried bananas wrapped in discarded computer printouts listing traffic movements on the Ho Chi Minh Trail. But today there is little to see in town. The Srithep, First, Chai Pattana, Winsor, and Nakhon Phanom hotels all offer air-conditioned rooms if you decide to break your tour here.

From Nakhon Phanom, Road 22 goes west about 86 km to Sakon Nakhon town. On the way you pass the village of **THA RAE.** There the largely Catholic population, including many Vietnamese, supports a diocese complete with a seminary.

It is not unusual to see military convoys moving along Road 22. The wild, remote terrain around Sakon Nakhon, particularly in the Phu Phan Mountains, harbors insurgents. Ordinary travelers will probably not notice anything unusual and need not fear hostilities.

* * *

SAKON NAKHON town itself seems totally removed from any hint of nearby guerrilla warfare. Spread out along a low plain that borders Nong Han, Thailand's largest lake, the town enjoys being the only northeastern province with plenty of water. For a delicious Thai meal in town, stop at Som Jai Restaurant for a full selection of curries. The Araya, Som-

Thailand's thousands of temples play an integral role in its daily life. Supplicants at Wat That Phanom (left) receive blessings from the resident monks. Merit-making devotees have richly endowed the temple with elaborate decorations such as carvings, paintings, tiled floors, and gold-leafed statues. The freshly painted spire of Wat Prathat Renu (above) is an example of the intricate art work that distinguishes contemporary Northeastern temples.

Major Archaeological Finds

kaeit, and Charoensuk hotels have air-conditioned rooms.

The ancient Khmers left monuments in Sakon Nakhon although their significance is so minor that only those with keen archaeological interest or vivid imagination should go see them. **Wat Choeng Chum,** in the town center, has a plain laterite *prang* of the 10th century hidden inside a brand-new white *prang.* You literally glimpse antiquity through a crack in the door. Outside of town, on Road 22 heading west for Udon, 3 km past the experimental rice station a sign points to **Wat Narai Cheng Weng,** built by a princess in the 11th century. Today, the survival of the crumbling sandstone *prang* is so precarious it looks as if Dr. Seuss drew its outline. But its carved lintels beautifully exemplify the Khmer Baphuon style. The *wat* supports a large school, so you may receive help from a novice studying English.

From Sakon Nakhon, Road 22 heads west toward Udon. About 110 km from Sakon Nakhon, in the dusty topland of the Northeast, a small sign in Thai points to **BAN CHIANG** located about 5 km north of the highway. The Thai-Lao farm community in Ban Chiang and nearby Pulu Village sits on what may be the most significant archaeological find in Southeast Asia in many years.

Although the people of Ban Chiang were long used to encountering pots, beads, and even human bones when digging around their houses, they paid little attention to the finds. Then in 1966, a young American named Steve Young showed some of the finds to the Fine Arts Department. Subsequent excavations have unearthed pottery and other artifacts dated by thermoluminescence at between 7,000 and 8,000 years old.

At first most archaeologists hesitated to venture broad theories about

Wat Cheong Chum
วัดเชิงชุม

21. Ban Chiang
บ้านเชียง

Wat Narai Cheng Weng
วัดนารายณ์เชงเวง

The little village of Ban Chiang sits on one of the most significant archaeological finds in Southeast Asia. Distinctive pottery decorated with bold red swirls (above, left) and human skeletons (above, right) have been dated at up to 8,000 years old; bronze objects predate those of the Middle East. At Nong Khai on the southern bank of the Mekong River (opposite), the younger set peddles cheerfully home from school in the late afternoon light.

the Ban Chiang find. But further study, mainly conducted by a team from the University of Pennsylvania has convinced many of the skeptics that an agrarian bronze-making civilization first appeared not in Mesopotamia or China, but in Southeast Asia.

The Thai government has cracked down on the illegal digging and sale of Ban Chiang artifacts, but villagers may approach visitors offering to sell green or dark blue beads, metal bracelets, pottery, and even human bones. Do not buy any of these items; you can be arrested for the unlicensed possession of antiques.

From Ban Chiang, Road 22 continues 47 km west to **UDON THANI** which grew quickly with the influx of American airmen during the 1960s. Ten years ago, the air in Udon was often thick with red dust raised by military trucks bouncing over the town's pothole dirt roads. Now motorcycles and flashy cars zoom over asphalt streets punctuated by increasing numbers of traffic lights. You wonder what will be the long-term cultural effects of so many bars, dance halls, and massage parlors that sprang up during the war.

From Udon, Route 2 runs north 53 km to reach **NONG KHAI** on the southern bank of the Mekong. Many buses and interprovince taxis travel to Nong Khai.

Quiet Nong Khai town has few attractions other than the wide Mekong and a forgettable monument marking the end of the Friendship Highway. In some years, usually during September or October, monsoon rains swell the river, causing it to overflow its bank and damage crops and property in lowlying sections of the province. When the water level drops in the dry season, islands appear in midstream, and on weekends local residents take food, drink, and radios out to *pai-tio* on the sandbars.

Road 210 runs west of Udon 143 km to the rugged, beautiful province of **LOEI**. What is now the traveler's delight was once the civil servant's nightmare; in the Thai bureaucracy, being assigned to Loei was like going to Siberia, for Loei in the old days was a jungle outpost that meant fever, cold weather, little comfort, and poor security.

Enroute, stop at the **ELEPHANT CAVE** *(Tham Erawan)* about 54 km before Loei and 2 km off the road on the right. Despite its isolation, the monastery there is well organized. Signs in English entreat visitors "Please keep the law of Buddhist brother." A new and life-size statue of Erawan, the triple-headed elephant of Thai mythology, marks the steep stairway and rocky path to the cave's entrance. Prehistoric artifacts have been found here, but all that distinguishes the cave, apart from its size and an occasional cobra

emerging from the rocks, is an elephant's skull. The climb up is rough.

Road 210 continues west to finally reach the town of Loei. A minor agricultural boom has not changed Loei's shy simplicity. Some shop houses display signs of the Siam Cement Co., but thankfully the town has not yet turned concrete as so many other provincial capitals have done. The usually placid Loei River flows through the center of town. At the Thai Udom and the Sahrai Thong, the town's only hotels, you can find inexpensive rooms.

To plunge further into the Loei wilderness, 50 km west on Road 203 takes you to **PHU RUA** ("Boat Mountain"). The road cuts through heavy banks of red laterite, past a sawmill and fields of kenaf and cotton, the latter being the province's big money spinner. About 30 km west of town on the way to Phu Rua, a *sala* refreshment area overlooks chains of

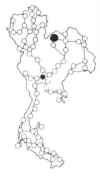

25. Loei
เลย (ตัวเมือง, จังหวัด)

Elephant Cave
ถ้ำช้าง

24. Phu Rua
ภูเรือ (ตัวเมือง, อำเภอ)

234

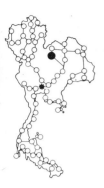

bluish hills. In December the mountains lie under thick blankets of smoke as farmers burn back the forest. Phu Rua itself is about 1,370 meters high. There is a rough road to the top which affords a view of the surrounding national forest. From Phu Rua hardy travelers can take a spine-jolting bus ride south on Road 203 to Lom Sak, then on to the provincial capitals of Phitsanulok or Phetchabun.

To see the Mekong near where it once again becomes the Thai-Lao border, drive 53 km north of Loei to **CHIANG KHAN.** A boat can be hired for the 4-km ride downstream to the Kuang Kud Ku rapids, worthwhile if only for the sheer sense of being locked in the deeper heart of Southeast Asia.

No experience in the Loei area can match the crisp beauty of **PHU KRADUNG NATIONAL PARK,** the most memorable escape in Northeast Thailand. Phu Kradung came to public attention only 50 years ago during the reign of King Rama VI. Today it is rarely visited on weekdays; students who have endured a 12-hour bus ride from Bangkok come on weekends to savor the invigorating cool, dry air. Some say the mountain's name derives from the mysterious sound of a bell *(kradung)* that supposedly grows louder on holy days. Others believe the name is a corruption of *krating,* the wild bulls which used to inhabit the remote plateau until hunters killed them off.

The entrance to Phu Kradung lies about 50 km southeast of Loei on Road 201 that goes to Chum Phae. About 3 km from the entrance you arrive at the park office where you can arrange for porters, store excess equipment, and park your car. Bring along tennis shoes, a wind breaker or

The climb to the top of Phu Kradung in Loei province is arduous, but the cool air, extensive wildlife, and spectacular views in the national park make the effort worthwhile.

sweater, packaged food (only one noodle shop operates on weekends), toilet articles, a camera, and a walking stick, if you are so inclined — for Phra Kradung, a plateau lying between 1,200 and 1,500 meters, beckons the naturalist-at-heart to set out down the trail. The park provides bedding and blankets in cabins that hold up to eleven people. Unless you are a champion hiker, let the porters carry everything up the 5-km trail to the plateau. (You can even hire four porters and a sedan chair for the climb!)

The climb is not easy but well worth the effort. After the fourth kilometer there is a cabin with cold water. Stop here, for the last kilometer is the toughest. Ladders negotiate the steepest boulders; views of the valley mitigate the strain. Once you make it up to the plateau you forget the tiring climb.

Atop Phu Kradung, clear and mostly level paths crisscross the 60-square-kilometer tableland. Rare birds, including hornbills, woodpeckers, and pheasants, may be seen; and even wild elephants and panthers somehow manage to climb up. Most of the fauna is quite shy.

The park's cabins and upper offices are located 3 km from a small radar station and a helicopter pad. Pick up a mimeographed map of trails and set off on nature walks. A good day begins before dawn with a chilly stroll to **Liem Pha Nok Hain** cliff to watch the sunrise. It is a long way down to the jungle where gibbons hoot. Spend part of the day finding the six waterfalls north of the cabins. About an hour before sunset, head for the serene setting of **Liem Pha Makdouk,** about 2 km west of the radar station.

From Phu Kradung you can take Road 210 to Khon Kaen and rejoin the Friendship Highway for the return trip to Bangkok; or return to Loei and cut across country on a rough road to Phitsanulok for a trip to the North.

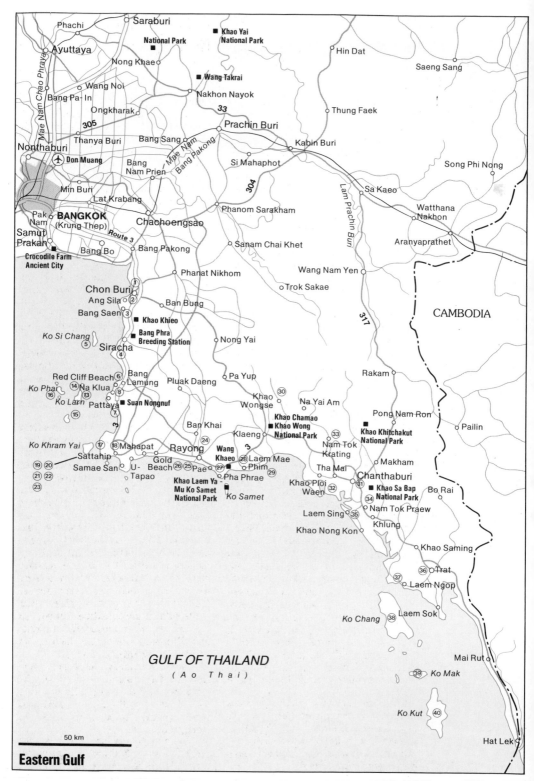

Phachi
Saraburi
Ayuttaya
Nong Khae
■ Khao Yai
National Park
■ National Park
Hin Dat
Saeng Sang
Wang Noi
■ Wang Takrai
Bang Pa-In
Nakhon Nayok
Thung Faek
Ongkharak
33
Prachin Buri
Song Phi Nong
Thanya Buri
Bang Sang
Kabin Buri
Nonthaburi
305
Bang
Nam Prien
Si Mahaphot
Sa Kaeo
✈ Don Muang
304
Watthana
Nakhon
Min Buri
Lat Krabang
Aranyaprathet
Pak
Nam
BANGKOK
(Krung Thep)
Phanom Sarakham
Chachoengsao
Samut
Prakan
Bang Bo
Bang Pakong
Sanam Chai Khet
Wang Nam Yen
■ Crocodile Farm
Ancient City
Phanat Nikhom
Trok Sakae
CAMBODIA
Chon Buri
①
Ang Sila
②
Ban Bung
Bang Saen
③
■ Khao Khieo
Nong Yai
Ko Si Chang
⑤
■ Bang Phra
Breeding Station
Siracha
④
Rakam
Bang
Lamung
Pa Yup
Pluak Daeng
Red Cliff Beach⑥
Na Klua
⑭
⑧
Khao
Wongse
㉚
Na Yai Am
Pong Nam Ron
Ko Phai⑯
⑬
Ko Larn
Pattaya
⑦
■ Suan Nongnuf
Ban Khai
Khao Chamao
Khao Wong
National Park
Pailin
⑮
Klaeng
㉝
■ Khao Khitchakut
National Park
Makham
Ko Khram Yai
⑰ ⑱Mahapat
Rayong
Nam Tok
Krating
Sattahip
⑲ ⑳
Samae San
Gold
Beach㉖㉕
Wang
Khaeo ㉘
3
Laem Mae
Tha Mai
Chanthaburi
U-
Tapao
Pae㉗
Phim
㉙
㉛
Khao Sa Bap
National Park
Bo Rai
㉑ ㉒
■ Khao Laem Ya-
Mu Ko Samet
National Park
Pha Phrae
Khao Ploi
Waen
㉜
㉞
Nam Tok Praew
㉓
Ko Samet
Laem Sing
㉟
Khlung
Khao Nong Kon
Khao Saming
Khao Samet
㊱
Trat
㊲
Laem Ngop
Ko Chang
㊳
Laem Sok
GULF OF THAILAND
(A o   T h a i)
Mai Rut
㊴ Ko Mak
Ko Kut
㊵
50 km
Hat Lek

Eastern Gulf

238

A Burgeoning
Resort Area

A graceful, curving stretch of brilliant white sand, lapped by gentle waves; in the sea a few white sailboats, a lone water-skier cutting like a knife through the sparkling water, and a tropical island surrounded by the darker blue of a coral reef; landward, all along the beach, luxurious modern hotels set in lush gardens, splendid private villas, and restaurants altogether serving a dozen or so different cuisines. This is the Eastern Gulf at Pattaya, arguably the greatest success story in the history of Southeast Asian resorts — at the very least one of the most remarkable. Barely more than two decades ago this lovely beach was a little-known retreat for a handful of rather adventurous foreigners and Thais from Bangkok, who braved the drive over poor roads to spend a weekend by the sea. There were no hotels then, luxury or otherwise, only a few collections of bungalows for rent, a rough clubhouse for a group of sailing enthusiasts, a couple of good seafood restaurants, and a small fishing village that gave the place its name. Apart from the beach, the main thing it had to recommend was its greater proximity to the capital than the more traditional resort of Hua Hin on the other side of the gulf, where the royal family passed their summer holidays, and where most of the wealthier families had hot-season villas. Seafront property in Pattaya in those days could be had for a song, and few if any entrepreneurs ever thought of the place in terms of tourists. Then, in the early '60s, the boom came. Partly it was due to a general boom in trade and tourism at that time, partly to the new, low-cost package tours whose members were as interested in

At the port of Klong Dan (previous pages), just outside of Bangkok, the day's catch is unloaded onto the docks. Fishing is a major industry along the Eastern Gulf, which is dotted with such busy commercial centers.

finding sea and sun as in seeing the standard attractions in Bangkok. In addition, with the establishment of the vast U-Tapao air base and the deep-water port at Sattahip, just beyond Pattaya, a new superhighway was built linking the area with the capital, cutting the driving time from over three to under two hours. The first major hotel, the Nipa Lodge, went up; and in the astonishingly short space of only three or four years the whole place was transformed. Now there are close to a dozen international-class hotels each of which has more than 200 rooms; a night life to rival Bangkok's when it comes to color and variety; restaurants that meet the standards of any in the capital; and facilities for such aquatic sports as waterskiing, scuba diving around the offshore islands, sailing, deep-sea fishing, parasailing — an exhilarating sport where you are towed up in the air behind a speed boat — and windsurfing.

The development of Pattaya as a resort opened up the whole Eastern Gulf Coast of Thailand, an almost unbroken stretch of beaches that goes down to Trat, the narrow finger of land that joins Cambodia. Other, less spectacular resorts than Pattaya have been built at Bang Saray and Rayong, farther down the coast than Pattaya. Close to Bangkok, about half an hour before Pattaya, Bang Saen has become the favorite seaside place for middle-class Thai families. According to dedicated skin divers, the waters of the gulf get clearer the farther down the coastline you go, the best of all being those off Chanthaburi Province, where the coast starts curving in toward Cambodia.

Some visionary developers now foresee the transformation of the whole region into a Thai Riviera, with hydrofoils as well as air-conditioned buses plying back and forth to Bangkok.

Although tourism has brought the Eastern Gulf Coast prosperity in a new form, it is far from being the

region's sole source of income. Other, older industries in the area have long played an important part in the Thai economy. Much of the seafood consumed or exported by Thailand comes from Eastern Gulf ports, and some of the largest fruit orchards are located between Rayong and Chanthaburi. The latter province is the country's major center for gem mining, especially of sapphires, both blue and black, which are probably Thailand's best bargain in precious stones. Some rubies are also mined there, though the best ones reputedly come from across the Cambodian border. Cities like Si Racha and Chon Buri, if somewhat lacking in visual charm, are nonetheless important commercial centers, with many plants for processing and canning the produce of the region. Si Racha, in particular, is noted as the home of a fiery hot chili sauce bearing its name that is a prominent feature of Thai dinner tables. Among the newer east coast industries, the growing of orchids for export in the form of cut flowers or plants prospers in dozens of huge nurseries, covering many hectares, some with more than half a million brilliantly blooming plants. The mushroom growth of this industry in recent years has pushed Thailand into the number-one spot among orchid exporters in Southeast Asia. The port at Sattahip, originally built as part of the American effort in the Vietnam War, is the biggest in the country and now handles a large part of Thailand's commercial shipping.

All this industry notwithstanding, the main lure of the Eastern Gulf for the average visitor to Thailand is its sun and sand and plentiful tourist facilities. Some of the older

A fishmonger at the morning market of Ban Amphur proudly displays some of the small fish that figure prominently in the Thai diet. In one form or another they find their way into almost every meal of all classes.

Leaving Bangkok

hands in Bangkok, resentful at having to share their once-private pleasures with so many strangers, grumble that Pattaya has been "ruined" and issue dire warnings about "uncontrolled" development. A controversy about the lack of proper planning has raged for several years, and a conservationist group has been leading the fight against indiscriminate building of shop houses and hotels in the resort. To the average tourist, however, the Eastern Gulf still seems a long way from the overcrowded resorts of America and Europe, and most visitors go home singing praise of the region just southeast of the capital.

* * *

The Eastern Gulf lies within easy reach of Bangkok. Buses leave from the Eastern Bus Terminal on Sukhumvit Road for the main cities on the Eastern Gulf: Chon Buri, Si Racha, Sattahip, Rayong, Chantha-buri, and Trat. Air-conditioned tour buses leave several times daily for the resorts of Bang Saen and Pattaya, and seats can be booked through tour companies such as Ital-Thai in Raj-prasong Shopping Centre and Diet-helm Travel, Ploenchit Road. Airplanes do not serve the Eastern Gulf, as it is only a few hours by road from the capital.

The main route for travel along the Eastern Gulf Coast is Sukhumvit Highway, which becomes Route 3 outside of Bangkok. Route 3 officially originates at the busy Bangkok intersection near the Erawan Hotel on Ploenchit Road; one kilometer to the east, over the railroad tracks, it becomes Sukhumvit. On Sukhumvit past the numbered *sois*, the home of Bangkok's western population, the traffic gradually thins out. Beyond

Fishermen offload their catch at the beach of Lam Mae Phim, typical of the many alluring beaches along the Eastern Gulf which now attract numerous visitors from everywhere.

the Phra Kanong Canal, the highway reaches the suburb of Bangna. From there a new shortcut to Bang Pakong cuts 20 km off the journey south by avoiding Pak Nam (or Samut Prakarn) at the wide mouth of the Chao Phya River.

Branching left and heading southeastward at Bangna, the fast shortcut offers fewer sights and less upcountry atmosphere than the old road, which arcs slightly seaward, passes the Ancient City, the Crocodile Farm (see "Bangkok Surroundings"), and Klong Dan, and beyond Pak Nam follows a scenic *klong* for 75 km.

Life along the old Sukhumvit *klong* seems resistant to most change, its traditional tranquillity shattered only by the occasional roar of a long-tailed boat and the silent sprouting of another television antenna. Framed by coconut trees, nipa palms, and bougainvillea, diamond-shaped fishing nets on the end of long counter-weighted poles perch over the canal's waters. Huge water jars sit at the feet of the stairways which climb up stilts to the thatched-roof huts above. Boys in tucked-up sarongs play *takraw*; girls shampoo in the *klong*. Old ladies sell fruit and the well-known chestnutlike *luk jak*. Along the right-hand side of the highway, stretch mangrove flats where villagers gather wood to make into charcoal, while their children catch crabs in the mud. As civilization steadily encroaches, factories compete with the quaint village *wats* for space along the highway.

On the old Sukhumvit Road,

about 12 km past Pak Nam and 3½ km past the Crocodile Farm turn-off, a seafood restaurant beckons from a marshy bank. Years ago, when the single good road south from Bangkok went just this far, the restaurant's fresh breezes, tangy food, and seclusion drew the capital's high society for evening feasts or just relaxed conversation. Today you can share in the local nostalgia by ordering splendid dishes of shrimp *(gung)*, crab *(poo)*, and oyster *(hoy)*.

At the 56-km-stone, Route 3 arrives at the busy fishing port of Klong Dan just a short way from the sea. The old highway then curves east to merge with the new road at Bang Pakong. The road swings south once more and heads for the distant hills of Chon Buri.

* * *

A pleasant and industrious town of about a quarter of a million people, mainly merchants, traders,

The numbers in the margin in this section refer to the map on page 238.

Young girls (opposite) enjoy an evening stroll along the beach at Pattaya. Once a sleepy fishing village visited by only a few sun-and-sea lovers from Bangkok, Pattaya has now developed into a Thai Riviera with dozens of luxury hotels overlooking the blue waters of the Gulf. The old Sukhumvit Klong (right), just outside Bangkok on the way to the Eastern Gulf, still offers views that have changed little over the years.

and craftsmen, **CHON BURI** for most tourists is but a lunch-stop on the way south to Pattaya. Most of Thailand's oyster population breeds on the Chon Buri coast and farther south along the gulf. Outside the town, about 3 km to the north, sits a hilltop monastery known as **Wat Buddhabat Sam Yot**, "Buddha's Footprint Mountain of Three Summits." Built amid green trees by an Ayuthaya king and renovated during the reign of King Chulalongkorn, it was once used to conduct a royal "Water Oath of Allegiance."

Near the center of Chon Buri, sits a colossal gold-mosaic image of the Buddha, belonging to **Wat Dhamma Nimitr**. The largest in the Eastern Gulf region and the only one in the country depicting the Buddha in a boat, the 40-meter-high statue recalls the story of the Buddha's journey to the cholera-ridden town of Pai Salee. Through inspiration and compassion, the Buddha cured many of the afflicted. On the same hill is found the local Chinese Buddhist Society, surrounded by the burial shrines of prominent members.

Those interested in the historical arts will want to stop in the midst of Chon Buri near the old market at a temple gate flanked by fruit sellers. The oldest and most important *wat* in the province, **Wat Intharam** presents an antiquated front: several buildings feature up-turned curved bases typical of the Ayuthaya period. The original wooden pedestals and roof decorations have disintegrated; but the roof replacement, also of an older, interesting style, has *cho-fas* (upturned eaves characteristic of royal and religious Thai architecture) with angels in molded stucco. Patterns composed of antique porcelain decorate the window arches. Within the *bot*, murals portray *devas* ("gods") in the upper panels, and the

1. Chon Buri
ชลบุรี (ตัวเมือง, จังหวัด)

Wat Buddhabat
วัดพุทธบาทสามยอด

Wat Intharam
วัดอินทาราม

Wat Dhamma Nimitr
วัดธรรมนิมิตร

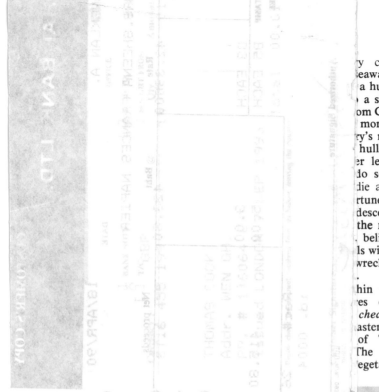

y called **Ruh Sam Pao.**
...eaward, its walls have the
...a huge hull which some say
...a shipwreck in which emi-
...om China were lost.

...more than 300 cells for the
...y's residents are also in the
...hulls. Many of the residents
...er leave, although they are
...do so, because they believe
...die at Ruh Sam Pao brings
...rtune. The old women of
...descent, some of whom have
...the monastery for 20 years
...believe that when they die
...ls will be carried to sea, past
...wreck of their fellows, back

...hin the monastery are two
...es of the giant Nakhon
chedi. A Thai monk heads
...astery, in which the Chinese
...of Teochew is commonly
...The residents *kin jeh*, "eat
...egetarian."

A sailor near Chon Buri (opposite) decorates the prow of his boat with colored cloths and flowers, following an old custom of placating the all-important goddess of the sea. Indispensable mortars and pestles for the Thai kitchen (above, left) are produced nearby at Ang Sila. South of the town, at the monastery of Luh Sam Pao, a nun's chamber has been built in the shape of a boat (above, right); sweet-smelling wreaths and joss sticks adorn the prow.

South of Chon Buri 18 km on the road past Ang Sila, the beach at **BANG SAEN** is a carnival each weekend and merry madness during the hot season. A profusion of multi-colored beach umbrellas, black inner tubes, and wrinkled watermelon rinds cover the sandy beach that is a favorite with Thai tourists. By Sunday night, Bang Saen is again a sleepy hollow of quiet beach bunga-lows and restaurants.

The T.O.T. runs the Bang Saen Beach Hotel which has a swimming pool and comfortable, if not plush, rooms. Near the beach there are also bungalows under coconut trees. **Bang Phra Golf Course** can be found nearby, on the left off Sukhumvit Highway, just past the Bang Saen market. The golf course has a motel, a lodge, a swimming pool, and a bar called the 19th Hole. The caddies, by the way, are all girls. Longest in Thai-land at 7,249 yards, the 18-hole course

lies in beautiful hills.

* * *

SI RACHA, 24 km south of Chon Buri, descends from the hills and extends into the sea on tentacle-like piers. Its famous hot sauce can be enjoyed overlooking the water at the Si Racha Restaurant, where fresh shrimp, crab, oyster, mussel, or aba-lone make fine dippings for the thick and tangy red liquid. An offshore rock supports a picturesque *wat* con-taining a lively mixture of Thai and Chinese Buddhist elements. Shrines honor a monk who spent many years atop the seaside hillock. An inevitable footprint of the Buddha, cast in alloy, graces the *wat*, and so do pictures of the beloved Chinese god-dess of mercy, Kuan Yin, and the Monkey God, possessed of magical powers in Chinese lore. The *wat* over-looks arrow-shaped fish traps made of nipa palm — a construction so functional that it has endured for

3. Bang Saen
บางแสน (หาด)
4. Si Racha
ศรีราชา (ตัวเมือง, อำเภอ)

Bang Phra Golf Course
สนามกอล์ฟบางพระ

centuries in Southeast Asia. Large tankers carrying crude oil from the Persian Gulf stream past Si Racha to the TORC Petroleum Refinery, 8 km south of town, which fuels Bangkok's growth and development. From the longest pier at Si Racha, boats ferry passengers to the nearby island of **Koh Sichang**. The weather-beaten diesel fishing boats rent for not less than 400 baht per round trip and take less than one hour to reach the island.

* * *

Before the Chao Phya River was dredged and a channel cut through the bar at the river's mouth, ocean-going vessels unloaded their cargo and passengers at **KOH SICHANG**. Today the island is quiet; there are no sailors' brawls at the merchant marine club; and the coffers of the customs house, once filled to the brim, gather dust. Koh Sichang's waters, clear from November through January, offer snorkelers and scuba divers a glimpse of abundant sea life. The dilapidated piers at the old refueling station make an interesting dive, and so does the nearby rusty shipwreck, both best explored with experienced divers. On the northern side of the island a lovely beach stretches beneath the sky.

* * *

Just 5 km from Si Racha at the 120-km-stone on the Sukhumvit Highway, the road on the right leads to the sea and **RED CLIFF BEACH**. Here is a moderately priced Thai resort with bungalows of one, two, or three bedrooms. As Red Cliff Beach is popular with locals, it is less expensive and less pretentious than Pattaya farther down the road, but nevertheless has pleasant seaside scenery, an enclosed salt-water swimming area with sand beach, a Thai night club, a small golfing area, and a restaurant that serves European, Thai, and Chinese food.

A couple takes a siesta on the sandy beach at Bang Saen (opposite) shaded by coconut palms. Only an hour or so from Bangkok, Bang Saen is a favorite resort with Thai tourists, who come in crowds on weekends during the hot season. Spacious Red Cliff Beach (above), not far from Si Racha, is another popular holiday spot that offers moderately priced bungalows beside the sea. During the week, both resorts are relatively empty and accommodations are plentiful.

The Thai Riviera

PATTAYA, everybody's paradise, is the premier beach resort in Thailand. Strange, because Pattaya really does not have much of a beach. However, this is mitigated by beaches on several small offshore islands and some hotels boast their own beaches. Swinging singles of any sex, contented families, and lovers of water sports all agree that Pattaya spells bliss. Everyone does his own thing and nobody is affronted. Air-conditioned coaches leave Bangkok daily and cover the 154 km to Pattaya in about three hours.

Basically, Pattaya consists of one straight 4 km road along the sea. The northern part of this is bordered, on one side, by 96 hotels, bars and restaurants. On the other side is the beach backed by wattle, flame and palm trees. Both sides of the southern quarter of this road are jammed with shops, bars and restaurants. A parallel road gives access to several hotels. Numerous short *sois* joining these two thoroughfares have their share of nightclubs, shops, bars and restaurants. Transport up and down the beach is by "5-baht" buses — small open-sided trucks seating about a dozen persons.

Many bars are nothing more than open-air kiosks with about a dozen stools and two or three bargirls. From these bars you can keep an eye on the activity or temporarily leave your drink for some spontaneous shopping.

South Pattaya starts to swing when the sun sets. Traffic practically comes to a halt. Scores of food stalls and itinerant vendors selling Buddhas and leather belts, amulets and bracelets move in. Fruit and flower stalls further brighten the scene. Jewelers do a brisk trade in sapphires and rubies. Tailors cajole customers into having a dress or safari suit run-up in 24 hours. Music blares from bars and stores selling pirated cassettes. The biggest and best bars — best because they are the most raucous — are the Marine, Grace and Simons. They

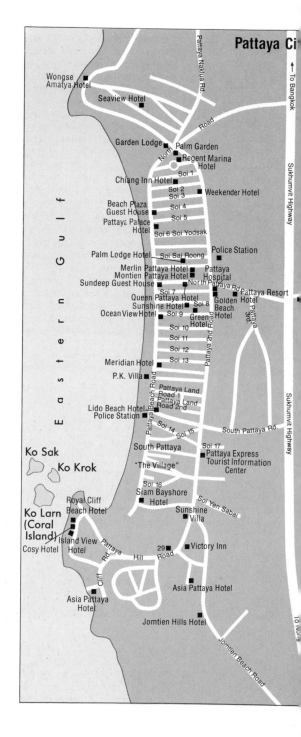

250

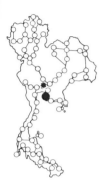

7. Pattaya
พัทยา
8. Na Klua
นาเกลือ

Palm Beach
หาดป่าล้ม

Pattaya Beach
หาดพัทยา

South Pattaya
พัทยาใต้

Tourists enjoy the creature comforts of South Pattaya, Thailand's foremost luxury resort.

stretch out over the water and you can share your beer with mosquitoes and lovely Thai girls. And if Eros is shooting his arrows there is no saying what will happen.

Pattaya is paradise for the lover of water sports. Ski-boats and sail boats, snorkeling and scuba-diving equipment, and water scooters can be rented. The adventurous will try parasailing. You are strapped into a parachute harness and then attached to one end of a tow rope, the other end of which is connected to a speedboat. The air current lifts your parachute and up, up you go to be granted a bird's-eye view of Pattaya. No training or skills are required and it is perfectly safe. Windsurfing is just as exciting but demands much skill. The keen angler can test his skills in landing groupers and red snapper, mackerel and bonito, sailfish and barracuda. Nearly all the large hotels have immaculate tennis courts and 10 km east of Pattaya is the Siam Country Club which boasts what is probably the best golf course in the Kingdom.

Those less athletically inclined and those who tire of sunbathing need not be bored. Excursions are organized to such places as sapphire mines, an orchid farm and an elephant kraal. Evenings can be spent at the movie house which shows English soundtrack films only; and the top hotels all have discos featuring live music.

Accommodation ranges from deluxe international hotels — the Royal Cliff Beach is a resort in itself — to simple bungalow units cooled by sea breezes rather than air-con, where you are able to do your own cooking. Not that dining is a problem. Dozens of food stalls, where the adventurous may dine *al fresco* for nearly nothing, line the main drag in South Pattaya. At the up-end of the market many restaurants offer international cuisine.

Island Hopping and
Scuba Diving

One of Pattaya's prime virtues lies hidden underwater. Within a week, it is possible to arrive as a neophyte and depart as a certified scuba-diver. One of the best ways to achieve this status is to visit Steven's Dive Shop, at the north end of Pattaya Beach, where professional instructors provide a boat, equipment, and a skin diving course. The instructors belong to both the National Association of Underwater Instructors and the Professional Association of Diving Instructors. Their courses are least expensive per person for a group of at least four.

Although some of the islands off Pattaya can at times become "crowded" with divers in favorite spots, there are altogether enough interesting undersea areas to provide plenty of space for all adventure seekers. Boats may be rented for the day at a price depending on the size and facil-

ities of the vessel and the visitor's bargaining prowess. Rates are generally better on weekdays and during tourist lulls, when a buyer's market prevails. Dive shop employees or owners can furnish tips on boat rental. Take along beverages kept chilled in an ice chest for sipping under the awning. The boats chug along at a leisurely pace just fast enough to reach the nearest group of islands in less than an hour. For the impatient there are speedboats.

Among the favorite nearby islands are the twins **KOH LARN** and **KOH SAK**. The first island is larger and more developed, though less spoiled, and now boasts several hotels and bungalows at Nuan Beach, and an 18-hole golf course as well. Be sure to sample some of the mouthwatering freshly caught crab and King Mackerel served at the simple little shops on Koh Larn. Good diving beckons in the whole area. Fifteen meters or so

13. Koh Larn
เกาะล้านและ
14. Koh Sak
เกาะสาก

down in the clear waters off the southern end of Koh Larn flourish beautiful coral formations and an abundance of colorful and exotic marine life. To the north of Koh Sak lies a shallow bay with both sandy and coral areas only 7 to 10 meters deep.

The tropical fish in these waters make one realize that an aquarium is only a peephole into a vast universe. Easily recognizable are the tube worms that sprout from the coral like tiny Christmas trees in fabulously varied colors. Eye-catching orange and white clownfish live in curious symbiotic rapport with the orange anemone, bringing food to the anemone in exchange for the protection of its stinging tentacles to which the clownfish are immune. Everywhere dances and shimmers a profusion of colors and shapes: soldierfish, damselfish, green parrot wrasse, polka dot grunts, batfish, and huge

friendly groupers.

Diving naturally calls for precaution; and the wise diver takes care to look and photograph rather than to touch or step on, especially when meeting up with the spiny sea urchin or the well-camouflaged stonefish. A less obvious danger is the tropical sun, the strength of which is often underestimated by visitors from temperate lands; a T-shirt protecting one's tender back allows the day's snorkeling to be recollected in tranquillity that evening.

Southwest of Koh Larn, about another hour or so by boat, lies **KOH LIN**. Although quite small, this island has many good diving spots. On the sea bottom are a relatively recent wreck, good coral formations, and fascinating sea life. Due west of Koh Larn, at about the same distance away as Koh Lin, is **KOH PAI**. Here, in water as deep as 25 meters or more, are found strikingly beautiful fish, coral and shells.

Several quiet areas lie just south of Pattaya towards Sattahip. These include a seaside retreat for the royal family (closed during visits by the king), and the Varuna Yacht Club where Thai helmsmen compete in a variety of classes of small sailboats. About 6 km south of Pattaya is the usually quiet **Y.M.C.A. BEACH**. The beach may be reached from Sukhumvit Highway by making a right turn at the 56-km-stone (measured from Chon Buri). Another tranquil spot, with a fine view of the sea and offshore islands, is a cliff that runs to the right of the highway up a track just beyond the 68-km-stone. One way to visit these places is to rent a motorcycle at Pattaya Beach. Resist the temptation to zoom through the changing of gears.

Boats with awnings (facing page) can be rented for excursions to offshore islands near Pattaya. There the clear waters (left) offer a new world of exploration for enthusiasts of spear fishing and scuba diving.

South of Pattaya

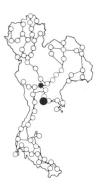

Overlooking a scenic bay containing scattered islands, the little fishing town of **SATTAHIP** about 20 km south of Pattaya grew up overnight to become an attractive, busy deep-water port. In the heart of town a large, modern temple rests on turquoise pedestals, while in the commercial center, a boisterous market brims with fresh fish, fruit, and vegetables.

The shop signs Apollo Optical, Man Fashion, and Florida Shoemaker beam the prosperity reaped from nearby military bases. The economic influence of the American military, however, once considerable when B-52 bombers and their crews were stationed at nearby U-Tapao, quickly evaporated, and along with it many of the gaudy trappings designed for the off-duty serviceman.

The Royal Thai Navy with headquarters in Sattahip is in charge of much of the coast between Pattaya and Sattahip. Sukhumvit Highway passes the Thai Naval Academy at the 167-km-stone.

In Sattahip, stroll past the shops or drop in for an *o liang* (the great local version of sweet iced coffee that came from French colonial Cambodia), have a spicy curry near the market, or browse over teak elephants in the souvenir shops, where you may find the perfect keepsake.

* * *

Six km past Sattahip, a broad, modern road on the right leads to the large. Thai military base. When the base is reached, turn right again and then, after 1 km, turn left along the fence at the side of the base. The road, which again turns right after a couple of kms, deterioriates and 8 km further on ends at Samae San.

Jetties poke out from the hill-backed fishing town of **SAMAE SAN** into the translucent turquoise bay, rimmed by an immediate archipelago of five islands. White and purple squid dry in the sun near the long wooden piers which have nautical gasoline stations. Near the docked boats, fishermen spend their time repairing nets or catching up on their laundry. On the village's single road, husky women tend their kitchens and sundries stores, some with games machines and juke boxes.

Few out-of-towners ever reach the lovely white beaches of the nearby islands, and those who have want to shield them from publicity. Visitors may rent a boat for approximately 200 baht per day to explore the islands' tree-lined beaches and neighboring reefs. Boats of shallow draft enter the bay between the islands of **KOH AI RAET** and **KOH SAMAE SAN**, the latter mountainous with bright white beaches and a

17. Sattahip
สัตหีบ
18. Samae San
แสมสาร

19. Koh Ai Raet
เกาะอ้ายแรต

20. Koh Samae San
เกาะแสมสาร

Amulets and tattoos help protect this fisherman (right) when he is at work in the Gulf of Thailand. His catch is likely to include such delicacies as baby squid, which at Rayong ends up barbecued (facing page).

small fishing hamlet surrounded with coconut trees. To the west is **KOH KHAM** and beyond **KOH CHUANG**, fringed with a tabletop coral reef, and **KOH CHAN**, where the beach has an itchy reputation for sand flies.

* * *

Situated 221 km from Bangkok, **RAYONG** is split in two by an estuary, unseen from the Sukhumvit Highway which plows through the commercial district of sundries shops, coffee stalls, and a forest of high TV antennas. A right turn at the stop light just past the air-conditioned O-Tani Hotel leads across a dilapidated bridge to an older but just as industrious fishing village that is strung along a strip of land between the beach and the estuary.

Rayong is famed for its *nam pla*, or "fish sauce," the sine qua non of Thai condiments. Producing

the sauce is a cottage industry in Rayong, and many homes have backyard factories. A small silver fish that abounds in the gulf is allowed to decompose for about seven months to produce the ruddy liquid that is filtered and bottled on the spot. Every Thai eating establishment, from the fancy restaurant to the humble noodle stall, serves the fish sauce, sometimes mixed with sliced chilies (called *prik nam pla*). Indeed, *nam pla* is a staple food throughout Southeast Asia: many poor farmers have raised their families in difficult times on a diet of plain rice flavored only with fish sauce.

* * *

On busy days, about 20 km east of Rayong, the wharfs of **BAN PAE** are covered with quiltwork thrown up by Poseidon. Dressed in weathered black shirts, straw hats, and sarongs, women spread out square carpets of

tangerine-colored shrimp to dry in the sun. Though the sight is compelling, the smell may overpower the newcomer, as the sun quickly decomposes the scraps and leftovers that will be used for chicken and crocodile feed.

This scenic fishing port is sheltered to the west by an outcrop of rocks, and by the island of **KOH KEO PISADAN** (also called Koh Samet) to the south. The island is remembered by students of Thai literature as the place where Sunthorn Pu, an undaunted romantic poet who lived in the 19th Century, retired to compose some of his works. Now, the island is increasing in popularity as a resort island with cheap accommodation, good food and great beaches.

The coastal road leading directly south from Ban Pae, passing the local fish sellers and barber shops, is a lovely drive, bordered by palms and white beach. It enters the pine forest and national park of **BAN PHA PHRAE** which overlooks the rocky islets east of Koh Keo Pisadan.

Down the road 7 km lies **SUAN WANG KAEW** beach resort, where bucolic paths weave in and out among seaside gardens.

Past the Suan Wang Kaew Resort 10 km on the coastal road, the beach of **LAEM MAE PHIM** extends for kilometers against the low surf of the gulf. In front of the fishermen's shacks along the shore, women sell sugared treats and squid roasted on skewers. The dwellings are impermanent, with walls tacked together from scrapwood and hung with kitchen utensils. Housewives do their daily washing out of a water jar on the porch, while scruffy dogs scavenge in the sands, occasionally clashing in a storm of growls and toothy snarls, much to the amusement of the villagers.

27. Ban Pha Phrae
อุทยานแห่งชาติบ้านผ่าแพร่

Suan Wang Kaew
สวนวังแก้ว

26. Koh Keo Pisadan
เกาะแก้วพิสดาร
28. Laem Mae Phim
แหลมแม่พิมพ์

256

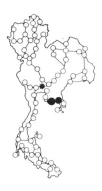

30. Khao Wongse
เขาวง

Just offshore Laem Mae Phim are two jagged islands called **KI PLAEM,** "Fish Droppings." They serve as a backdrop for weathered fishermen unloading the small silver fish used to make *nam pla*. To the left of a small promontory lie another three islands that provide a natural perspective, decreasing in size with distance. The nearest and largest **KOH MAN NAI**, is privately owned and has a sheltered beach on its western side, coconut groves, and clumps of old mango trees. There are little bungalows for rent and seafood restaurants, catering to busloads of young Bangkok students on holiday trips to Chanthaburi.

To return inland to Route 3, the Sukhumvit Highway, you take the road branching to the left after Laem Mae Phim, passing through dense rubber plantations and clusters of bamboo. Three kilometers farther the small village of Ban Kram centers around a large old tree that is the object of animistic worship; cloth is wrapped around it and nearby stands a spirit house.

* * *

On Route 3 at the 288-km-stone, a turn north along a small town street leads to a rough dirt road (check conditions beforehand during the rainy season) and 13 km later to an inland adventure at Khao Wongse.

Villagers say that people have tried to take photographs from the mystic jagged peaks of **KHAO WONGSE**, but when they returned to Bangkok their film mysteriously was blank. The gray-streaked outcrop dominates the valley of red laterite dust and humble farmlands. To the left of the simple *wat* and Chinese shrine lying at its base, Buddhist monks recite scripture in their living quarters fashioned out of crevices in the cliff face.

Khao Wongse is full of caverns. One old woman, her face powdered white to cool her skin after bathing, has lived there since childhood, but claimed she has not yet seen all the caves. In Tam Plak, a hollow near the *wat*, water continues to drip on the brow of the stalagmite image of **Lord Buddha**. Worshippers visit the cave to offer prayers, light yellow candles, shake divining sticks, and read their fortunes.

Village children happily offer their services as guides to those who wish to climb to the top of Khao Wongse. The path jumps over tree roots and boulders, dried leaves, and brilliant red bugs and breaks out upon a succession of small, contemplative clearings, where the children ring temple bells to mark their ascent. Villagers claim that crocodiles live in underground streams, and that some of the cave walls gleam with diamonds.

A sailor climbs to the crow's nest (facing page) near one of the islands called Ki Plaem, just offshore. Villagers (left) enjoy Thai chess.

Chanthaburi and Surroundings

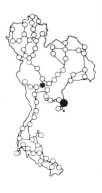

Farther south along the Eastern Gulf, about 330 km from Bangkok lies **CHANTHABURI**, a town with a raffish air of prosperity. Gem fever continually grips the place; local gossip buzzes with news of big finds — the proverbial 10,000- or 20,000-baht stones. Even the income from polishing small gems comes as an economic windfall by local standards.

Motorcycles clog the streets, another immediately noticeable sign of the town's wealth. It seems that everyone has a bike, and for good reason. Many of the youngsters who pick fruit in the nearby orchards where no buses go, afterwards zoom back into town for an afternoon of profitable gem polishing. Nearly every shop in Chanthaburi has a row or rows of wooden lathes. The gem mines, rubber plantations, and fruit orchards provide a livelihood for many residents, including a large number of ethnic Chinese and Vietnamese. Chanthaburi now has several air-conditioned hotels, such as the Muang Chan, Chanburi, Kasemsarn, and Travel Lodge.

The nearest gem mining area, at **KHAO PLOI WAEN** ("Hill of the Sapphire Ring"), is reached by a slightly indirect route that leads out of the market and goes 11 km to the port, where the Chanthaburi River empties into the gulf. Back towards town 4 km a road on the left goes 4 km to Ban Kacha, with the sapphire-laden slopes of Ploi Waen on the left. Here, under jackfruit trees, miners and middlemen haggle over the price of gems. The open pits gouged out of the hillside are two to 10 meters deep.

Organized tours are conducted of the Chanthaburi mining areas, including a find-it-yourself tour in which visitors can prospect on their own, keeping whatever gems they un-

31. Chanthaburi
จันทบุรี (ตัวเมือง, จังหวัด)

Gems are cut and polished (above) in small shops throughout Chanthaburi. At the open mines of Khao Ploi Waen, a gem dealer displays with pride polished blue sapphires, the most famous stone found in the area.

earth. Check with the local tour agencies.

About 5 km south of Chanthaburi stands Khai Nern Wong, "Camp on a Small Circular Hill," where King Taksin retreated after the fall of Ayuthaya in 1767, to regroup his forces, recruit new soldiers, and construct a fleet of warships. Afterwards he returned north to defeat the Burmese invaders. On the same hill are the remains of a fortress built by King Rama III. In spots around the hill derelict cannons point emptily at the now silent jungle. Several of the artillery pieces are of great size; locals claim they could protect the mouth of the Chanthaburi river about 11 km away. Today, spirits are believed to still keep watch in the ruined stronghold.

Also of interest in Chanthaburi is the French-style Church of the Immaculate Conception, the largest in Thailand, built around 1880. It is still active, and attended by the Thai-Vietnamese community of Chanthaburi, the members of which migrated to Thailand over the last two centuries. The descendants of these immigrants engage in a number of businesses, foremost of which is the making of reed products, such as mats, handbags, and tableware, which are woven in attractive shapes and patterns. Many are made in their homes and some of the best can be ordered from the nuns of the church. There is also a reed-ware factory in the city.

Chanthaburi residents are fortunate in having two good waterfalls relatively near. Directly opposite the Chanthaburi turnoff on the Sukhumvit Highway at the 324-km-stone, a dirt road leads inland and goes for 22km through orchards of rambutan, strong-smelling durian, oranges, and litchis; then the road turns right and goes another 3 km to

An old cannon (left) still menaces intruders at the old fortifications outside Chanthaburi. The town's French-style cathedral (above), built around 1880, has an active congregation of Thai-Vietnamese Catholics.

reach **NAM TOK KRATING** ("Bull Waterfall") a cascading series of small falls tumbling over granite for some 400 meters. Trees dedicated by Thai officials, enclosed by white picket fences, decorate the area. A painted map hangs on a tree, pointing out hideaways up a rocky path that winds to the side of the falls. On weekends and holidays the falls attract many visitors, but on weekdays one can find repose next to the small pools and cascades.

Farther down Route 3, near the 347-km-stone, inland lies another popular waterfall, **NAM TOK PRAEW**. Beyond makeshift shacks in which women sell sticky rice and durian jam is a simple gray *chedi* overlooking the fall.

The *chedi* commemorates a consort of King Chulalongkorn who drowned while being rowed up the Chao Phya River to Bang Pa-In. Her death was particularly tragic, since her attendants could have saved her had they not been forbidden by custom to touch the body of a royal person.

Young people like to swim in the pools here, and the area is seldom deserted in daylight. While boys in shorts and sarongs do flips into the cool water, modest girls sit fully covered under the big splash. The fish are more daring and come nibbling at the feet dangling in the water. During the durian season, busloads of Thais from as far as Bangkok roar in to see the falls and bargain for the seductive fruit.

The province of Trat, just beyond Chanthaburi and centered about 400 km from Bangkok at the end of the Sukhumvit Highway, or Route 3, extends between the Gulf of Thailand and the Cambodian border like a mandarin's fingernail. The road from Chanthaburi sweeps through a green panorama of paddy, rubber trees, and marshland. For a

33. Nam Tok Krating
น้ำตกกระทิง

34. Nam Tok Praew
น้ำตกพริ้ว

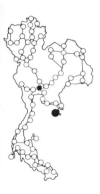

good view of the sea, take the turnoff at the 348-km-stone (just past the turnoff for Nam Tok Praew) for the 16-km trip to Laem Sing.

Named for a lion-shaped island offshore, **LAEM SING** is a small fishing town with two remnants of a brief French colonial presence at the turn of the century: a red brick Customs House and "Chicken Dung Prison."

Return to Route 3 for the remaining 75 km drive to the town of **TRAT**. The provincial capital itself is undistinguished, but trips to scenic islands begin 16 km down the road at **LAEM NGOP**. There you can rent a boat to **KOH CHANG**, Thailand's third largest island, famed for wild boar and the **MAIYOM WATER-FALL**. Off the northern tip of Koh Chang some of the largest sharks in the gulf cruise near a rock outcrop. Your rented boat can sail on to **KOH MARK** and **KOH KUT** which offer clear-water lagoons for good diving. Stock up on provisions in Trat for the island trips. In the town itself, the Thai Rong Roj Hotel offers modest lodging if you wish to stay overnight while exploring the Eastern Gulf's most far-flung province.

Depending on conditions in the area, one may make a diversion toward Bangkok on Road 317, which leaves Route 3 northeast of Chantha-buri and hugs the Cambodian border all the way to Sa Kaeo, east of Bangkok. Many new settlers farm the jungled hills, but most activity is scarce and the countryside mostly wild and unpopulated. On the way, places of interest include the waterfall on Khao Soi Dao, "Mountain of the Harvest of Stars," about 66 km from Route 3; and Wat Tham Lek Khaw Chaka, a cave monastery about 140 km north of Route 3.

The waterfall of Nam Tok Praew (facing page) tumbles into a pool which is a popular place for bathing and picnicking. During the durian season, busloads of Thais from Bangkok come down on outings. Playing at being a skipper (above), a little boy enjoys the gentle surf at Koh Chang, one of Thailand's largest island, famed for its wild boar, and picturesque waterfall; nearby islands offer clear-water lagoons which are ideal for diving.

South Thailand

264

A stretch of pure white sandy beach lies, this time, on an island off the west coast in far South Thailand. On one side of the island, steep rocky limestone cliffs rise sheer from the indigo waters of the Andaman Sea looking like strange seagoing prehistoric monsters. On the other side, a simple fishing village looks suspiciously like a postcard of an unreal tropical paradise. But it is very real and even mundane to the people who live on it and derive their livelihood there. Lithe young men, who have never heard of vertigo, scale to the top of the interior of enormous caves via rickety bamboo ladders to harvest tiny glutinous nests of a certain kind of swift. These are prized by Chinese all over the world as the principal ingredient of the delicacy known as bird's nest soup and South Thailand is reputed by connoisseurs to have the purest and tastiest of this delectable gourmet's delight. The fishermen from the village go out with their nets in the evening, return in the early morning with the dependable treasures of the sea, their lives as inexorably paced by the rhythms of nature as those of the farmers in the Central Plains, more than 1500 kms away.

There are countless large and small islands like this one scattered down the narrowing strip of land that leads to Malaysia, its eastern coast on the Gulf of Thailand, the other on the Indian Ocean. Except for some of the larger islands like Koh Samui (*koh* in Thai means "island") and Phuket which is now being developed as a major tourist center, few are ever seen by visitors, their tropical beauties known only to those who live and work around them.

Thailand's South, a long arm of land containing 14 provinces, is a

The many spires of a venerated temple (previous pages) strain toward a scorching tropical sky at the southern town of Nakhon Si Thammarat, far down Thailand's gulf coast.

richly beautiful area of wild jungle and rocky mountains and broad beaches of powdery sand. It offers the visitor excellent recreation, seafood, skindiving, and spectacular scenery — it is the unheralded, untrammeled part of the country that can provide some of the most rewarding vacations.

In many ways the South is a different world from the rest of the country, especially the farther south you go: different in climate, religion, and industry. Shady plantations of rubber trees are more common than rice paddies. As the visitor enters the four most southern provinces — Betong, Pattani, Narathiwat and Yala — the gilded dome of a Muslim mosque becomes a more familiar sight than the sloping roof of a Buddhist temple. Especially in the provinces near the border where the people speak Malay as well as Thai, and throughout the region, there is a distinctive southern dialect, as well as a southern cuisine that resembles Malaysia's more than that of central Thailand. The southern rainy season — two of them, in fact — is wetter and longer than in the rest of the country, the wettest months of all being December and January.

Like the North, the South was for many years semiautonomous, governed by its own rulers, separated from the capital by both culture and distance. Only within the present century has the South become an integrated part of the Thai kingdom.

It has had its own problems, too. Many of its people have felt cut off from the mainstream of Thai culture, misunderstood by the rulers in far-off Bangkok. One result of this has been a small but worrying separatist movement composed of radical Moslems who would like to see the distant provinces joined to Malaysia. After long neglect of this problem, the government is now taking positive steps to relieve the sense of alienation: officials who are sent to the South from other parts of the country are

now encouraged to learn the local customs and dialect; a southern university has been established; and the royal family recently built a palace at Narathiwat, not far from the border, from where the time is spent traveling among the people of the region. In addition to the Southern Railway Line, modern superhighways now run from Bangkok to the Malaysian border, making the South more accessible than ever before.

The South is rich in natural resources and is, after Bangkok, Thailand's most prosperous region. Rubber, the country's second largest export product after rice, thrives in the humid climate, and there are thousands of hectares of coconut plantations. Tin is mined in the South and all Thailand's tin is refined in Phuket's huge smelter. Haadyai, the railway terminus of the South, is one of the fast-growing cities in Thailand, a brash, brassy, boom town, attracting not only business men seeking to cash in on local industry, but also thousands of Malaysian tourists lured by its free-swinging night life. (Malaysians constitute the largest single group of tourists coming to Thailand, incidentally, and the majority of them come for the pleasures of Haadyai.) Tourism is a fairly recent part of southern development, but if forecasts are correct, it will prove an important one in the near future. For many years, the principal means of getting to the area was the railway, and that was convenient to only a few of the most scenic spots along the peninsula; the only dependable way up until 1976 of getting to the lovely islands of the gulf was to take a freighter of the Thai Navigation Department — still a very pleasant trip if one has the time — and getting to Phuket, on the Andaman Sea, was a major journey. The

Turbaned against the sun, a boatman steers along the narrow peninsula of South Thailand; tourism is a recent development in this prosperous area.

new highways, regular flights by the domestic airline, and a causeway connecting Phuket with the mainland have changed all that, and the incredible natural beauty of the southern beaches are becoming known in the travel world. *Time* Magazine in a recent Asian travel story listed Phuket among a small number of destinations still unspoiled by package tours. Despite the apparent serenity, a number of important resort projects for that idyllic island are already under construction or on the drawing board. "The South is the coming place," says a travel agent in Bangkok. "A few years ago hardly anyone had heard of it. Now everybody wants to go there."

* * *

Thai Airways (not to be confused with Thai International) has daily flights from Bangkok to Phuket, Trang, Haadyai, Pattani and Narathiwat. Most of these provincial capitals are also linked by flights of Thai Airways.

Thailand's State Railway offers daily express service leaving Bangkok's central Hua Lampong Station in the late afternoon for the South. Although designated "express," this is no scenery-blurring train; its leisurely pace affords a good view of green rice paddies, *klong*-side villages, abrupt mountains, and growing towns. Each stop provides a sampling of local food. Hawkers rush to the train's windows selling fresh fruits, *kanoms* (or "sweet") wrapped in banana leaves, barbecued meats, dried squid, and the ubiquitous iced drinks served in plastic bags.

Travelers in no particular hurry should break their journey in several provinces to see attractions otherwise passed after dark. However, the

The seascape at Phangnga Bay, filled with limestone outcrops which seem to spring out of the calm inland waters, has the haunting delicacy of a classic Chinese watercolor painting.

traveler must note that on a journey of 200 km he can break his journey once and once only and then for no longer than 48 hours. You can set off from railway towns on bus, taxi, or boat for a varied and thorough appreciation of the South. When booking seats do not overlook second-class passage, which on many trains equals the comfort of first-class. For those rushing on to Peninsular Malaysia, the express (Express 11) leaves Bangkok on Mondays, Wednesdays and Saturdays in the afternoon and arrives at Butterworth (the terminal for the Malaysian island of Penang) about 24 hours later. Connections can then be made with trains for Kuala Lumpur and Singapore.

The young and resolute might prefer to board one of the air-conditioned coaches of the many companies which make the run from Bangkok to the South. Bangkok to Phuket takes about 14 hours; Bangkok to Haadyai about 20 hours.

Alternatively, South Thailand may be approached from Peninsular Malaysia. Thai Airways has five flights a week from Penang to Phuket: three of these are via Haadyai. Malaysian Airlines has flights from Penang to Haadyai on Fridays and Sundays. Trains depart Butterworth for Haadyai en route to Bangkok on Monday, Wednesday and Friday at 7:55 a.m. The trains arrive at Haadyai after a 4½-hour journey. Quicker by far are the buses from Butterworth to Haadyai and faster still are the "shared" taxis. The latter depart Butterworth when they have a full load of five persons; fares are very reasonable.

Those approaching the South from Malaysia's east coast (Kota Bharu) would cross the Thai-Malaysia border to the station of Sungai Kolok from where it is a two-hour journey to Yala.

During low tide, this broad secluded beach covered with shells extends to the offshore islands, at Hat Noparat Thara near Krabi.

Entering the South

If you are leaving Bangkok by car, the main roads lead to the South's first attractions: Phetchaburi Province and the beaches and hills near Hua Hin. On the way South, you can include a visit to the Rose Garden and Nakhon Pathom (see "Bangkok Surroundings"), or take a shortcut and go directly to Phetchaburi.

The provincial capital of **PHET-CHABURI**, 165 km south of Bangkok, has several worthwhile sights. As you approach the town on Route 4, turn left at the T-junction just outside the town, continue past a rocky hill on the right, cross the railroad tracks, and stop under the shady trees for a visit to **Khao Luang Cave**. Here you will see huge stalactites and many Buddha images, illuminated around midday by a natural shaft of light, presenting an inspiring scene.

As Route 4 enters Phetchaburi town, *naga*-topped walls frame the ascent to a **Palace built by King Mongkut** in the last century. Several buildings surrounding the hillside palace afford a fine vista of the city, its river, rice fields, and the mountainous Burmese border to the west.

Farther south on Route 4, 17 km from Phetchaburi, a dirt road on the right leads to **Kang Krachan Dam** (also called Ubol Ratana Dam after King Bhumibol's eldest daughter). The road first follows a canal, then passes an older dam, and finally comes to the earthen walls of Kang Krachan. The Irrigation Department usually grants permission to tourists to stay at its bungalow overlooking the scenic reservoir and to take boats up the reservoir to the river.

Some 35 km south of Phetchaburi is **CHA-AM**, a beach long favored by Thais but only recently discovered by foreigners. The Regent Cha-am and Regent Lodge hotels make the most of Cha-am's casaurina-fringed beach.

1. Phetchaburi
เพชรบุรี (ตัวเมือง, จังหวัด)
2. Kang Krachan Dam
เขื่อนดินแก่งกระจาน

Khao Luang Cave
ถ้ำเขาหลวง

3. Hua Hin
หัวหิน (ตัวเมือง, อำเภอ)

The numbers in the margin in this section refer to the map on page 264.

About 30 km further south lies **HUA HIN**, Thailand's oldest major beach resort. It was put on the map in 1910 by Prince Chakrabongse, brother of Rama VI, who led a party of international royalty down the peninsula to hunt game. Here, King Prachadipok (1925-1935) built a palace called Klai Klangwan, meaning "far from worries." Fittingly, he was vacationing here on June 24, 1932, when a bloodless coup toppled him, replacing 700 years of absolute monarchy with a constitutional one.

A 1932 *Guide to Bangkok* called the resort, "the most popular with travelers . . . longing for a game of golf." In those days, golf traps were imprinted with tiger pawprints. To-day, Hua Hin's well-tended 18-hole golf course is considerably tamer.

Remnants of the 30s linger at the Railway Hotel. Recently renovated, it has retained its air of gentility, with ceiling fans and gardens filled with a menagerie of animals clipped from the bushes. A bit south, the Royal Garden Hotel, appeals to those with a taste for modern amenities. The Hua Hin beach is wide but unremarkable. Boys rent small ponies for short rides down the wide beach.

Hua Hin town lacks the charm of the Railway Hotel. Its shops sell plastic blow-up porpoises and ducky tubes, seashells artfully fitted into vases and ashtrays, beachware, and floppy hats. However for a bit of lively local color, stroll down to the pier in the morning or evening, order a drink in one of the coffee shops, and watch the fishermen unload their catches and women stoop to examine and bargain for a wide variety of fresh seafood, including an occasional shark or stingray.

Leave Hua Hin by heading south again on Route 4. About 22 km from the town, the highway crosses Pranburi River, then enters a town by the

Limestone hills (facing page) rise near Petchaburi, the first provincial capital as you enter South Thailand. Farther down, children (above) play in the placid water near Hua Hin, one of the country's oldest beach resorts and still popular with Bangkok residents who like the quiet, old-fashioned atmosphere of the place; a royal palace at the resort, built by King Rama VII, bears the evocative name Klai Klangwan, meaning "far from worries."

same name. A road to the left leads to Pak Nam Pranburi situated 8 km away at the river-mouth. Children play under stilt-houses while fishermen hang their nets to dry on wooden racks.

On Route 4 south of Pranburi you begin to glimpse the jagged outline of the **NATIONAL PARK OF KHAO SAM ROI YOT** (Mountain of 300 Peaks). Turn left down a dirt road and continue 14 km to the limestone outcrops. The gorges and caves here used to shelter highwaymen who robbed unwary travelers; their haunts were cleared out long ago. Now deer and monkeys roam the picturesque park.

The sky above Khao Sam Roi Yot is fondly remembered in the annals of the Chakri Dynasty. On August 18, 1868, King Mongkut, an astute mathematician and astronomer, brought the governor of Singapore and members of the Bangkok court to

this place to view a total eclipse of the sun which he himself had foretold. The king's prediction, to the astonishment of local astrologers, was only four minutes off. News of this event helped to discredit the superstition that an eclipse happened when a giant swallowed the sun and disgorged it when impelled by gongs and general noisemaking.

Ninety-one kilometers south of Hua Hin, down a road that branches left just before the 323-km-stone, **PRACHUAP KHIRI KHAN** faces a scenic little harbor enclosed by knoblike hills. As you enter Prachuap, a hill rises to the left and seems, in certain light, to reflect a patch of sky. In fact, on **Khao Chong Krachok** ("Mirror Mountain") a natural arch lets you see through to the sky on the other side. Steps, 395 in all, lead up the hill to a small monastery surrounded by frangipani trees. Within the *chedi* are special Buddha relics

4. Khao Sam Roi Yot
เขาสามร้อยยอด

5. Prachuap Khiri Khan
ประจวบคีรีขันธ์ (ตัวเมือง, จังห

Khao Chong Krachok
เขาช่องกระจก

which were bequeathed to the state by Rama I and Rama IV and are used in the coronation of Chakri kings.

Continue on the road to town, pass the administrative offices, then turn left on to a road that leads to the northern end of the beach. Beach bungalows shaded by trees serve as a pleasant stopover if you wish to break your journey here. Near the end of the jetty that pokes far out into the bay, Pla Mong Restaurant serves delicious seafood — crab salad, deep-fried fish, lobster — to diners seated around a concrete patio overlooking the water.

From Prachuap, 27 km south on Route 4 at the 350-km-stone, turn right continuing for 7 km to reach **HUAY YANG WATERFALL.** The cascade spills over 120 meters of boulders in a jungle setting not far from the Burmese border. The waterfall is located in an area called Thap Sakae District which is famous for its infor-

mal trading. Burmese cross the mountainous frontier to swap animals or produce for manufactured goods that are scarce in their own country.

About 35 km beyond Thap Sa kae District lies the town of **BANG SAPHAN** which is divided into two by the southbound railway tracks. As you enter the town, turn left and 12 km later the road ends at the edge of a wide, pretty bay rimmed by a 6-km-long beach. The green outcrop of Khao Mae Pamphung marks the northern end of the beach; Koh Thalu Island lies off its southern extremity. If you do not mind sand in your shoes, enjoy some seafood and drinks served on the wooden tables right on the beach.

Back on Route 4, south of Bang Saphan, the countryside becomes more lush, mountainous, and overgrown. In cleared spots, rubber plantations spread beneath limestone

The South offers a wide variety of scenic views over the ever-present sea. A hillock looks down upon a finger of land near Prachuap Khiri Khan (left), where bungalows line the white-sand beach. At a temple on the same hill (above, left) pilgrims have adorned a footprint of the Buddha with gold leaf. The strenuous fishing life along the southern coast produces handy people, such as this fisherwoman wearing a traditional hat at Bang Saphan (above, right).

Crossing the Isthmus

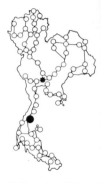

cliffs that appear sporadically down the Kra Isthmus and far into the Malay Peninsula.

Around 490 km south of Bangkok, Route 4 comes to an important junction where it branches right and goes to the Indian Ocean on the coast of South Thailand. The left branch leads to Chumphon provincial capital, while straight ahead 76 km away is the seaport of Lang Suan which lies at the beginning of a recently completed highway linking Bangkok to the towns of Surat Thani, Nakhon Si Thammarat, and Songkhla.

Left at this junction marked by signs and gas stations, a road goes 8 km to **CHUMPHON** which is noted for its cut-rate bird's nest soup. The city itself has little of scenic interest; but east of it lies **PAK NAM CHUMPHON** at the mouth of the Chumphon River, a fishing port that has boats for hire by the hour for trips to nearby islands where swallows build the nests so highly prized in Chinese cuisine. During the mating season from March through August authorized collectors climb high up the cliffs to fetch the delicacies. The island of Lanka Chio is especially famous. Merchants bid for concessions to take the nests, and even hire gunmen to guard their stake. It is fascinating to watch the gathering of nests, but be sure to let the guards know you are just looking. The island-dotted coastal waters here make for exciting sailing too.

From the provincial capital of Chumphon, Route 4 strikes out west across the narrowest neck of the Kra Isthmus, then veers south and follows the Pak Chan River through Kra Buri on the way to Ranong.

About 12 km beyond Kra Buri, turn left just before the 504-km-stone to reach **Tham Prakayang,** a temple in a cavern. If you have no flashlight, the monks will usually lend one for the dark ascent in the image-filled cave. One totally black Buddha gazes upon you through mother-of-pearl eyes. A limestone and wooden stair-

case leads up and out of the cave to well-worn paths trodden by monks who meditate amid the isolated foliage atop the outcrop.

South of Tham Prakayang, the highway begins to cut briskly over jungled hills and crosses a wide river. Soon after the 597-km-stone, **PUNYABAN WATERFALL** lies just next to the road. Truck drivers stop, don their sarongs, and take a quick bath in the splashing water. This is a popular domestic tourist spot. A tea-house serves snacks near the falls. Climb a path to the left of the falls for a good view of the scenic countryside: the Pak Chan estuary, nearby islands, and the mountains of the southern tip of Burma.

At the 612-km-stone turn right near the Thara Hotel to enter the provincial capital of **RANONG**. The hotel itself has one of Ranong's main attractions: hot mineral water piped in from nearby thermal springs. To reach the springs, travel up the side-road left of the river behind the hotel. The road follows a rocky riverbed bordered by thatch huts and banana trees. After 1 km, on the right stands a small shrine to the spirit of the springs. A well encloses the main outlet which pours forth 500 liters per minute of 70°C sparkling mineral water. You can cross a suspension bridge leading over the river to a little park. Or you can climb the hill behind the shrine to a small *wat* enclosed by a lovely, deep-shaded forest.

Continuing up the road past the hot springs, you reach the village of **HAT SUPIN** in tin-mining country: stark landscapes of white silt, bamboo scaffolding, deep pits, and gouged-out cliff faces. In open cast mining, gushing water carves holes in the earth. The mineral-laden water is filtered through a platform sieve supported by a bamboo framework. The

10 Punyaban Waterfall
น้ำตกบัญญาพรรณ

8. Pak Nam Chumphon
ปากน้ำชุมพร
11. Ranong
ระนอง (ตัวเมือง, จังหวัด)

12. Hat Supin
หาดสุปิน

9. Tham Prakayang
ถ้ำพระขาหย่ง

The evening market (right) bustles at the mouth of the Ranong River.

276

tin ore is then sorted out of the mud and sand. In the morning you can watch sturdy women carrying wooden bowls to pan tin in the river, while their husbands work in the chalk quarry behind the village. One of Thailand's major exports (after rice, other crops, and natural rubber), tin is mined all along the Indian Ocean coast of the Kra Isthmus. Much of the production, which ranks second in the world, comes from private businesses like those around Hat Supin.

A small sign with fish painted on it points the way to **Wat Hat Supin** where children rush up to sell sweet popcorn. Visitors feed the popcorn to hundreds of carp that swarm in a pool by the side of the temple.

Drive back to Ranong, then take the 3-km-long road to **PAK NAM RANONG** on the sea. There boats unload fish at a modern wharf and trucks dump tonnes of crushed ice

on emptied decks. From this port some boats sail the Indian Ocean as far as Pakistan in search of fish.

Ranong Island, with its houses on stilts and fishing boat anchorage, lies directly opposite Pak Nam Ranong. You can rent boats on the mainland for island trips.

Return to Route 4 and continue south past Kapoe, Khuraburi, and the 776-km-stone, the last road marker showing the distance from Bangkok. About 4 km north of Takua Pa there is a junction with Road 401 leading east to Surat Thani and Chaiya.

A great drive full of ups, downs, and sharp corners, Road 401 zigzags over and around the cloud-cloaked limestone pinnacles of the Kra Isthmus. For the first 37 km, it traverses the wide valley of the Takua Pa River, passing tin mining camps flanked by mountains. Then the road enters the hills and plunges through a

remarkable series of streaked lime-stone precipices and splintered rocks — some of the most breathtaking scenery in Thailand. Rarely do you see another vehicle. The old dream of a canal across the Isthmus linking the Indian Ocean and the Gulf of Thailand seems unlikely to material-ize in this wild setting.

For a midway rest, stop 59 km from the start of Road 401 at **Wat Thamwaran**, just to the left of a small river. The *wat* provides a simple shel-ter for monks who meditate near a cave that opens on the other side of the outcrop to a serene spot on the riverbank.

Approaching Surat, as the Thais call it, Road 401 leaves the hills and enters dense rubber plantations. About 120 km from the Route 4 turnoff, Road 401 bends right for the final 12 km into the town of **SURAT THANI**, a busy ship-building, fish-ing, and mining center lying on the

right bank of the Tapi River. Surat itself has little worth seeing, but is the point of departure for worthwhile sidetrips. The first sidetrip is for those interested in ancient history who should here board the north-bound train for an hour's trip to Chaiya.

A small, sleepy town of unpaint-ed wooden buildings, a 60-second pause for the Bangkok express, it could be any small town of South Thailand. But **CHAIYA** is the subject of a dispute claiming it to be the capital of a once great empire. A group of historians now believe that the capital of the Srivichaya empire, described by the wandering Chinese Monk, I Ching, in A.D. 671, was not Palembang in Sumatra, but Chaiya. In fact, they claim, the date previous-ly accepted as the founding of the em-pire in Palembang was actually the date it was conquered by Chaiya, and even the name Chaiya, they believe, is

Wat Thamwaran
วัดธรรมาวาส
15. Chaiya
ไชยา (ตัวเมือง, อำเภอ)

14. Surat Thani
สุราษฎร์ธานี (ตัวเมือง, จังหวัด)

Wat Mahathat
วัดมหาธาตุ

Suan Mok
สวนโมก

Wat Wieng
วัดเวียง

Wat Long
วัดลอง

Wat Kaeo
วัดแก้ว

a contraction of Srivichaya.

Only a few traces of this mighty empire, which once stretched from Java through Malaysia to Thailand, remain today. Less than 2 km out of town stands **Wat Mahathat**, one of the most revered temples in Thailand. Its central *chedi* is claimed to be over 1,300 years old and is a direct visual link between Chaiya and the Srivichaya period. A small museum adjoining the *wat* has some interesting relics from the vicinity.

Closer to town is **Wat Wieng**, where an inscription was found, dated A.D. 755 and erected by a King Vishnu. It was the erroneous attribution of this inscription, 50 years ago, to a different location that led to the hypothesis that Palembang was the Srivichaya capital. Two other *wats*, **Wat Long** and **Wat Kaeo**, equidistantly spaced from Wat Wieng, mark the sites of the Srivichaya edifices. Today only Wat Kaeo holds

a dim reminder of a forgotten past with the crumbling wall of a once great stupa. All that is known is that it was built to commemorate a victory. Perhaps the shattered remains of a Buddha, peering through a mist of cobwebs from his lonely niche, knows the truth.

A few kilometers farther west from these historic remains, a small hillock rises from the flat countryside. Here stands a Buddhist retreat named **Suan Mok**, as new as Chaiya's past is old. The walls and columns inside the central building are covered with an eclectic series of paintings that span everything from the history of Buddhism to Aesop's fables. Suan Mok owes a surrealistic touch to a wandering Zen Buddhist, Emanuel Sherman, whose search for enlightenment led him from the United States to Japan and Thailand, eventually ending on the island of Phangan off the Thai coast. After his death

Crossing the Kra Isthmus, the narrowest point on the southern peninsula, the highway zigzags over and around impressive limestone pinnacles (facing page). A good place to make a cool stopover along the way is the cave temple of Wat Thamwaram (above, left), where a simple shelter is provided for monks who come to meditate. Children also enjoy playing in the cave and its serene surroundings, and one bold youngster poses au naturel (above, right).

Idyllic Islands

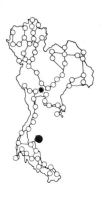

local artists covered one wall with illustrations to portray Sherman's epigrams.

Bas-reliefs telling the story of the Buddha decorate the outer walls. They were modeled locally from photos of the Indian originals. Suan Mok's quirky touch continues into its adjoining structures. In what could almost be a bilingual pun, the *bot* really is a boat. A large concrete ship serenely sails the sea of suffering to eventual nirvana. Suan Mok's abbot is a much respected man whose followers flock from all over Thailand, and his lay brother is one of the chief proponents of the Chaiya capital theory.

From Suratthani it is 20 km to Ban Don, and 70 km to Don Sak from which boats depart from **KOH SAMUI**, the largest island in the western portion of the Gulf of Thailand, and for **KOH PHA-NGAN** a short distance north of Koh Samui.

Several times daily, buses make the one-hour journey from the railway station at Suratthani to Ban Don. Speedboats leave Ban Don at 9 a.m., and 11 a.m. (50 baht) for a three-hour journey to Samui. Another leaves at 12:30 p.m. for Ban Don and Pha-ngan, 45 minutes further on (60 baht).

The overnight boat leaves Ban Don at 11 p.m., arriving at Samui at 6 a.m. (50 baht for a four-person cabin). An express boat takes just two hours and leaves at 8:30 and 10:30 a.m. (60 baht).

The newer, faster route is to take a one-hour, 70 km bus ride (20 baht) from Suratthani to the Lame Kula Pier at Don Sak. Ferries depart at 9 a.m. and 4 p.m., taking just one hour to reach Koh Samui (40 baht).

About 250 sq km or the size of Penang, Samui is one of the prettiest islands in the Gulf. Superb beaches, hills, jungles and waterfalls provide scenic variety rivalled by few other

16. Koh Samui
เกาะสมุย

Ban Don
บ้านดอน

Regular ferries (above) ply the waters between Ban Don on the coast and the idyllic tropical island of Koh Samui (right), 32 km away. The largest island in the western Gulf of Thailand, Koh Samui is also one of the most beautiful and unspoiled; its economy is based on coconuts, reputedly the best in Thailand, and the aroma of roasting coconut flesh pervades the island. In addition to the six-hour ferry a speedboat makes the trip in only three hours.

islands. For the moment, it is the domain of the backpackers but its natural beauty mark it for future tourism development, beginning with an airport slated for the late 1980s.

Samui's lifestyle is relaxed, its people are even more relaxed. Coconuts are the mainstay of the island's economy, a well-developed economy which utilizes labor-saving devices in the form of monkeys trained to climb up the tall trees and pluck the coconuts. The smell of roasting coconut meat, rich and pleasant, pervades the island.

Aside from a hotel on Yai Noi Bay, Na Thon Bay, and another at Chawaeng Bay, accommodation comes in the form of simple bungalows costing less than US$2 per night. There's no shortage of them; there are a total of 104 complexes at 11 beautiful beaches.

Simple food is cheap and delicious on Koh Samui. At the morning market you can breakfast on noodles and mild coconut curry for a few baht. Hawkers sell an endless variety of coconut and rice sweets. Try the coconut and date paste balls covered with sweet dough and deep fried. Fruits grown on the island — coconuts (the main export), papayas, bananas, mangoes (in season), pineapples, and jackfruit — are incredibly cheap.

The main activity for visitors on Koh Samui is "beaching." The beaches have it all: long stretches of dazzling white sand littered with cowries and crawling with harmless crabs; warm, clear water; and a sun that never quits, except in December when the rains claim that distinction.

A fleet of *song tao*, small pickup trucks converted to taxis with two parallel rows of seats at the back, serve Koh Samui. Cheap and fast, they never refuse a fare and load up until passengers are hanging off the

17. Ban Ang Thong

บ้านอ่างทอง

tailgate and roof. Visitors can organise a "do-it-yourself" island tour. For about 50 bath a head half a dozen persons can pile into a *song tao* or, alternatively, make a similar round-the-island tour by boat for about the same price. Rent a motorcycle; a paved 52-km road around the rim of the island makes driving a pleasure.

Worth visiting are **Na Muang Falls**, **Hin Ngu Temple** with its huge seated Buddha and a tiny beach with "grandmother" and "grandfather" rocks, both of which are explicitly phallic.

An excursion worth making is a visit to the small villages that are dispersed throughout Koh Samui. More than 32,000 people live on the island and that is an enormous amount of hospitality. Near the mountains are coconut plantations and lush forests where the occasional path cuts through to a cluster of beautiful, yet simple, hardwood homes.

There is a remarkable sense of peace on Koh Samui. The island and the sea produce an abundance of food and the forests provide bamboo and wood for shelter. Life seems easy. There are several schools on the island and the wealthier families send their bright children to universities on the mainland. And whoever decides not to aspire to an intellectual or commercial career in the modern cities of Thailand knows there are planty of coconuts in the forests.

* * *

To the north is **KOH PHA-NGAN**, an island even more remote but with the same type of bungalow accommodations as found at Koh Samui.

For 200-300 bath; one can hire a fishing boat to carry a large number of passengers to explore nearby islands. One of the most popular is the Angthong National Park, a one-hour boat journey northwest of Samui. It boasts a huge inland lake with water the green of glacial lakes.

Route 4 continues down the peninsula along the Indian Ocean passing through the small district town of **TAKUA PA**. Over a thousand years ago, Takua Pa was a port for Indian traders who settled along the coasts of the Malayan Peninsula when the region was called Suvannabhumi, Land of Gold. Some scholars think the Indians sought shortcuts to the South China Sea. Unearthed statues have helped trace caravan routes across the Kra Isthmus to Surat Thani. Two 7th-century Dvaravati statues found on an island in the mouth of the yellowish Takua Pa River, add to the archaeological evidence. Today Takua Pa has little claim to fame except as the district center of a rich tin

20. Takua Pa
ตะกั่วป่า (ตัวเมือง, อำเภอ)

An islander on Koh Samui nimbly scales a coconut tree to cut it down; every part of the tree finds a use—the flesh of the nut for food, the fronds for thatching and matting, and the trunk for timber and fuel.

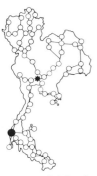

18. Bang Sak Beach
หาดบ้านสาก

21. Lam Pi Waterfall
น้ำตกลำปี

19. Khao Luk Beach
หาดเขาลูก

mining area. Travelers can stop here for a bite to eat on the way to Phuket.

About 13 km south of Takua Pa, tire tracks branching off Route 4 to the right under some casuarina trees lead to **BANG SAK BEACH** on a wide bay. Behind a refreshment stand, a thatched palm screen encloses a freshwater well for bathing and changing clothes. With its turquoise waters and white sand, isolated Bang Sak Beach lacks only Tahitian drums to complete an idyllic Polynesian setting.

Soon after Bang Sak, the road rises from sea level and meanders along jungled cliffs. In gaps between the trees, wide white beaches and small fishing fleets appear below. Farther out at sea, barges are engaged in small-scale mining.

About 36 km from Takua Pa, as the highway completes a twisting descent back to the sea, **KHAO LUK BEACH** lies immediately to the right.

About 30 families live most of the year in the natural shelter of this cove. The men do not fish; with the aid of air pumps and goggles, they dive for tin. Like nautical prospectors, they stay under water one or two hours at a time, loading tin-bearing sand into buckets. Workers hoist the full buckets onto bamboo rafts and sieve their contents.

Every June the powerful monsoon churns up the ocean and halts the tin diving off Khao Luk. The mining families abandon their huts to the destructive lashing of wind and sea until the monsoon relents.

Returning to Route 4, south about 69 km from Takua Pa, a reddish dirt road to the left, just before a small school on the other side of the highway, marks the entrance to **LAM PI WATERFALL**. Follow the dirt road 2 km through a rubber plantation to the three-part fall and clear pool perfect for bathing.

The thirty-odd families who live on the sheltered beach of Khao Luk (above, left) do not earn their living by fishing, as one might expect, but by diving offshore for tin-bearing sand on the bottom of the sea; operations are halted in June each year by the powerful monsoon storms. About 30 kilometers away a drive through a rubber plantation takes you to the waterfall of Lam Pi (above, right), at the foot of which is a clear pool that is ideal for bathing.

Up-and-coming Resort

Fifty km south of Takua Pa is the town of Khok Kloi, with the road to Pang-nga leading to the left. Another 30 km south, one crosses the Sarasin Bridge onto the island of **PHUKET**, washed by the warm waters of the Andaman Sea and one of the prettiest islands in Asia. The term "tropical paradise" is overused but justified.

Unlike many islands, Phuket's beauty is not limited to its beaches. About the size of Singapore, it offers beautiful beaches on the down slope of a range of hills covered in jungle, coconut and rubber plantations, and picturesque villages. On the other side of the beaches are reefs teeming with marine life. In short, it enjoys the best of three worlds.

The road from the Bridge to the town of Phuket passes the airport before arriving at the intersection with the roads to Surin Beach and Phak Chit. Here, stand two bronze women warriors, drawn swords in hands. The pair are the sisters, Chan and Muk, who led an army to repel Burmese invaders, an 18th-century battle which preserved Phuket's independence.

Phuket's wealth comes from four principal sources. Its waters and the interior areas are rich tin lodes, major contributors to Thailand's position as the world's third largest tin exporter. Rubber is also a major moneyearner as are coconuts and rice.

Tin built the town of Phuket, home for some 50,000 Thais. For the most part, the town is a non-descript collection of three-story shophouses. In the northeastern section of the town, however, one finds the legacy of the tin barons that give the town what charm it has. Here are the baronial houses built in the European fashion and set in large lawns, testament to the vast wealth of Phuket's heyday in the early years of this century.

The streets in the inner city are lined with old-style shophouses built

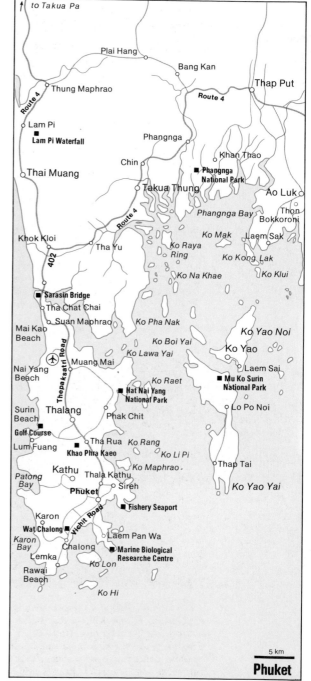

in what is known as the Sino-Portuguese style similar to Songkhla and Penang. Three stories high, and built by middle-income Chinese, the ground floor is a shop and reception hall, the upper floors are for the large families. The large signs with big characters over the doors identify the family and clan residing within.

Several downtown buildings suggest European influence, indeed, some of the early history of the town involves Europeans. In 1786, the founder of Penang, Captain Light of the East India Company, was offered a package deal of both islands by the Sultan of Kedah suzerain of the area. But for Britain's lack of finances to capitalize on the deal, Phuket might well have become a British colony.

The Chartered Bank building, Thai Airways office and others with their arched loggias resemble the buildings of colonial Singapore and Penang. These old buildings lend a charm to Phuket that is otherwise missing. Of note is the brightly-painted **Put Jaw Chinese Temple** just past the market on Ranong Road. Like many similar Chinese shrines elsewhere in Asia, its central altar is dedicated to Kuan Yin, the goddess of mercy.

Outside of the town, the only building worthy of note is **Wat Chalong**. It sits 6 km further south on the Phuket Bypass, a ring road of sorts that runs west of Phuket town. The opulently-decorated temple is famed for the gold leaf covered statue of Luang Pho Chaem, the wat's abbot at the turn of the century. He was renowned for his skill in setting bones, a craft which proved very useful when armies of Chinese from Malaysia attempted to take over the town and its tin mines. Once the smoke had cleared, Luang Pho was awarded a special ecclestical title for his services in healing those injured

Chinese immigrants have played an important part in the development of many of the leading towns and cities of the South. On the wealthy, tin-mining island of Phuket, the Temple of Put Jaw (above, left), the oldest and largest, is dedicated to Kuan Yin, the Goddess of Mercy. Colorful and distinctive festivals, such as fire-walking rituals, are held annually at this gaudily-decorated temple, under the supervision of the resident priests (above, right).

in the clashes.

Phuket's glory, however, lies in its beaches and it has a wealth of them. All are located on the western side of the island; the eastern shore is comprised primarily of rocky shoals.

The most developed is **PA-TONG** due east of Phuket town. In the early 1970s, Patong was little more than a fishing village on a wide crescent of sand. It has however made up for lost time, with a vengeance. Gone is the village, replaced by an entire town with hotels, supermarkets, shopping arcades, and a range of amenities.

The beach is dotted with colorful parasols and the bay with yachts. Unlike most of the other Phuket beaches, Patong has a wide range of water sports facilities including windsurfing, sailing, and boogie boards. One can rent scuba gear and even take lessons leading to PADI certification. These shops offer diving trips into the bay or west to the Similan Islands, considered one of the best diving areas in Asia with crystal clear blue water and a multitude of marine life. One can also snorkel at the reef on the southern end of Patong Bay or at Kata Noi, two beaches to the south. Phi Phi island is also an ideal snorkeling area.

Patong has a full array of restaurants specializing in seafood prepared Thai-style. The prize item on the menu is the giant Phuket Lobster, a monster of the deep with enough meat to feed a couple. Patong also has open-air bars with hostesses and a discotheque. To the north are Surin and Singh beaches.

SURIN is dominated by the Pansea Resort. **HAAD SINGH** is a beautiful beach, reputedly with a murderous undertow which accounts for its lack of accommodation. Instead, there is a nine-hole golf course kept cropped to the proper height by a

Rawai Village
หมู่บ้านราไว

Laem Ka Noi
แหลมข่าน้อย

286

herd of water buffaloes who, by being moving hazards, wreck havoc with any serious golfer's game. An 18-hole golf course is to be completed on the island by the late 1980s.

Further north near the airport is **NAI YANG** beach. Set in the heart of Nai Yang National Park, it is cooled by casaurina trees. It recently acquired a major hotel but otherwise accommodation is limited.

Beyond Nai Yang is Phuket's longest beach, **MAJ KHAO** where each December through February, giant sea turtles struggle ashore at night to lay their eggs in holes they dig in the sand.

South of Patong is **KHARON** beach and, past a small ridge running a finger into the sea, Kata beach. Kharon has a large hotel but is otherwise occupied by small villages of bungalows. Not as developed as Patong, Kharon and Kata both have clean, wide beaches. They appeal to the holidaymaker interested in relaxing, soaking up the sun, swimming and enjoying excellent seafood.

KATA is the site of Asia's second Club Med, a tribute to its beauty. There are other bungalow complexes as well as some good restaurants. Water sports facilities are limited to windsurf boards, sailboats and hobies.

Over the hill from Kata is **KATA NOI** (Little Kata). It has a large hotel, white sand and a superb snorkeling area at the southern end of the beach.

At the southwestern edge of Phuket is one of its prettiest beaches: **NAI HARN**. Nai Harn is a strand of sand nestled between two tall hills, fronted by a calm sea and backed by a lagoon; an idyllic setting if there ever was one. It boasts the island's most expensive hotel and cheapest bungalows, all on the same beach. Water sports facilities are limited but the beach is so beautiful no one cares. Nai Harn is renowned for its sunsets.

A word of warning about Phuket: during the monsoon season

(May–October), many of the beaches develop a particularly vicious undertow and care must be taken when swimming.

Within sight of Nai Harn is a stunning vantage point for viewing the sunset: **Promthep Cape**, a tall hill carpeted in date palms and bright yellow grasses, plunging into a sea hissing against its rocky shore. Around the corner from Promthep, at the end of the highway from Phuket town is Rawai whose foreshore is a mass of rocks that lie exposed during low tide. It is then that shell hunters venture forth, turning over the stones in search of specimens.

RAWAI is one of the island's two *Chao Lay* or sea gypsy villages. The sea gypsies were once nomadic fishing families, roaming from island to island, setting up housekeeping until they decided to move on. Their men are skilled fishermen both above and below the water. From a young

Tribes of exotic sea gypsies preserve their own way of life on Koh Sireh near Phuket town. Anthropologists believe these independent people are related to the fisherfolk of the Andaman Islands.

age they can dive to great depths in search of the giant lobsters, staying there for up to three minutes. They are a simple people who adhere to animistic beliefs.

The village, and that at **Koh Siray** east of Phuket town, are not terribly clean. Most families live in thatched huts set on stilts and protected by tin roofs, with the livestock living beneath the floor. There is not a lot to see in either village. East of Phuket town, the Phuket Aquarium houses a variety of colorful well-displayed Andaman Sea fish and coral.

Transportation around the island is by blue-and-white buses that leave from the Phuket market for every point on the island. The cost is 10 baht per person. Small, four-wheeled vehicles called tuk-tuks, carry four passengers in comfort and cost about 150 baht depending on destination.

Here, as in Samui, the preferred vehicle is the motorcycle. Phuket has numerous roads that lead into picturesque little villages (the town itself is reputed to have had the first paved road in the kingdom). In the waters off the eastern coast are numerous pearl farms which welcome visitors. Most grow what are known as "half pearls" but one, on Koh Naka Noi, grows the full-sized South Sea pearls worth thousands of dollars. It also claims to have produced the world's largest pearl.

Koh Naka Noi
เกาะนากาน้อย

Phuket is the departure point for journeys to the amazing Pang-nga Bay and Koh Phi Phi a few hours east by boat.

About 30 km northeast of Khok Kloi on the mainland north of Phuket, a road on the left leads to **SUAN KU** with a limestone cave filled with dozens of Buddha images. Light streaming in through an opening gives the cave a mystical aura.

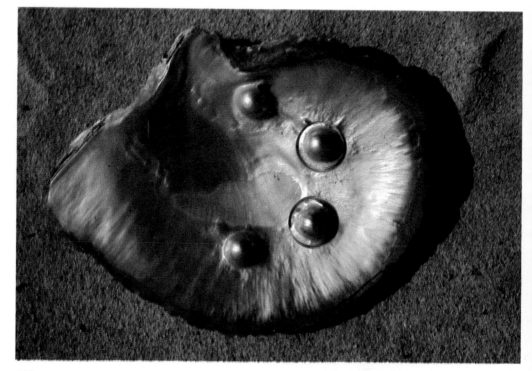

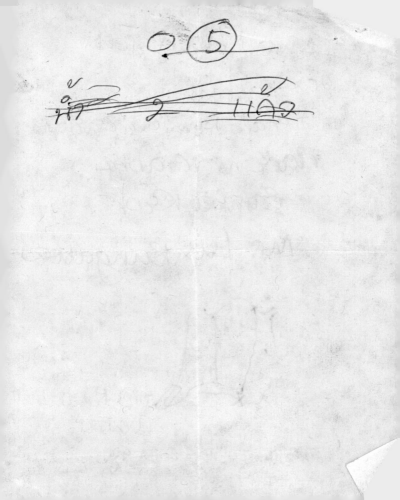

Kho Phangan

40k ~~Post~~ troul / ~~Kho~~ Samoi
Hard Rim overdeveloped

Place nn Crabbe
Bamboo Rest.

Mr. Lux Bungaloes

HAD RM
DONT
GO.

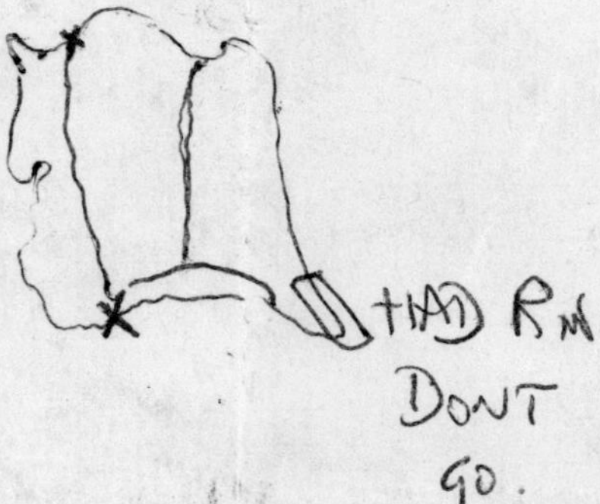

Island Interlude

23. Phangnga Bay
อ่าวพังงา

Khao Kien
เขาเขียน

Koh Pannyi
เกาะปันหยี

Tham Lawd
ถ้ำลอด

Route 4 soon enters Phangnga's small provincial town where your choice of lodgings is limited to several lackluster Chinese hotels. If they seem below standard, remember that the sights in **PHANGNGA BAY** will more than make up for the dearth of good lodging in town. As there may be a number of tourists in town at the same time, it is always a good idea to arrange your boat rental the afternoon or evening before setting out for the bay. To do this, go 6 km back towards Khok Kloi and turn left for 4 km to the Phangnga Customs House and a small village where fishing and tourist boats are rented.

Enroute to Phangnga Bay, the boat glides along glassy, green riverways flanked by mangrove swamps. Old ladies under big hats paddle past in narrow boats piled with bananas. The boatman stops at green signs naming the islands after the shape of their silhouettes (such as Koh Ma Chu or "Puppy Island").

Just before the mouth of Phangnga River, the boat approaches the base of the mountain **KHAO KIEN** where a cavern contains primitive paintings depicting human and animal forms like the cave drawings of Lascaux. To the right lies a large rock island called **KOH PANNYI** where an entire Muslim fishing village stands on stilts over the water.

The boat proceeds into a maze of islands, one more astonishing than the next, where part of the James Bond movie *Man With The Golden Gun* was filmed. Highlights of this "lost world" setting include:

THAM LAWD: On a seeming collision course with a huge limestone outcrop, the boat slips into a barely discernible, overgrown entrance to a cave. For more than 50 meters you slide under giant stalactites. Rocks protruding from the water appear to

The clear waters around Phuket are good for pearl farming (facing page); a large pearl farm is maintained on Koh Naka Noi, an island just thirty minutes off the eastern coast of Phuket. Towering limestone outcrops (above left), carved by weathering and then flooded by a rise in the sea level, stand in Phangnga Bay, one of Thailand's most scenic spots. Primitive, ancient paintings (above, right) adorn the walls of the cave on the island of Khao Kien in the bay.

have been sliced by a machete-wielding god.

THAM NAK: A twisted stalagmite at the entrance resembles a *naga* serpent, giving this cave its name. Green stalactites burst from the ceiling like a frozen waterfall. The whole mountain-island seems from the outside to drip with streaked limestone. Scenes from numerous Thai movies have been filmed here.

KOH THALU: *Thalu* means to pass from one side to the other, in this case not over the mountain, but under it. The boat squeezes through a cave filled with stalactites.

KOH KHAO PING GUN: This is the spot to shut off the motor, to swim and picnic. A small beach overlooks another island, **KOH TAPOO**, which looks like a thorny spike drilled into the sea. Behind the beach is a huge rock slide: the mountain seems to have split in two. The halves appear to lean against each other. Locals say they are two lovers. A small staircase leads to a cavern above the water where limestone formations look like a large mound of solidified spilled glue.

Several onshore caves in Phang-nga are worth visiting. Approached from town, **THAM RUSSI** or "Hermit Cave" lies on the left 2 km before the Customs House turnoff. A stalagmite in the approximate shape of a hermit has been embellished by human hands with a long white beard, a saffron cloth around the shoulder, and a cane. Many believe the *russi* has power to cure the sick and predict winning lottery numbers.

Unusual labyrinthine grottoes weave through Tham Russi. In a parklike atmosphere, lovers stroll over bridges crossing pools within the cave that is well-appointed with neon lights and even toilet facilities.

Continuing 500 meters down the road, passing the governor's office on

Tham Nak
ถ้ำหนัก

Tham Russi
ถ้ำฤาษี

Koh Thalu
เกาะตาลู

Koh Khao Ping Gun
เกาะเขาพิงกัน

Koh Tapoo
เกาะตะปู

The Southwest Coast

The seascape at Phangnga Bay is filled with a fantastic array of weathered limestone outcrops and islands.

the left, you see a blue sign pointing out a trail towards **Wat Tham Pong Chang**, "Temple-Cave in the Elephant's Stomach." A claustrophobic tunnel to the left of a pool leads into a small shrine adorned with statues of three sacred elephants.

Just 2 km from Phangnga on Route 4 you reach a fork where a sign points right, 85 km to Krabi. Beyond the fork the road rises into a winding pass through giant limestone hills and fertile valleys. At the foot of the pass on the right, you are greeted by the humble visage of a Buddha statue at **Wat Kirirong**, at the entrance to a hollow under huge cliffs.

South of Wat Kirirong the horizon continues to defy gravity in places where huge rocks rise above the jungle in seemingly towering upheavals. About 45 km from Phangnga the road squeezes between two gargantuan rocks and glides into the town of **AO LUK**, 40 km before Krabi. Turn-

ing right at the main junction in town, you go 2 km to reach **THAN BOKKORONI NATIONAL PARK**, one of the most beautiful in Thailand. Like a scene from *Lost Horizon*, the park funnels through lofty cliffs. In one spot an underground stream rises amid lush vegetation at the base of a mountain. Gravel paths snake beneath cliff faces covered in green vines punctuated by red hibiscus. The bay of Ao Luk is fascinating with its huge limestone rocks towering majestically above calm, green waters.

Returning to Route 4 you can stop at **Ban Thong Agricultural Station** where botanists breed new strains of rubber, coffee, and tea. Continuing along Route 4, you wind through dense stands of rubber trees. Strips of white latex hang drying from bamboo poles in front of many houses. Unlike Malaysia with its vast plantations, Thailand has a multitude of small, privately owned groves.

About 25 km south of Ao Luk, still traveling beneath and around unpredictable limestone "eruptions," you pass **Naichong Rubber Experimental Station.**

By taking Route 4 all the way toward Krabi (the highway actually bypasses the provincial capital 5 km to the north of it), you miss a scenic sidetrip. If you have an extra few hours, turn right about 7 km beyond the Naichong Station. Continue for 6½ km, then left for 11½ km through small farming villages not far from the sea. A white sign points to Hat Noparat Thara Beach 7 km down a dirt road.

The usually deserted broad beach of **HAT NOPARAT THARA** faces rocky islands half a kilometer off-shore that can be reached on foot at low tide. Along the beach casuarina trees extend for kilometers, providing shade for occasional benches. The sand varies in texture from sugar-like fineness to a grainier composition of millions of tiny shells.

Drive back 7 km to the sideroad and go 3 km farther to another white sign, this one marking the 9 km road to **SUSARN HOI ("SHELL CEMETERY") BEACH**. This is not a sand beach; rock slabs, made of petrified shells 25 million years old, feel like irregular concrete slabs underfoot. Many of the nipa huts along the beach sell choice pieces of petrified cones.

Back on the sideroad to **KRABI**, you enter the town behind the province's administrative offices on a hill overlooking the port. From there you can drive to the Krabi River and the wharves. Old black junks with yin and yang talismans painted on their bows will often berth at Krabi after voyages from Singapore or Penang. From the docks you can catch boats to Koh Phi Phi, the island of high cliffs and curious cave drawings.

27. Susarn Hoi Beach
หาดสุสานหอย

28. Krabi
กระบี่ (ตัวเมือง, จังหวัด)

26. Hat Noparat Thara
หาดนพรัตน์ธารา

Scenic, unexplored beaches run for kilometers along the coast around Trang and Krabi, on the Andaman Sea. The sand varies in texture from sugarlike fineness to a grainy composition of shells, and the water is often limpidly blue. The beach at Noparat Thara (above) looks out on a line of rocky offshore islands that can be reached by foot at low tide. A bit farther down the coast past Trang stretches Pak Mong Beach (opposite), where the scenery is memorable.

Turquoise waves caress a beach so dazzlingly white it is almost painful to the eye. Colorful fishing boats bask in a wide, sheltered bay. Called **KOH PHI PHI**, this island paradise, fringed with secluded beaches and surrounded by clear, warm waters, lies south of the fishing town of Krabi.

From Krabi, the boat follows a seemingly aimless path to avoid the mud banks. Koh Phi Phi is visible ahead as soon as you hit the open sea, and gradually the morning mist clears to reveal an undulating island with a high, rocky, tree-covered headland at the southern tip. No regular boats make the four-hour trip out from Krabi, but if you ask at the wharves, there usually is someone planning on going. Alternatively, boats leave regularly from Phuket's Chalong Bay for the four-hour journey.

The tiny population of Koh Phi Phi lives in a scattering of fishing huts. Walking northeast down the coast, you will find a string of a half-dozen beaches with thatched bungalows of the type (and price) found on Samui. Small beach-side restaurants serve seafood prepared European or Thai style.

When exploring the island, you will not fail to be impressed by the huge kilometer-long rock that rears out of the sea south of the island. The sea funnels down between the steep cliffs of this barren island and the equally formidable ramparts of Koh Phi Phi's headland, creating a choppy swell that can be frightening in the small boat that ferries you across. A flimsy jetty, suspended from overhanging rock by a tangle of ropes, projects out over the sea. Clamber along it and you find yourself in a huge, dripping cavern. A web of bamboo scaffolding reaches up, disappearing into the gloomy upper recesses. Men climb up these precar-

ious ladders to collect swallow's nests which are sold as an expensive delicacy for the gourmet. One glance at the shaky supports reaching up in darkness to the ceiling of the cave is enough to explain why bird's nest soup is very expensive.

The cave's denizens provide a more mundane product in the guano that coats the cave floor and fills the air with its distinctive odor. On the cave wall close to the entrance are a mysterious series of paintings depicting a variety of sailing ships.

* * *

For kilometers around Krabi on the mainland, eerie limestone outcrops erupt from the earth trailing a green canopy of vegetation behind them. They are the land-based kin of the islands that dot the sea around Phi Phi. To soften the blow of returning to "civilization," Krabi has an excellent and inexpensive little hotel with a downstairs restaurant that has

that small town rarity, an English menu. It promises such unusual delicacies as "four things soup in a firepan" or "assorted duck's feet."

As you head southeast from Krabi on Route 4, the land gradually flattens. Dike-enclosed rice fields appear on both sides of the road. Seemingly abandoned suitcases and boxes on the roadside designate bus stops; would-be passengers wait patiently under banana trees nearby.

Only a fanatical spelunker would venture off Route 4 to investigate the minor caves at **KHAO PINA**. All fanatics should turn left 92 km from the Krabi junction down a dirt road leading 1½ km to a small temple at the base of a tall staircase climbing up to two caves. Bring your own flashlight. An unexpected statue of a Thai official dressed in a white, medalfestooned jacket and blue pants stands stiffly before a chapel.

Back on Route 4, you pass

Khao Pina
เขาปิ่นา

Folk art decorates the southern countryside everywhere you go along the road. There is a simple and playful artistry about many of the statues, such as this pastel Buddha just north of Krabi (above, left). An unexpected statue of a Thai official (above, right) stands stiffly before the chapel at Khao Pina. Trang's Chinese heritage is revealed at the elaborately decorated Teochew shrine at Ban Bangrok (facing page), dedicated to a red-faced god of war.

30. Trang
ตรัง (ตัวเมือง, จังหวัด)

Pak Mong Beach
หาดผาม่อง

Ban Bangrok
บ้านบางรก

Surin Park
สวนสุรินทร์

through Huai Yot 108 km from Krabi and go another 28 km to **TRANG** provincial capital. Everyone gets down to business in Trang, one of the smaller but prosperous links in the chain of largely Chinese southern towns. Many of the Teochew-speaking immigrants sought work here panning tin but wound up running the rubber trade.

Trang's Chinese heritage is reflected in monuments at the northern approach to the city. In **BAN BANG ROK**, 3 km north on Route 4, a Teochew shrine honors Kwan Tee Hun, a red-faced, bearded god believed to have the power to prevent or start war. Tortoises, symbolic of longevity, sun themselves around the pool in the main hall. Farther south on Route 4 a dragon gate guards the city.

The provincial town itself is drab. Trang Hotel offers air-conditioned rooms, but its dining room downstairs appears dark and dreary. The town does boast one celebrated restaurant, however, just to the right of the post office one block north of the railway station. Its owner proudly serves hot Chinese plum wine, roasted cashews, thick spring rolls and excellent fried fish. Eel imported from Kwangtung, prepared with pork in heavy gravy, called *pla thua na*, is the specialty of the house.

When in Trang you can take a number of interesting sidetrips. **PAK MONG BEACH** lies on the Indian Ocean off Road 4046 (the Sikao Road) just after the 28-km-stone from Trang. It is a long bumpy trip but the scenery and sunsets are memorable. **SURIN PARK**, which lies a short distance west of Trang on Route 4, has a beatiful large pond surrounded by well-kept gardens. Going northeast from Trang through Huai Yot will take you through a beautiful winding valley and to Nakhon Si Thammarat.

The Deep South

A long main street runs through the ancient city of **NAKHON SI THAMMARAT**, or Nakhon, as the Thais call it for short. Painted wooden shop houses, a new museum, Thai-style administrative buildings, a store selling shadow-play puppets, and several temples line this street. The Thai Hotel near the market has air-conditioned rooms.

Nakhon was an important city in the Dvaravati and Srivichaya empires. A few Dvaravati sculptures remain in **Wat Mahathat**, one of the oldest temples in Thailand, on the southern outskirts of town. The *wat* features a 77-meter-high *chedi* with a top covered by 270 kilograms of gold. To the right of the *chedi*, a temple museum houses a great assortment of delicate gold and silver offerings. Next to the *wat*, the Viharn Luang, with its inward-leaning columns, presents a fine example of Ayuthaya period design.

Thailand's nielloware industry began in Nakhon. You can observe some of the craftsmen who started it all about 50 years ago at the original Nakhon shop on Chakrapetch Road. Niello looks like enamel, but in fact is a black alloy that fills spaces between lines of silver or gold in objects ranging from ashtrays to royally commissioned jewelry.

When the road north from town is improved, the trip to Sichon on the Gulf of Thailand will reward visitors with scenic views and Srivichaya artifacts. Until then, visit the cave that once sheltered King Taksin when he fled from the Burmese. Take the road across the railroad tracks to Lan Saka Village, turn right at the first fork, and go 9 km to the cave where the view of the countryside is nothing short of magnificent.

* * *

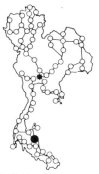

31. Nakhon Si Thammarat
นครศรีธรรมราช (ตัวเมือง, จังหวั

Wat Mahathat
วัดมหาธาตุ

32. Khao Chong Reserve
เขตรักษาพันธุ์สัตว์ป่าเขาช่อง

33. Phatthalung
พัทลุง (ตัวเมือง, จังหวัด)

An all-weather highway linking Nakhon Sri Thammarat to Songkhla recently has been completed. It runs through numerous lemon orchards and past several dusty arenas where fighting bulls are trained. But an alternative to the new road is the older Route 4 which leads to Phatthalung by going through the provincial capital of Trang.

Enroute to Phatthalung on Route 4, about 20 km east of Trang, the **KHAO CHONG NATURE RESERVE** encompasses slightly tamed jungle, a rocky creek, and a waterfall. Drive into the reserve but do not panic if you encounter soldiers brandishing weapons. The reserve also hosts a military camp. Khao Chong represents part of Thailand's nascent conservation and ecology movement. Students at the Nature Education Center here can study southern animals in a natural rain forest environment. The small zoo houses a sampling of local fauna, like the Binturong civet, Prevost squirrel, Brahminy kite, hog badger, and some endangered species including the white-handed gibbon which is usually captured by killing a mother with young.

The hog badger has an interesting connection with southern bull fighting, which is the regional entertainment and occasion for gambling that involves no matador, but just two bulls in a locked-horns pushing contest. The hog badger's meat does not taste good, but the unfortunate long-clawed mammal is occasionally shot for the fat on its nose. A bull with this wild-smelling fat rubbed on its horns, it is claimed, can intimidate and defeat any opponent. Naturally, the use of this fat is regarded as cheating.

From the Khao Chong Nature Reserve, drive 34 km to **PHATTHALUNG**. Along this stretch of Route 4, a few motorists have been relieved of their cash and valuables by bandits

Adorned with gold leaf, a Buddha image gazes out serenely at Wat Mahathat one of the oldest and most revered temples in Thailand, just outside the ancient city of Nakhon Si Thammarat (facing page). Old cannons (above, left), now playthings, line the front of the administrative buildings of the city. A white-faced gibbon (above, right) is one of the many native animals of the South that can be seen at the Khao Chong Nature Reserve, not far from Trang.

but such occasions are rare. You will likely only see Thai Army soldiers camped in tents between rows of rubber trees.

Route 4 to Phatthalung zigzags under towering jungle trees, past pink earthen rock, up and down the mountainous watershed along the center of the isthmus. About 3 km before Phatthalung, the highway branches south to Haadyai. You continue straight, past the provincial administrative offices, then bear left on the road to Khuan Khanun ("Jackfruit Hill") and **Wat Ku Ha Sawan**. This temple was recently renovated, but behind its yellow buildings a staircase climbs up to a large grotto lighted by a natural arch. A delightful obese, laughing Buddha marks the entrance. Around a copper-leafed Bodhi tree are gathered dozens of Buddha images. Light from the arch glints off the gold leaf on the statues. To the right of the *wat* lies another

cave formerly inhabited by a hermit monk. His personal collection of images remains there.

To visit another temple and the northern end of the inland sea, take the road leading east from town. **Wat Wang** ("Palace Temple") is 8 km from the city on the left side of the road. An attractive *chedi* graces the front of the temple courtyard. Inside the temple proper are unrestored frescoes dating back about 200 years.

Continue down the road another 7 km to Ban Lampam where the water of the inland sea, 70 km from its entrance to the Gulf of Thailand, is fresh.

A short boat trip from Phatthalung town leads to **THAM MALAI**, a cave lying between the province's two famous peaks: Broken-Hearted Mountain and Broken-Headed Mountain. Legend says these represent two women turned to stone in punishment for jealousy. Catch the

Wat Wang
วัดวัง

Wat Ku Ha Suwan
วัดคูหาสวรรค์

Tham Malai
ถ้ำมาลัย

Behind a building at Wat Ku Ha Sawan (above) sits a delightful laughing Buddha (right). At Haadyai, a bull fight (facing page) means that the beasts compete against each other, in locked-horn wrestling.

34. Haadyai
หาดใหญ่ (ตัวเมือง, อำเภอ)

Songkhla Nakharin
มหาวิทยาลัยสงขลานครินทร์วิโรต

Rubber Research Center
ศูนย์วิจัยยางพารา

boat behind the train station for the 15-minute ride to Tham Malai. A monk caretaker will turn on a generator to light up the cave that features some good stalactites.

As Phatthalung offers no really good hotels, head back to Route 4 and turn south for Haadyai.

* * *

HAADYAI, the commercial capital of south Thailand, is a growing city, frontier in style, with rubber and tin in its surrounding areas and a thriving night life. Because prices of many items (including night life) are lower in Thailand than in Malaysia, Haadyai has become a shopping and sybaritic haven for Malaysians who pour across the border on buying sprees.

Few hotels can have more musical outlets than the Sukhontha. Three big bands, each with a galaxy of singers, swing every night in the hotel's clubs and discos and, in addition, a

group performs in the coffee shop. The hotel also has a Pink Lady — a massage parlor. Other massage parlors, branches of Bangkok organizations, are the Atami and Chao Phya.

Haadyai has several points of interest for those recovered sufficiently from their revels of the previous night. In the town at Wat Haadyai Nai is the third largest reclining Buddha in the world. Do not just admire the exterior of this giant who sits atop a 3 meter high base. Ascend this pedestal and enter into the Buddha's innards where lungs and shrines sit side by side.

On the outskirts of the town, en route to Songkhla, is the **Rubber Research Center**, serving all the Thailand, where graft and tapping methods are tested, and then experimental studies for their high yield are made on rubber trees. Small-holding farmers come to study at the center where there is a rubber processing

laboratory. (Telephone one day in advance to request a tour.)

Next to the research center is the **Songkhla Nakharin University,** set on 120 hectares and spectacular in its architectural style. A pumpkin-shaped building containing the auditorium and laboratories is surrounded by a moat. Arched windows in the pumpkin catch breezes from all directions and channel them through the building to provide natural air conditioning. An exhaust pump in the center sucks the warm air out.

Sunday is the day for bullfights. However, do not envisage a *corrida* with *matadors* and *picadors:* bull fighting Thai style is a contest which pits one humpbacked bull against another. Two animals are brought face to face. They lower their heads, practically interlock their horns and paw the ground. Each pushes against the other. The fight may last minutes or a couple of hours. It ends when one bull gains the ascendancy by pushing the other back, back, back or when one simply turns and takes flight. He, sensible fellow, has heard that "the bull who fought and ran away lived to fight another day." Betting on "Yellow Baby" and "Elvis" is heavy.

For food try the Haivathene at 69 Themanoonvithi Road. People come all the way from Bangkok to salivate over the shark's fin soup and reservations are needed. Other specialities are poached duck and fried pigeon. Several large open-air restaurants serve superb seafood to the accompaniment of raucous live music and go-go girls. Try the Ton-Nga Chang with its imaginative decor.

Other than to Songkhla, Haadyai has no taxis, but buses will take you anywhere in town — a door to door service — for 5 baht. The railway station has a bath and changing room and an attractive swimming pool can be found behind City Hall.

Songkhla and to Malaysia

35. Songkhla
สงขลา (ตัวเมือง, จังหวัด)

Majimawat Temple
วัดมัชฌิมาวาท

If Haadyai is brash then **SONG-KHLA** is discreet, like the inexpensive restaurant in Paris (now, alas, no more) that one passes on to a friend with the promise not to tell anyone lest it be spoiled. Indeed, Songkhla is the main reason for the international traveler visiting Haadyai. Trains, buses and taxis cover the 25 km between the two towns. The really adventurous can make arrangements to make the journey by water.

Built on a peninsula, Songkhla is an old Chinese city peacefully surrounded on three sides by water. However, only the seaward (eastern) side is suitable for sunning and swimming. The north part of the beach is backed with lush casuarina trees and here one finds such unlikely traffic as monks is saffron robes and humpbacked bulls being prepared for the bullfights. The focal point of the beach is a bronze statue of a mermaid immediately opposite the Samila

Hotel, the only hotel of distinction in Songkhla. The hotel also serves as the clubhouse for the *Thongyai Golf Course*. Immediately northwest of the mermaid, and on the sandy beach, are a score of seafood restaurants. Select your meal from uncooked displays including 35-cm-long tiger prawns and then, while waiting for it to be cooked, relax in colorful deck chairs alongside low tables.

Three km south of the Samila Hotel is a small, extremely active fishing village inhabited mainly by Muslims. But it is the fishing boats rather than the fisher people who fascinate. It would be difficult to beat these *gorlae* for sheer pizzaz and imagination: captivating folk art in a riot of color and a multitude of visual themes cover them stem to stern.

Beyond the fishing village lies the rock beach of **Kao Seng** whose fame rests on a precariously poised giant boulder called **Nai Bang's Head.** If

Jammed with visitors, popular Samila Beach (left) faces the gentle inlet at Songkhla and boasts more than twenty seafood restaurants where one can select one's meal from the day's catch. Over on the Gulf, another stretch of beach is lined with graceful casuarina trees and is generally more deserted (above, left). At a Muslim village about 3 km down the coast, fishing boats with finely decorated sterns (above, right) wait on the sand to head out to sea.

you manage to push it over then you might be fortunate enough to uncover the millionaire's treasure reputedly hidden below. Inland from the beach is the **Banloa Coconut Plantation** where one can watch trained monkeys who, on demand, climb trees and bring down selected coconuts.

Then visit **Wat Kho Tum,** built among enormous boulders on a near-by hilltop. See Buddha's footprint in a cave and a sleeping Buddha reclining underneath an overhanging rock. Around the corner from this is **Wat Maeche,** a charming sandy spot where Buddhist nuns reside. The nuns, often young, with white robes and shaven heads, grow flowers, rise at 4:00 a.m. to meditate, and read philosophy before setting out for alms.

Across the road from the entrance to the Samila Hotel is **Khao-Noi** — a topiary garden — with realistic fighting bulls, birds in flight, and an elephant that is elephantine in size, sculpted out of yew. Around the corner from this, on Sukhum Road, in the late afternoon, you will find gatherings of monkeys. They have come down from the hilltop to sit, hands on knees, scratching or blinking, seeming to philosophize like old men. Continue towards the lake to Viehienchom Road from where a steep path and steps lead in 20 minutes to the top of **Mount Tangkuan** where stand the ruins of an ancient *chedi*. The panorama is spectacular and the amazing activity at the wharves along the lake give credence to Songkhla's claim to being the busiest fishing port in all Asia.

A pleasant excursion is to **Kho Yor** situated in **Thale Sap** or **Songkhla Lake,** one of the largest lakes in Southeast Asia. Actually, it is a deep inlet rather than a lake, being connected to the sea, and its waters are brackish. En route to Yor Island a stop

Banloa Coconut Plantation
สวนมะพร้าวบ้านเลา
Wat Kho Tum
วัดเขาทุ่ม
Wat Maeche
วัดแม่เจ

302

36. Pattani
ปัตตานี
37. Yala
ยะลา
38. Narathiwat
นราธิวาส

may be made at the Fisheries Station where enormous white *pla kapong* are bred. Kho Yor is renowned for its locally woven cotton and has a number of ancient Buddhist monuments. But the real joy is the tranquility of the idyllic landscape in comparison to which gentle Songkhla becomes a bustling frenetic metropolis.

Another excursion by boat is to the offshore islands of **Maew** and **Nu (Cat and Rat)**. Nu is the larger and has some pleasant picnic spots and bathing beaches.

Songkhla boasts two museums. The chock-a-block museum in the **Majimawat Temple** (popularly called **Wat Klant**) is in marked contrast to the spic-and-span, recently renovated **Old Governor's Palace**, a beautifully proportioned Chinese mansion of 1878. The latter contains an excellent collection of ceramics and documented remains, recovered by scuba divers

from an ancient wreck in the Gulf of Thailand. The Majimawat museum collection ranges from early Thai five-color pottery and 200-year-old shell boxes of the Buket style to a pre-electric fan that operates on gas. You are on your own, though, because there are no labels and the monk in charge speaks only Thai. The 200-year-old marble Buddha gracing the altar inside the temple of the same complex lacks the pure gold lotus that it once wore on its head, as the lotus crown is now safely stored in a vault. Chinese lions, a gift of some rich Chinese in the early days, guard the doorway opening on to the interesting murals within. Some show scenes of Songkhla while others depict European sailors and a steam boat.

Lift your eyes as you walk along Nakorn Noak Road and Nakorn Nai Street: old Chinese families living in the lovely Sino-Portuguese shop-houses are reputed to be extremely rich and conservative.

From Songkhla there are two basic routes to Malaysia. The shorter and most frequently traveled road follows approximately the railway line to the western Malaysian cities of Alor Star and Butterworth. From Haadyai, Route 4 leads directly south to the border, or if you wish to visit every provincial capital, head west of Route 4 towards Ratphum District. This side trip leads to the remote and unspoiled provincial town of Satun.

The adventurous traveler with time to spare might wish to make his way towards Malaysia's east coast. En route the provincial Thai capitals of Pattani, Yala and Narathiwat may be visited. Many residents of these towns are Chinese but the majority of the people are Malay. Mosques can be seen and the Malay language is commonly spoken. Of interest near Yala are the Silpa caves. The large cave of **Tham Koo Ha Pimak** contains a 25-meter-high Buddha, considered a holy pilgrimage site by southern Thais. It is surely an apt place to conclude your Thai adventure.

Almost every accessible cave in Thailand is believed to be the dwelling place of spirits and provides a setting for a grotto temple. An example is Silpa Cave near Yala which contains interesting Buddha images.

GUIDE IN BRIEF

Traveling to Thailand

By Air

The great majority of visitors arrive and depart by air on more than 35 international airlines, which have scheduled flights and chartered tours to Thailand. Bangkok's Don Muang International Airport has been improved so that customs clearance and passport checks are relatively fast. A US $300 million expansion program, including construction of a new international passenger terminal, is currently in progress and is expected to be completed by 1988. Remember that Bangkok airport tax for outgoing passengers on international routes is 150 baht per person.

Although nearly all air passengers arrive and depart from Bangkok, there are at least two other recommended alternative ways of entering the country by air. You can fly to southern Thailand — to Haadyai, or the resort island of Phuket — on Thailand's domestic airline, Thai Airways, from Penang or Kuala Lumpur. (Do not confuse this domestic airline with Thai International.) Malaysian Airlines (MAS) flies the same route. Passengers from Hong Kong on Thai International can fly direct to the northern city of Chiang Mai and to Phuket without going through Bangkok, and those from Singapore can arrive directly at Phuket.

See Appendix for listing of airline officers in Bangkok.

Arrival

From Don Muang Airport, there are various ways to get downtown to Bangkok (22 kilometres south). Via the newly-open expressway (toll fee: 10 baht per car), it is a 30 to 45 minute drive away.

Two limousine services are run by Thai International. Air-conditioned sedans offer 24-hour service, while buses leave every half-hour. Tickets cost 300 baht and 100 baht respectively; further information on exact routes and destinations can be obtained in the arrival lobby.

Public taxis and buses will also take you to Bangkok. Do not be in a hurry to hop into a taxi, though, as taxis here are not metered. Be sure you first agree on a fare, normally between 180 and 200 baht. Bus fares are 3.50 baht for a regular bus and 15 baht for an air-conditioned bus. Pick-up points for public taxis and buses are just outside the airport gate.

About 800 metres from the airport, across the often-crowded highway, is the Don Muang Railway Station. A train service runs from here to Bangkok at a fare of 4 baht. However, this is recommended only for visitors with light luggage.

By Sea

In this day of hurried leisure, passenger liners are finding themselves in dire straits. Currently the only way to reach Bangkok by sea is via freighters, which generally make a point of providing excellent accommodation and food at a fare rather less than cruise ships. From Europe, companies such as Ben Line Steamers, Polish Ocean Lines and Nedloyd ship out to Bangkok. From the United States, Pacific Far East Line, American President Lines and State Lines go to Bangkok. There are also many ships sailing regularly from Japan, Hong Kong and Singapore. Inquire with local travel agents for schedules and fares.

By Rail

Except when it rains so hard that railroad tracks are submerged, Thai trains are reliable. You can get first-class, air-conditioned sleeper going anywhere within the country for less than 500 baht (US$22). There are railroads between Singapore, Malaysia and Thailand. A two-day rail odyssey originating in Singapore offers third-class sit-ups, second-class sleepers and first-class, air-conditioned compartments. Magic Arrow Express leaves Singapore Sunday, Tuesday and Thursday at 8:10 a.m. and arrives at Kuala Lumpur 3:35 p.m. the same day. North Star Night Express then leaves Kuala Lumpur Sunday, Tuesday and Thursday at 9:30 p.m. and arrives at Butterworth (on the main road opposite the island of Penang) at 6:47 a.m. the next morning. the International Express bound for Bangkok then takes over the last link, leaving Butterworth at 7:40 a.m. on Monday, Wednesday and Friday to arrive in Bangkok within 24 hours.

There is a dayliner service between Butterworth and Haadyai in southern Thailand. There is no seat number on the ticket, however, and you can find yourself riding "second-class standing" for the four-hour trip. For the same price, take a shared taxi instead.

On the east side of Malaysia, you can take a train to Kota Bharu, do the short distance to the border by road, and meet the Thai railhead at Sungai Kolok.

By Road

Thailand is currently experiencing an automotive boom. Roads are being improved and extended into the more remote provinces, but apart from the southern road links with Malaysia, Thailand is virtually road-locked.

At present there is no road access to and from Burma, a missing link in the Asian Highway that stretches from Turkey to Singapore. If and when Burma opens its land frontiers, Mae Sot — a small town in the northwestern province of Tak — will be the point of entry.

There are three main roads crossing the Thai-Malaysian border in the south. Inexpensive taxis and minibuses ply the routes between major towns. Malaysia closes its border at 6 p.m. daily, so plan your itinerary in accordance. In case you are driving yourself or renting a car, Malaysia prohibits any vehicle from Thailand that does not have an insurance policy. Most cars in Thailand do not.

Travel Advisories

Passport

All foreign nationals entering Thailand must be in possession of a valid passport.

Visas

All foreign nationals can stay in Thailand for up to 15 days without a visa. For a longer stay a visa must be obtained from Thai embassies or consulates abroad. Tourist visas cost US$5; applications must be accompanied by three passport sized photos. Visas are granted for a period of 60 days, with a possible extension of another 60 days upon request. However, getting an extension is such a hassle that visitors tend to sidestep requirements (which include presenting a resident sponsor with a guarantee-bond of US$250) by simply leaving the country and obtaining another tourist visa.

Nationals of the following countries are allowed entry into the country for a period of 15 days:

American Continent: Argentina, Brazil, Canada, Mexico, U.S.A.

Asia: Brunei, Burma, Indonesia, Israel, Japan, Jordan, Korea, Kuwait, Malaysia, Oman, Philippines, Saudi Arabia, Singapore, Turkey.

Australia and the Pacific Area: Australia, Fiji, New Zealand, Papua New Guinea, West Samoa.

Africa: Algeria, Egypt, Kenya, Sudan, Tunisia, Yemen.

Europe: Austria, Belgium, Denmark, Finnland, France, Germany, Greece, Iceland, Ireland, Italy, Luxemburg, Norway, Spain, Sweden, Switzerland, Great Britain and Northern Ireland, Yugoslavia.

Re-entry visa

A person who wishes to leave Thailand and return before expiry of his tourist visa must first obtain a re-entry visa. This can be done Monday to Friday from 8:30 a.m. to 3:30 p.m. at the Immigration Division, Soi Suan Plu, South Sathorn road (tel: 286-9222); or Saturday, Sunday and government holidays between 8:30 a.m. and 3:30 p.m. at the Tourism Authority of Thailand, Rajdamnoen Avenue. Cost of a re-entry visa is 500 baht, and it must be accompanied by one photo.

Exit visa

An exit visa is normally not required.

Validity of visa

A visa is a valid for one entry within 60 days from the date of issue. A transit visa is valid for 30 days and a non-immigrant visa 90 days. Should the holder of the visa be unable to enter Thailand within this period, Thai embassies or consulates generally will extend the visa for a period not exceeding the period of validity of the applicant's passport, nor exceeding a period of six months.

Health Regulations

Incoming visitors (except those arriving from Europe, Australia, the United States, Japan and within Asia) need an International Certificate of Health, showing a smallpox vaccination within the last three years, **if** arriving from an infected area. Yellow fever inoculations are required by persons coming from or going to contaminated areas; children less than a year old are exempted.

Transit/Transfer

If you are a transfer passenger, you must immediately reconfirm your next flight at the airport transfer counters located in the Transit Lounge, which is next to the Departure Lounge on the first floor. While waiting for next departure time, you are free to shop at the duty-free shops in this lounge.

If you are on transfer to a domestic flight, clear through customs and leave the building. The domestic terminal, a one-story building providing facilities for domestic passengers is located at a distance of about one miles (1.6 km) from the international terminal. IRF charges between terminals: 80 baht limousine; 20 baht bus.

Departure

You can arrange to be picked up from your hotel by Thai International's air-conditioned sedan (tel: 511-0121 ext. 455 or 277-0111). Alternatively, buses depart every 30 minutes, from 6 a.m. to midnight, from the Silom Road Air Terminal. Those staying near the Bangkok Railway Station or Samsen Railway Station can take the train to Don Muang Railway Station. Taxis and public buses are also available. See Arrival section above.

Departing passengers are required to pay airport tax when checking in. International: 150 baht. Domestic: 20 baht.

Customs

As with most countries, Thailand prohibits visitors bringing in illicit narcotic drugs and explicit pornography. Firearms require a permit from the Police Department. Goods that may be imported duty-free include 200 cigarettes, one liter of wine or spirits, a camera with five rolls of film, and a reasonable amount of personal effects. Persons taking up residence in Thailand can bring in used household wares duty-free. Used cars cannot be imported. Pet animals can usually be cleared through customs upon arrival at the airport. Visitors arriving by sea must apply to the Disease Control Division, Livestock Department, Ministry of Agriculture, Phya Thai Road (tel: 252-6944). Veterinary vaccination certificates are necessary.

Visitors are permitted to bring in any amount of foreign currency for personal use but must fill in a currency declaration form for larger sums. No one can bring in or take out of Thailand more than 500 baht. Holders of family passports are permitted to export 1,000 baht.

Currency

The unit of currency in Thailand is the *baht* (pronounced "baad"). One US dollar is equivalent to 26.00 baht (in early 1987). One baht is divided into one hundred *satang*. Coins are valued at 25 satang (smaller gold coin), 50 satang (bigger gold coin), one baht (smaller nickel coin) and five baht (bigger nickel coin). The 25-satang coin is commonly called a *salehng*. Paper notes are valued at 10 (brown color), 20 (green), 50 (blue), 100 (red) and 500 (purple) baht.

If you have traveler's checks in American dollars, they can be cashed at banks in all provincial capitals; so there is no need to carry unmanageable amounts of baht notes with you outside of Bangkok. Traveler's checks in other currencies, however, are best cashed in Bangkok. As a rule, hotel exchange rates are poorer than those offered by banks and authorized money changers.

Keep in mind that most hotels do not accept personal checks. Most major hotels accept credit cards: the American Express card is most widely welcomed. Smaller hotels, shops or restaurants accept only cash.

Getting Acquainted

Government and Economy

Thailand is a constitutional monarchy. The head-of-state since 1946 has been King Bhumipol Adulyadej. Prime Minister Prem Tinsulanonda has held office since March 1980.

Almost 55 million persons make their homes in Thailand: nearly five million of them live in Bangkok. Rice is the major export crop. More than three million tons is exported annually, ranking second in the world. Thailand is the world's largest exporter of tapioca, second largest of rubber, and the fifth largest producer of tin. Teak, sugar cane, maize, tobacco and cotton are other important export crops. And fisheries rank high in the economy.

The gross national produce (1984) is US$38.5 billion. The per capital income (1984) is US$73.3.

Geography

Thailand comprises an area of 198,455 square miles, about three-fourths the size of the American state of Texas. It stretches from forested mountains with narrow fertile valleys in the North, and a dry plateau adjacent to the Mekong River in the Northeast: across the fertile alluvial basin of the Chao Phya river, where most of the population lives; to a long finger of beaches and rain-forest down the Isthmus of Kra and Malay Peninsula in the South.

Climate

Although Thailand is situated well within the tropics, there is a wide climatic range, depending on the time of year and the part of the country. The Central Plains (including Bangkok), the hilly North, and the arid, flat Northeast share the same seasonal patterns. The so-called hot season spans March, April and May, although many foreign residents argue that it is hot throughout the year when it is not raining. Daytime temperatures in the hot season are in the 30°C (86°F) range and can reach 40°C (104°F), especially in the Northeast.

In June, the southwest Monsoon ushers in the rainy season with slightly lower temperatures but higher humidity. Many travelers unfamiliar with Asia have a misconception of the monsoon and expect months of unbroken cloudy, rainy weather. In Thailand, the monsoon season amounts to five months of unpredictable weather. Some days bring erratic rainstorms while others are clear and sunny. November ushers in the cool season, particularly in the North where night temperatures can drop to 8°C (46°F). Bring a sweater or jacket if traveling there between November and February.

The long isthmus in South Thailand, which straddles the Gulf of Thailand and the Indian Ocean, has a climate similar to that of Malaysia — subtle seasonal variations with the weather generally warm, humid, and sunny year-round. Rain is possible almost any time.

Clothing

Light and loose clothes are best suited to Thailand's climate. For the hot season, pack clothes that provide adequate protection from the direct sun — cotton is best, and umbrellas and sunglasses are highly recommended. For the rainy season, it is wise to carry clothes that dry quickly after a sudden downpour. For the four months from November to February, warmer clothes (at least a sweater and warm socks for the chilly nights) are necessary in the North and other hilly regions, as there is no central heating or even household fireplaces.

Bangkok is highly westernized in its business and social dress, with provincial centers following suit. Certain restaurants require jackets and ties for dinner. At traditional ceremonies and formal gatherings, however, Thai women often prefer to don their ethnic silk costumes.

Hygiene

In a country where people are as personally neat and cleanliness-conscious as the Thais, there are relatively few health hazards stemming directly from poor sanitation. In Bangkok, visitors will spend much of their time in air-conditioned hotel rooms, restaurants, stores, bars and tour buses that are usually quite sanitary. For the more ambitious sightseer Bangkok has certain minor hazards — like most cities of five million people — which prove to be more unpleasant than unhealthy. These include the pungent smell of stagnant canals and the noxious exhaust of cars and buses. Walking in Bangkok can often be dangerous particularly at street crossings; you can greatly minimize the risk by staying on sidewalks and in crosswalks.

Tap water in Bangkok is considered relatively safe, but to be doubly sure, drink purified bottled water. Small shops and mobile vendors abound, selling all sorts of cool drinks to quench thirst and curiosity. Unless you are accustomed to tropical climes where slight diarrhea is common, you may wish to avoid this kind of drink. If you really must satisfy your curiosity, avoid crushed ice and ask for ice cubes instead. They are much safer.

Travelers who have never reckoned with the tropical sun should keep in mind that noon is not the wisest time to sunbathe: you will earn a burn in just 15 minutes. You can get sunburnt even on a cloudy day in Thailand. If you are out touring, exposed to the elements, wear a straw hat or carry a paper parasol. If you spend much time moving around in the sun (sweating a lot in the process) and start feeling a little weak and dizzy, you probably need more salt. Either carry salt tablets with you or do as the Thais do — mix salt in your lemonade or Coke.

Visitors traveling upcountry may encounter another minor malady. Since there is no familiar Western food in most provincial capitals except in the downtown areas, the traveler may have to eat native Thai food. This can have as many chili peppers in it as a salad has cucumbers. The result could be what the Thais call "walking stomach" (diarrhea). Prevention: Eat Chinese food instead, more bland but less volatile, or ask for food without hot peppers. Cure: Take one or two Lomotil pills.

Time conversion

Thailand Standard Time is seven hours ahead of Greenwich Meridian Time. Arriving in Bangkok from Hong Kong or Singapore, that means you would set your watch back one hour upon arrival. International time differences are staggered as follows:

Thailand	12 noon today
Hong Kong	1 p.m. today
Tokyo	2 p.m. today
Sydney	3 p.m. today
Hawaii	7 p.m. yesterday
Los Angeles	9 p.m. yesterday
New York	12 midnight today
London	5 a.m. today
Paris	6 a.m. today
Bonn	6 a.m. today
New Delhi	10.30 a.m. today

Business Hours

As in most Asian countries, Thai people like to begin their days early. In this way, they can beat the midday heat, having attended to important matters first thing in the day.

Government offices: Most government offices are open Monday through Friday from 8.30 a.m. to 4.30 p.m. with a noon-to-1 break for lunch. The best time to do business is generally as early as possible; the worst time is after 3 p.m.

Banks: Hours are Monday through Friday, 8.30 a.m. to 3.30 p.m. See Appendix for full listing of major banks in Bangkok.

Post offices: The General Post Office or GPO (Prisanee Klang), situated on New Road, is open from 8 a.m. to 6 p.m. weekdays and 8 a.m. to noon weekends and holidays. Its several branch offices in Bangkok also operate during these hours. But up-country post offices close at 4.30 p.m.

Department stores: Major stores usually open at 10 a.m. and close at 7 p.m. Smaller stores usually stay open 12 hours a day, seven days a week. The only time of year when shops close en masse for three or four days is during Chinese New Year in February.

Public holidays: Some dates vary with the lunar calendar, but this schedule will give you an approximate idea of dates when most offices and shops will close:

New Year's Day	January 1
Chinese New Year	early-mid February
Maka Puja	mid-late February
Chakri Day	April 6
Songkran	
(Thai New Year)	April 13-15
Coronation Day	May 5
Visakha Puja	mid-late May
Asalaha Puja	mid-late July
Queen's Birthday	August 12
Ok Pansa	mid-late October
Chulalongkorn Day	October 23
Loy Krathong	November full moon
King's Birthday	December 5
New Year's Eve	December 31

Embassies and consular services

Nearly every nation in the world has an embassy, consulate or diplomatic mission in Bangkok. Each of these offices has full facilities to assist their citizens with any needs or problems.

A full listing of embassies and consulates can be found in this book's appendix. Major offices include the United States Embassy at 95 Wireless Road (tel. 252-5040); the German Embassy at 9 Sathorn Tai Road (tel. 286-4223); the French Embassy at Customs House Lane (tel. 234-0950); the British Embassy at 1031 Ploenchit Road (tel. 252-7161); and the Australian Embassy at 37 South Sathorn Road (tel. 286-0411).

Electricity

Thailand operates on 220-volt, 50-cycle AC power. Most modern hotels will provide transformers for guests with 110-volt appliances. Up-country, however, transformers are hard to find. In some areas, electrical outlets of any voltage are unavailable. Travelers would be wise not to rely on electric shavers and hair dryers, but should stay well stocked on razor blades and thick hair-drying towels.

Tourist Information

The Tourism Authority of Thailand (TAT), located near Rajdamnoen Boxing Stadium, is a government agency established to serve the needs of visitors. While the main offices keep government hours (see above), the Tourist Information Service remains open on Saturdays, Sundays and holidays.

In addition to its Bangkok headquarters, the TAT has branch offices in Pattaya, Phuket, Korat, Chiang Mai, Kanchanaburi and Haadyai. There are overseas bureaus in New York, Los Angeles, London, Paris, Frankfurt, Tokyo, Rome, Sydney, Hong Kong, Singapore and Kuala Lumpur.

TAT OVERSEAS OFFICES

United States

Tourism Authority of Thailand, 5 World Trade Centre, Suite No. 2449, New York, N.Y. 10048, U.S.A. Tel: (212) 432-0433; Cable: THAITOUR NEW YORK; Telex: 667612 TOT UW.
Tourism Authority of Thailand, 3440 Wilshire Blvd., Suite 1101, Los Angeles, CA 90010, U.S.A. Tel: (213) 382-2353, 54-55; Cable: THAITOUR LOS ANGELES; Telex: 686208 TTC LSA.

Japan
Tourism Authority of Thailand, Hibiya Mitsui Building, 1-2, Yurakucho 1-Chome, Chiyoda-Ku, Tokyo 100, Japan. Tel: (03) 580-6776-7, 508-0237; Cable: THAITOUR TOKYO; Telex: J33964 TATTYO.

Tourism Authority of Thailand, Hirano-Machi Yachiyo Bldg., 5F 2-8-1 Hirano-Machi, Hicashi-Ku, Osaka 541, Japan. Tel: (06) 231-4434; Fax: (06) 231-4337; Tlx: J64675.

Germany
Thailandisches Fremdenverkehrsburo, Bethmannstr. 58/IV., D-6000 Frankfurt/M.1, West Germany. Tel: (069) 295-704, 295-804; Cable: THAITOUR FRANKFURT/M., Telex: 413542 TAFRA D.

Australia
Tourism Authority of Thailand, 12th Floor Royal Exchange Bldg., 56 Pitt Street, Sydney 2000, Australia. Tel: (02) 277-549, 277-540; Cable: THAITOUR SYDNEY; Telex: 23467 THAITC AA.

England
Tourism Authority of Thailand, 9 Stafford Street Cnr. Albemarle Street, London WIX 3 FE, England. Tel: (01) 499-7670, 499-7679; Cable: THAITOUR LONDON; Telex: 298706 THAITR G, TAT/LON.

Singapore
Tourism Authority of Thailand, C/O Royal Thai Embassy, 370 Orchard Rd., Singapore 0923. Tel: 235-7901, 235-7694; Cable: THAITOUR SINGAPORE; Telex: 39428 TATSIN RS.

France
Office National Du Tourisme De Thailande; 90 Avenue Des Champs-Elysees, 75008 Paris, France. Tel: 4562-8656, 4562-8748; Cable: THAITOUR PARIS; Telex: 650093 TATPAR F.

Malaysia
Tourism Authority of Thailand, C/O Royal Thai Embassy, 206 Jalan Ampang, Kuala Lumpur, Malaysia. Tel: 248-0958; Telex: TATKL 31089.

Hong Kong
Tourism Authority of Thailand, Room 401, Fairmont House, 8 Cotton Tree Drive, Central, Hong Kong. Tel: (5) 8680732, 8680854.

Italy
Tourism Authority of Thailand, C/O Thai Airways International Limited, Via Barberini, 50 00187 Rome, Italy.

Transportation

Air Travel
Thai Airways (do not confuse it with Thai International) links major cities throughout the country with its fleet of Beoing 737s. In the North, it flies daily to Chiang Mai, with less frequent stops at Phitsanulok, Phrae, Nan, Lampang, Chiang Rai and Mae Hongson. In the Northeast, there are daily flights to Ubon Rajthani, and other stops in Udon, Nakhon Phanom, Khon Kaen and Loei. The southbound schedule includes the island resort of Phuket, as well as Haadyai, Trang and Pattani.

Thai Airways also has regular flights to Penang and Kuala Lumpur in Malaysia, and weekly flights to Hanoi, Vietnam. For reservations call 281-1633 in Bangkok.

Automobiles
It is possible to rent cars with major agencies in Bangkok. Indeed, there are 43,840 kilometers of national and provincial highways in Thailand, and another 12,000-or-so kilometers under construction. But most signs are in the Thai language only; driving can be hazardous for the uninitiated; and other forms of transportation are universally recommended to visitors. Chauffeur-driven rentals are usually best.

Buses
Air-conditioned coaches and ordinary buses run from Bangkok to every town in Thailand. All told, 2,744 buses are operated by the state Transport Company over 134 routes to all 72 provinces; and another 2,246 buses operate on 147 routes within or between the provinces.

In Bangkok, there are three major bus terminals:

Northern and Northeastern routes: Taladmochit, on Paholyothin Road, tel. 282-6660.

Eastern route: Ekamai on Sukhumvit Road, tel. 392-2520. This is the route that goes to Pattaya and points beyond.

Southern route: Sam Yaek Fai Chai on Charansanitwongse Road in Thonburi, tel. 411-1337.

There are also numerous private buses and coaches that ply routes between major cities. Check with local agencies for schedules and fares.

Trains
Thai trains are comfortable and reliable, though they are crowded all year round. The State Railway of Thailand runs international express, express, rapid, ordinary and diesel railcar services in three passenger classes over an extensive and well-maintained network. Costs are very reasonable. You can choose from third-class situps, second-class air-conditioned situps (with reclining chairs), second-class sleepers, and first-class air-conditioned compartments. For information and reservations, call the Bangkok Railway Terminus at 233-7010, or Hua Lampong Station at 223-3762.

Waterways

Thailand has an estimated three million kilometers of navigable waterways. Most visitors limit their water travel to trips around Bangkok, or possibly the daily launch to Ayuthaya on the Oriental Queen. Cost of that excursion is 650 baht including lunch. Hotels in Bangkok and all provincial capitals can arrange localized excursions.

The Thai Navigation Company has three passenger-cargo ships that travel south from Bangkok, down the Gulf of Siam and South China Sea, to Koh Samui, Songkhla, Pattani and Narathivat. Departures are Wednesday and Saturday. Full nine-day cruise rates average about 1,000 baht.

City Transportation in Bangkok

Buses: The Bangkok Metropolitan Transit Authority (BMTA) runs city buses. They are cream-colored with blue stripes, though you sometimes can hardly make out the cream because of the mud and dust. Most have route numbers in front and on the back, but again the dust sometimes obscures these numbers. The buses are usually very crowded during the rush hours in the morning and afternoon, but are relatively vacant at other times during the day. Bus fares start at 1.50 baht for the first 10 kilometers, with an additional one baht for the next 10 kilometers.

Air-conditioned buses, also run by the BMTA, link major places in Bangkok. They are quite comfortable and not so crowded. Fares start at five baht for the first eight kilometers and two baht for each additional kilometer. Consult the Tourist Information Service for detailed information on routes.

Taxis: There are two kinds of taxis: air-conditioned and non air-conditioned. An air-conditioned taxi usually charges 10 baht more than an ordinary one. However, the air-con cabs are more comfortable, safer, and usually in better operating condition than the others.

Make sure you and the driver agree on a fare before you get into the cab. Bargaining is essential, as taxis do not have meters. Many drivers do not speak English, so it is a good idea to have your hotel desk write down your destination in Thai and suggest the approximate fare. Short trips usually are a minimum of 30 baht; a trip from the Grand Palace to the major hotel districts should be 50 to 60 baht.

Pedicabs: Commonly known as *sam-lor* or *tuk-tuk*, they consist of a motor-scooter around which a two-seat carriage has been built. They are worth trying for short trips. Prices start at 10 baht; again, bargaining is essential.

Boats: Numerous ferries and express boats ply the Chao Phya river and major klongs. In addition, several day and night cruises can be booked through major hotels. Going rate for renting private jet-boats along the river bank is about 300 baht per hour, regardless of the number of passengers.

Accommodations

There is no telling just how many hotels there are in Thailand. They exist all over the country and their standards range from deluxe international inns to small, simple establishments catering to on-the-move hitchhikers.

Fluctuations in exchange rates and rampant inflation make it virtually impossible to pinpoint hotel rates. As a general rule, rates are highest in luxury hotels found in resort cities and provinces like Bangkok, Chiang Mai and Pattaya. It is always advisable to call ahead or check with a travel agent about the latest prices. Most lodgings add a 10½ percent hotel tax and a 10 percent service charge.

You may rest assured that finding a hotel that suits your needs and budget is never a task. The list in the Appendix presents some of the hotels, in alphabetical order, within each province. This will give an idea of what is available and where.

Communications

Thailand is fully equipped with modern telecommunications services. Mail service is reliable. Most major hotels provide telex and cable services.

Mail: A local letter requires 1.25 baht stamp and an aerogramme costs 6.25 baht per sheet. Air mail postcards are 7.50 baht to the United States, 6.50 baht to Europe and Australia; five-gram letters are 9.50 baht to the U.S.A., 8.50 baht to Europe.

Telephone: You can make local calls from any telephone. A Bangkok telephone has seven digits (for example 392–4824). Calling upcountry requires dialing first, the area code, then, the number. You can easily find an area code in the English-language telephone directory. Local calls can be made on the ubiquitous red public phones: cost is one baht with a three-minute cut. For international calls dial 100. A call to Europe or America costs about US$15 person-to-person, US$11.25 station-to-station, for three minutes.

For directory assistance, dial 13.

Cable: The General Post Office provides around-the-clock cable service.

Telex: Major hotels provide telex services. Also, the General Post Office provides around-the-clock services.

News Media

Thailand is a modern country with thriving press, radio, television and film industries.

Press: In Bangkok there are 13 Thai language dailies and three English ones — *The Bangkok Post*, *The Bangkok World* and the *Nation Review*. *The Post*, at eight baht per copy, provides the best coverage of international events; the *Nation*, at seven baht, is best for Thai politics and syndicated columns. *The World* is priced at three baht. Also available are the *International Herald Tribune* (10 baht) and *The Asian Wall Street Journal* (10 baht).

Upcountry there are provincial newspapers that are published every 15 days, to coincide with the lottery results. However, these local newspapers don't render much interest to travelers, and Bangkok-based newspapers are available throughout the country.

Radio: The pace of Thai AM radio, to unattuned Western ears, is even more nerve-racking than that of most Western pop radio. In some upcountry towns the single station broadcasts at four different frequencies; even the hilltribe people of the North tote portable radios. The FM fare is generally better, with classical music, interviews, features, and the BBC news. Certainly the most program variety is found on the shortwave bands, where you can pick up Indian music, Vietnamese polemics, or the Voice of America, which also broadcasts world news in simplified English. Here are some channels that broadcast in English:

Chulalongkorn University FM 101.5 MHz. Provides classical music daily from 9:30 to 11 p.m.

FM 107. Provides from jazz to disco music from 6 a.m. to 2 a.m.

. Radio Thailand. Broadcasts in English for 4½ hours a day on FM (VHF) 97.0 MHz., SW 11.905 and 9.655 MHz.

British Broadcasting Company. The BBC broadcasts its World Service in English to Thailand from 5 to 7:30 p.m., SW on 6.195, 9.410, 9.570 and 11.955 MHz. Additionally, from 7:30 to 10:30 a.m. on 11.955, and news also on 15.380 from 9 to 10 a.m. Evening broadcasts are from 4 p.m. to 1:45 a.m. on 6.195 and 9.740; until 12:45 a.m. on 11.740; until 6:15 p.m. on 15.280; until 8:30 p.m. on 17.770 MHz.; and until 9:30 p.m. on 21.550 MHz.

Voice of America. VOA broadcasts in English from 5 to 8 a.m. on SW 9.770, 11.760 and 15.185 MHz; from 6 to 10 p.m. on 6.110, 9.760, 15.160 and 21.615 MHz.

Television: Thailand was the first country in Southeast Asia to begin regular TV transmission, and since that epic day in 1955, the Thais have become no less hooked on this medium than citizens of more developed countries. The Thais produce their own soap operas, and broadcast Japanese, Chinese, British as well as American series, usually with the Thai soundtrack dubbed in. However, you can tune into the original soundtracks on FM radios.

For original soundtracks;
Channel 3 : 105.5 MHz
Channel 7 : 103.75 MHz.
Channel 9 : 107 MHz.

You can also watch local and international news (via satellite) on Channels 3 and 9 at 8 p.m. with English translation on 107 MHz.

Cinema: Thailand has a prosperous film industry supported by throngs of admiring fans. Most movies go to a great lengths — two hours or more — to include all variety of entertainment at one sitting: musical comedy, violent action and romance. The same faces keep turning up, bigger than life, with familar scripts and familiar roles. For example, when a certain popular actor was injured while filming a scene, production was halted on 14 different movies he was making simultaneously. Although Thai feature films are generally slap-dash and slapstick, several notable exceptions have been well-received by resident foreigners and were shown at international film festivals.

In Bangkok, many American and European movies draw bigger crowds than Thai features. To comfortably accommodate the ever-burgeoning crowds of escapists, Thailand can rightly boast having some of the best cinemas anywhere, and at the best prices — 20 to 60 baht per person. Most foreign films, except when shown upcountry, are left with the original soundtrack, with Thai and Chinese subtitles added. Upcountry provincial capitals often have an English sound-room at a distance that rarely lends enchantment: beyond the plate-glass window, the Thai audience is treated to a live translation done by a versatile person who impersonates four or more different voices. For those who relish Chinese or Japanese "inner power" flicks, they abound throughout Thailand's movie world. Some theaters exclusively feature martial-arts epics on their marquees. Most have English subtitles.

Places of Worship

Thailand is primarily a Buddhist country. However, it has very high religious tolerances and it welcomes the practice of any other religion within the country. Hence, a Buddhist temple and a Catholic church on the same road is not an uncommon sight. Here are some non-Buddhist places of worship.

Calvary Baptist Church, Soi 2, Sukhumvit. Road, Tel: 251-8278.
Holy Redeemer Church (Roman Catholic), 123/19 Soi Ruam Rudee, Tel: 252-5097.
The Evangelical Church, Soi 10, Sukhumvit Road, Tel: 251-9539.

Christ Church (Anglican/Episcopal Services), Convent Road, Tel: 234-3634.

German Church service, Victory Monument, Tel: 391-0551.

Hindu Temple (Wat Khek), Pan Road, Off Silom Road.

Wat Sirikurusing Saha (Sikh), 565 Pahurat Road, Tel: 221-1011.

Bahai Faith, 77/1 Soi Lang Suan, Off Ploenchit Road, Tel: 252-5355.

Health and Emergencies

There are Western-educated doctors and dentists in Bangkok and Chiang Mai. Your hotel or the Tourist Information Center can assist you in making and keeping appointments.

Major hospitals with English-speaking staffs in Bangkok are as follows:

Bangkok Christian Hospital, 124 Silom Road (tel: 233-6981).

Camillian Hospital, 423 Soi 55 Thonglor, Sukhumvit Road (tel: 391-0136).

Chulalongkorn Hospital, Rama IV Road (tel: 252-8131).

Paolo Memorial Clinic and Hospital, 670/1 Phaholyothin Road (tel: 279-7040).

Phrommitr Hospiral, 12 Soi Prommitr. Sukhumvit Road (tel: 391-8383).

Police Hospital. 492/1 Rajdamri Road (tel: 252-8111).

Saint Louis Hospital, 215 Sathorn Tai (tel: 233-8180).

Seventh Day Adventist Hospital, 430 Pitsanuloke Road (tel: 281-1422).

For police assistance or other emergency help, contact your hotel desk or the Tourist Authority of Thailand.

Dining Out

"Thai foods," an expert on the subject writes, without mincing words, "are very, very hot." If you find a Thai cook pondering over a simmering pot of *gaeng pet.* "hot curry," chances are you will catch her resolutely adding another handful of tiny green chilies, called in Thai *prick kee nu,* a single one of which would be enough to blast the average *farang* out of his chair.

Not all Thai foods are so hot, of course. There is a wide range of native sweets, including delicate custards in ripe coconut and sugary confections wrapped in banana leaves, as well as a number of only moderately seasoned noodle dishes; but the fundamental fact remains that the Thais like their food highly spiced, especially the curries. A half dozen or so different kinds of chilies are used with what may appear to the uninitiated as abandonment, the hottest of all being a deceptively pretty little orange one called *prik kee nu luang*. Restaurants catering to foreign tourists have learned their lesson and produce a kind of watered-down version

that Thais regard with undisguised amusement.

Actually, curry is only one small part of Thai cuisine, which, on closer acquaintance, reveals itself as immensely varied and complex — so complex, indeed, in its proper preparations that you rarely get it in restaurants, which generally offer only basic dishes and Thai-Chinese concoctions. Aside from chilies, the basic seasoning of Thai food are coriander (fresh and sprinkled on nearly everything), garlic, basil, cardamom, and a small, round, pealike vegetable that is a form of eggplant. There are also a number of basic sauces that appear at every dinner, the most essential being *nam pla*, or fish sauce.

Since the majority of Thai dishes are either soft or soupy, chopsticks are not used at a Thai dinner; a large spoon and a fork are usually the only utensils provided, the fork being used to push the food onto the spoon. A large platter of rice is the mainstay of the meal, with five or six smaller bowls of curry, vegetables, fish, soup, and the like set around it. You put a pile of rice in the middle of your plate and then add a little of each dish to it.

The different regions of Thailand have their own distinctive cuisines, and while certain basic dishes are similar there are many variations. Chiang Mai food, for example, is milder than that of the Central Plains where glutinous rice (eaten by hand) is usually included. In the South, curries predominate. Northeasterners enjoy a number of specialties that may give fastidious *farang* eaters cause for thought, like pig's head and frog curry, but many Thais insist that cooking in the Northeast is the best in the country.

Eating in Bangkok

The problem of eating in Bangkok, as one gourmet has observed, is not so much where as what. The city probably has a more diversified selection of restaurants than any other capital in Asia, with the possible exception of Tokyo, with a range running from cheeseburgers to sukiyaki and almost everything in between. Within a relatively small area you can eat Mexican, French, German, Italian, Scandinavian, Hungarian, Japanese, Vietnamese, Korean, English, American, Laotian, Filipino, Indian, Indonesian, Swiss, Burmese and Austrian — and not, in most cases, vague approximations but the real thing, prepared by cooks from the country in question. Half a dozen provinces of China are represented, from bland Cantonese to spicy Szechuanese, offering not only such splendors as Peking Duck but esoteric oddities like duck tongues and chicken breast stuffed with bird's nest.

You can dine on Central, Northern, Southern, and Northeastern Thai food, either in fairly basic surroundings or in lavish, air-conditioned comfort while watching a show of folk and classical dancing. Your hotel bookshop will probably have a number of restaurant guides to help you make a choice; one that is recommended is *Eating Out In Bangkok* by Harry Rolnick, a highly personal but dependable compilation by a long-time resident of Bangkok. The listing of restaurants in the Appendix of this book serves as a brief and easy guide to some of the places in which you can experience the various types of cuisine available.

Except for weekends, reservations are usually unnecessary, even at the fanciest restaurants; only one hotel restaurant requires a jacket and tie.

Roadside Kitchens:

Inveterate snackers, Thais like to eat when the mood strikes them, at almost any hour of the day or night. Their philosophy regarding food is, quite simply, "Eat when you are hungry." Wherever you go in Thailand you will see them around a noodle vendor's bicycle or at one of the temporary sidewalk stalls that spring up as if by magic wherever people are likely to be working or passing by — eating a bowl of rice noodles garnished with a bit of fried meat and coriander, a delicate little pancake folded around a sugary sweet, or a deep-fried banana fritter.

These portable kitchens, using only the basics in equipment — usually only a brazier of charcoal and a few pots and pans — turn out culinary delights remarkably complex by any standards.

A Thai Menu

Appetizers

peanuts	tua
cashews	met mamuang himmapan
salty dried beef	nua sawan
crispy pork skin	kaab muu
crispy noodles	mee krob
deep-fried shrimp	gung tawt krob
shrimp chips	khao kriep gung
barbecued pork	muu satay
spring rolls	poh pia

Soups and Noodles

rice soup (with chicken pork, shrimp, or egg)	kow tom
rice porridge (with chicken and shredded ginger—egg optional)	jok
clear soup (with celery and bean curd)	tom juut
lemon shrimp soup	tom yaam gung
wanton soup	geo nam
white-noodle soup (with fish balls, pork, chicken, or duck)	kwit-teo nam (luuk chin, muu, gy, pet)
yellow-noodle soup	bami nam
hot white noodles	kwit-teo hehng
dry yellow noodles	bami hehng
crispy yellow noodles	mii grawp
fried wanton with greens	geo raat naa
fried white noodles	kwit-teo raat naa
fried yellow noodles	bami raat naa
fried noodles (with egg and bean sprouts)	kwit-teo pat ty

Rice

dry white rice	kow plow
Chinese rice soup	kow tom plow
sticky rice	kow neo
fried rice with shrimp and vegetables	kow pat gung
fried rice with pork	kow pat mu
fried rice with egg	kow pat ky dow raat naa

Main Dishes

omelette with pork	ky yat sy
sweet and sour (chicken, pork, fish, shrimp)	preo waan (gy, muu, pla, gung)
barbecued chicken	gy yaang
deep-fried chicken	gy tawt
sliced chicken and rice	kow man gy
fried chicken and cashews	gy pat met mamuang
fried chicken with mint and cloves	gy pat by gaprow
Thai chicken curry	gaeng gy
Indian chicken curry	gaeng garii
beef in oyster sauce	nua pat nam man hoy
ginger beef	nua pat king
partly boiled egg with seasoning	kai luak

Sauces and Spices

fish sauce (substitute for salt)	nam pla
light soy sauce	nam sii iw kow
dark soy sauce	nam sii iw dam
red spicy sauce	nam prik
sweet plum sauce	nam buay wan
vinegar with chilies	nam som
dried chili flakes	prik kee nu bon
salt	glua
black pepper	prik ty
ginger	king
garlic	gratiam
curry	gaeng

Sweets (Kanom)

sticky rice baked in bamboo	kow laam
mango and sticky rice with coconut sauce	kow neo mamuang
brown sticky rice	kow neo deng
banana fritters	gluay tawt
bananas in sweet coconut milk	gluay buad chee
egg custard	kanom maw gang
Chinese tarts	kanom pia
peanut brittle	tua dut
fruit, beans, or jelly with sweet juice and shaved ice	tubtim krab

Drinks

to take out	sy tung
ice water	nam yen
cold Chinese tea	nam keng plow
hot Chinese tea	nam cha rawn
iced tea with sugar	cha dam yen
iced tea with lemon	cha manow
hot tea with sweet milk	cha rawn
hot pekoe tea with lemon	cha rawn kab manow
iced black sweet coffee (Chinese)	o-liang
iced Thai coffee with sweet milk	gafeh yen
hot Thai coffee with sweet milk	gafeh rawn
instant coffee	nesgafeh
hot ovaltine with sweet milk	owaltin rawn
iced ovaltine	owaltine yen
bottled soybean milk	wytamilk
fresh milk	nom sot
iced lemonade with salt	nam manow
iced lemonade without salt	nam manow (my sy glua)
fresh orange	nam som sot
coconut milk	nam maprow

Shopping

Shopping is a pleasure, not only because of the variety of things to buy but also, nowadays, because of the ubiquity of Bangkok's air-conditioned shopping centers where it is possible to get a good deal of your buying done without being laid out by the heat. The following are some of the things Thailand is noted for, both the quality and the price, in most cases, being superior to anywhere else.

Thai fabrics. Thai silk is too well known to need any introduction; suffice to say that it is here, in quantity, in assorted weights, in meters, or made up into clothes and other items. It may, however, be useful to note that the quality of silk is not always uniform, and in some shops that offer suspiciously good bargains, the cloth may have been cleverly interwoven with rayon or some other synthetic; stick to the better-known shops unless you are good at telling. Handwoven Thai cotton is less famous and unjustly so, for it is a soft but durable material that is wonderful for dresses, upholstery, and other uses. In many shops you can get the cotton in the same colors and prints as the silk, at around 40 to 50 baht a meter.

Jewelry. Gold in Thailand is considerably cheaper than in Europe or the United States, and the craft of making modern jewelry — as distinct from the traditional Thai designs — has progressed to the point where many tourists now rank Bangkok ahead of Hong Kong. Best buy among native stones is the sapphire, blue or black, star or plain: also you can sometimes find good rubies from Cambodia and Burma. Most stones are less expensive than in the West. For something different, look at the Thai princess ring, which has nine tiers set with nine different precious and semi-precious stones.

Handicrafts. If you are going to Chiang Mai, where most of the Thai handicrafts come from, wait and buy them there. Otherwise, look for the hilltribe embroidery, lacquerware, painted umbrellas, wood carvings, basketwork, and delightful fish mobiles made of woven bamboo which Thai mothers hang over cribs as pacifiers. The government-sponsored Narayana Phand, on Larn Luang Road in Bangkok is a good place to buy most of these.

Celadon. This was originally made in Thailand during the Sukhothai period, died out, and was revived about 20 years ago. Vases and lamp bases are good buys; complete dinner sets are also available as well as a variety of souvenir pieces.

Dolls. For collectors, there is a wide selection in a classical dance costumes or depicting the various hilltribes of the North.

Bronzeware. Long one of the most popular buys with tourists, bronzeware now comes in plain, modern designs as well as the traditional Thai ones. You can get everything in it from complete cutlery sets to salad bowls; look also for bronze temple bells to hang on a terrace or patio. At several shops you can get bronzeware that has been siliconized so that it will not tarnish.

Spirit Houses. There are some charming ones in the shape of little Thai-style houses which are not too bulky to send or carry.

Antiques. Read the section on Bangkok's Nakorn Kasem in Chinatown for added information on these. Best buys are Chinese porcelains and furniture, carvings from Thai temples, Sawankhalok (a porcelain made near Sukhothai in the 14th century), old Thai paintings, silver betel-nut boxes, Burmese tapestries and wooden figures. Fakes abound, especially in Buddha images, so know what you are doing or go to the best shops. For most Buddhist art of Thailand, a permit is required from the Fine Arts Department before the pieces can be taken out of the country. The good shops will take care of this complicated job for you.

The Central Department Store, with its fire branches in Silom, Chidlom, Wangburapa, Ladya and Ladpraw, is the best place for a visitor who does not have enough time to go around the country to shop for gifts from various provinces. It also has goods from all over the globe. Prices are fixed; credit cards and personal checks are accepted. **Thai Daimaru** has two branches: one in Rajdamri Arcade on Rajdamri Road and the other at Phra Kanong on Sukhumvit Road. It sells mostly imported goods from Japan. Prices are fixed; credit cards and checks are accepted. **The Mall Shopping Center** on Rajdamri Road offers for sale goods from all around the world at fixed prices. **Robinson Department Store** has three branches: Rajdamri, Victory Monument and Siam Square. You will find a good range of ready-made clothes here at fixed prices.

Those who like bargaining will find small or big shops on almost every street of Bangkok offering everything from rubber bands to jewelry. A few big shops accept credit cards and checks but most prefer cash.

Festivals & Fairs

The ceaseless pursuit of *sanuk* in Thailand guarantees a plenitude of festivals, fairs, seasonal sports, and similar pleasures, as well as a number of more solemn religious ceremonies. The greatest concentration of these comes in the cool season, from November through February, but something or other is going on most months of the year.

Most of Thailand's annual events, especially religious holidays, are determined by the Thai lunar calendar. Therefore it is impossible to provide exact dates for these happenings well in advance. (The Tourist Authority of Thailand does publish each year a revised calendar of festivals.) Thailand has adopted the Western calendar for official purposes, but the years are still numbered as well according to the Buddhist Era, which began in 543 B.C. So A.D. 1977 is the year B.E. 2520. The following is a list of some of the annual highlights to look for on your visit.

JANUARY

New Year's Eve and Day are official holidays; as in the West the night of the 31st is a time for celebration. In Bangkok, all the leading hotels stage some sort of festivity, usually of the paper-hat-and-noisemaker variety. But if you want to join celebrating Thais go either to Khao Din (Dusit) Zoo or to Sanam Luang, the big field across from the Temple of the Emerald Buddha. A word of caution about the latter: the pushing, squeezing, and general high spirits can get fairly enthusiastic if you go into the middle of the crowd and it may not appeal to the sedate and fainthearted.

Outside Bangkok, Chiang Mai is the best place for New Year's, for there is a three-day **Winter Fair** with gala parades, beauty contests, and all sorts of northern amusements.

Usually held in January — though sometimes in February, depending on the organizing committee — is the **Red Cross Fair,** normally opened by the king and queen, in Amporn Gardens near the old Parliament building. There are stalls operated by foreign embassies, Thai film stars, government departments, and various universities, as well as performances of folk and classical dancing and other nightly entertainment. All proceeds go to the Thai Red Cross, whose honorary president is the queen.

FEBRUARY

Maka Puja, an important Buddhist holiday, is celebrated toward the end of this month, depending on the moon. It commemorates the miraculous occasion when 1,250 of the Buddha's disciples gathered without prior arrangement to hear him preach. On this day Thai temples are crowded, and the faithful gain merit by such acts as releasing caged birds. The day's ceremonies culminate in a candlelight procession around the *bot*, the main temple building.

Chinese New Year falls on the first day of the first Chinese lunar month, usually in February. No gay celebrations fill the streets as in other countries. For Thailand's several million Chinese the occasion calls for family reunions, feasts, gift giving, and the only time-out all year from the paramount matters of business. Most Chinese shops close for three or four days. Chinese Buddhist temples, near Yaowaraj Road in Bangkok and in Thonburi, are crowded with devotees, offering prayers for good fortune.

Phra Buddhabaht Festival finds Buddhist devotees flocking to the Shrine of the Holy Footprint near Saraburi, 136 km north of Bangkok. Originally built in the 16th century, the famed shrine annually attracts pilgrims who flock to honor what is believed to be a gunuine footprint of the Buddha. According to legend, a hunter discovered the footprint filled with water which had miraculous curative power.

MARCH

There is no official holiday in March, but this month (and April, too) happens to be the best time for **Kite Flying** because of the breezes that spring up nearly every afternoon on even the hottest days. In Bangkok there are official kite-fights every weekday afternoon from 4:30 until dusk at Sanam Luang. Restaurants are set up on the Thammasat University side of the field, and for the price of a beer or a soft drink you can relax in deck chairs and watch the overhead activity.

APRIL

Chakri Day on April 6 is a national holiday which commemorates the founding of the Chakri

dynasty of which the current ruling monarch is the ninth king. People take flowers and incense to the Temple of the Emerald Buddha to pay respect to former kings of the dynasty. The Pantheon, a building on the temple grounds adjoining the Grand Palace, housing the statues of each king, is open to the public only on this day of the year.

The highlight of this month is **Songkran,** the old Thai New Year, which takes place between the 13th and 15th. Songkran is essentially a religious holiday, marking the beginning of the Buddhist year. Traditional Thais observe it by going to temple, sprinkling water on Buddha images, and giving their houses a thorough cleaning. However, over the years decidedly secular manifestations have been added to the holiday, the principal one being the freedom to throw water on anyone who happens to be passing by — not altogether unwelcome, if you are prepared for it, since April is the hottest month of the Thai year. Everyone is fair game for a sudden drenching, especially in Chiang Mai, where many of the old traditions are still observed. Such carefree water throwing is uncommon in Bangkok, but a popular place near the capital is at Phra Pradaeng, down near the mouth of the Chao Phya River. It is best to go to Phra Pradaeng by boat, since the road traffic gets congested, once there, you will see parades, boat races, and folk dances — and also probably come back soaking wet.

MAY

Coronation Day on the 5th is a national holiday marking the anniversary of the coronation of His Majesty King Bhumibol Adulyadej. Inside the Royal Chapel of the Grand Palace, high-ranking government officials pay their respects to the king.

The Ploughing Ceremony takes place around the middle of this month in Sanam Luang in Bangkok. As previously noted, this is a basically Hindu ceremony celebrating the beginning of the rice-planting season; seeds that have been blessed are ritualistically sown, and the coming harvest is predicted by Brahman priests.

Visakha Puja, another important Buddhist holiday, comes on the full moon day of the sixth lunar month, which usually falls in May. Perhaps the most sacred of all Buddhist days, this celebrates the birth, death, and enlightenment of the Buddha. In the evening at nearly every temple, there are processions of people carrying candles; one of the loveliest of all Thai festivals.

JULY

Asalaha Puja marks the beginning of **Buddhist Lent** *(Khao Pansa)* — three months during which monks must remain in their temples and strictly observe their religious duties. It is also the time that most young Thai men choose to enter a monastery for a temporary stay that may last anywhere from a week to the full three months; and almost anywhere you go in Thailand you will come across a *buat nang,* or "ordination ceremony." As with so many Thai ceremonies, this is a combination of the high-spirited (on the eve of his ordination the novice customarily gives a festive party for all his friends) and the deeply religious (he exchanges his white supplicant's robes for the priest's saffron ones, thereby bidding symbolic farewell to the world which can be deeply moving).

The Buddhist Lent period also marks a temporary halt to most festivals in Thailand, for these are the rainiest months and it is risky to schedule outdoor events until the cool season starts and the rain stop.

AUGUST

The **Queen's Birthday** on the 12th is a public holiday throughout Thailand, when Her Majesty Queen Sirikit makes offerings to monks at Chitralada Palace and attends various religious ceremonies.

OCTOBER

Ok Pansa, during this month, is the end of Buddhist Lent and the beginning of the *kathin* season. *Kathins* are ceremonies in which groups of people go to various temples to present robes and other gifts to the resident monks. All over the country you see supplicants along the roads, either in buses or on foot, usually accompanied by music and dancing. The most spectacular of all *kathins* in the past was when the king went by river in the gilded royal barges to Wat Arun, but this has not been held for years due to the condition of the barges; plans have been announced, however, to revive it in the near future, and if this comes about visitors will be able to see one of the world's truly great spectacles.

The 23rd of this month is **Chulalongkorn Day**, commemorating the death of King Rama V. Thousands of people go on this day to his statue in front of the old Parliament Building to lay wreaths in homage to his memory.

NOVEMBER

This is the best of all festival months in Thailand with various fairs, large and small, going on all over the country. One of the most beautiful is **Loy Krathong**, which takes place on the night of the full moon of the twelfth lunar month, the exact date of which varies each year. A *krathong*, traditionally, is a small, lotus-shaped boat containing a candle, incense sticks, and often a coin; both adults and children place them in the rivers and canals to honor the water spirits and, some believe, carry away their sins. The best places in Bangkok to enjoy this charming celebration are on the river, along Klong Saen Sap (the one that runs behind the British Embassy), or around the lakes at Khao Din Zoo and Lumpini Park. Thousands of people from all over the country also go to Chiang Mai for Loy Krathong, where it is a city-wide festival; the Ping River that runs through the middle of Chiang Mai is a magical sight as countless *krathongs*, some of them huge, elaborate affairs, drift downstream twinkling along the dark waters.

The **Golden Mount Fair** is another major November event in Bangkok. Around Wat Sakhet are dozens of little food stalls, open-air theaters, and shops; and the Golden Mount is alive with light as people carry candles in a procession to the top.

Close to the time of Loy Krathong is the Hindu celebration called **Deepavali**, or the Festival of Lights. At this time most of the Hindus in Bangkok,

and many from the countryside, come to the ornate little Indian Temple on Silom Road in Bangkok to watch various entertainments, including feats of self-mutilation performed by pious zealots.

Also around Loy Krathong time is the large, six-day **Phra Pathom Chedi Fair** in Nakhon Pathom, west of Bangkok (less than an hour's drive). This takes place at the largest *chedi*, or pagoda, in Thailand, and people come from all over to this fair, regarded as one of the best of the year.

Some time in November is the **Elephant Round-up**, staged by the Tourist Authority of Thailand and the local government of Surin Province, at which hundreds of elephants put on a spectacular show that has become a great favorite with tourists. Special air-conditioned trains make the overnight trip from Bangkok to Surin, and sheltered viewing stands and an English commentary are provided for ticket-holders.

Also of possible interest is the **Trooping of the Colors** on the 8th, when contingents of the army, navy, and air force parade in review at Bangkok's Royal Plaza often before the king.

DECEMBER

The King's Birthday on December 5 is a national holiday, and most of Bangkok is decorated with colored lights, flags, and portraits of the king in honor of the occasion. The best places to enjoy the decorations are along Rajadamnern Avenue and around the Grand Palace.

Christmas is not celebrated in Thailand, except by the tourist hotels, the few Thai Christians, and of course many members of the foreign community.

Nightlife

The nighttime world of Thailand needs no introduction. Night life is as important to Bangkok visitors as sandy beaches are to Hawaii or cherry blossoms to Japan.

Thai nightlife is centered around nightclubs, bars, massage parlors and — more recently —, discotheques, all of which exist in almost all corners of the country.

Musical entertainment, provided by pop groups or solo vocalists, is available at the larger hotels. It is difficult to know just what is featured since hotels rotate their acts. Call to check first.

For a cheaper way to enjoy an evening drink and perhaps a meal with musical accompaniment, there are many open-air restaurants around Bangkok — especially along Lard Prao Road — where live bands play music of Thai modern genre and (occasionally) Western.

If your idea of a well-spent evening is jiving to the latest sounds, drinking and chatting with beautiful hostesses, visit any of the bars and nightclubs on Patpong Road or Soi Cowboy (off Soi 21, Sukhumvit Road). These bars are famous for their open and friendly bargirls. Most of them also stage floor shows, with the first show starting about 10 p.m. Some have "Happy Hours," early evening sessions when drinks are offered at half price; and "Movie Time," when video recordings of rock and pop groups are shown.

Fancy trying Bangkok's famed massage parlors? Try those along Patpong II Road (the small road parallel to the main Patpong Road) or on Petchburi Road. A massage will cost from 120 baht per hour upwards although much depends on the class of establishment . . . and how elaborate a massage you require.

Courtesy and Custom

Some customs are important to keep in mind during a visit to Thailand. The Thais are far too genial and easygoing to expect a *farang* ("foreigner") to observe all their ways, but here, as anywhere, it helps to have a few general ideas about the *dos and don'ts* of polite society.

Perhaps the one area (besides showing proper respect for the monarchy) where they *can* be sticky is regarding behavior in a temple. Visitors are required to remove their shoes before entering the building containing the principal Buddha image, which is the one where people will be sitting about the floor paying homage to the Buddha. Women are not allowed in the monks' quarters, nor should they hand anything directly to a monk. (Should the occasion arise when a woman *has* to give something to a monk and no man is around to perform the service, she places the object on a table or on the ground and then the monk is free to pick it up for himself.) What few unpleasant incidents there have been involving foreigners in *wats* have arisen because the Thais felt some deliberate insult had been given to their religion. One, a few years ago, came about when some visitors to the ruins of Sukhothai were photographed sitting on the head of a huge Buddha image — a double insult actually, since the head is considered the most sacred part of the body. Another resulted from a singularly insensitive team of fashion models who not only posed provocatively but even changed their clothes in the compound of Wat Phra Keo.

Greetings

When Thais meet one another, they do not usually shake hands. The customary greeting is the *wai,* with the hands raised as if in prayer. Traditionally, the higher the hands are held the more respectful is the *wai,* so that by observing two people you can tell theoretically their respective ranks. But rank is a complicated matter in Thailand, involving, as it does, such things as age, occupation, and social position. For an outsider, it is enough to make the gesture.

As the feet are the lowest part of the body, it is considered rude in Thailand to point your feet at anybody, especially if the gesture is deliberate. Most Thais strive mightily to avoid doing so even accidentally, and as a result you seldom see people with their legs crossed, or if they are, they tend to keep the toes pointed carefully toward the floor.

Dress

Thais are extremely neat in their appearance, and even in a slum it is rare to see anyone who is really dirty or unkempt; mechanics, covered with grease and grime at the end of the day, emerge from their evening bath as spotless as if they had never come within reach of an engine. (All Thais bathe at least once a day and usually twice.) To say that someone is *mai rieb-roi* ("not neat") is almost as serious as saying that he is *mai suparb* ("not polite"), and very often it is the same thing; disorderliness can be regarded as rude in certain circumstances. Although among some younger, westernized Thais — the kind you see roaming about Bangkok shopping centers — it is considered smart (*sa-mart*) to dress in the loose, semi-hippie garb of Western teenagers, to the great majority of the population it is simply *mai rieb-roi.* Similarly, to conservative Thais, there are polite and impolite colors — a brightly colored dress is acceptable on a young girl but not on an older woman, who ought to wear somber shades or pastels. (There are even certain colors for certain days; Sunday, for example, is the only day on which almost anyone can wear red without being considered *mai-suparb* in the extreme.) As a general rule, of course, foreign visitors are not included in all these strictures, and as long as you look reasonably presentable (even in a *mai-suparb* color) you are not likely to get a second look on the street. It *is* frowned upon, however, for a woman to wear shorts in public particularly in a temple, or to show too much of the rest of her body either for that matter.

In Public

It is common to see two Thai men holding hands as they walk along the street — a sign, incidentally, of simple friendship; nothing else — but very rare to see a man and woman doing it, for public displays of affection between the sexes is an old and strong taboo. During the Vietnam war, when Bangkok was a major rest and recreation center for thousands of American servicemen, one of the most frequent criticisms leveled at them was their public behavior with bar girls, innocent though most of it was by American standards. The experience has left many well-bred Thai girls wary about even being seen with a *farang* for fear she will be held in contempt by others.

Names

Surnames are a relatively recent innovation in Thailand, having been introduced only fifty-odd years ago during the reign of King Rama VI. Before that, people were called simply by a single name, followed by an explanation, if necessary, such as "son of . . ." or "from the town of . . ." Even today the average Thai last name is usually so long and complex that it is seldom used; thus Mr. Kraisri Nimmanahsominda is called, simply, Mr. Kraisri. *Khun,* in Thai, is the equivalent of either Mr. or Miss or Mrs., and is used for both men and women. You may encounter titles of Thai royalty, which in descending order are Mom Chao (M.C.), Mom Rajawong (M.R.), Mom Luang (M.L.).

Expressions

Three Thai expressions, Thai soul talk in fact, to remember: *mai pen rai, pai-tio, sanuk*. None of them can be translated into English with great precision, but all of them are important to understanding the Thai heart and character.

Mai pen rai is usually rendered into English as "never mind," and in many cases this seems a fair enough translation. You forget something you said you would do for a friend and he responds to your apologies with *mai pen rai*, meaning. "Don't worry about it; it doesn't matter; stay cool." But *mai pen rai*, as more than one writer on Thailand has pointed out, suggests a state of mind as well as a specific reaction to a situation. In that sense, it can be seen as an extension of the Buddhist philosophy — a shrugging off of the unimportant, the merely transient. To a certain, rigid kind of Western mind it can be an exasperating attitude, particularly when applied to matters he regards as important. But to others it is an essential part of the relaxed atmosphere of Thailand — the reluctance to get overexcited about things (certainly things one cannot do anything about, such as making a late train hurry or a canceled flight airborne), the tendency to accept difficulties casually, the preference for laughter over tears.

Sanuk means "fun," but as in the case of *mai pen rai* this literal translation gives only a shadow of its real extended meaning and the role it plays in Thai life. The Thai love of *sanuk*, their *joie de vivre*, is deeprooted and irrepressible and pervades almost every aspect of their daily existence. Without really thinking, they tend automatically to divide the experiences of life into those that are *sanuk* and those that are not, or *mai sanuk*; and to classify something in the latter category is a very grave criticism indeed. Going *pai-tio* is *sanuk*. So is going to a movie, to a festival, to a wedding, to visit an old friend, to have a bowl of noodles at a good restaurant, almost any kind of trip. Work, on the other hand, is not *sanuk*, at least not if it is totally unrelieved and — most damning criticism of all — "serious." A highly qualified lecturer arrived a few years ago to take up a post at one of Thailand's leading universities. On paper, and in fact, he was an acknowledged authority on his subject, which he had taught successfully in several famous institutions abroad. He bombed in Thailand almost from the start because his students, with pitiless accuracy, labeled him as *mai sanuk*. "He just *taught*," one of them said later, after the professor had left in total bewilderment. "He didn't even smile." A Japanese manufacturing company ran into the same opposition when it tried to duplicate the efficient, production-line techniques that worked so well back home; the Thai workers became "bored" (another devastating term of criticism) with the unrelieved routine, and since boredom is very definitely *mai sanuk* the plant came perilously close to disaster. It was only when they injected a little *sanuk* into the process — piped-in music, snack breaks, games between various departments — that things began to take a turn for the better.

The Thai fondness for *sanuk* does not, as some outsiders may mistakenly conclude, indicate a frivolous mentality, a refusal to face up to the less palatable realities of life; rather, it reveals an ingrained sense of joy, without which life for the Thais would be a drab and meaningless affair. They are willing to work hard when it is necessary (look at the labor gangs along the roads, where women are carrying the same loads as men under the sweltering sun), and to fight bravely, too, in emergencies (visit one of the military hospitals and see the soldiers wounded in battles against Communist insurgents in the South); but they see no point in either work or fighting that is devoid of joy — those road workers, as likely as not, will be cracking jokes and devising small but vital ways to make the labor a little less of a routine.

Pai-tio reflects another aspect of Thai life, one much less readily translatable. Generally speaking, to *pai-tio* means to go for a stroll, to wander about with no particular aim, to go see what's up, to take the evening air, to stand around a movie theater and watch people — but already the possibilities, the variations, stretch into infinity. It may be best to put it this way: whenever you see Thais on foot outside their homes or places of work, unless they are walking *very* purposefully the chances are that they are going *pai-tio*. Outside of a monastery, the desire for solitude mystifies Thais, who delight in putting on their best clothes and going to some public place to observe the activity. A foreigner who expressed surprise at the crowded movie theaters in Thailand despite the television antennas that loom over almost every house was told, "But you can't *see* people at home." To see people, you have to go *pai-tio*. Places to *pai-tio* vary in quality. The most traditional are the marketplaces, where almost everybody goes to buy or just to look; in Bangkok, on Saturday and Sunday (the most popular *pai-tio* days), the great Weekend Market at the Chatuchak Park on Paholyothin Road is crowded with people, the great majority of whom are simply there to *pai-tio*.

Conversation

Finally, a word should be said about the avid curiosity of Thais concerning subjects that are not normally regarded as suitable topics of conversation in most Western countries. Not long after meeting you, for instance, a Thai friend might suddenly inquire, "How much did that shirt cost?" Or how large your salary is; or how old you are; or whether you are married and, if not, why. Such questions, personal as they may sound, are not regarded as rude but as simply a way of showing interest; they would ask the same questions of another Thai. You are not necessarily required to give correct answers, or any answer at all as long as you accompany your refusal with a friendly smile to show that you have not been offended. One *farang* resident of Bangkok has worked out a standard reply to questions about his salary. He simply smiles and says, "Not enough."

The Thai Language

History. When the first Thais began emigrating from southern China to North Thailand, they naturally brought language with them. Akin to Chinese, their words were tonal and monosyllabic. However, as the Thais moved south into the Central Plains they conquered and merged with the Mons and Khmers thereby absorbing certain words of their languages. Perhaps the most radical changes occurred when the Thai language borrowed elements from Sanskrit and Pali, ancient languages of India that Buddhist monks had introduced to the Mons and Khmers. These languages of the scriptures are nontonal and polysyllabic and their influences are today most evident in the complicated grammar of literary Thai. Sanskrit, Pali, and Khmer are the primary sources of a special vocabulary called *rachasap* — the Thai court language used in the presence of royalty. Interestingly, those royal words which are of Khmer origin are at present in common use in Cambodia. Thai language has also been influenced to a lesser extent by the Malays and immigrant Chinese.

The Thais have had an alphabet since A.D. 1283, when Ramkamhaeng of the Sukhothai dynasty instituted a writing system modeled by an Indian one with Khmer characters. The modern Thai alphabet has 44 consonants, 24 vowels, and four diacritical tone marks. Thai is written from left to right.

Dialects. Each of Thailand's four main regions has its own dialect: Northern Thai, Northeastern Thai (Lao), Central Thai (with several subdialects), and Southern Thai. They are almost as different from each other as are the Romance languages, Spanish, Portuguese, and Italian. However, standard Thai, a synthesis of central dialects, is the one language taught in schools throughout the country and recognized as the official government medium.

Grammar. Spoken Thai in all regions is grammatically simple in comparison with European languages. Each word is complete in itself — there are no prefixes or suffixes, no genders for nouns, no articles, no plurals, and no verb conjugations of any kind. There are no set rules making Thai words belong to a particular part of speech, so a word may be used as a noun, verb, adjective, or adverb, depending upon its position in the sentence.

Verb tenses are indicated (if at all) by several fixed auxiliaries before the verb: *ja* for the future, and *gamlang* (meaning "energy") for the present continuous. The past tense is usually indicated by a time phrase.

The basic word order of a sentence is subject-verb-object, with modifiers following each appropriate word. For instance: "He (*kow*) eats (*gin*) rice (*kow*) fried (*pat*)."

In the case of question tags, such as "There isn't much time, is there?" a Thai will often respond to the form with "Yes," while an English speaker would respond to the *meaning* with "No." So double-check such answers, if you are not sure.

Lyrics. Many common Thai words when translated literally bespeak a muse or a minstrel. Some examples:

spirit's clothes = butterfly
slow forest = cemetery
sky cries out = thunder
sky fire = electricity
walking stomach = diarrhea
rice scarce and fruit dear = famine

Tones. Tones were originally adopted to differentiate between identical monosyllabic words. Without tones, the meaning of *my my my my?* could be little more than emotive; but giving each word a separate tone, and thus a meaning of its own, makes the sentence clearly ask: "Does new silk burn?" "Clearly" to a native speaker, that is. Central Thai has five tones that are relatively easy to distinguish, compared with the tones of other regions. (Northern Thai has seven tones that vary greatly from province to province.) For simplicity, the guide below does not indicate the five tones of Central Thai. The visitor who seriously desires to learn the Thai language needs to befriend and win the heart of a sympathetic bilingual native to help give voice to the proper cues.

Consonants. There are 20 consonant sounds in Thai, all of which are close to English sounds though several fall somewhere in between two English consonant sounds, as indicated below.

p	This sound falls between *b* and *p*. It occurs in English only after *s*, as in the word *space*. Say *space* three times then drop the *s*.
t	This sound falls between *d* and *t*. It occurs in English only after *s*, as in the word *stay*. To practice *t*, say *stay* several times, then drop the *s*.
j	This sound falls between *j* as in *jet* and *ch* as in *chop*.
ng	Unlike in English this sound can begin a word in Thai. To practice it, say *singer* several times, then drop the *si—er*.
g	a hard sound as in *go*, but sometimes falls closer to *k*.

All other consonant sounds are pronounced as they would be in English.
Note: When the three sounds *t*, *p*, and *k*, appear at the end of a word, there is no follow-through of breath as there often is in English. These consonants are sometimes aspirated, as in *phai,* "to paddle," in contrast to a hard *p* in *pai-tio,* "to stroll."
It is common to hear *l* substituted for *r* in Thai, especially in Bangkok.

Vowels. Thai vowel sounds are rather more difficult than the consonants; for some sounds there is no equivalent in English, nonetheless a rough guide is presented below.

i	as in *sip*
ii	as in *seep*
e	as in *bet*
eh	as in *bat*
uh	as in *earn* (without the *r*)
a	as in *pun*
aa	as in *pal*
u	uu as in *pool*

o	as in *so*	
ai,y	as in *pie*	
u	no equivalent; approximated by a guttural *u*.	
ow	as in *cow*	
aw	as in *paw*	
iw	as in *you*	
ew	as in Elmer Fudd's pronunciation of Merry (*mewy*)	
eo	as in *Leo*	
oy	as in *toy*	
uy	as in *we*	

Politeness. In the Thai language there are a number of words used to convey mood rather than meaning. Two such essential words in polite speech are the particles *krap* (used by men) and *ka* (used by women) for statements and questions. For extreme politeness, you would say them after every request and reply. To attract someone's attention a man would say *kun krap* and a lady *kun ka*. Thais in addition often omit the pronouns *poom/chan* (*I*) and *kun* (*you*) for an added touch of discreetness.

Useful Expressions

Note: Alternative pronunciations are given within parentheses.

Numbers

1.	one	*nung*
2.	two	*sawng (sorng)*
3.	three	*sam (sarm)*
4.	four	*sii*
5.	five	*ha*
6.	six	*hok*
7.	seven	*jet (chet)*
8.	eight	*beht (paet)*
9.	nine	*kow*
10.	ten	*sip*
11.	eleven	*sip-et*
12.	twelve	*sip-sawng (-sorng)*
15.	fifteen	*sip-ha*
20.	twenty	*yii-sip*
21.	twenty-one	*yii-sip-et*
25.	twenty-five	*yii-sip-ha*
30.	thirty	*sam (sarm)-sip*
31.	thirty-one	*sam (sarm)-sip-et*
40.	forty	*sii-sip*
50.	fifty	*ha-sip*
100.	one hundred	*nung roi (roy)*
200.	two hundred	*sawng (sorng) roi (roy)*
1,000.	one thousand	*pan (ban)*
10,000.	ten thousand	*muun*

Days of the week

Sunday	*wan athit*
Monday	*wan jan (chan)*
Tuesday	*wan angkaan*
Wednesday	*wan put (bhut)*
Thursday	*wan paruhat*
Friday	*wan suk*
Saturday	*wan saw (sao)*
today	*wan ni*
tomorrow	*phrang (brung) ni*
everyday	*thuk wan*
when?	*mua rai?*

Greetings and Civilities

hello, good morning, goodbye	*sawatii (sawadee) krap/ka*
excuse me, pardon me	*kaw toot (khor thot)*
never mind	*mai pen rai*
Please come in.	*Chuhn (choen) kow.*
Please sit down.	*Chuhn (choen) nang.*
May I come in?	*Kow dai mai?*
How are you?	*Sabai di rue?*
Well, thank you	*Sabai di, kawpkun (khorpkhoon)*
thank you	*kawpkun (khorpkhoon)*
I cannot speak Thai.	*Puut (phoot) thai mai dai.*
Please speak slowly	*Proht(d) puut cha-cha.*
May I take a photo?	*Tai ruup dai mai?*
What do you call this in Thai?	*Phasa thai ii riak waa arai?*
Where do you live?	*Yoo tii nai?*
no	*mai*
not, not good	*mai dai*
very good	*dee mark*

Directions and Travel

where	*tii nai*
left	*sai*
right	*khwa*
straight ahead	*trong pai*
slow down	*cha-cha*
stop here	*yud (yut) tii nii*
drive	*khab (khap)*
be careful	*ra wang*
fast	*rew*
What street is this?	*Nii thanon arai?*
What town is this?	*Nii muang arai?*
How many kilometers to ...?	*Gii kiilo by (pai) ...?*
Wait a few minutes	*Khoi deo.*
I want to go to ...	*Yaak ja (cha) by (pai) ...*
entrance	*khao*
exit	*ork*
bus station	*sathani rot meh*
railway station	*sathani rot fai*
airport	*sanam bin*
gas (petrol) station	*pam namman*
hotel	*rongrem*
police station	*sathani tamruat*
embassy	*sathan thut*
taxi	*thaksii*
pedicab	*samlor*
motorized pedicab	*thuk-thuk*
long-tailed boat	*hang-yao*
river ferry (fast boat)	*rua rew*
canal	*klong*
bridge	*saphan*
lane	*soi*
street	*thanon*
village	*ban*
town	*muang*
city	*nakhon*
island	*koh*
beach	*hat*
hill	*khao*
mountain	*phukkhao (doi)*

At the hotel

hotel	*rongrem*
Do you have a double room?	*Mii hawng (horng) kuu mai?*
I want air conditioning.	*Ow hawng (horng) air.*
I want to see it first.	*Yaak ja duu hawng (horng) gawn.*
Do you have a cheaper room	*Mii hawng (horng) tuuk gwaa (kwa) nii mai?*
Wake us at 7 a.m.	*Pluuk row ton jet mong chow.*
Where is the lavatory?	*Suam tii nai?*
Where is the bathroom?	*Hawng (horng) naam tii nai?*

Ordering & Bargaining

Do you have ...?	*Mii ... nai?*
yes	*mii*
no	*mai mii*
I want ... please	*Ow ... krap/ka.*
I want more ...	*Ow iik ...*
How much is this?	*Nii raka towry (thao-rai)?*
How much per meter?	*Met la towry (thao-rai)?*
I want to buy 4 meters.	*Tawng-gan (torng-kan) sii met.*
How much of a discount?	*Ja lot towry?*
Do you have something cheaper?	*Mii tuuk gwaa (kaa) tii mai?*
Do you have another color?	*Mii sii uhn mai?*
Do you have a smaller size?	*Mii kanaat lek gwaa (kwa) nii mai?*
O.k. I'll take it.	*Toklong.*
Wrap it for me.	*Haw hai duai.*
Bill please.	*Gep taang, krap/ka.*
No chilies please.	*Yaa sai prik na.*

Other handy words

enough	*paw*
a lot	*maak-maak*
too much	*maak kuhn pai*
who	*krii*
what	*arai*
when	*muarai*
where	*tii nai*
how old?	*aayuu towrai?*
yes, right	*chai*
no, not right	*mai chai*
comfortable, well	*sabai*
not well, sick	*mai sabai*
cold weather	*now*
cold temperature	*yen*
hot	*rawn (rorn)*
water	*nam*
spicy hot	*pet (phet)*
delicious	*aroy*
sweet	*waan*
sour	*preo*
hungry	*hiw how*
thirsty	*hiw nam*
fresh	*sot*

ripe	*suuk*
sleepy	*nguang nawn*
young	*awn*
old (age)	*geh*
new/old	*my/gow*
big	*yy*
small	*lek*
to like	*chawp*

Further Reading

History

Cady, John F., *Southeast Asia: Its Historical Development*. New York: McGraw-Hill, 1964.

Chakrabonse, Prince Chula, *Lords of Life*. London: Alvin Redman, 1960.

Coèdes, George, *The Indianized States of Southeast Asia*. Translated by Susan Brown Cousing and edited by Walter F. Vella. Honolulu: East-West Center Press, 1968.

Coèdes, George, *The Making of South East Asia*, translated by H.M. Wright. Berkeley and Los Angeles: University of California Press, 1966.

Damrong Rajanubhab, H.R.H. Prince, *History of Siam Prior to the Ayudhya Period*. Bangkok: Siam Society, 1920.

Hall, D.G.E., *A History of South-east Asia*. Third edition. London: Macmillan, 1968.

Hutchinson, E.W., *1688: Revolution in Siam*. Hong Kong University Press.

Jumsai, M.L. Manich, *History of Thailand and Cambodia*. Bangkok: Chalermnit, 1970.

Jumsai, M.L. Manich, *Popular History of Thailand*. Bangkok: Chalermnit.

Moffat, Abbot Lew, *Mongkut, the King of Siam*. Ithaca, New York: Cornell University Press, 1961.

Samudavanija, Chai-Anan. *The Thai Young Turks*. Singapore: Institute of Southeast Asian Studies, 1982.

Wood, W.A.R., *A History of Siam*. London: T. Fisher Unwin, 1926.

Wyatt, David K., *The Politics of Reform in Thailand: Education in the Reign of King Chulalongkorn*. New Haven: Yale University Press, 1969.

People

Collis, Maurice, *Siamese White*. London, 1936.

Seidenfaden, Erik, *The Thai Peoples*. Bangkok: Siam Society, 1967.

Skinner, G. William, *Chinese Society in Thailand*. Ithaca, New York: Cornell University Press, 1957.

Young, Gordon, *The Hill Tribes of Northern Thailand*. Third edition. Bangkok: Siam Society, 1966.

Religion

Bruce, Helen, *Nine Temples of Bangkok*. Bangkok: Chalermnit.

Bunnag, Jane, *Buddhist Monk, Buddhist Layman*. Cambridge: Cambridge University Press, 1973.

Dhani Nivat, Prince, *A History of Buddhism in Siam*. Bangkok: Siam Society, 1965.

Keyes, Charles F., *The Golden Peninsula: Culture and Adaptation in Mainland Southeast Asia.* New York: Macmillan, 1977.

Tambiah, S.J., *Buddhism and the Spirit Cults in Northeast Thailand.* Cambridge: Cambridge University Press, 1970.

Wells, K.E., *Thai Buddhism: Its Rites and Activities.* Bangkok: Police Press, 1960.

Arts and Culture

Diskul, M.C. Subhadradis, *Art in Thailand: A Brief History.* Bangkok: Silpakorn University, 1970.

LeMay, Reginald, *The Culture of South-east Asia.* London: George Allen & Unwin, 1954.

Rajadhon, Phya Anuman, *Essay on Thai Folklore.* Bangkok: DK Books.

Warren, William, *The House on the Klong.* Tokyo: Weatherhill. Photos by Brian Brake. The Jim Thompson art collection.

Wray, Joe and Elizabeth; Rosenfield, Clare; and Baily, Dorothy; *Ten Lives of Buddha.* Tokyo: Weatherhill. Handsome book on traditional *jataka* painting.

General

Amranand, Pimsai, *Gardening in Bangkok.* Bangkok: Siam Society.

Cooper, Robert and Nanthapa, *Culture Shock: Thailand. Singapore: Times Books, 1982.*

Hanks, Lucien M., *Rice and Man: Agricultural Ecology in Southeast Asia.* Chicago: Aldine, 1972.

Hollinger, Carol, *Mai Pen Rai.* Boston. Houghton Mifflin. Expatriate life in the 1950s.

Ingram, J.C., *Economic Change in Thailand, 1830–1970.* Palo Alto, California: Standford University Press, 1971.

Lekagul, Boonsong and Cronin, Edward, *Bird Guide of Thailand.* Bangkok: Kuruspha.

McCoy, Alfred W., *The Politics of Heroin in Southeast Asia.* New York: Harper and Row, 1972.

Mulder, Niels, *Everyday Life in Thailand.* Bangkok: DK Books.

Pramuan Sarn Staff, *All about Thailand.* Bangkok: Pramuan Sarn Publishing House.

Vella, Walter F., *Chaiyo!* Honolulu: University of Hawaii Press, 1979.

Warren, William and Riboud, Marc, *Bangkok.* New York: Weatherhill.

Warren, William, *The Legendary American.* Boston: Houghton Mifflin. The story of silk czar Jim Thompson.

Young, Ernest, *The Kingdom of the Yellow Robe.* London: Archibald, Constable, 1907.

Appendix

Accommodation

BANGKOK

Airport Hotel, 333 Chert Wudthakas Road, Don Muang, tel: 566-1020 (10 lines), 556-1021 (10 lines). 300 rooms overlooking tropical gardens and a pool. 24-hour coffeeshop, 3 restaurants, and video lounge. Connected to the airport by skybridge and bus shuttle services.

Ambassador, 171 Sukhumvit Road (Soi 11), tel: 251-5141. Has Western, Japanese, Chinese, Thai and seafood restaurants, 3 bars and 2 coffee houses; 24-hour room service and basement nightclub. In the center of the commercial and entertainment districts.

Asia, 296 Phya Thai Road, tel: 281-1433. Easy access to town, poolside snacks. European-Chinese-Japanese cuisines.

Bangkok Center, 328 Rama IV Road, tel: 235-1780. Situated near the Chinatown district just across the road from Hua Lampong railway station. Coffee shop and restaurants.

Bangkok Palace, City Square, Petchburi Road, tel: 251-8874. Swimming pool, two restaurants, coffee shop. In the heart of Bangkok within walking distance from Rajdamri shopping arcade.

Century, 9 Rajprarob Road, tel: 252-9755. European-Chinese-Japanese cuisines. Friendly atmosphere.

Continental, 971 Phaholyothin Road tel: 278-1596. European, Oriental and Thai cuisines and all the usual amenities.

Dorchester, 21 Soi Kotoey, Pratipat, tel: 279-2641. Restaurant, coffee shop, swimming pool and shopping arcade.

Dusit Thani, 946 Rama IV Road, Saladang Circle, tel: 233-1130. One of Bangkok's top hotels. Several restaurants and varied cuisines. Has discotheque and sauna in addition to all the standard amenities. Located in business and entertainment area.

Erawan, 494 Rajdamri Road, tel: 252-9100. One of Thailand's better hotels, it has a tropical garden and Continental restaurant, post and travel offices and a full range of other services.

Federal, 27 Sukhumvit Road (Soi 11). tel: 252-5143. Centrally situated in a residential area with all facilities.

First, 2 Petchburi Road tel: 252-5010. European, Chinese and Thai cuisines and round-the-clock coffee shop. Features a nightclub and "sightseeing" counter. Conveniently situated in center of movie district.

Florida, 43 Phya Thai Square, tel: 245-3221. Undistinguished but pleasant and homely. Features all the usual amenities in addition to being close to a delightful Laotian nightclub.

Fortuna, 19 Sukhumvit Road (Soi 5), tel: 251-5121. Situated in the center of the bar district and somewhat unprepossessing but boasts all the standard amenities.

Golden Dragon Hotel, 20/21 Ngarmvongwan Road, tel: 588-4751. Restaurant and coffee shop. Swimming pool, fifteen minutes from the airport.

Grace, 12 Sukhumvit Road (Soi 3), Nana North, tel: 252-9170. In the center of the bar district and known for its exotic coffee shop. Provides all facilities.

Hilton International Bangkok, Nai Lert Park, North Wireless Road, tel: 252-3622, 252-7380. 400

luxurious rooms and suites with private balconies. Swimming pool, pool-side bar, 4 restaurants, health club, tennis and squash courts.

Honey, 31 Soi 19 (Soi Wattana), Sukhumvit Road, Tel: 252-7111: Restaurant, coffee shop, swimming pool.

Hyatt Central Plaza, 1695 Phaholyothin Road, tel: 5131590-65.

Impala, 9 Soi Kasem (Soi 24), Sukhumvit Road, tel: 391-0038. Restaurant and coffee shop. Conference rooms, car rentals and the usual amenities.

Imperial Hotel, Wireless Road, tel: 252-8070, 252-8079. Pleasant and luxuriously appointed, has shopping arcade and spacious garden.

Indra Regent, Rajprarob Road, tel: 251-111. Medium class international-type hotel with European, Chinese, Thai cuisines and a splendid coffee shop.

The Landmark Hotel and Plaza, 138 Sukhumvit Road, tel: 2524819, 251-1556.

Liberty, 215 Sapan Kwai, Pratipat Road, tel: 270-9606. Dining room, bar, coffee shop, swimming pool, travel agency and shopping arcade.

Majestic, 97 Rajadamnern Avenue, tel: 281-5000 Garden, nightclub and garage. Pleasant and close to government ministries and UN offices.

Malaysia, 54 Ngam-du-plee Road, Rama IV Road, tel: 233-4980. Dining room, bar, swimming pool. Has the usual amenities.

Mandarin, 662 Rama IV Road, tel: 233-4980. Conveniently located near railway station. All standard amenities including European, Chinese, Japanese and Thai cuisines.

Manhattan, 13 Soi 15, Sukhumvit Road, tel: 252-7141. European, Chinese, Japanese, Korean and Thai cuisines. Round-the-clock coffee service, beer garden and a very friendly atmosphere.

Manohra, 412 Suriwongse Road, tel: 234-0570. European and Thai cuisines. Quiet and friendly. Near the Post Office and souvenir shops.

The Menam, 2074 New Road, Yannawa, tel: 289-3814, 289-3818. 800 deluxe rooms and suites. 4 restaurants serving Thai, Chinese, Japanese and European cuisine, a seafood restaurant, poolside bar, disco, tennis and squash courts.

Metro, 1902 New Petchburi Road, tel: 391-1736. All the usual facilities plus a 24-hour bar and restaurant service.

Miami, 2 Sukhumvit Road (Soi 13), tel: 252-5140. Bar, coffee shop, swimming pool, travel agency and money changer.

Miramar, 777 Mahachai Road, Minsen Corner (Samyod Road), tel: 222-1711. Bar, restaurant and coffee shop, 2 conference rooms, travel agency and money changer. Located in Chinatown and business center of Bangkok.

Montien, 54 Suriwongse Road, tel: 234-8060. International standard class hotel with luxury appointments; situated in the center of the entertainment district.

Morakot, 2802, New Petchburi Road, tel: 314-0761. Dining room, bar, coffee shop, swimming pool, travel agency and shopping arcade.

Narai, 222 Silom Road, tel: 233-3350. International standard class hotel. Boasts a revolving-roof restaurant, European and Asian cuisines. German beer cellar and Italian coffee shop.

New Empire, 572 Yawaraj Road, tel: 234-6990. Chinese restaurant, European and Thai food. Free transportation from hotel to airport.

New Fuji, 299-301 Suriwongse Road, tel: 234-5364. One of the smaller hotels with no swimming pool catering somewhat to middle-class Japanese. Provides one of the nicest and cheapest meals in the city.

New Nana, 4 Soi Nana Tai, Sukhumvit Road. Restaurant, 24-hour coffee shop, bar, conference rooms, swimming pool, money changer, taxi service.

Oriental, 48 Oriental Avenue, New Road, tel: 234-8620. Bangkok's (and the world's) best known top-class hotel with a historic past associated with personages like Joseph Conrad and Somerset Maugham. Special appeal is its site overlooking the Chao Phya river.

Park, 6 Sukhumvit Road (Soi 7), tel: 252-5110. Restaurant serving European and Chinese food. Bar, money changer and the usual amenities.

Peninsula, 295/3 Suriwongse Road, tel: 234-3910. Medium-type hotel with all the standard facilities.

President, 135/26 Gaysorn Road, tel: 252-9880. International standard hotel. Conveniently situated in the center of town. Has all facilities with European and Thai cuisines.

Prince, 1537/1 New Petchburi Road, tel: 251-3318. Somewhat far from town but has all facilities and reasonable rates.

Princess, Charoen Krung Road, tel: 234-2951. Medium-type hotel with standard facilities.

Rajah, Sukhumvit Road (Soi 4), tel: 252-5102. All facilities with European, Chinese and Thai cuisines.

Rajsubhamitra, 269 Larn Luang Road, tel: 281-3644. An unassuming place with attractive monthly rates. Besides standard services has a roof garden. European, Chinese, Thai cuisines.

Rama Gardens, 9/9 Vibhavadi Rangsit Road, tel: 597-1113. Only eight minutes from the airport. Two swimming pools, four restaurants and a nightclub. Gardens and health club.

Ramada, 1169 New Road, tel: 234-8971. Dining room, nightclub cocktail lounge, coffee shop and tea lounge.

The Regent Bangkok, 155 Rajdamri Road, tel: 251-6532. One of Bangkok's top deluxe hotels. Western, Thai, Japanese and Chinese restaurants; coffee shop, swimming pool and fitness club.

Reno, 40 Soi Kasemsan 1, Rama I Road, tel: 252-6121. Restaurant, swimming pool.

Rex, 762/1 Sukhumvit Road, tel: 391-0100. Very reasonable rates for the service offered, which is nearly everything.

Rich, 136/14 Sukhumvit Road, tel: 252-9174. Small in size but easy on the purse. Has all the basic amenities plus a swimming pool.

Rose, 118 Suriwongse Road, tel: 233-7695. Favored for brief stays of short duration.

Royal, 2 Rajadamnern Avenue, tel: 222-9111. One of Bangkok's oldest hotels conveniently close to government ministries, UN offices and temples. All facilities available.

Royal Orchid Sheraton, Captain Bush Lane, Sophya

Road, tel: 234-3100. All its 780 rooms have views over the adjacent Chao Phya river. Swimming pool, sauna, massage, bars, nightclub and lounge. Continental and Japanese restaurants.

Sakol, Soi 2, Phya Thai Road, tel: 252-8161. All the standard facilities at reasonable rates.

Shangri-la Hotel, 89 Soi Wat Suan Plu, New Road, tel: 235-6310-2. 650 rooms, 47 suites, restaurants, poolside snack bar, banquet/function facilities, health club and sports facilities.

Siam, 1777 New Petchburi Road, tel: 252-5081. Medium-class hotel with all the standard facilities.

Siam Inter-Continental, Srapatum Palace Property, 967 Rama I Road, tel: 252-9040. International-standard hotel set in pleasant garden surroundings with miniature zoo, tennis courts, mini-golf range. Do not confuse with Siam Hotel (preceding entry).

Suriwongse Hotel, 31/1 Suriwongse Road, tel: 233-3223. With restaurant.

Swan Hotel, 31 New Road. Air-conditioned rooms with a swimming pool.

Tawana Sheraton, 80 Suriwongse Road, tel: 253-35160. Located in center of entertainment district, excellent service with all facilities.

Thai, 78 Prachatipat Road, tel: 281-3633. Medium-class hotel with most standard facilities. European and Chinese cuisines. Close to government ministries and UN offices.

Trocadero, 343 Suriwongse Road, tel: 234-8920. Dining room, bar, coffee shop. Has all the usual amenities. Two minutes to General Post Office.

Viengtai, 42 Tani Road, Banglampu, tel: 281-5788. Close to UN and government ministries.

Victory, 322 Silom Road, tel: 233-9060. Restaurant, coffee shop, swimming pool, money changer and the usual amenities.

Windsor, Soi 20, Sukhumvit Road, Tel: 258-0160. All facilities plus car-rentals and tennis court.

World, 1996 New Petchburi Road, Tel: 3924340. Dining room, bar, swimming pool, conference room.

YMCA, 27 Sathorn Tai Road, Tel: 2865134. All facilities including sports. Some cottages also available. Variety of European, Chinese and Thai food.

CENTRAL THAILAND

ANG THONG
Bua Luang, Tambol Posa, 16 rooms.
Suvapan, Amphoe Muang, 35 rooms, air-conditioned.

KANCHANABURI
Luxury, Tambol Ban Nua, 17 rooms.
Muang Thong, Tambol Ban Nua, 36 rooms.
Prasobsuk Bungalow, Tambol Ban Nua, 33 rooms.
River Kwai Jungle Rafts, Tambon Saiyoke, (Bangkok reservation: 11 Sukhumvit 49, 49-10 Soi Plukmit, Tel: 3923641). 34 rooms.
River Kwai Village, 284/3-16 Sang-Chooto Road, Tambol Ban Nua. Tel: 511565, (Bangkok reservation: 2346840). 60 rooms, air-conditioned. Conference room.
Wang Thong, 60/3 Sang Chooto Road. Tel: 511739. 20 rooms.

LOPBURI
Asia Lopburi, 1/17-8 Surasak Road, Tel: 411892.

111 rooms, air-conditioned.
Muang Thong, Surasongkram Road, 48 rooms, air-conditioned.
Nett, 17/1-2 Rajdamnoen, Tel: 411738. 41 rooms, air-conditioned.
Taipei, 24/6-7 Surasongkram Road, Tel: 411524. 105 rooms, air-conditioned.
Vidoonsi, 388 Naraimaharaj Road, Tel: 411009. 50 rooms, air-conditioned.

NAKHON PATHOM
Mit Phaisarn, Phra Pathom Chedi, 59 rooms.
Mitsumpan, Lungphra Road, 23 rooms, air-conditioned.
Rose Garden, Km 32 Petchkasem, (Bangkok reservation, 4/8 Sukhumvit Soi 3, Tel: 2515735). 106 rooms, air-conditioned. 25 bungalows.
Sirichai, 37-41 Saiphra Road, Tel: 241800. 25 rooms.

NONTHABURI
Golden Dragon, 20/21 Ngamwongsvarn. 114 rooms, air-conditioned.
Hotel 73, Tambol Suan Yai. 19 rooms.
Mitr Sukchai, Tambol Suan Yai. 18 rooms.

PATHUM THANI
Chom Krao, 1/3 Tambol Ta Ram. 36 rooms.
Mit Phaisarn, 146/12 Tambol Bang-Proke. 20 rooms.
Pattamarom, 145-155 Tambol Bang-Proke. 22 rooms.
Teke Heng Chong, 74-76 Tambol Ta Ram.

PETCHABURI
Khao Wang, 36 Tambol Klong Kra-Sang, 49 rooms.
Petchkasem, 14 Tambol Rai Som, 50 rooms.
Regent Cha-Am, 849/21 Cha-Am Beach, tel: (032) 471483-9. (Bangkok office: Regent House Building, 183 Rajadamri Road, Patumwan, tel: 252-1497, 252-8319.) 400 rooms, lounge, restaurant, coffee house, banquet/function facilities, golf course, pool and water-sports facilities.
Sales Villa Bungalow, 285 Ruamchit Road, Cha-am Beach, (Bangkok reservation, Tel: 2818308).
Santi Suk Bungalow, Km 206 Nang Ramperk, Cha-am Beach, (Bangkok reservation, Tel: 2511847 Ext. 13, 17). 43 rooms.

PHRA NAKHON SI AYUTHAYA
Cathay, Tambol Hor Rattana Chai, 26 rooms.
Thai Sena, 286 Senanawin 2 Road, 17 rooms.
Thai Thai, 13/1 Naresuan Road, Tel: 251505. 25 rooms, air-conditioned.
U-Thong, 86 U-Thong Road, Tel: 251136. 65 rooms.
Vieng Fah, Tambol Pratu-chai. 22 rooms.

RATCHABURI
Araya, Tambol Na Muang, Amphoe Muang. 80 rooms, air-conditioned.
Kasen Suk, Tambol Ban Pong, Amphoe Ban Pong, 24 rooms.
Lucky, Tambol Ban Pong, Amphoe Ban Pong, 51 rooms.
Namsin, 2-16 Krai Petch Road, Tel: 337551. 75 rooms, air-conditioned.
Sala Thai, Tambol Na Muang, Amphoe Muang, 44 rooms, air-conditioned.
Si Ban Pong, 8 Sangchooto Road, Amphoe Ban Pong. 30 rooms, air-conditioned.
Siri Sumpan, Tambol Ban Pong, Amphoe Ban Pong. 47 rooms.

Siroj, 139-141 Amarin Road, tel: 337021. 24 rooms, air-conditioned.

Zin Zin, 32/4-7 Railway Road, Tel: 337474. 50 rooms, air-conditioned.

RIVER KWAI see KANCHANANBURI

SAMUT PRAKAN

Bunthomtip, Tambol Sam Rong Nua, Amphoe Muang, 20 rooms.

Charoen Suk, Tambol Pak Nam, Amphoe Muang, 24 rooms.

Hom Huan, Tambol Sam Rong Nua, Amphoe Muang, 20 rooms.

Kwanchai, Amphoe Phra Pradaeng, 32 rooms.

New Sisawai, Amphoe Phra Pradaeng, 42 rooms.

Phra Pradaeng, Amphoe Phra Pradaeng, 30 rooms.

Sukumvit, Tambol Pak Nam, Amphoe Muang, 36 rooms.

SAMUT SAKHON

Kasem, Sethakit Road. 46 rooms.

Viengtai, Tambol Mahachai, Amphoe Muang. 19 rooms, no air-conditioning.

Wiangthai, Sukhontip Road. 19 rooms.

SAMUT SONGKHRAM

Mae Klong, 526/10-13 Petchsamut Road. 20 rooms.

SARABURI

Keo Un, 1741/7-8 Paholyothin Road, Tel: 211222. 169 rooms, air-conditioned.

Saen Suk, 209/1 Tambol Pak Preaw. 81 rooms.

Saraburi, 497 Tambol Pak Preaw. 81 rooms.

Supsin, Amphoe Muang, 46 rooms.

Thanin, Amphoe Phra Phutthabat, Tel: 266088. 45 rooms, air-conditioned.

SINGBURI

Chaophya, Tambol Bangbhutsa. 44 rooms, air-conditioned.

Phitsanulok, 28 Naresuan Road, Tel: 258425. 60 rooms.

Samai Niyom, Tambol Nai Muang. 33 rooms.

Unhachak, 66-67 Phya-Lithai Road, Tel: 258387. 34 rooms.

PHRAE

Nakhon Phrae, Tambol Nai Wiang. 100 rooms, air-conditioned.

Paradorn, 177 Yantrakijkosol Road. 25 rooms, air-conditioned.

Sawasdikarn, 76-78 Yantrakijkosol Road. 30 rooms.

Tang Sri Paiboon, 84 Yantrakitkoson Road. 49 rooms, air-conditioned.

Thepwimarn, Tambol Nai Wiang. 51 rooms, air-conditioned.

PICHIT

Buraparat, Amphoe Taphan Hin. 23 rooms.

New Hua Hin, Amphoe Taphan Hin. 51 rooms, air-conditioned.

Phaisarn, 522-526 Busaba Road. 19 rooms.

Taphan Hin, 7/17 Daeng Thong Di Road. 21 rooms, air-conditioned.

SUKHOTHAI

Chinwat, 1, 2, 3 Nikornkasem Road. 46 rooms.

Phong Prasert, 92/6 Nilornkasem Road. 30 rooms. air-conditioned.

Roong Fah, 8 Singhawat Road. 14 rooms.

Sawasdipong, 56/2-56/15 Singhawat Road. 28 rooms.

Sukhothai, 15/5 Singhawat Road. 40 rooms.

TAK

Bhumiphol Guest House, Bhumiphol Dam, (Bangkok reservation, Tel: 4243805). 31 rooms.

First, Tambol Mae Sot. 38 rooms.

Mae Ping, 321 Tambol Nong Luang. 46 rooms.

Sgnuan Thai, 619 Tak Sin Road, Tel: 511265. 37 rooms.

Siam, 185 Tambol Mae Sot. 70 rooms.

Tak, 8/9 Tambol Nong Luang, Tel: 511234. 29 rooms.

Thavisak, 561/8 Mahatthai Bamrung, Tel: 20235. 32 rooms, no air conditioning.

UTTARADIT

Chai Fah, Tambol Thasao, Amphoe Muang. 14 rooms, air-conditioned.

Thanothai, 149-153 Kasemras Road. 27 rooms, air-conditioned.

Uttaradit, 24-28 Rasanarn Road. 28 rooms, air-conditioned.

Vanich, 1 Sri-Uttara Road. 74 rooms, air-conditioned.

NORTHEASTERN THAILAND

BURI RAM

Grand, 137 Niwat Road. 71 rooms, air-conditioned.

Krung Rome, Amphoe Muang. 75 rooms, air-conditioned.

Maitrichitr, 169/2-169/4 Soonthornthep Road. 18 rooms, air-conditioned.

CHAIYAPHUM

Charoen, Yutti Dham Road. 18 rooms, no air-conditioning.

Lert Nimit, 336 Harurthai Road. Tel: 811053. 38 rooms, 15 bungalows.

Lert Nimit Co., Ltd., 447 Niversrat Road. Tel: 811522. 80 rooms, air-conditioned.

Phaiboon, Yutti-Dham Road. 20 rooms.

Saeng Petch, Tambol Nai Muang, Amphoe Muang. 25 rooms.

KALASIN

Mit Wattana, Tambol Kalasin, Amphoe Muang. 36 rooms.

Sang Thong, Kalasin Road. 31 rooms, air-conditioned.

Saeng Chai, Amphoe Kushinarai. 12 rooms, air-conditioned.

Saeng Fah, Amphoe Muang. 20 rooms.

Thai Thong, 107/7-8 Phirom, Tel: 811661. 28 rooms.

KHON KAEN

Chatchai, Tambol Nai Muang, Amphoe Ban Phai. 27 rooms.

Choo Charoen, Thambol Nai Muang, Amphoe Ban Phai. 54 rooms.

Grand, 39 Soi Samaki-Utid. 70 rooms, air-conditioned.

King's, Tambol Nai Muang, Amphoe Muang. 99 rooms.

Kosa, 250-252 Srichan Road, Tel: 236772. 115 rooms, air-conditioned.

Lilla, Tambol Nai Muang, Amphoe Muang. 46 rooms, air-conditioned.

Mung Korn Thong, 41/1-6 Na Muang Road, Tel: 236411. 40 rooms, air-conditioned.

Queen's, 207-9 Maliwan Road, Chumpare. 120 rooms.

Roma, 50/2 Klang Muang Road, Tel: 236276. 97 rooms, air-conditioned. Conference room for 500-800 persons.

Royal, Tambol Nai Muang, Amphoe Muang. 20 rooms, air-conditioned.

Sawasdi, Na Muang Road, Tambol Nai Muang. 68 rooms, air-conditioned.

Thani Bungalow, Tambol Nai Muang, Amphoe Muang. 113 rooms.

Vanchai 2, Tambol Nai Muang, Amphoe Ban Phai. 44 rooms.

LOEI

Porn Sin, 93 Kaew Asa Road. 15 rooms.

Sarai-thong, Ruamchitr Road. 43 rooms.

Thai Deam, 122/1 Charoen Rat Road, Tel: 811763. 55 rooms, air-conditioned.

MAHASAKHAM

Pattana, Tambol Talad, Amphoe Muang. 70 rooms.

NAKHON PHANOM

Chai Pattana, 550 Fuang Nakhon Road. 42 rooms, air-conditioned.

First, 370 Sithep Road, Tel: 511253. 63 rooms, air-conditioned.

Nakhon Phanom, 528/39 Abhibarn Buncha Road, Tel: 511253. 57 rooms, air-conditioned.

Rose Garden, Nakorn Pathom. (Bangkok Office: 4/8 Soi 3, Sukhumvit Road, tel: 253-2276, 253-6295-7.) 80 rooms, restaurants, banquet/reception facilities, shopping arcade, pool, tennis courts, golf course and Thai Village Show.

Sithep, 708/11 Sithep Road, Tambol Nai Muang, Tel: 511036. 56 rooms, air-conditioned.

Windsor, 692/19 Bamroang Muang Road, Tel: 511538. 60 rooms, air-conditioned.

NAKHON RATCHASIMA

Chumphol, Tambol Nai Muang, Amphoe Muang. 69 rooms.

Chomsurang, 2701/2 Mahad-Thai Road. 119 rooms, air-conditioned.

Fah Sang, 112-114 Mookhamontri Road, Tel: 242143. 77 rooms, air-conditioned.

Fah Thai, 849/851 Pho Klang Road, Tel: 242533. 90 rooms, air-conditioned.

Korat, 4014 Asdang Road, Tel: 242444. 121 rooms, air-conditioned.

Lak Muang, Tambol Nai Muang, Amphoe Muang. 83 rooms, air-conditioned.

Sakol, Tambol Nai Muang, Amphoe Muang. 82 rooms.

Siri, Tambol Nai Muang, Amphoe Muang. 60 rooms.

Singburi, 882/18-21 Khunsan Road, Tel: 511752. 110 rooms, air-conditioned.

Thavorn Panich, Amphoe Muang. 23 rooms.

SUPHAN BURI

K.A.T., 433 Near Police Station, Prapanvasa Road, 51 rooms.

Kalaket, Tambol Tha Piliang. 32 rooms.

Petch, Tambol Tha Piliang. 40 rooms.

Si Muang, 531-536 Prapanvasa Road. 39 rooms.

Si Suphan, Tambol Tha Piliang. 47 rooms.

Suksan, Tambol Tha Piliang. 60 rooms.

UTHAI THANI

Hua Thai, Tambol Uthai Hong. 13 rooms.

Phiboon Sook, Tambol Uthai Hong. 40 rooms.

Prasertsri, Tambol Ban Rai. 12 rooms.

NORTHERN THAILAND

CHAI NAT

Arunothai, Tambol Nai Muang. 30 rooms.

Nam Chai, 63/22 Tambol Nai Muang, Tel: 411725. 57 rooms, air-conditioned.

Suk Sawasdi, Tambon Nai Muang. 41 rooms, air-conditioned.

Thepchoom Boonma, Tambol Nai Muang.

CHIANG MAI

Anodad, 57-59 Rajmaraka Road, Tel: 235353, 150 rooms, air-conditioned.

Chiang Inn, 100 Changklan Road, Tel: 235655, (Bangkok Reservation, Tel: 2516883). 175 rooms, air-conditioned.

Chiang Mai President, 226 Vichayanon Road, Tel: 235116, (Bangkok reservation, Tel: 3147776). 150 rooms, air-conditioned.

Diamond, 33/10 Charoen Prated Road, Tel: 234155. 145 rooms, air-conditioned.

Dusit Inn, 112 Chang Klan Road, tel: (053) 251633-7. (Bangkok Office: Dusit Thani, Rama IV Road, tel: 233-1140, 233-1130.) 200 rooms, minibars, restaurants, lounge and banquet/function facilities.

Muang Mai, 502 Huey Kaew Road, Tel: 221392. 155 rooms, air-conditioned.

New Asia, 55 Rajawongse Road, Tel: 235288. 204 rooms, air-conditioned.

Orchid Chiang Mai, 100-102 Huay Kaew Road. Tel: 222099. Situated near city center, 5 km from Chiang Mai Airport. Has 24-hour room service, swimming pool, sauna, tennis courts, golf facilities, nearby, bars, lounges and disco. Restaurants and coffee houses which serve continental, Japanese and Thai dishes.

Porn Ping, 46-48 Charoen Prated Road. 152 rooms, air-conditioned.

Poy Luang, 146 Super Highway Road, Tel: 234633, (Bangkok reservation, Tel: 2520200. 225 rooms, air-conditioned.)

Prince, 3 Tai Wang Road, Tel: 236396. 112 rooms, air-conditioned.

Railway, 471 Charoen Muang Road, Tel: 236463, (Bangkok reservation, Tel: 2230341). 76 rooms, air-conditioned, 8 bungalows.

Rincome, 301 Huay Kaew Road, Tel: 221044, (Bangkok reservation, Tel: 2526118). 158 rooms, air-conditioned.

Rintr, 99/9 Huay Kaew Road, Tel: 22-1483, (Bangkok reservation, Tel: 251-1870).

Sri Tokyo, 63 Chang Klan Road. 144 rooms, air-conditioned.

Sumit, 198 Rajpakinai Road, Tel: 235996, (Bangkok reservation, Tel: 2794525). 165 rooms, air-conditioned.

Surawongs, 110 Changklan Road, Tel: 236789. 168 rooms, air-conditioned.

CHANG RAI

Krung Thong, 412 Sanambin Road, Tel: 311033. 112 rooms, air-conditioned.

Rama, 331/4 Trairat Road, Tel: 311344. 43 rooms, air-conditioned.

Ruang Nakhon, 25 Ruang Nakhon Road, Tel: 344566. 61 rooms, air-conditioned.

Siam, Amphoe Muang. 54 rooms.

Suknirum, 424/1 Bunpakarn Road. Tel: 311055.

105 rooms, air-conditioned.

Wiang Inn, 893 Pholyothin Road. Tel: 311551. 112 rooms, air-conditioned.

KAMPHAENG PHET

Chakunglao, Near Ping River. 120 rooms.

Chong Sawasdi, 180 Tesa Vichit Road. 29 rooms.

Naowarat, Near Ping River. 100 rooms.

Nittayaprapa, 118/1 Tesa Road, Amphoe Muang. 32 rooms.

Phet, 99 Vichit Road Soi 3, Amphoe Muang. Tel: 711283, (Bangkok reservation, Tel: 2516512).

Rajdamnoen, 892 Rajdamnoen Road, Tel: 217029. 74 rooms.

LAMPANG

Asia Lampang, 229 Boonyawat Road, Tel: 217844. 64 rooms, air-conditioned.

Siam, 260/29 Chatchai Road. 84 rooms, air-conditioned.

Sri Sgna, Tambol Suandong, Amphoe Muang. 35 rooms, air-conditioned.

Tip Chang, 54/22 Thacrownoi Road, Muang District, Tel: 218-078. 125 air-conditioned rooms. Swimming pool, coffeeshop, restaurant and a cocktail lounge.

LAMPHUN

Chamchantr, Tambol Viangthong, Amphoe Muang. 17 rooms.

Notanon, 51/2 Tambol Nai Muang. 15 rooms.

MAE HONG SON

Meitee, 55 Khunrum Prapas Road, Tambol Chomkham. 38 rooms, air-conditioned.

Mit Aree, Tambol Mae Sariang, Amphoe Mae Sariang. 18 rooms.

Mitniyom, 90/1 Khunrum Prapas Road. 44 rooms, air-conditioned.

Sguan Sin, 35 Singhanat Road. 28 rooms.

Singhanat, Singhanat Road, Amphoe Muang. 25 rooms, no air conditioning.

Suk Somchai, Singhanat Road. 16 rooms, air-conditioned.

NAKHON SAWAN

Anodad, 479-483 Kosi Road, Tel: 212856. 153 rooms, air-conditioned.

Irawan, 1-5 Matulee Road, Tel: 212070. 43 rooms, air-conditioned.

New White House, 2 Matulee Road, Tel: 212157. 48 rooms.

Sala Thai, 221-225 Tambol Pak Nam Pho. 40 rooms.

Toek Lueng, 24-44 Tambol Pak Nam Pho. 50 rooms.

Visanu 2, 30 Uttakavee Road, Tel: 212932. 117 rooms, air-conditioned.

NAN

Amornsir, Tambol Nai Wiang. 26 rooms.

Nan Fah, 436-438-440 Sumon Thevaraj. 24 rooms.

Suk Kasem, Anantaworaritdej Road. 60 rooms, air-conditioned.

Thevaraj, 466 Sumon Thevaraj Road, Tel: 710095. 115 rooms, air-conditioned.

PHAYAO

Chai Kwan, 53 Tah Kwan Road. 10 rooms.

Chiang Kham, 643 Tambol Yuan, Amphoe Chiang Kham. 32 rooms.

Siriphan Bungalow, 648/2 Kwan Phayao, Tel: 431314. 20 rooms.

Tharn Thong, 55-57-59 Donsnam Road, Tel:

431302. 94 rooms.

Wattana, 69 Donsnam Road. Tel. 431086. 34 rooms.

PHETCHABUN

19 Hotel, Tambol Chi-smor-tod. 42 rooms.

Pen Silpa 1, 333/8 Wajee Road, Amphoe Lomsak. 28 rooms.

Pen Silpa 2, Wajee Road. 16 rooms.

Phetch Siam, Tambol Chi-smor-tod. 72 rooms.

Srichai, Tambol Lom Sak, Amphoe Lom Sak. 70 rooms.

Wilawan, Kotchaseni Road, Tambol Kong Thoon. 17 rooms.

PHITSANULOK

Amarin Nakhon, 3/1 Chao Phya Phitsanulok, Tel: 238588. 124 rooms, air-conditioned.

Hor Fah, 73/1-5 Phya-Lithai Road, Tel: 258484.

Nanchao, 242 Boromttrailoknarth Road, Tel: 25-951.

Sri Pattana, 3571/5 Suranari Road, Tel: 242944. 183 rooms, air-conditioned.

Thai Hotel, Tambol Nai Muang, Amphoe Muang. 69 rooms.

Thai Hotel 2, Tambol Nai Muang, Amphoe Muang. 60 rooms.

Thai Pokphan, 104-106 Asadang Road, Tel: 242454. 66 rooms.

NONG KHAI

Banterngchitr, 626 Banternchit Road. 27 rooms.

Phantawee, 1241 Haisoke Road. 39 rooms, 6 bungalows.

Phoonsap, Meechai Road. 20 rooms.

Prachak Bungalow, 1178 Prachak Road. 28 rooms, air-conditioned.

Thong Wichit, 1244 Banterngchit Road. 32 rooms.

ROI ET

Bua Luang, Talad Roi Et. 36 rooms.

Bungalow 99, Tambol Nai Muang. 32 rooms, air-conditioned.

Niyom, Tambol Nai Muang, Amphoe Muang. 50 rooms.

Suriya, Tambol Nai Muang. 41 rooms.

Thiende, Tambol Nai Muang. 42 rooms.

Tokyo, Phoenchit Road. 58 rooms.

SAKON NAKHON

Araya, 1432 Prem Preeda Road. 49 rooms, air-conditioned.

Charoen Sook, 636 Charoen Muang Road. 40 rooms, air-conditioned.

Krong Thong, 645/2 Charoen Muang Road. 38 rooms, air-conditioned.

New Hotel, 22 Thanasarn Road, Tel: 511341. 56 rooms, air-conditioned.

Saeng Charoen, Tambol Nai Muang. 46 rooms.

SI SA KET

Nittrakarn, 370 Si Sa Ket Road, Amphoe Muang. 44 rooms.

Phothong, 1055/11 Railways Road, Tambol Muang Tai, Amphoe Muang. 20 rooms.

Prom Phimarn, Amphoe Muang. 80 rooms, air-conditioned.

Santisook, 370 Si Sa Ket Road, Amphoe Muang. 68 rooms, air-conditioned.

Thai Serm Thai, 370 Si Sa Ket Road, Amphoe Muang. 34 rooms.

SURIN

Angsupan, 155-161 Tanasarn Road, Amphoe Muang. Tel: 511302. 59 rooms, air-conditioned.

Erawan, 37 Kroong Sri Road, Tel: 511328. 24 rooms.

Krung Sri, Kroong Sri Road. 65 rooms.

Memorial, 186 Lak Muang Road, Tel: 511288. 56 rooms, air-conditioned.

New Hotel, 22 Thanasarn Road, Tel: 511341. 56 rooms, air-conditioned.

Saeng Charoen, 155-161 Thanasarn Road, Tel: 511302. 62 rooms, air-conditioned.

UBON RATCHATHANI

Bordin, 14 Phalochai Road, Tel: 254209. 171 rooms, air-conditioned.

Pathumrat, 173 Chayang-kul Road. Tel: 254417. 145 rooms, air-conditioned.

Rajthani, 229 Khuan Thani Road, Tel: 254599. 107 rooms, air-conditioned.

Siam, 94 Phalochai Road, Tel: 254771. 62 rooms, air-conditioned.

Thong Poonpan, Upparaj Road. 67 rooms, air-conditioned.

Ubon Pattana, 333 Ubonkit Road, Tel: 254333. 126 rooms, air-conditioned.

UDON THANI

Chaiyaporn, 209-211 Mak Khang Road, Amphoe Muang, Tel: 220913. 77 rooms, air-conditioned.

Charoen, 549 Phosri Road, Amphoe Muang, Tel: 221332. 120 rooms, air-conditioned.

King's, Tambol Mak Khaeng, Amphoe Muang. 135 rooms.

Krung Thong, 195-199 Phosi Road, Amphoe Muang, Tel: 221161. 85 rooms.

Mapakdi, Tambol Mak Khaeng, 45 rooms.

Pracha Pakdi, 156/8 Prachak Road, Amphoe Muang, Tel: 221805. 45 rooms.

Siri Udon, 79-91 Amphoe Muang Road, Tel: 221816. 130 rooms, air-conditioned.

Sri Chai, Tambol Mak Khaeng. 29 rooms.

Subhamitr, Tambol Mak Khaeng. 60 rooms.

Udon, 81-85 Mak Khaeng Road, Tel: 221628. 80 rooms, air-conditioned.

Victory, 60 Phosi Road, Amphoe Muang, Tel: 221462. 49 rooms, air-conditioned.

YASOTHORN

Arun Pattana, Amphoe Muang. 18 rooms, no air conditioning.

Surawej Wattana, 128/1 Changsanit Road. 30 rooms, air-conditioned.

Udom Pharn, Uthai Rermmit Road. 35 rooms.

Yos Nakhon, Uthai-Ramariti Road. 64 rooms, air-conditioned.

EASTERN THAILAND

CHACHOENGSAO

Chachoengsao, Tambol Na Muang. 45 rooms.

Mitsampan, Tambol Na Muang. 37 rooms.

Yenchitr, Tambol Na Muang. 29 rooms.

CHANTHABURI

Chai Li, Tambol Wat Mai, Amphoe Muang. 60 rooms.

Chanthaburi, Amphoe Muang. 70 rooms, air-conditioned.

Eastern, Tambol Bangkaja, Amphoe Muang. 142 rooms, air-conditioned.

Kasemsan 1, 98/1 Benjamarachuthid Road, Tel: 311100. 36 rooms, air-conditioned.

Kasemsan 2, Tambol Wat Mai. 120 rooms.

Kiatkajohn, Tambol Wat Mai, Amphoe Muang. 63 rooms.

Muangchan, 257-259 Srichan Road, Tel: 311116. 120 rooms, air-conditioned.

NAKHON NAYOK

Khao Yai, Tambol Hintang, (Bangkok reservation, Tel: 2825209). 30 bungalows, 18 motels, 9 guest houses.

Panjai, 352/1 Suwanansorn Road, Opp. Nakhon Nayok Hospital. 48 rooms, air-conditioned.

Tansamai, Tambol Nakhon Nayok. 30 rooms.

Tansamai, Tambol Ta Chang. 35 rooms.

PATTAYA

Asia Pattaya, Pattaya Beach, Tel: 418577, (Bangkok reservation, Tel: 2820121). 270 rooms, air-conditioned.

Bang Saray, 17/1 Na Chomtean (Bangkok reservation, Tel: 2863407). 52 rooms, air-conditioned, garden beach, swimming pool, and fishing and skiing facilities.

Cobra Cabana, Jomtien Beach. (Bangkok Office: 82 Sukhumvit 23, Tel: 258-4040/7/9/. Beach resort, restaurant, windsurfing center, cat and dinghy sailing.

Grand Palace, Pattaya Beach, Tel: 418-319, 418-487 (Bangkok reservation, Tel: 234-8971, 234-8975). Private beach and swimming pool, tennis courts, coffeeshop and restaurant.

Koh Larn Vac, Larn Island, (Bangkok reservation, Tel: 2453221 Ext. Koh Larn Vac). 78 rooms.

Merlin Resort, Pattaya Beach, Tel: 418755, (Bangkok reservation, Tel: 2330802). 360 rooms, air-conditioned.

Montien Pattaya, Pattaya Beach, Cholburi. Tel: 418155. Ong Pattaya Bay; water sports facilities, 24-hour room service, swimming pools, tennis courts, restaurants and coffee houses serving Japanese, Oriental and Western cuisines.

Nipa Lodge, Pattaya Beach, Tel: 418321, (Bangkok reservation, Tel: 2526118). 138 rooms, air-conditioned.

Ocean View, 382 Pattaya Beach, Tel: 418084, (Bangkok reservation, Tel: 2529590). 115 rooms.

Orchid Lodge, Pattaya Beach (Bangkok Office: 15/F, Amarin Tower, 500 Ploenchit Road, tel: 252-6045, 252-6087, 252-6118, 252-6694).

Pattaya Inn, Pattaya 380 Sukhabhibarn Road, Tel: 418400, (Bangkok reservation, Tel: 2513844). 120 rooms.

Pattaya Palace, Pattaya Beach, Tel: 418319, (Bangkok reservation, Tel: 2341010) 220 rooms, air-conditioned.

Regent Marina Hotel, North Pattaya Road, Cholburi, tel: 418-015, 419977-8. (Bangkok Office: 440/3-4 Sukhumvit Road, Soi Thonglor 55, tel: 3902511-2.) 220 rooms, restaurant, coffee house, swimming pool bar, sports and convention facilities.

Royal Cliff, Pattaya Beach, Tel: 418344, (Bangkok reservation, Tel: 2453037). 520 rooms, air-conditioned.

Royal Garden Resort, 218 Beach Road, Tel: (038) 4181267, 418122. (Bangkok booking office, Tel: 2518659). 115 rooms.

Seaview Pattaya, Pattaya Beach (in Soi Wongamatya on Pattaya-Naklua Road), Tel: 419-317, 419-189 (Bangkok reservation, Tel: 251-1555). Private beach, swimming pool, tennis courts, coffeeshop and restaurant.

Siam Bayshore, Pattaya Beach, Tel: 418677, (Bangkok reservation, Tel: 2512458). 274 rooms, air-conditioned.

Siam Bayview, Pattaya Beach, Tel: 418-728, 418-729. (Bangkok reservation, Tel: 251-8798). 300 rooms and suites. Swimming pool, seafood restaurant, coffeeshop, tennis courts.

Sugar Hut, Jomtien Beach, tel: (038) 418374-5. (Bangkok Office: Khun Naulnoi, tel: 252-3415.) Thai style bungalows, restaurant, room service.

Sugar Palm Beach, P.O.Box 80, tel: (038) 418-079. (Bangkok Office: 82, Sukhumvit 23, tel: 258-4040, 258-4047.)

Tropicana, 98-9 Pattaya Beach, Tel: 518566, (Bangkok reservation, Tel: 2529187 Ext. 216). 116 rooms, air-conditioned.

Wongse Amatya, Pattaya Beach, Tel: 418118, (Bangkok reservation, Tel: 278-4375, 278-5343.)

PRACHIN BURI

Ammuey Suk, 110/1 Rat Utit Road, Amphoe Aranyaprathet, 53 rooms, air-conditioned.

Kasem Suk, 4-5-6 Chitasuwan Road. 14 rooms.

Kavee, Tambol Sa Kaew, Amphoe Sa Kawe. 36 rooms.

King's, 65/7, 65/8 Rajdamri Road, Amphoe Muang. 61 rooms air-conditioned.

Prom Charoen, Tambol Kabin Buri, Amphoe Kabin Buri. 22 rooms.

Sirimonkol, Tambol Kabin Buri, Amphoe Kabin Buri.

RAYONG

Asia Mai, Tambol Tha — Pradu. 65 rooms.

Rayong, Tambol Tha — Pradu. 46 rooms.

Rayong O-Tani, 169 Sukumvit Road, Tel: 611161. 117 rooms, air-conditioned.

Sahayon, Tambol Cherng Noen. 36 rooms.

Tawan Ok, Tambol Tha — Pradu. 34 rooms.

Wang Kaew, Km. 248, Bangna-trat, Amphoe Klaeng, (Bangkok reservation, 153/2 Soi Mahad Lek Luang 1, Rajdamri Road, Tel: 2510836). 62 rooms; conference room for 150 persons.

TRAT

Muang Trat, 11/1-11/2 Sukumvit Road, Tel: 511191. 80 rooms, air-conditioned.

Tang Nguan Seng, Amphoe Muang. 52 rooms.

Thai Roong Roj, 296 Viwattana, Tel: 511141. 76 rooms, air-conditioned.

SOUTHERN THAILAND

CHUMPHON

Sri Chumphon, 127/22-24 Saladaeng Road. 100 rooms, air-conditioned.

Pornsawan Home, 110 GP4 Paknam — Chumporn. Tel: 52-1031 (Bangkok reservation. Tel: 468-5360).

Suriya, 125/24-26 Saladaeng Road. 26 rooms.

Thai Prasert, 202-204 Saladaeng Road. 47 rooms.

HAT YAI

Asian Hotel, 55 Niphat Utit 3 Road, Hat Yai, Songkla, Thailand, Tel: 245938/245271/245455.

Cathay, 93/1 Niphat Utit 2 Road, Tel: 243106.

Emperor Hotel, 1 Tanrattanakorn Road, Hat Yai, Tel: 245698/245709.

Grand, 443/1 Phetchkasem Road, Tel: 243286.

Hat Yai Motel, 58/4 Sangsi Road, Tel: 244207. 144 rooms air-conditioned.

Hor Fah, 124/8 Damnoen Witi Road, Tel: 243444.

33 rooms.

King's 126-134 Niphat Utit 1 Road, Tel: 243966. 66 rooms.

Kosit, Niphat Utit 2 Road, Tel: 244576. 182 rooms, air-conditioned.

Lam Thong, 42 Damnoen Witi Road, Tel: 244433. 100 rooms, air-conditioned.

Metro, 86 Niphat Utit 2, Tel: 244422. 151 rooms, air-conditioned.

Nora, 216 Thammanoon Vithi Road, Tel: 244944. 192 rooms, air-conditioned, restaurant, shops, travel agency.

Rama President, 420 Petchkasem Road, Tel: 244477. 110 rooms, air-conditioned, located in residential area, close to airport and railway terminal, dining room, cocktail lounge, swimming pool.

Sukhontha, 26 Saneha-Nuson Road, Tel: 243999. 204 rooms, air-conditioned, restaurant, bar, nightclub.

Yong Dee, 99 Niphat Utit 3 Road, Tel: 244499. 101 rooms, air-conditioned.

KOH SAMUI

Chao Koh, 29/4 Bandon-Samui, Surat Thani 8400, Tel: 077-42124. (Bangkok reservation, 84 Soi Udomsuk Sukhumvit 103 Prakanong. Tel: 3983933).

Coral Bay, P.O. Box 19 Koh Samui, Surat Thani 84000. (Bangkok reservation, Tel: 2797573 12/1, 14 Soi Suntisavee Pradhipat Rd.)

Nara Lodge, 81 Bo-Phut, Koh Samui, Surat Thani, 84000. (Bangkok reservation, Tel: 2774240. Telex: 67434 SSSAMUI TH).

Pansea, 38 Borbhud, Koh Samui, Surat Thani 84000. (Bangkok reservation, 21 Flr. Chanissara Tower, 942/163 Rama IV. Tel: 2356075, 2350676. Telex: 87654 WOLDWID).

KRABI

Kittisak, 9 Sri Phangnga Road. 18 rooms.

Thai, 2/1 Adisorn Road. 27 rooms, air-conditioned.

Viengthong, 2 Uttarakit Road, Tel: 611188. 80 rooms, air-conditioned; conference room for 100 persons.

NAKHON SRI THAMMARAT

Burapha, Tambol Klung. 33 rooms.

Muang Thong, 1459/7-9 Charoen Wattana Road, Tel: 356177. 52 rooms.

Nakhon, 1477/5 Yommaraj Road, Tel: 356318. 42 rooms.

Nakhon Tak Sin, Sri Praj Road, Amphoe Muang. 150 rooms, air-conditioned. Conference room for 500 persons.

Neramit, 1629-1631 Neramit Road, Tel: 356514. 75 rooms, air-conditioned.

New Sir Thong, Tambol Tha-wang. 41 rooms.

Seri, Amphoe Muang. 52 rooms, air-conditioned.

Siam, 1407/17 Chumroen Vithi Road. 67 rooms, air-conditioned.

Soon Thorn, Tambol Sichol. 40 rooms.

Suntisook, Tambol Sichol. 80 rooms.

Taksin Hotel, Sriprach Road. 120 rooms, Tel: 356121.

Thai Hotel, 1369/1375 Rajdamnoen Road, Tel: 356451. 115 rooms, air-conditioned.

Thai Wattana, Tambol Pak Prak. 15 rooms.

Thiem Fah, Tambol Sichol. 41 rooms.

Yaowaraj, Tambol Klung. 53 rooms.

NARATHIWAT

Lilla, 28-32 Saritwongse Road, Amphoe Sungai Kolok, Tel: 611188. 72 rooms, air-conditioned.

Merlin, 40 Charoenket Road, Amphoe Sungai Kolok, Tel: 611003. 96 rooms, air-conditioned.

Merry (Madee), 19/4 Chuenmanka Road, Amphoe Sungai Kolok, Tel: 611122. 31 rooms, air-conditioned.

Rex, 6/1-2 Chumroon Nara Road, Amphoe Muang. Tel: 511134. 40 rooms, air-conditioned.

Tak Sin 1, 3 Pracha Samran Road, Amphoe Sungai Kolok. Tel: 611083. 39 rooms, air-conditioned.

Tak Sin 2, 4 Pracha Samran Road, Amphoe Sungai Kolok, Tel: 611085. 49 rooms, air-conditioned.

Tanyong, 20-28 Sopapisai Road, Amphoe Muang, Tel: 511477. 92 rooms, air-conditioned.

Thai Eak, 43 Wongse Witee Road, Amphoe Sungai Kolok, Tel: 611052. 37 rooms, air-conditioned.

Thani, 4/1 Chuenmanka Road, Amphoe Sungai Kolok, Tel: 611046. 72 rooms, air-conditioned.

Un Un, 183/1-2 Pracha Viwat Road, Amphoe Sungai Kolok, Tel: 611058. 48 rooms, air-conditioned.

PHANGNGA

Lak Muang, 1/2 Petchkasem Road, Tel: 411125. 26 rooms, air-conditioned.

Padoang, 22-24 Tambol Takua-Pa. 32 rooms.

Rak Phangnga, Petchkasem Road. 36 rooms.

Rattanapong, Petchkasem Road. 30 rooms.

Takua-Pa, 178/6-8 Tambol Takua-Pa. 27 rooms.

Tan Prasert, 23/1-2 Tambol Takua-Pa. 30 rooms.

PHATTHALUNG

Hoh Fah, 56-58 Posa-ard Road, Tel: 611045. 42 rooms, air-conditioned.

Kink Fah, 210/1-2 Rames Road. 27 rooms.

Phatthalung 2, Tambol Khoohasawan. 26 rooms.

PHUKET

Bungalow Nai Harn, Had Nai Narn. 100 rooms.

Coral Beach Hotel, Patong Beach, Kata District, Phuket (Bangkok Office: 45/F, Amarin Tower, 500 Ploenchit Road, Tel: 252-6045, 252-6087, 252-6118, 252-6694).

Club Med, Kata Beach, Phuket (Bangkok Office: The Peninsula Plaza, Ground Floor, 153 Rajdamri Road, Tel: 253-0108. Telex: 21608 TH).

Imperial, 52 Phuket Road, Tambon Talat Yai, Tel: 212311. 41 rooms, air-conditioned.

Kakata Inn, 27 Rasda Road, tel: 212-892. (Bangkok Office: Tel: 258-9246-7, 258-1928.) 95 traditional bungalows, restaurant, beach bar, windsurfing school and daily tours.

Karon - On - Sea, P.O. Box 131, Phuket Post Office 83000, tel: (076) 211066, 211077, Ext. 8027. Family standard bungalows and restaurant.

Kata Tropicana (Bungalow), Had Kata, (Phuket Office; 64/11 Krung Thep Road, Tel: 211606). 63 rooms.

Kata Villa, Had Kata, (Phuket Office, 2 Krabi Road, Tel: 211014). 20 rooms.

Le Meridien Phuket, Karon Beach, Muang District, Phuket (Bangkok Office: 37 Soi Somprasong 3, Petchaburi Road, Tel: 251-4707, 252-3919. Telex: 87489 TH).

Pansea, Tel: 211856. (Bangkok Office: 4th Floor, Air France Bldg., 3 Patpong Road. Tel: 2337115-9.) 100 rooms, air-conditioned, restaurant, bar, beach-side cafe, golf course, pool and sports facilities.

Patong Beach Bungalows, 96/1 Pisit Road, Had Patong, (Phuket Office, 55 Phuket Road, Tel: 211426). 104 rooms, air-conditioned.

Pearl, 42 Montri Road, Tel: 211091, (Bangkok reservation, 1035/4 Pleonchit Road, Tel: 2516527).

Phuket Cabana (Bungalow), Had Patong, (Phuket Office, 63 Phuket Road, Tel: 211932. 29 rooms.

Phuket Island Resort, 73/1 Rasada Road, Tel: 211421. (Bangkok reservation, Tel: 252-5320.) 194 rooms, air-conditioned. Conference room for 300 persons.

Phuket Merlin Hotel, 158/1 Jawaraj Road, 220 rooms, air-conditioned, Tel: 211618.

Phuket Sin Thavee, 89 Phang-nga Road, Tel: 211186. 139 rooms.

Phuket Yacht Club, Nai Harn Beach. (Bangkok Office: 37 Soi Somprasong 3, Petchburi Road, tel: 251-4681, 251-4685/6.) 120 rooms, air-conditioned, 3 restaurants, 1 lounge.

Rawai Bungalows, Wiset Road, Tambon Rawai, Tel: 211205 (Bangkok reservation, Tel: 5855860). 30 rooms.

Sea View (Bungalow), 3 Had Patong, (Phuket Offices 351/1 Yaowaraj Road, Tel: 211346). 27 rooms.

Thavorn, 74 Rasada Road, Tel: 211333. 200 rooms, air-conditioned.

PRACHUAP KHIRI KHAN
AND HUA HIN BEACH RESORT

Chatchai, 59/1-3 Petchkasem Road, Amphoe Hua Hin. 35 rooms, air-conditioned.

Damrong, 46 Petchkasem Road, Talat Chatchai, Hua Hin, Tel: 511574. 30 rooms, air-conditioned.

Royal Garden Resort, 107/1 Phetkasem Beach Road, tel: (032) 511881-4. (Bangkok booking office: 17 Sukhumvit Soi 11, tel: 2518659, 2524638, 2528252.) 171 rooms, mini bar, restaurants, lounge, disco, sports facilities and tours available.

Le Sofitel Central Hua Hin, 1 Dammennkasem Road, Hua-Hin, Prachuap-Khirikhan 77110, Tel: (032) 511012, 511015. Telex: 78313 CETRAC TH. (Bangkok Office: 21/Flr. Charn Issara Tower, Rama IV Road, Tel: 233-0256. Telex: 87654 WOLDWID TH.

Namsin, 40/8-10 Petchkasem Road, Hua Hin, Tel: 511051. 20 rooms.

Prakarn Siri, Amphoe Pranburi. 84 rooms.

Saflom, Hua Hin Beach, Tel: 511890, (Bangkok reservation, Tel: 2515735). 46 rooms, air-conditioned.

Suksun, 131 Soosuek Road, Amphoe Muang. Tel: 510131. 92 rooms.

Supamit, 19 Amnuaysin Road. Tel: 511208. 36 rooms.

Tessaban Bungalow, Chaitalay Road, Tel: 510157. 36 rooms.

RANONG

Asia, Ruangraj Road. 51 rooms.

Charoen Sook, Ruangraj Road. 51 rooms.

Rattanasin, Ruangraj Road. 44 rooms.

Sin Ranong, Ruangraj Road. 104 rooms, air-conditioned.

Sook Somboon, Tambol Bangrin. 36 rooms.

Suriyanant, Ruangraj Road. 31 rooms.

Thara, 2/2 Petchkasem Road, Tel: 811510. 65 rooms, air-conditioned.

SONGKHLA

Rado, 59 Sanehanusorn Road, Hat Yai, Tel:

245266. 96 rooms, air-conditioned. Conference room for 40 persons.

Railways, 1 Dhamnoon Witee Road, Hat Yai, Tel: 244766. 46 rooms, air-conditioned. Conference for 200 persons.

Sakol, 47-8 Sanehanusorn Road, Hat Yai, Tel: 245256. 91 rooms, air-conditioned.

Samila, 1/11 Rajdamnoen Road, Samila beach, Tel: 311289. 75 rooms, air-conditioned.

SATUN

Rian Thong, 124/1 Samantapradit Road. 25 rooms.

Satun Thani, Tambol Piman. 50 rooms.

Udom Sook, Tambol Piman. 33 rooms.

Muang Thong, 282/6-10 Na Muang Road, Tel: 272960. 180 rooms, air-conditioned.

Phanfah, 247/5 Na Muang, Tel: 272287. 57 rooms.

Surat, Tambol Talad. 40 rooms.

Tapee, 100 Chonkasem Road, Tel: 272575. 120 rooms, air-conditioned.

SURAT THANI

Siam Tara Hotel, 1/144 Donnok Rd., Muang Surat Thani 84000, Tel: 077-273740-3.

Siam Thani Hotel, 180 Punpin Rd, Muang Surat Thani 84000. (Bangkok Reservation: Liberty Hotel 215 Pradhipat, Bangkok 10400, Tel: 2710724).

Tapee Hotel, 100 Chonkasem Rd., Bandon Surat Thani 84000, Tel: 077-272575.

Wang Tai Hotel, 1 Talad Mai Rd., Muang Surat Thani 84000, Tel: 077-273410-6.

TRANG

Bungalow Caesar, Amphoe Muang. 27 rooms.

Koteng, Rama 6 Road. Tel: 218148. 56 rooms, air-conditioned.

Nara, Amphoe Muang. 34 rooms.

Queen's, 85-89 Visetkul Road, Tel: 218522. 150 rooms, air-conditioned.

Sahathai, Amphoe Muang. 30 rooms.

Trang, 134/2-5 Visetkul Road, Tel: ·218229. 64 rooms, air-conditioned.

YALA

Fah Un Roong, 130 Chantarothai Road, Amphoe Betong. 38 rooms.

Hua Un, 352/1 Siriroj Road, Tambol Satang, Tel: 212771. 47 rooms, air-conditioned.

Keng Thai, 33 Chaya chavalit Road, Amphoe Betong. 32 rooms.

Sri Yala, 20 Chai Charas Road, Tel: 212170. 91 rooms, air-conditioned.

Tepvimarn, 31-37 Sri Bamroong Road, Tel: 212796. 84 rooms, air-conditioned.

RESTAURANTS
Bangkok

Thai cuisine

Bussaracum, 35 Soi Pipat 2, Convent Road, tel: 235-8915.

Chitpochana, 1082 Paholyothin Road, tel: 279-5000. Also 62 Soi 20, Sukhumvit Road, tel: 391-6401.

Datchanee, 18/2-4 Parchathipathia Road, tel: 281-0640.

Djit Pochana-Oriental, 489 Charoen Nakorn, tel: 234-8632 ext. 3133.

Lemon Grass, 5/1 Soi 24, Sukhumvit Road, tel: 258-8637.

Silom Village Restaurant, Opp. Swasdee Tennis Court, Sukhumvit Soi 31, tel: 258-4502.

Spice Market, The Regent Bangkok, 155 Rajdamri Road, tel: 251-6127.

Srithandorn, 197 Soi 101, Ladprao, tel: 377-6189.

Thai Food Restaurant, opposite Planetarium, corner Soi 61, Sukhumvit Road, tel: 391-1360.

Thanying, 10 Pramuan St., Silom Road, (opposite Bangkok Christian College) tel: 236-4361.

The Toll Gate (Palace Cuisine), 245/2 Soi 31, Sukhumvit Road, tel: 391-3947.

Thon Tum Rub, 15-17 Sukhumvit Soi 8, Sukhumvit Road, tel: 253-5745.

Your Place, 25 Soi 33, Sukhumvit Road, tel: 391-0158.

Zezavo Jungle Food, 50/3 Ngamvongwan Road, tel: 588-2267.

Other Asian cuisine

Akamon (Japanese), 233 Soi 21, Sukhumvit Road, tel: 391-8144.

Café India, 460/8 Surawong road, tel: 233-0419.

The Cedar (Lebanese), 138 Sukhumvit Soi 49, tel: 392-7399.

Chinatown (Cantonese), Dusit Thani Rama IV, tel: 233-1130, 336-0450-9.

Grand Shangri-la (Chinese), 154/4-5 Silom Road, tel: 234-2045.

Himali Cha Cha (Indian), 1229/11 New road, tel: 235-1569.

Rose La Moon (Chinese), 165/5-6 Soi 21, Sukhumvit Road, tel: 391-7351.

Seoul (Korean), 47 Rajprasong Road, tel: 252-9285.

Shochiku (Japanese), 62/9-10 Soi Thaniya, off Silom Road, tel: 233-9694.

Tien Tien (Chinese), 105 Patpong Road, tel: 234-8717.

Vietnam Restaurant, 82-84 Silom Road, tel: 234-6174.

The Whole Earth (Vegetarian), 93/3 Soi Lang Suan, Ploenchit Road, tel: 252-5574.

European cuisine

La Brasserie (French), The Regent Bangkok, 155 Rajdamri Road, tel: 251-6127.

Le Cristal (French), The Regent Bangkok, 155 Rajdamri Road, tel: 251-6127.

Le Metropolitain (French), 135/6 Gaysorn Road, tel: 252-8364.

L'Opéra, 55 Soi 39, Sukhumvit Road, tel: 258-5605.

Ma Maison (French), Hilton International, 2 Wireless Road, tel: 253-0123.

The Two Vikings (Scandinavian), 2 Soi 35, Sukhumvit Road, tel: 391-8364.

Chiang Mai

Ban Suan (Thai), 51/3 Chiang Mai-San Kampaeng Road.

Chalet (French), 71 Charoenprathet Road.

Charueng Jungle Food, 5 Superhighway (Airport Road).

Doi Den (Thai), Nimmanhemindr Road.

Fuang Far (Thai), Suriwongse Road.

Le Cog d'Or (French), 18-20 Chaiyapoom Road.

The Whole Earth Restaurant (Vegetarian), Sri Donchai Road.

Pattaya

Akamon (Japanese), Pattaya 2 Road, tel: 419598.
Bencharong (International), at Royal Wing, Royal Cliff Beach Resort.
Café India (Indian), Post Office Lane, Beach Road, tel: 419679.
Dolf Riks (International), Srinakhon Shopping Centre, tel: 418269.
Kare Sai Garden (Thai), Naklua Road, North Pattaya.
Krua Suthep (Thai), Pattaya 2 Road, tel: 419888.
La Gritta (Italian), Orchard Lodge, Beach Road, tel: 418161, 418323.
Nang Nual (Thai), Sunset Avenue, South Pattaya, 418478, 418708.
Restaurant Market (variety), South Pattaya, 419694.
Seafood Pattaya (Thai), South Pattaya.
Suan Tarn (Thai), at Cobra Cabana, Jomtien Beach.

BANKS IN BANGKOK

Asia Trust Bank, 80-82 Anuwong Road, tel: 222-2171.
Bangkok Bank, 333 Silom Road, tel: 234-3333.
Bangkok Bank of Commerce, 171 Suriwong Road, tel: 234-2930.
Bangkok Metropolitan Bank, Yukol 2 Road, tel: 282-3281.
Bank for Agriculture, Mansion 1, Rajadamneon Klang Avenue, tel: 281-3622.
Bank of America, 2/2 Wireless Road (adjacent to Hilton International Bangkok), tel: 253-0112.
Bank of Asia for Industry & Commerce, Samyek Charoen Krung, 601 New Road, tel: 222-5111.
Bank of Canton, 197/1 Silom Road, tel: 234-7030.
Bank of Korea, 16 Soi 20, Sukhumvit Road, tel: 391-8605.
Bank of Tokyo, Thaniya Building, 62 Silom Road, tel: 233-0790.
Bank of Ayudhya, 550 Ploenchit Road, tel: 252-8171.
Banque de l'Indochine et de Suez, 142 Wireless Road, tel: 252-2111.
Bharat Overseas Bank, 221 Rajawong Road, tel: 221-8181.
Chartered Bank, Saladaeng Circle, Rama IV Road, tel: 234-0821.
Chase Manhattan Bank, 965 Rama I Road, Siam Center, tel: 252-1141.
Four Seas Communications Bank, 231 Rajawong Road, tel: 222-2161.
Government Housing Bank, 77 Rajadamnern Avenue, tel: 281-5155.
Hong Kong and Shanghai Banking Corp., Siam Center, 965 Rama I Road, tel: 251-3252.
International Commercial Bank of China, 95 Suapa Road, tel: 221-8121.
Krung Thai Bank, 53 Sukhumvit Road, tel: 251-2032.
Laem Thong Bank, opp. Phitphan Phanich Building, tel: 233-9730.
Mercantile Bank, 63 Silom Road, tel: 233-5996.
Mitsui Bank, Boon-Mit Building, 138 Silom Road, tel: 234-3841.
Siam City Bank, 1101 New Petchburi Road, tel: 252-4425.
Siam Commercial Bank, 1060 New Petchburi Road,

tel: 251-9111.
Thai Danu Bank, 393 Silom Road, tel: 233-9160.
Thai Development Bank, 20 Yukol 2 Road, tel: 281-3533.
Thai Farmers Bank, 400 Paholyothin Road, tel: 270-1122; 142 Silom Road, tel: 234-7050.
Thai Military Bank, 34 Phayathai Road, tel: 282-2727.
Union Bank of Bangkok, 624 Yawaraj Road, tel: 233-4740.
United Malayan Banking Corp., 3rd Floor, Hua Kee Building. 107-9 Suapa Road, tel: 221-9191.
Wanglee Bank, Cathay Trust Building, 1st Floor, 1016 Rama IV Road, tel: 233-2111.

DIPLOMATIC MISSIONS

Argentine Embassy, 5th Floor, Thaniya Building, 62 Silom Road, tel: 234-6911, 234-6913. Office hours: 8.30a.m.—1p.m.
Australian Embassy, 37 South Sathorn Road, tel: 286-0411. Office hours: 8.30a.m.—4.20p.m.
Austrian Embassy, 14 Soi Nandha, off Soi Atta-karnprasit, Sathorn Tai Road, tel: 286-3011, 286-3037.
Bangladesh Embassy, 6-8 Charoenmitr, Soi 63, Sukhumvit Road, tel: 391-8069, 391-8070. Office hours: 8.30a.m.—4.30p.m.
Belgian Embassy, 44 Soi Phya Pipat, Silom Road, tel: 233-0840, 233-0841. Office hours: 8.30a.m.—1p.m.
Brazilian Embassy, PIM Building, 8/1 Soi 15, Sukhumvit Road, tel: 251-6043. Office hours: 8.30a.m.—4p.m.
British Embassy, 1031 Ploenchit Road, tel: 252-7161, 252-7169. Office hours: 8a.m.—4.30p.m.
Bulgarian Embassy, 11 Soi Lampetch, Hua Mark, tel: 314-3056. Office hours: 8a.m.—2p.m.
Burmese Embassy, 132 Sathorn Nua Road, tel: 233-2237, 234-2258. Office hours: 8.30a.m.—12.30p.m. and 1—4.30p.m. (Monday to Thursday); 8.30a.m.—12 noon and 1—5p.m. (Friday).
Canadian Embassy, 11th Floor, Boonmitr Building, 138 Silom Road, tel: 234-1561, 234-1568. Office hours: 8a.m.—4.30p.m.
Chilean Embassy, 15 Soi 61, Sukhumvit Road, tel: 391-4858. Office hours: 9a.m.—5p.m.
Chinese Embassy, 57 Rajadapisek Road, tel: 245-7032, 245-7039. Office hours: 8a.m.—12 noon and 1—4.30p.m.
Czechoslovakian Embassy, 7th Floor, Silom Building, Rm. 705, 197/1 Silom Road, tel: 234-1922, 233-4535. Office hours: 8a.m.—3p.m.
Danish Embassy, 10 Soi Attakarn Prasit, Sathorn Tai Road, tel: 286-3930, 286-3932, 286-3936. Office hours: 8a.m.—1p.m.
Dominican Consulate, 92/6 Changwattana Road, Laksee, Bangkaen, tel: 579-3537, 579-1130. Office hours: 9a.m.—1p.m.
Egyptian Embassy, 49 Soi Ruam Rudee, Ploenchit Road, tel: 252-6139, 252-7767. Office hours: 9a.m.—2.30p.m.
Finnish Embassy, 3rd Floor, Vithayu Place, 89/17 Wireless Road, tel: 252-3636, 252-3637.
French Embassy, Customs House Lane, tel: 234-0950, 234-0956. Office hours: 8a.m.—1.30p.m.
German Embassy, 9 Sathorn Tai Road, tel:

286-4223, 286-4227. Office hours: 8a.m.—1p.m.

The Consulate General of the Hellenic Republic (Greece), 3rd Floor, President Travel Service Building, 412/8-9 Siam Square, Rama I Road, tel: 252-1681, 252-1686. Office hours: 9a.m.—12 noon and 1:30—3p.m.

Hungarian Embassy, 28 Soi Sukchai, off Soi 42 Sukhumvit Road, tel: 391-7906. Office hours: 8a.m.—4p.m. (Monday to Thursday) and 8a.m.—2p.m. (Saturday).

Indian Embassy, 46 Soi Prasarnmit, off Soi 23, Sukhumvit Road, tel: 233-5065. Office hours: 8.30a.m—12:30p.m. and 1—4p.m.

Indonesian Embassy, 600-602 Petchburi Road, tel: 252-3135, 252-3139. Office hours: 7:30 a.m.—12 noon and 1—4 p.m.

Iranian Embassy, 9th Floor, Shell House, 140 Wireless Road, tel: 251-4925, 252-0205. Office hours: 8:30 a.m—4 p.m.

Iraqi Consulate, 47 Pradipat Road, Samsen Nai, Phya Thai, tel: 279-1893. Office hours: 8:30 a.m.—3:30 p.m.

Israeli Embassy, 31 Soi Lang Suang, Ploenchit Road, tel: 252-3131, 252-3134. Office hours: 8 a.m.—3:30 p.m. (Monday to Thursday); 8 a.m.—3 p.m. (Friday).

Italian Embassy, 92 Sathorn Nua Road, tel: 234-9718, 234-9230. Office hours: 8:30 a.m—1:30 p.m.

Japanese Embassy, 1674 New Petchburi Road, tel: 252-6151, 252-6159. Office hours: 8:30 a.m.—12 noon.

Korean Embassy, 28/1 6th Floor, Phraphavit Building. Surasak Road, tel: 234-0723, 234-0726. Office hours: 8 a.m.—12 noon and 2—5 p.m.

Embassy of the (Lao) People's Democratic Republic, 19 Sathorn Tai Road, tel: 286-0010, 286-3362. Office hours: 8 a.m.—12 noon and 2—4:30 p.m.

Malaysian Embassy, 35 Sathorn Tai Road, tel: 286-1390, 286-1392, 286-7769. Office hours: 8:30 a.m.—12:30 p.m. and 2—4:30 p.m.

The Consulate of Monaco, 3rd Floor, Nailert Building, 888 Petchburi Road, tel: 252-8106 Ext. 46. Office hours: 9 a.m.—12 noon and 2—4 p.m.

Nepalese Embassy, 189 Soi Puengsuk, Soi 71, Sukhumvit Road, tel: 391-7240. Office hours: 8 a.m.—12 noon and 1:30—4:30 p.m.

Netherlands Embassy, 106 Wireless Road, tel: 252-6103, 252-6105. Office hours: 8 a.m.—2:30 p.m. (Monday and Wednesday to Friday); 8 a.m.—12:30 p.m and 2—5 p.m. (Tuesday).

New Zealand Embassy, 93 Wireless Road, tel: 251-8165.

Norwegian Embassy, 20th Floor, Chockchai Building, 690 Sukhumvit Road, tel: 392-1164, 392-1160. Office hours: 9 a.m.—2:45 p.m.

The Honorary Consulate of Sultanate of Oman, 134/1-2 Silom Road, tel: 235-8868. Office hours: 8 a.m.—2 p.m.

Pakistan Embassy, 31 Soi Nana Nua (Soi 3), Sukhumvit Road, tel: 252-7036, 252-7038. Office hours: 8 a.m.—3:30 p.m.

Peru Consulate, Louis T. Leonowens Building, 723 Siphya Road, tel: 233-5910, 233-5917, 234-5840. Office hours: 8:30 a.m.—12 noon.

Philippines Embassy, 760 Sukhumvit Road, opposite Soi 47, tel: 391-0008, 391-0211. Office hours: 8 a.m.—12 noon and 1—5 p.m.

Polish Embassy, 61 Soi Prasanmit, Soi 23, Sukhumvit Road, tel: 391-0668, 391-2356. Office hours: 8 a.m.—2 p.m.

Portuguese Embassy, 26 Bush Lane, tel: 234-0372, 234-2123. Office hours; 8:30 a.m.—1:30 p.m.

The Embassy of the Socialist Republic of Romania, 39 Soi 10, Sukhumvit Road, tel: 252-8515. Office hours: 8:30 a.m.—2:30 p.m. (Monday to Friday); 8:30 a.m.—12 noon (Saturday).

Saudi Arabia Embassy, 10th Floor, Boonmitr Building, 139 Silom Road, tel: 233-7941, 233-7942. Office hours: 8:30 a.m.—2 p.m.

Singapore Embassy, 129 Sathorn Tai Road, tel: 286-2111, 286-1433. Office hours: 8:30a.m.—12 noon and 1—4:30p.m.

Spanish Embassy, 103 Wireless Road, tel: 252-6112, 252-8368. Office hours: 8:30a.m.—1:30p.m.

Sri Lanka Embassy, 7th Floor, Nai Lert Building, 87 Soi 5, Sukhumvit Road, tel: 251-8534, 252-4164. Office hours: 8:30a.m.—12 noon, 1—4:45p.m.

Swedish Embassy, 11th Floor, Boonmitr Building, 138 Silom Road, tel: 234-3891, 234-3892, 233-0295.

Swiss Embassy, 35 North Wireless Road, off Ploenchit Road, tel: 252-8992, 252-8994. Office hours: 8a.m.—4p.m.

Turkish Embassy, 153/2 Soi Mahadledk Luang 1, Rajdamri Road, tel: 251-2987, 251-2988.

Union of Soviet Socialist Republic Embassy, 108 Sathorn Nua Road, tel: 234-9824, 234-2012. Office hours: 7:30a.m.—4:15p.m. (Monday); 7:30—3:15p.m. (Tuesday to Friday).

United Arab Republic Embassy, 49 Soi Ruamrudee, tel: 252-6139. Office hours: 9a.m.—2p.m.

United States of America Embassy, 95 Wireless Road, tel: 252-5040, 252-5049. Office hours: 7:30a.m.—12 noon and 1—4:30p.m.

Yugoslavia Embassy, 28 Soi 61, Sukhumvit Road, tel: 391-9090, 391-9091. Office hours: 8:30a.m.—4:30p.m.

Vatican Holy See, Apostolic Nunciature, 217 Sathorn Tai Road, tel: 233-9109, 235-7269. Office hours: 8:30a.m.—1:30p.m.

Vietnamese Embassy, 83/1 Wireless Road, tel: 251-7203, 251-5836, 251-5837. Office hours: 8:30a.m.—4:30p.m.

AIRLINE OFFICES IN BANGKOK

Aeroflot Soviet Airlines, 7 Silom Road, Reservation and ticketing: tel. 233-6965, 233-6967. Airport: tel. 286-0190 ext. 111.

Air Canada, 1053 New Road. tel. 233-5900. Airport: tel. 286-0190, ext. 293, 294.

Air France, 3 Patpong Road, Ticketing: 236-0157, 233-7119 ext. 248, 258, 268. Reservation: tel. 236-0158. Airport: tel. 286-0190 ext. 113, 114.

Air India, 287 Silom Road, Ticketing: 233-8950, 233-8954 ext. 156, 158. Reservation: tel. 234-7558, 233-4525. Airport: tel. 286-0190 ext. 121, 122.

Air Lanka, 1 Patpong Road. tel: 235-6800, 235-0133, 235-0134. Airport: tel. 286-0190 ext. 332.

Air New Zealand, c/o World Travel Service, 1053 New Road. tel: 233-5900, 233-5909. Airport: tel. 286-0190 ext. 145

Air Pacific, 3rd floor, Chongkolnee Bldg., 56

Surawongse Road. tel. 234-0300, 235-2448.

Alia Royal Jordanian Airlines, Yada Bldg., 56 Silom Road. Ticketing: 235-3970, 235-3979.

Alitalia, 138 Silom Road. tel. 233-4000, 233-4004. Reservation: tel. 234-5253, 234-5257. Airport: tel. 286-0190 ext. 132.

American Airlines, c/o Berli Jacker Travel Office, 542/1 Ploenchit Road. tel. 252-1181, 252-1185, 252-8744.

Bangladesh Biman, Ground and 6th floors, Chongkolnee Bldg., 56 Suriwongse Road. tel. 233-6178. Airport: tel. 286-0190 ext. 25

British Airways, 2/F, Charn Issara Tower, 942/ 81 Rama IV, Bangkok 10500, tel. 236-8655.

British Caledonian, c/o Berli Jucker Travel Office, 542/1 Ploenchit Road. tel. 252-1181, 252-1185, 252-8744.

Burma Airways, 208 Surawong Road. tel: 234-9692, 233-3052. Airport: tel. 286-0190 ext. 266.

Canadian Pacific Airlines, 89/12 Bangkok Bazaar, Rajdamri Road. tel. 251-0063, 251-0064.

Cathay Pacific Airways, 109 Surawongse Road. tel. 235-6022, 235-6026. Reservation: tel. 233-6105, 233-6109. Airport: tel. 286-0190 ext. 156.

China Airlines, Siam Centre, Rama I Road. Ticketing: tel. 251-9656, 251-9659. Reservation: tel. 252-1748, 252-1749. Visa Section: tel. 251-7978. Airport: tel. 286-0190 ext. 160.

Continental Airlines, 5th floor, Dusit Thani Bldg., Rama IV Road. tel. 233-0566, 234-7876, 234-7878.

Delta Airlines, Getz Corporation, 62/21 Thaniya Road. tel. 233-1840, 233-1843.

Egypt Air, 120 Silom Road. Ticketing and reservation: tel. 233-7601, 233-7603. Airport: tel. 286-0190 ext. 274.

Fiji Air, 3rd floor, Chongkolnee Bldg., 56 Surawongse Road. tel. 234-0300, 235-2448.

Finnair, c/o Berli Jucker Travel Office, 542/1 Ploenchit Road. tel. 252-1181, 252-1185, 252-8744.

Flying Tiger Lines, c/o Thai Airways International, 3rd floor, Don Muang Airport, tel. 286-0090 ext. 272, 233-0566, 234-7876.

Garuda Indonesian, 944/19 Rama IV Road. tel. 233-0540. Reservation: tel. 233-0981, 233-0982. Airport: tel. 286-0190 ext. 170, 171.

Gulf Air, 9 Dejo Road, Bangkok 10500, tel. 235-5605, 235-1397.

Hawaiian Airlines Inc., c/o Berli Jucker Travel Office, 542/1 Ploenchit Road, tel. 252-1181, 252-1185, 252-8744.

Japan Air Lines, Patpong Road, tel. 234-9105, 234-9119. Reservation: ext. 125, 153. Ticketing: ext. 134, 135, 136. Airport: tel. 286 0190 ext. 135, 136, 137.

KLM Royal Dutch Airlines, 2 Patpong Road. tel. 233-5150, 233-5160. Reservation: ext. 36, 37, 38. Ticketing: ext. 31, 32, 33. Airport: tel. 286-0910 ext. 191.

Korean Airlines, 946 Dusit Thani Building, Rama IV Road. tel. 234-9283, 234-9289. Reservation: ext. 21, 25. Ticketing ext. 31, 33. Airport: tel. 286-0910 ext. 222, 233.

Kuwait Airways, 159 Rajdamri Road. tel. 251-5854, 251-5857. Airport: tel. 286-0190 ext. 388.

Lao Aviation, 56 Chongkolnee Bldg., Surawongse Road, tel. 233-7950. Reservation: tel. 234-0300.

Lot Polish Airlines, 485/11-12 Silom Road. tel.

235-2223, 235-2227, 235-7092. Airport: tel. 286-0190 ext. 274.

Luthansa German Airlines, 331/1-3 Silom Road. tel. 234-1350, 234-1359. Airport: tel. 286-0190 ext. 211, 213.

Malaysian Airlines System, 98-102 Surawong Road. tel. 234-9795. Reservation: 234-9790. Airport: tel. 523-7270, 523-7271.

Northwest Orient Airlines, 965 Rama I Road. tel. 251-9652, 251-9654.

Pakistan International Airlines, Thai Style Bldg., Suriwongse Road. Ticketing and reservation: tel. 234-2961, 234-2964. Airport: tel. 286-0190 ext. 129.

Pan American World Airway, Maneeya Building, 518/2 Ploenchit Road, Bangkok 10500, tel. 252-7309.

Philippine Airlines, 4th Floor, Chongkolnee Bldg. Reservation: tel. 233-2351, 233-2352. Airport: tel. 286-0190 ext. 190, 191.

Quantas Airways, 11/F, Charn Issara Tower, 942/51 Rama IV, Bangkok 10500, tel. 236-0102.

Royal Brunei Airlines, c/o Thai Airways International, Silom Road. Ticketing: tel. 234-3111, 234-3119.

Royal Nepal Airlines, 1/4 Convent Road. Reservation: tel. 233-3921, 233-3924. Airport: tel. 286-0190 ext. 152.

Sabena Belgian World Airlines, 11th floor, CCT Building, 109 Suriwongse Road. tel. 233-5940, 233-5941. Airport: tel. 286-0190 ext. 273, 274.

SAS Scandinavian Airlines System, 412 Rama I Road. tel. 252-4181. Airport: tel. 523-6121 ext. 134.

Saudi Arabian Airlines, Ground Floor, CCT Bldg., 109 Surawongse Road. tel. 235-7930, 235-7939.

Singapore Airlines, 62/1-4 Silom Road. Ticketing: tel. 235-1580, 235-1589. Reservation: tel. 235-1570, 235-1579.

Swissair Transport, 1 Silom Road. tel. 233-2930, 233-2934. Reservation: tel. 233-2935, 233-2938. Airport: tel. 286-0190 ext. 225.

Tarom Romanian Air Transport, Zuellig Bldg., 1-7 Silom Road. tel. 235-2668, 235-2669.

Thai Airways, 6 Larn Luang Road. tel. 281-1633, 282-7151. Reservation: tel. 281-1626, 281-1093. Weekends and holidays: tel. 281-1737, 281-1989, 281-1626, 281-1633. Airport: tel. 523-6201 ext. 290.

Thai Airways International, 89 Vipavadee Rangsit Road. tel. 511-0121. Ticketing: tel. 513-0121. Reservation: tel. 233-3810. Airport: tel. 286-0190 ext. 273, 274.

Trans Mediterranean Airways, 4th floor, CTI Bldg., 462-472 Sukhumvit Road. tel. 390-2481, 390-2485. Airport: tel. 286-0190 ext. 169, 177.

Trans World Airlines, 142/23 Soi Suksavithaya, Sathorn Nua Road, Bangkok 10500, tel. 233-7290-1.

Union de Transports Aeriens (UTA), 3 Patpong Road, tel. 233-7100, 233-7119. Ticketing: ext. 18, 28, 38. Reservation: ext 22, 33, 44. Airport: tel. 286-0190 ext. 262.

United Airlines, 183 Rajdamri Road, Bangkok 10500, tel. 251-6006, 251-7500.

Western Airlines, 501 Dusit Thani Bldg., Rama IV Road, tel. 233-0566, 234-7876.